CATCH-UP MATH

Get your child back on track!

Multiplication ◎ Division ◎ Factors ◎ Area

Multiples ◎ Fractions ◎ Decimals

Number Patterns ◎ Measurement

Using Angles ◎ Classifying Shapes

Publishing Credits
Corinne Burton, M.A.Ed., *President* and *Publisher*
Emily R. Smith, M.A.Ed., *SVP of Content Development*
Véronique Bos, *VP of Creative*
Lynette Ordoñez, *Content Manager*
Avery Rabedeaux, *Assistant Editor*
Kevin Pham, *Graphic Designer*

Image Credits: all images from iStock, Dreamtime, and/or Shutterstock

A division of Teacher Created Materials

5482 Argosy Avenue
Huntington Beach, CA 92649
www.tcmpub.com/shell-education
ISBN 979-8-7659-7014-0

This Edition is for sale in North America (including Canada) only.
From material first published and copyright Pascal Press.

Printed by: **418**
Printed in: **USA**
PO#: **PO9308**

CONTENTS

CONTENTS

ABOUT CATCH-UP MATH

The Catch-Up Math series enables children to start from scratch when they are struggling with grade-level math. Each book takes math back to the foundation and ensures that all basic concepts are consolidated before moving forward. Lots of revision and opportunities to practice and build confidence are provided before moving on to new topics.

Each new topic is introduced clearly with simple explanations, examples, and trial questions (with answers) before children move to the Practice section. To help students understand difficult topics, instructional videos are included throughout the book.

A QR code on a topic page provides access to the video.

This book has 13 chapters that cover a variety of mathematical concepts. The chapters are:

1 Whole Numbers
2 Addition
3 Subtraction
4 Multiplication
5 Division
6 Fractions
7 Decimals
8 Patterns and Algebra
9 Length
10 Angles
11 Shapes
12 Area
13 Volume and Capacity

★ A review section that can be used as assessment and to check students' progress is included at the end of each chapter.

★ Answers are at the back of the book.

How to Use This Book

Children can work through the pages from front to back or choose individual topics to reinforce areas where they are struggling.

The topics are introduced with:

- clear instructions, using simple language
- completed examples and incomplete examples for students to tackle before moving on to the **Your Turn** sections
- videos linked by QR codes to provide additional instruction and clarify difficult concepts

Each Your Turn section contains a SELF CHECK for students to reflect and give self-assessment on their understanding.

HOW TO USE THE QR CODES IN CATCH-UP MATH

A unique aspect of the Catch-Up Math series is the **instructional videos**.

The videos further explain and clarify various mathematical concepts. The videos are simply accessed via QR codes and can be watched on a phone o or tablet. Or, view all the videos by following this link: tcmpub.digital/cu-math5.

Access the video by scanning the QR code with your device

SCAN to watch video

Each video shows the page from the book. An instructor talks through the concepts and examples and demonstrates what children need to do. The solutions to the examples are presented before children tackle the Your Turn sections. This careful instruction ensures that children can confidently move on to the following Practice questions. Children should be encouraged to check their Your Turn answers before moving on.

25 instructional videos included!

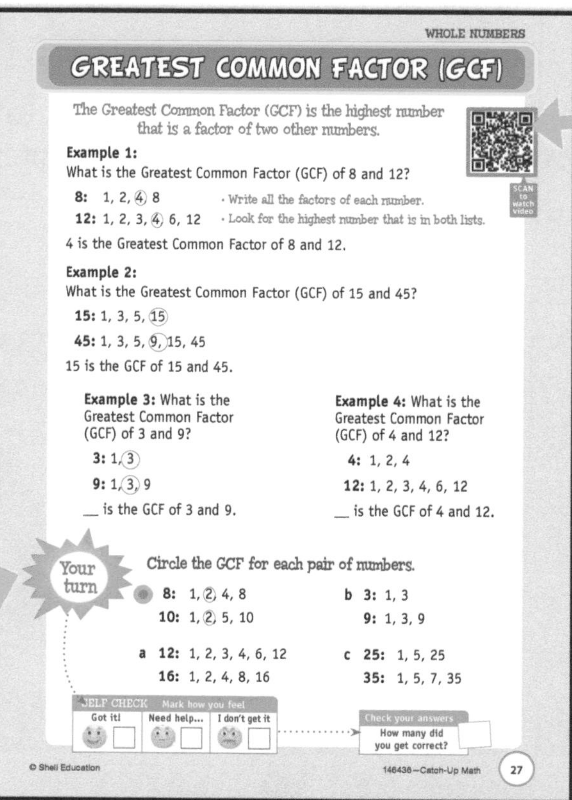

WHOLE NUMBERS

GREATEST COMMON FACTOR (GCF)

The Greatest Common Factor (GCF) is the highest number that is a factor of two other numbers.

SCAN to watch video

Example 1:
What is the Greatest Common Factor (GCF) of 8 and 12?

8: 1, 2, (4), 8 • Write all the factors of each number.
12: 1, 2, 3, (4), 6, 12 • Look for the highest number that is in both lists.

4 is the Greatest Common Factor of 8 and 12.

Example 2:
What is the Greatest Common Factor (GCF) of 15 and 45?

15: 1, 3, 5, (15)
45: 1, 3, 5, 9, (15), 45

15 is the GCF of 15 and 45.

Example 3: What is the Greatest Common Factor (GCF) of 3 and 9?

3: 1, (3)
9: 1, (3), 9

__ is the GCF of 3 and 9.

Example 4: What is the Greatest Common Factor (GCF) of 4 and 12?

4: 1, 2, 4
12: 1, 2, 3, 4, 6, 12

__ is the GCF of 4 and 12.

Your turn

Circle the GCF for each pair of numbers.

8: 1, (2), 4, 8
10: 1, (2), 5, 10

b **3:** 1, 3
9: 1, 3, 9

a **12:** 1, 2, 3, 4, 6, 12
16: 1, 2, 4, 8, 16

c **25:** 1, 5, 25
35: 1, 5, 7, 35

SELF CHECK Mark how you feel
Got it! | Need help... | I don't get it

Check your answers
How many did you get correct?

© Shell Education 146436—Catch-Up Math 27

Scan this to access the video.

After watching the video, children can confidently complete the Your Turn section.

MATH SKILLS

This book contains key math skills from both second and third grade to help your child catch up to grade level.

Grade 4 Math Skills	Pages
Recognize that a digit in one place represents ten times the digit to its right (e.g., the digits in 77 are worth 70 and 7).	9–12, 15–18
Read and write numbers using numerals, words, and expanded form. Compare the values of the numbers using > (greater than), < (less than), and = (equal to) up to 1,000,000.	13–14, 19–22
Round multi-digit whole numbers to any place.	23–24, 40–41, 50–51
Find factor pairs for numbers under 100. Understand that a number can be broken into its factors.	25–32, 56–57
Add and subtract multi-digit numbers using the standard algorithm.	38–41, 44–51
Multiply a multi-digit number by a one-digit number.	58–65
Divide a multi-digit number by a one-digit number.	76–93
Explain why fractions are or are not equivalent, and write equivalent fractions.	102–109
Add and subtract fractions with like denominators.	110–111
Write fractions as decimals to the tenths and hundredths places.	114–117
Create a pattern with numbers or shapes that follow a given rule.	132–136
Know relative sizes of units within one system of measurement (metric or customary).	144–149, 152–153, 198–203, 215–222
Use the formulas to calculate area and perimeter of shapes.	154–157
Understand that angles are formed when two line segments or rays share an endpoint. Identify angles as acute, obtuse, or right.	162–176
Measure angles using a protractor. Draw angles when given a specific measurement.	170–172
Solve addition and subtraction problems to find unknown angles.	173–176
Use attributes to identify and categorize shapes.	182–191
Identify parallel and perpendicular lines in shapes.	184–185
Recognize and draw lines of symmetry.	192–193
Calculate the area and perimeter of shapes.	198–207

MATH SKILLS (CONT.)

Grade 5 Math Skills	Pages
Understand that in a multi-digit number, a digit in one place is ten times the value of the digit to its right and $\frac{1}{10}$ of the value of the digit to its left.	9–12, 15–18
Read and write multi-digit numbers up to 1,000,000 using numerals, words, and expanded form. Compare the values of the numbers.	13–14, 19–22
Fluently add and subtract multi-digit numbers using the standard algorithm.	38–41, 44–51
Multiply multi-digit whole numbers using the standard algorithm.	60–61, 66–69
Read, write, and compare the values of decimals to the thousandths place. Write decimals in expanded form.	110–125
Create patterns with numbers that follows a given rule.	132–136
Solve numerical expressions and equations using the four operations.	137–140
Know relative sizes of units within one system of measurement (metric or customary) and provide examples.	144–149, 152–153, 198–203, 215–222
Convert measurements within the metric system and the customary system.	150–151, 217–222
Use for the formulas for area and perimeter in real-world problems that include rectangles.	154–157
Classify types of angles.	164–169
Accurately measure and draw angles using a protractor.	170–172
Apply rules for a type of shape to all shapes in that category.	182–191
Identify parallel and perpendicular lines in shapes. Use these lines to name shapes.	184–185
Recognize that three-dimensional shapes have volume. Measure volumes by counting unit cubes.	213–214

PLACE VALUE

THREE-DIGIT AND FOUR-DIGIT NUMBERS

Where a digit is in a number is called the place value.

A three-digit number has a hundreds place, a tens place, and a ones place.

Example 1:

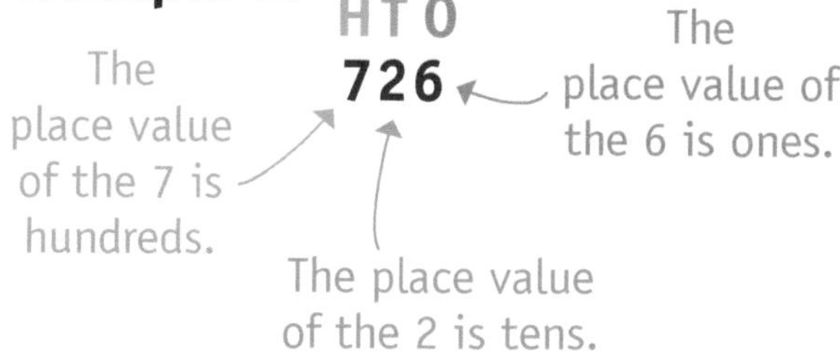

Example 2:

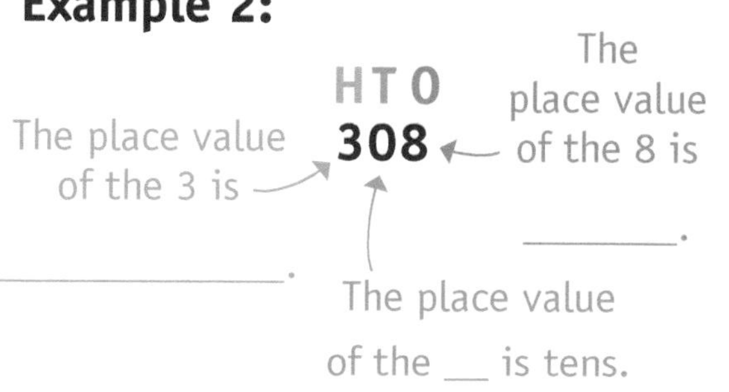

A four-digit number has a thousands place, a hundreds place, a tens place, and a ones place.

Example 3:

Th H T O

3,854

The place value of the 3 is thousands.

The place value of the 4 is ones.

The place value of the 8 is hundreds.

The place value of the 5 is tens.

Example 4:

Th H T O

8,614

The place value of the 8 is ________.

The place value of the __ is ones.

The place value of the 1 is ______.

The place value of the 6 is ________.

1 What is the place value of the 5?

- ● 523 hundreds
- **a** 3,275 ________
- **b** 5,961 ________
- **c** 152 ________
- **d** 2,053 ________
- **e** 1,295 ________

2 Circle the thousands in purple, hundreds in green, tens in blue, and ones in red.

● 2,897 **a** 5,921 **b** 253 **c** 320 **d** 4,815

SELF CHECK Mark how you feel		
Got it! ☐	Need help... ☐	I don't get it ☐

Check your answers

How many did you get correct? ☐

PRACTICE

Write the place value of each underlined digit.

- 3,724 tens
- **a** 5,236 ____________
- **b** 7,314 ____________
- **c** 257 ____________
- **d** 1,293 ____________
- **e** 1,036 ____________
- **f** 5,130 ____________
- **g** 108 ____________
- **h** 642 ____________
- **i** 7,398 ____________
- **j** 2,450 ____________
- **k** 3,706 ____________
- **l** 52 ____________
- **m** 3,254 ____________

2 Write the numbers in standard form.

- 6 thousands, 2 tens, 3 hundreds, 0 ones 6,320
- **a** 5 tens, 8 ones, 3 thousands, 4 hundreds ____________
- **b** 9 hundreds, 0 tens, 0 ones ____________
- **c** 6 ones, 5 tens, 7 hundreds ____________
- **d** 1 thousands, 4 ones, 8 hundreds, 3 tens ____________
- **e** 2 hundreds, 3 tens, 5 ones ____________

Color the digits in the thousands purple, hundreds green, tens blue, and ones red.

- **a** 8 4 3 5
- **b** 4 7 5 6
- **c** 6 6 5
- **d** 7 5 6
- **e** 8 3 7
- **f** 4 5 8 7
- **g** 9 2 6
- **h** 8 1 7 0
- **i** 6 1 0 9
- **j** 2 1 9
- **k** 2 0 1 3
- **l** 3 2 4
- **m** 5 9 6
- **n** 4 9 2 3

VALUE

THREE-DIGIT AND FOUR-DIGIT NUMBERS

The value of a number is how much a number is worth.
To find the value of a digit, look at where it is in a number.

For example, what is the value of the 3 in 7,310?
The 3 is in the hundreds column, so the value of 3 is 300.

Example 1:

In the number 593,
the value of 5 is 500,
the value of 9 is 90,
and the value of 3 is 3.

Example 2:

In the number 1,729,
the value of 1 is 1,000,
the value of 7 is 700,
the value of 2 is 20,
and the value of 9 is 9.

Example 3:

In the number 471,
the value of 4 is ____,
the value of ____ is 70,
and the value of 1 is ____.

Example 4:

In the number 8,235,
the value of 8 is ____,
the value of 2 is ____,
the value of ____ is 30
and the value of 5 is ____.

Circle the numbers where the value of 3 is 30.

537 (circled)   634   3,921   8,231

1,325   1,813   432   13

SELF CHECK Mark how you feel		
Got it! ☐	Need help... ☐	I don't get it ☐

Check your answers
How many did you get correct? ☐

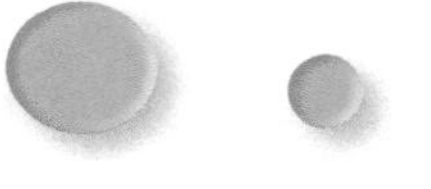

1 What is the value of 4 in these numbers?

- ● 3,247 40
- a 1,354 ____
- b 436 ____
- c 134 ____
- d 543 ____
- e 6,842 ____
- f 1,473 ____
- g 4,825 ____
- h 7,415 ____
- i 6,497 ____
- j 4,832 ____
- k 743 ____
- l 4,903 ____
- m 849 ____
- n 5,243 ____

2 Write a number that has a 5 with each given value.

- ● 50 4,953
- a 5 ____
- b 500 ____
- c 50 ____
- d 5,000 ____

3 Circle the digit with the least value, and underline the digit with the most value for each number.

- ● 5,382
- a 530
- b 1,037
- c 265
- d 2,589
- e 9,803
- f 1,009
- g 8,632
- h 582
- i 471
- j 4,936
- k 5,419
- l 873
- m 684
- n 3,781
- o 9,275

4 Circle the numbers with each matching value.

- ● The value of 5 is 50: 457 255 386 857 59 2,581
- a The value of 4 is 400: 342 439 5,543 477 1,472 415
- b The value of 6 is 6,000: 6,358 4,600 1,362 6,426 47 6,156
- c The value of 7 is 7: 1,297 1,732 407 372 5,470 1,357
- d The value of 3 is 30: 735 32 4,534 351 937 358

EXPANDED FORM

THREE-DIGIT AND FOUR-DIGIT NUMBERS

We expand a number by writing the value of each digit.

Example 1: Write 763 in expanded form.

763 = 700 + 60 + 3
(7 hundreds) (6 tens) (3 ones)

When a number is written this way, it is in expanded form.

Example 2: Write 2,852 in expanded form.

2,852 = 2,000 + 800 + 50 + 2
(2 thousands) (8 hundreds) (5 tens) (2 ones)

When a number has a zero in it, leave out that place value.

Example 3:

3,092 = 3,000 + 90 + 2
(3 thousands) (9 tens) (2 ones)

Leave out the hundreds.

Example 4:

Complete the expanded form.

8,243 = 8,000 + ____ + 40 + ____
(8 ______________) (2 hundreds) (____ tens) (3 ones)

Your turn

Write these numbers in expanded form.

347 = 300 + 40 + 7
= 3 hundreds + 4 tens + 7 ones

a 432 = ____ + ____ + ____
= ____ hundreds + ____ tens + ____ ones

b 3,065 = ____ + ____ + ____
= ____ thousands + ____ tens + ____ ones

SELF CHECK Mark how you feel

Got it!	Need help...	I don't get it
☐	☐	☐

Check your answers
How many did you get correct? ☐

PRACTICE

1 Write these numbers in expanded form.

- 2,538 = 2,000 + 500 + 30 + 8

a 857 = ____ + ____ + ____

b 329 = ____ + ____ + ____

c 1,093 = ____ + ____ + ____

d 1,834 = ____ + ____ + ____ + ____

e 506 = ____ + ____

f 4,370 = ____ + ____ + ____

2 Write these numbers in expanded form.

- 1,464 = 1,000 + 400 + 60 + 4

a 302 = ________________________

b 1,642 = ________________________

c 2,037 = ________________________

d 4,060 = ________________________

e 850 = ________________________

3 Match each number with its expanded form.

• 282	6,000 + 800 + 9
a 1,463	200 + 80 + 2
b 707	400 + 20 + 4
c 1,490	1,000 + 400 + 60 + 3
d 540	1,000 + 400 + 90
e 6,809	500 + 40
f 424	700 + 7

PLACE VALUE
FIVE-DIGIT NUMBERS

The place value is the value of a digit based on where it is in a number.

Example 1: This place value chart shows 89,374.

Ten Thousands	Thousands	Hundreds	Tens	Ones
8	9	3	7	4

The number 89,374 has:
- 8 ten thousands
- 9 thousands
- 3 hundreds
- 7 tens
- 4 ones

Look at the order—the largest place value is on the left and the smallest is on the right.

Example 2:
The number 74,351 has:
- ____ ten thousands
- ____ thousands
- ____ hundreds
- ____ tens
- ____ ones

Example 3:
The number 15,113 has:
- 1 ____________________
- 5 ________________
- 1 ________________
- 1 ________
- 3 ________

Trace the numbers in the ten thousands place in orange, the thousands place in purple, the hundreds place in green, the tens place in blue, and the ones place in red.

● 25,361   43,240   329   7,267   927

1,352   672   93   3,289   14   63,053

SELF CHECK Mark how you feel		
Got it! ☐	Need help... ☐	I don't get it ☐

Check your answers
How many did you get correct? ☐

PRACTICE

1 Circle ten thousands in orange, thousands in purple, hundreds in green, tens in blue, and ones in red.

- ● 36,285
- a 42,560
- b 95,390
- c 59,936
- d 99,363
- e 38,342
- f 67,429
- g 84,132
- h 53,931
- i 19,150
- j 10,000
- k 35,003
- l 62,415
- m 71,317
- n 59,020

2 Fill in the chart.

	Number	Ten Thousands	Thousands	Hundreds	Tens	Ones
●	52,059	5	2	0	5	9
a	63,000					
b	42,618					
c	86,254					
d	38,913					
e	71,352					

3 What is the place value of each underlined digit?

- ● 36,$\underline{2}$58 hundreds
- a $\underline{2}$4,736 ____________
- b 42,82$\underline{0}$ ____________
- c 3$\underline{0}$,745 ____________
- d 65,8$\underline{1}$2 ____________
- e 19,$\underline{0}$56 ____________
- f $\underline{2}$2,490 ____________
- g 7$\underline{3}$,592 ____________
- h 38,$\underline{2}$50 ____________
- i 53,2$\underline{5}$2 ____________
- j 84,25$\underline{6}$ ____________
- k 9$\underline{1}$,029 ____________
- l 83,$\underline{2}$43 ____________

VALUE
FIVE-DIGIT NUMBERS

The value of a number is how much it is worth.

Example 1:

TT Th H T O

25,967

The value of the 2 is 20,000.

The value of the 5 is 5,000.

The value of the 9 is 900.

The value of the 6 is 60.

The value of the 7 is 7.

Example 2:

TT Th H T O

78,496

The value of the 7 is ________.

The value of the 8 is ______.

The value of the 4 is _____.

The value of the 9 is _____.

The value of the 6 is _____.

1 Write a number where 6 has each given value.

●	60	363	c	6,000	________
a	600	________	d	60,000	________
b	6	________	e	60	________

2 Circle the numbers where 5 has a value of 50.

● (652) 5,632 54 64,357 15

2,593 3,156 3,205 50,326 25,937

SELF CHECK Mark how you feel

Got it!	Need help...	I don't get it
☐	 ☐	☐

Check your answers

How many did you get correct? ☐

PRACTICE

1 What is the value of each underlined digit?

●	32,651 30,000	d	99,062 ________	h	13,313 ________
a	36,324 ________	e	14,271 ________	i	95,449 ________
b	80,357 ________	f	52,437 ________	j	57,595 ________
c	71,352 ________	g	81,950 ________	k	25,311 ________

2 Use the digits 4, 9, 8, 5, 2 to make a five-digit number with:

●	9 ten thousands 94,852	c	4 thousands ________	f	2 tens ________
a	2 hundreds ________	d	9 ones ________	g	4 tens ________
b	5 ones ________	e	8 thousands ________	h	8 hundreds ________

3 Write each five-digit number in different ways.

a 53,428

● 53 thousands + 428

534 hundreds + ________

5,342 tens + ________

5 ten thousands + ________

b 56,320

● 563 hundreds + 20

56 thousands + ________

5 ten thousands + ________

5,632 tens + ________

EXPANDED FORM
FIVE-DIGIT NUMBERS

When a number is written to show the value of each digit, it is called an expanded number.

Example 1: Write 3,629 in expanded form.

3,629 = 3,000 (3 thousands) + 600 (6 hundreds) + 20 (2 tens) + 9 (9 ones)

Example 2: Write 59,284 in expanded form.

59,284 = 50,000 (5 ten thousands) + 9,000 (9 thousands) + 200 (2 hundreds) + 80 (8 tens) + 4 (4 ones)

Example 3: Write 85,409 in expanded form.

85,409 = ________ (8 ten thousands) + 5,000 (____ thousands) + 400 (____ hundreds) + ____ (9 ones)

Example 4: Write 16,265 in expanded form.

16,265 = ________ (1 ten thousand) + 6,000 (____ thousands) + 200 (____ hundreds) + ____ (6 tens) + ____ (5 ones)

Your turn

Complete the expanded numbers.

- 56,324 = 50,000 + 6,000 + 300 + 20 + 4

a 72,393 = 70,000 + 2,000 + ____ + 90 + 3

b 1,874 = ______ + 800 + 70 + 4

c 98,731 = 90,000 + 8,000 + ____ + 30 + 1

d 5,638 = 5,000 + 600 + ____ + 8

SELF CHECK Mark how you feel		
Got it! ☐	Need help... ☐	I don't get it ☐

Check your answers
How many did you get correct? ☐

PRACTICE

Match each number to its expanded form.

●	24,937	100 + 90 + 3
a	15,471	5,000 + 600 + 40 + 9
b	3,584	50 + 7
c	29,762	20,000 + 9,000 + 700 + 60 + 2
d	35,847	3,000 + 500 + 80 + 4
e	57	10,000 + 5,000 + 400 + 70 + 1
f	193	20,000 + 4,000 + 900 + 30 + 7
g	5,649	30,000 + 5,000 + 800 + 40 + 7

2 Write these numbers in expanded form.

● 75,389 = 70,000 + 5,000 + 300 + 80 + 9

a 22,387 = ____________________

b 91,476 = ____________________

c 89,295 = ____________________

d 73,049 = ____________________

Fill in the missing numbers.

● 62,583 = 60,000 + 2,000 + 500 + 80 + 3

a 74,860 = ________ + 4,000 + ____ + ____

b 81,060 = 80,000 + ______ + ____

c 16,036 = ________ + 6,000 + ____ + ____

d 97,398 = 90,000 + 7,000 + ____ + 90 + ____

e 23,529 = ________ + 3,000 + ____ + 20 + ____

f 54,207 = 50,000 + 4,000 + ____ + ____

GREATER THAN, LESS THAN, EQUAL TO

THREE-DIGIT, FOUR-DIGIT, AND FIVE-DIGIT NUMBERS

>	=	<
the symbol for greater than	the symbol for equal to	the symbol for less than

These symbols help you compare numbers.

Example 1: 25,374 [>] 21,320

25,374 is greater than 21,320.

Example 2: 12,347 [<] 42,135

12,347 is less than 42,135.

Example 3: 52,436 [=] 52,436

52,436 is equal to 52,436.

Example 4: 626 > 425

626 ______________ 425.

Example 5: 1,345 = 1,345

1,345 ______________ 1,345.

Example 6: 29,306 < 57,403

29,306 ______________ 57,403.

Write True or False.

- 32,357 < 33,295 True
- **a** 63,249 > 6,423 ________
- **b** 95,931 < 96,918 ________
- **c** 12,354 = 12,354 ________
- **d** 67,493 < 69,957 ________
- **e** 99,099 > 98,326 ________

Which number does the pointy end point to? That helps you tell the difference between < and >.

SELF CHECK Mark how you feel

Got it!	Need help...	I don't get it
 ☐	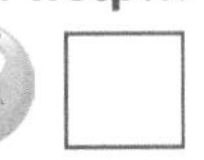  ☐	 ☐

Check your answers

How many did you get correct? ☐

PRACTICE

1 Write <, >, or = in the boxes, and cross out the incorrect words.

- 53,824 [>] 52,852 — because 53,824 is greater than / ~~less than~~ / ~~equal to~~ 52,852
- **a** 27,325 [ ] 53,725 — because 27,325 is greater than / less than / equal to 53,725
- **b** 49,243 [ ] 35,935 — because 49,243 is greater than / less than / equal to 35,935
- **c** 12,653 [ ] 12,653 — because 12,653 is greater than / less than / equal to 12,653
- **d** 59,731 [ ] 15,463 — because 59,731 is greater than / less than / equal to 15,463
- **e** 33,821 [ ] 97,328 — because 33,821 is greater than / less than / equal to 97,328

2 Write >, <, or = to make the statements true.

253 [<] 325	**e** 14,385 [ ] 14,835	**j** 842 [ ] 842
a 1,594 [ ] 1,495	**f** 25,849 [ ] 28,594	**k** 15,385 [ ] 15,385
b 6,327 [ ] 7,326	**g** 38,542 [ ] 24,583	**l** 5,738 [ ] 8,753
c 149 [ ] 941	**h** 98,990 [ ] 98,099	**m** 9,205 [ ] 9,025
d 1,873 [ ] 1,873	**i** 347 [ ] 743	**n** 47,382 [ ] 43,872

3 Put a check next to the correct statements and an X next to the incorrect statements.

347 < 754 ✓	**d** 8,491 < 8,194	**h** 9,801 > 9,108
a 1,254 = 1,254	**e** 8,648 > 8,846	**i** 12,534 > 13,435
b 389 < 983	**f** 5,347 < 5,743	**j** 58,934 < 54,983
c 7,621 > 8,723	**g** 1,263 < 1,362	**k** 72,105 > 75,107

ROUNDING TO THE NEAREST 100, 1,000, AND 10,000

Rounding is useful when you need to estimate an answer.

Round-down numbers					Round-up numbers				
0	1	2	3	4	5	6	7	8	9

Rounding to 100

1 Go to the hundreds column.
2 Write the round-up number above the hundreds.
3 Circle the number in the tens column.
4 Is it a round-up or round-down number?
5 Round the number.

Example 1: Round to the nearest 100.

9 ← up
8(5)7

900

Rounding to 1,000

1 Go to the thousands column.
2 Write the round-up number above the thousands.
3 Circle the number in the hundreds column.
4 Is it a round-up or round-down number?
5 Round the number.

Example 2: Round to the nearest 1,000.

6 ← up
45,(8)45

46,000

Rounding to 10,000

1 Go to the ten thousands column.
2 Write the round-up number above the ten thousands.
3 Circle the number in the thousands column.
4 Is it a round-up or round-down number?
5 Round the number.

Example 3: Round to the nearest 10,000.

3
2(4),556
down

20,000

Example 4:
Round 15,486 to the nearest 100.

5
15,4(8)6

____

Example 5:
Round 1,742 to the nearest 1,000.

2
1,(7)42

____

Round to the nearest 100.

3 ← up
37,2(9)5

37,300

a 5,834 ________

b 652 ________

SELF CHECK Mark how you feel

Got it!	Need help...	I don't get it
 ☐	 ☐	☐

Check your answers
How many did you get correct? ☐

PRACTICE

1 Round these numbers to the nearest 100.

- 6,873 (9, up) 6,900
- c 9,876 ______
- f 64,327 ______
- a 653 ______
- d 15,492 ______
- g 714 ______
- b 1,524 ______
- e 59,821 ______
- h 8,935 ______

2 Round these numbers to the nearest 1,000.

- 74,238 (5, down) 74,000
- b 2,738 ______
- d 16,423 ______
- a 1,543 ______
- c 6,735 ______
- e 41,470 ______

3 Round these numbers to the nearest 10,000.

- 64,372 (7, down) 60,000
- b 54,972 ______
- d 60,429 ______
- a 47,346 ______
- c 58,262 ______
- e 10,003 ______

4 Round these numbers.

	Nearest 100	Nearest 1,000	Nearest 10,000
37,342	37,300	37,000	40,000
a 68,437			
b 40,305			
c 23,036			

FACTORS

There are two ways to identify factors.

- **A factor is a number that divides into a larger number without leaving a remainder.**
  30 ÷ 6 = 5, so 5 and 6 are factors of 30.
- **We know that 6 × 5 = 30, so any numbers multiplied to get the product are factors of that product.**
  factor × factor = product

Example 1: What are the factors of 12?

We know 1 × 12 = 12, so 1 and 12 are factors.

2 × 6 = 12, so 2 and 6 are factors.

3 × 4 = 12, so 3 and 4 are factors.

We can write all the factors of 12 in order:

1, 2, 3, 4, 6, 12

Example 2: What are the factors of 21?

We know 1 × 21 = 21, so 1 and _____ are factors.

3 × 7 = 21, so 3 and _____ are factors.

We can write all the factors of 21 in order:

_____, _____, _____, _____

Your turn

Circle the factors of each number.

● Factors of 8:
(1) (2) 3 (4) 5 6 (8)

a Factors of 15:
1 2 3 5 7 8 9 15

b Factors of 9:
1 2 3 6 7 9

c Factors of 7:
1 2 3 4 5 6 7

SELF CHECK Mark how you feel		
Got it! ☐	Need help... ☐	I don't get it ☐

Check your answers
How many did you get correct? ☐

PRACTICE

1 Write the factors of these numbers.

- (example) 10 1, 2, 5, 10
- **a** 14 ______________________
- **b** 16 ______________________
- **c** 30 ______________________
- **d** 32 ______________________
- **e** 36 ______________________
- **f** 20 ______________________
- **g** 22 ______________________
- **h** 6 ______________________

2 Cross out the number that is not a factor of the first number.

- (example) **21:** 1, ~~2~~, 3, 7, 21
- **a** **27:** 1, 3, 6, 9, 27
- **b** **40:** 1, 2, 3, 4, 5, 8, 10, 40
- **c** **100:** 1, 2, 4, 5, 6, 10, 20, 25, 50, 100
- **d** **18:** 1, 2, 3, 4, 6, 9, 18
- **e** **24:** 1, 2, 3, 4, 6, 7, 8, 12, 24
- **f** **25:** 1, 2, 5, 25
- **g** **28:** 1, 2, 3, 4, 7, 14, 28
- **h** **5:** 1, 2, 5
- **i** **35:** 1, 5, 6, 7, 35
- **j** **49:** 1, 4, 7, 49
- **k** **33:** 1, 3, 10, 11, 33

GREATEST COMMON FACTOR (GCF)

The Greatest Common Factor (GCF) is the highest number that is a factor of two other numbers.

SCAN to watch video

Example 1:
What is the Greatest Common Factor (GCF) of 8 and 12?

8: 1, 2, (4), 8 • Write all the factors of each number.

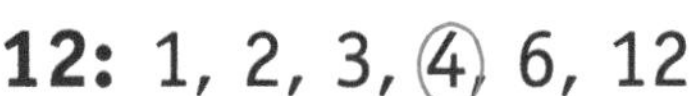
12: 1, 2, 3, (4), 6, 12 • Look for the highest number that is in both lists.

4 is the Greatest Common Factor of 8 and 12.

Example 2:
What is the Greatest Common Factor (GCF) of 15 and 45?

15: 1, 3, 5, (15)

45: 1, 3, 5, 9, (15), 45

15 is the GCF of 15 and 45.

Example 3: What is the Greatest Common Factor (GCF) of 3 and 9?

3: 1, (3)

9: 1, (3), 9

_____ is the GCF of 3 and 9.

Example 4: What is the Greatest Common Factor (GCF) of 4 and 12?

4: 1, 2, 4

12: 1, 2, 3, 4, 6, 12

_____ is the GCF of 4 and 12.

Circle the GCF for each pair of numbers.

8: 1, (2), 4, 8
10: 1, (2), 5, 10

b **3:** 1, 3
9: 1, 3, 9

a **12:** 1, 2, 3, 4, 6, 12
16: 1, 2, 4, 8, 16

c **25:** 1, 5, 25
35: 1, 5, 7, 35

SELF CHECK Mark how you feel

Got it!	Need help...	I don't get it
☐	 ☐	 ☐

Check your answers
How many did you get correct? ☐

PRACTICE

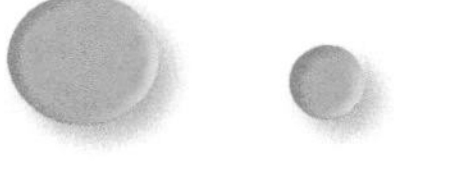

1 Find the Greatest Common Factor (GCF).

12: 1, 2, 3, 4, 6, 12
15: 1, 3, 5, 15
3 is the GCF of 12 and 15.

a 14: ______________________
21: ______________________
_____ is the GCF of 14 and 21.

b 21: ______________________
24: ______________________
_____ is the GCF of 21 and 24.

c 18: ______________________
36: ______________________
_____ is the GCF of 18 and 36.

d 10: ______________________
24: ______________________
_____ is the GCF of 10 and 24.

e 16: ______________________
20: ______________________
_____ is the GCF of 16 and 20.

f 22: ______________________
33: ______________________
_____ is the GCF of 22 and 33.

g 10: ______________________
30: ______________________
_____ is the GCF of 10 and 30.

h 9: ______________________
27: ______________________
_____ is the GCF of 9 and 27.

i 12: ______________________
18: ______________________
_____ is the GCF of 12 and 18.

MULTIPLES

A multiple is the number you get when you multiply two factors together.

12 is a multiple of 3 and 4 because 3 × 4 = 12. (3 = factor, 4 = factor, 12 = multiple)

12 is also a multiple of 1 and 12 because 1 × 12 = 12. (1 = factor, 12 = factor, 12 = multiple)

It is also a multiple of 2 and 6 because 2 × 6 = 12. (2 = factor, 6 = factor, 12 = multiple)

Every number has both 1 and itself as factors.

Example 1: What are the multiples of 3?

The multiples of 3 are the numbers you get when you multiply 3 by another number.

3 × 1 = 3, 3 × 2 = 6, 3 × 3 = 9, 3 × 4 = 12, 3 × 5 = 15, 3 × 6 = 18

The first six multiples of 3 are 3, 6, 9, 12, 15, and 18.

Example 2: What are the first five multiples of 5?

5 × 1 = ____, 5 × 2 = ____, 5 × 3 = ____, 5 × 4 = ____, 5 × 5 = ____

The first five multiples of 5 are ____, ____, ____, ____, and ____.

Write the first three multiples.

- 2: 2, 4, 6
- **a** 3: ____, ____, ____
- **b** 4: ____, ____, ____
- **c** 12: ____, ____, ____

SELF CHECK Mark how you feel		
Got it! ☐	Need help... ☐	I don't get it ☐

Check your answers
How many did you get correct? ☐

PRACTICE

1 Write the first eight multiples.

- 1: 1, 2, 3, 4, 5, 6, 7, 8

a 2: ___, ___, ___, ___, ___, ___, ___, ___

b 4: ___, ___, ___, ___, ___, ___, ___, ___

c 5: ___, ___, ___, ___, ___, ___, ___, ___

d 7: ___, ___, ___, ___, ___, ___, ___, ___

e 9: ___, ___, ___, ___, ___, ___, ___, ___

f 10: ___, ___, ___, ___, ___, ___, ___, ___

g 11: ___, ___, ___, ___, ___, ___, ___, ___

2 Cross out the number that is not a multiple of the first number.

- 5: 55, 60, 65, 70, ~~73~~, 75

a **10:** 90, 100, 110, 115, 120, 130

b **3:** 21, 24, 27, 28, 30, 33

c **6:** 6, 12, 18, 20, 24, 30

d **8:** 8, 16, 24, 32, 40, 46

e **12:** 12, 24, 28, 36, 48, 60

f **2:** 18, 20, 22, 23, 24, 26

g **4:** 36, 40, 44, 46, 48, 52

h **11:** 22, 33, 35, 44, 55, 66

i **7:** 21, 28, 35, 37, 42, 49

j **9:** 54, 56, 63, 72, 81, 90

LEAST COMMON MULTIPLES (LCM)

The Least Common Multiple (LCM) of two numbers is the smallest number that is a multiple of both numbers.

SCAN to watch video

Example 1:

What is the Least Common Multiple of 4 and 8?

Multiples of **4:** 4, (8), 12, 16 ...

Multiples of **8:** (8), 16, 24 ...

The LCM of 4 and 8 is **8.**

Finding the LCM can help you work with fractions and arrange things in equal groups.

Can you figure out how?

Example 2:

What is the Least Common Multiple of 8 and 12?

Multiples of **8:** 8, 16, (24), 32 ...

Multiples of **12:** 12, (24), 36, 48 ...

The LCM of 8 and 12 is **24.**

Example 3:

What is the Least Common Multiple of 2 and 4?

Multiples of **2:** 2, (4), 6, 8 ...

Multiples of **4:** (4), 8, 12, 16 ...

The LCM of 2 and 4 is _____.

Circle the LCM for each pair of numbers.

● **2:** 2, 4, 6, (8) ...
8: (8), 16, 24, 32 ...

b **2:** 2, 4, 6, 8 ...
3: 3, 6, 9, 12 ...

a **4:** 4, 8, 12, 16 ...
6: 6, 12, 18, 24 ...

c **1:** 1, 2, 3, 4, 5, 6 ...
6: 6, 12, 18, 24, 30, 36 ...

SELF CHECK Mark how you feel		
Got it! ☐	Need help... ☐	I don't get it ☐

Check your answers

How many did you get correct? ☐

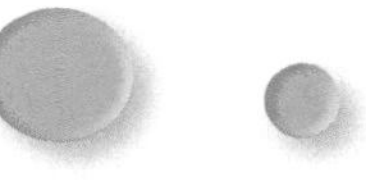

PRACTICE

1 What is the Least Common Multiple (LCM)?

2: 2, 4, 6, 8, (10)
5: 5, (10), 15, 20
The LCM is 10.

a 3: ______
4: ______
The LCM is ______.

b 5: ______
10: ______
The LCM is ______.

c 2: ______
6: ______
The LCM is ______.

d 3: ______
6: ______
The LCM is ______.

e 1: ______
4: ______
The LCM is ______.

f 4: ______
10: ______
The LCM is ______.

g 3: ______
5: ______
The LCM is ______.

h 2: ______
10: ______
The LCM is ______.

i 3: ______
9: ______
The LCM is ______

j 4: ______
8: ______
The LCM is ______.

WHOLE NUMBERS REVIEW

1 Fill in the number chart.

	Number	Hundred Thousands	Ten Thousands	Thousands	Hundreds	Tens	Ones
a	56						
b	250						
c	1,346						
d	8,007						
e	32,430						
f	40,003						
g	100,200						
h	840,937						
i	647,300						
j	420,030						

2 What is the place value of the 7 in these numbers?

a 473 ____________________

b 1,257 ____________________

c 4,732 ____________________

d 7,890 ____________________

e 20,700 ____________________

f 762,381 ____________________

g 27,392 ____________________

h 173,258 ____________________

i 27 ____________________

j 387 ____________________

k 7,321 ____________________

l 268,473 ____________________

REVIEW

3 What is the value of each underlined digit?

a 4,<u>8</u>27 __________

b 15,3<u>2</u>6 __________

c <u>2</u>9 __________

d 16<u>4</u> __________

e <u>2</u>4,985 __________

f 3<u>6</u>,438 __________

g <u>1</u>29,853 __________

h 4<u>5</u>7,906 __________

i 6,95<u>7</u> __________

j 47,<u>5</u>90 __________

k 531,2<u>8</u>5 __________

l <u>7</u>36,150 __________

m 1<u>6</u> __________

n 4<u>9</u>3 __________

4 Write these numbers in standard form.

a 3 hundred thousands, 2 ten thousands, 8 thousands, 5 hundreds, 6 tens, 9 ones __________

b 8 hundreds, 5 ones, 7 ten thousands, 6 hundred thousands, 4 thousands __________

c 5 thousands, 3 ten thousands, 6 hundred thousands, 3 ones __________

d 7 ones, 4 hundreds, 7 ten thousands, 2 hundred thousands __________

5 Color the digits in the hundred thousands yellow, ten thousands orange, thousands purple, hundreds green, tens blue, and ones red.

a 109,580

b 961

c 7,620

d 87,314

e 89

f 73,554

g 346

h 406,789

6 Write 6-digit numbers where the 7 is worth:

a 70 __________

b 7 __________

c 700 __________

d 700,000 __________

e 70,000 __________

f 7,000 __________

7 Write 6-digit numbers where the 5 is worth:

a 5,000 ____________ d 50,000 ____________

b 50 ____________ e 500,000 ____________

c 5 ____________ f 500 ____________

8 Circle the numbers where the value of 4 is 400.

236,400 4,372 23,436 24 643,825 437 6,840

14,593 983,402 127,483 1,438 14,383 1,534

9 Write these numbers in expanded form.

a 723 = ______________________________

b 1,439 = ______________________________

c 533 = ______________________________

d 25,295 = ______________________________

e 384,629 = ______________________________

10 Write these numbers in ascending order.

a 6,523; 3,526; 5,236; 5,623; 5,632

____

b 14,759; 41,579; 54,791; 91,547; 75,154

____

c 613,285; 582,316; 631,582; 531,682; 815,632

____

REVIEW

11 Write these numbers in descending order.

a 9,524; 4,529; 9,254; 5,429; 2,945

____

b 61,379; 97,316; 69,137; 67,139; 79,613

____

c 459,352; 253,954; 495,234; 942,355; 395,542

____

12 Write <, >, or = to make the statements true.

a 372 ☐ 273

b 249 ☐ 942

c 2,835 ☐ 5,382

d 7,263 ☐ 3,267

e 18,430 ☐ 10,834

f 29,372 ☐ 92,732

g 293,481 ☐ 934,812

h 76,439 ☐ 76,439

i 653,295 ☐ 625,395

j 843,252 ☐ 483,522

13 Round the numbers.

Round to	a 532,487	b 643,981	c 857,603
nearest 10			
nearest 100			
nearest 1,000			
nearest 10,000			
nearest 100,000			

14 Write all the factors.

a 12 ______________________

b 16 ______________________

c 18 ______________________

d 36 ______________________

15 Write the Greatest Common Factor (GCF).

a 8: ______________________

12: ______________________

The GCF is _____.

b 20: ______________________

24: ______________________

The GCF is _____.

c 15: ______________________

18: ______________________

The GCF is _____.

16 Write the first five multiples.

a 2: ___, ___, ___, ___, ___

b 8: ___, ___, ___, ___, ___

c 5: ___, ___, ___, ___, ___

d 9: ___, ___, ___, ___, ___

e 10: ___, ___, ___, ___, ___

f 7: ___, ___, ___, ___, ___

17 Find the Least Common Multiple (LCM).

a 3: ______________________

4: ______________________

The LCM is _____.

b 2: ______________________

3: ______________________

The LCM is _____.

ADDING WITH AND WITHOUT REGROUPING

FOUR-DIGIT NUMBERS

Here are examples of adding 4-digit numbers with 2-digit, 3-digit, and 4-digit numbers, with and without regrouping.

	4-digit + 2-digit	4-digit + 3-digit	4-digit + 4-digit
Without regrouping	**Example 1:** $\begin{array}{r} 3,042 \\ +\quad 53 \\ \hline 3,095 \end{array}$	**Example 3:** $\begin{array}{r} 6,381 \\ +\quad 608 \\ \hline 6,989 \end{array}$	**Example 5:** $\begin{array}{r} 4,573 \\ +5,321 \\ \hline 9,894 \end{array}$
With regrouping	**Example 2:** $\begin{array}{r} 5,6{}^{1}39 \\ +\quad 45 \\ \hline 5,684 \end{array}$	**Example 4:** $\begin{array}{r} 5,{}^{1}4{}^{1}82 \\ +\quad 159 \\ \hline 5,641 \end{array}$	**Example 6:** $\begin{array}{r} {}^{1}5,{}^{1}9{}^{1}47 \\ +2,655 \\ \hline 8,602 \end{array}$

Example 7:

$$\begin{array}{r} 2,537 \\ +\quad 98 \\ \hline \end{array}$$

Example 8:

$$\begin{array}{r} 9,008 \\ +\quad 990 \\ \hline \end{array}$$

Example 9:

$$\begin{array}{r} 6,837 \\ +1,895 \\ \hline \end{array}$$

Solve these addition problems.

●
$$\begin{array}{r} {}^{1}3,{}^{1}8{}^{1}54 \\ +\quad 156 \\ \hline 4010 \end{array}$$

a
$$\begin{array}{r} 2,152 \\ +\quad 215 \\ \hline \end{array}$$

b
$$\begin{array}{r} 5,354 \\ +1,345 \\ \hline \end{array}$$

c
$$\begin{array}{r} 6,824 \\ +5,495 \\ \hline \end{array}$$

d
$$\begin{array}{r} 1,579 \\ +\quad 43 \\ \hline \end{array}$$

e
$$\begin{array}{r} 8,097 \\ +\quad 49 \\ \hline \end{array}$$

SELF CHECK Mark how you feel

Got it!	Need help...	I don't get it
☐	☐	☐

Check your answers

How many did you get correct? ☐

PRACTICE

1 Solve.

Example:

Th	H	T	O
4	[1]3	[1]5	7
+		5	3
4	4	1	0

a

Th	H	T	O
5	9	8	1
+		3	8

b

Th	H	T	O
5	6	2	5
+		4	3

2 Add the numbers in each problem.

Example: 7,[1]0[1]95 + 56 = 7,151

a 8,973 + 24

b 6,261 + 49

c 8,789 + 39

3 Solve.

Example: 7,531 + 246 = 7,777

b 5,816 + 347

d 4,382 + 341

f 6,920 + 189

a 8,994 + 538

c 6,243 + 185

e 5,711 + 399

g 4,920 + 239

4 Add.

Example: 4,925 + 1,031 = 5,956

b 6,789 + 2,345

d 8,573 + 5,480

f 7,267 + 5,243

a 5,431 + 1,542

c 9,990 + 7,348

e 9,324 + 1,588

g 9,373 + 2,779

ROUNDING TO ESTIMATE ADDITION ANSWERS

We can use rounding to get an answer that is close to the actual answer.

Round each number to the nearest 10, and then add to estimate the answer.

Example 1:

138 + 21 is about 160

140 | 20

Example 2:

142 + 57 is about ____

____ | ____

Round to the nearest 100 to estimate the answer.

Example 3:

346 + 287 is about 600

300 | 300

Example 4:

415 + 695 is about ____

____ | ____

Your turn

Estimate the answers.

- Round to the nearest 10. 514 + 32 is about 540 (510 | 30)

a Round to the nearest 100. 215 + 168 is about ____ (____ | ____)

b Round to the nearest 10. 547 + 98 is about ____ (____ | ____)

SELF CHECK Mark how you feel

Got it!	Need help...	I don't get it
☐	☐	☐

Check your answers

How many did you get correct? ☐

PRACTICE

1 Estimate the answers by rounding each number to the nearest 10.

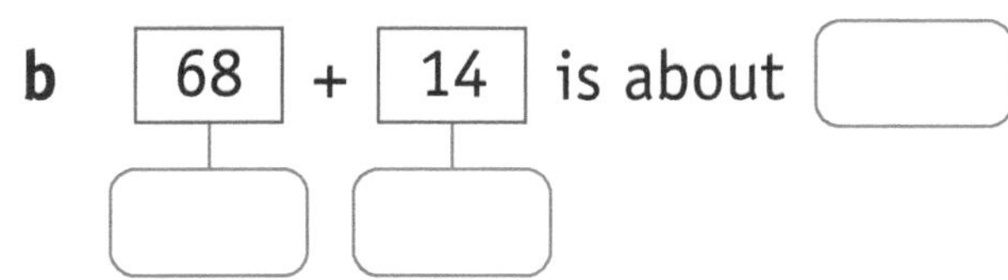

154 + 38 is about 190
(150) (40)

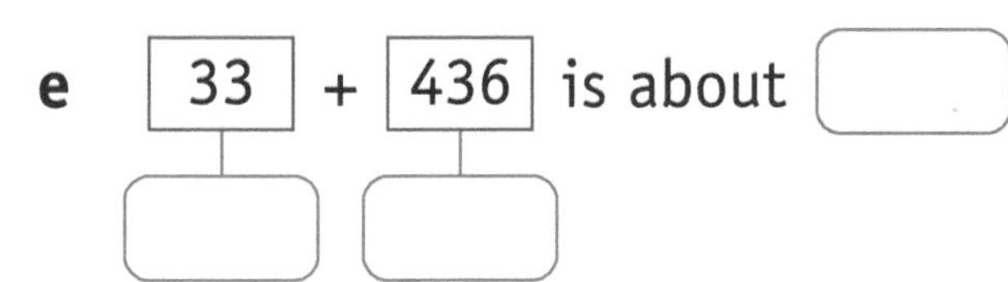

c 281 + 36 is about ____

a 63 + 45 is about ____

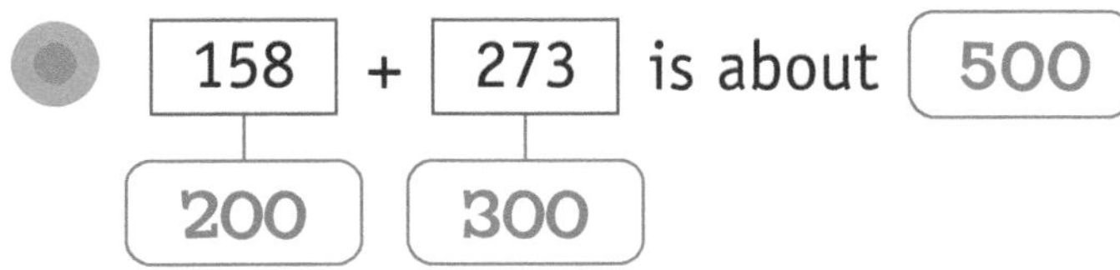

d 26 + 584 is about ____

b 68 + 14 is about ____

e 33 + 436 is about ____

2 Round each number to the nearest 100 to estimate the answers.

158 + 273 is about 500
(200) (300)

a 519 + 647 is about ____

b 595 + 235 is about ____

c 909 + 367 is about ____

d 435 + 815 is about ____

ADDITION REVIEW

1 Add these numbers.

a	b	c	d	e
36 + 52	57 + 22	72 + 15	43 + 25	17 + 91

2 Solve.

a. 735 + 121	c. 532 + 415	e. 1,382 + 1,411	g. 3,253 + 1,512
b. 424 + 61	d. 732 + 142	f. 2,461 + 1,327	h. 4,210 + 1,037

3 Complete these addition problems.

a. 74 + 39	e. 76 + 89	i. 709 + 899	m. 9,501 + 3,389
b. 26 + 89	f. 135 + 429	j. 457 + 753	n. 6,206 + 8,549
c. 45 + 76	g. 576 + 836	k. 628 + 946	o. 7,385 + 7,493
d. 35 + 58	h. 897 + 123	l. 2,436 + 5,820	p. 7,825 + 3,093

4 Round these numbers to the nearest 10 to estimate the answers.

a 27 + 32 is about ☐

b 48 + 61 is about ☐

c 143 + 58 is about ☐

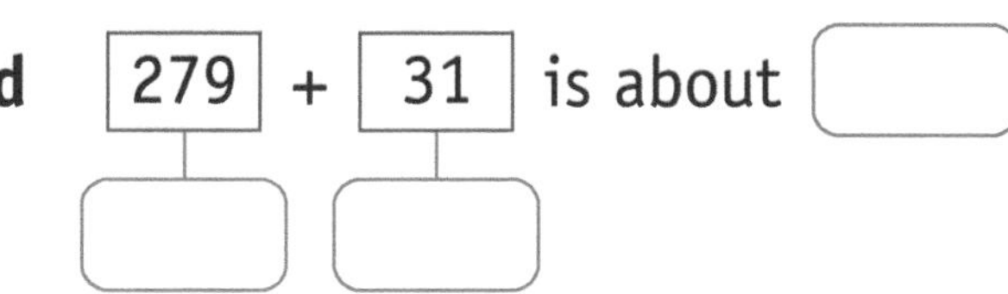

d 279 + 31 is about ☐

5 Round these numbers to the nearest 100 to estimate the answers.

a 327 + 141 is about ☐

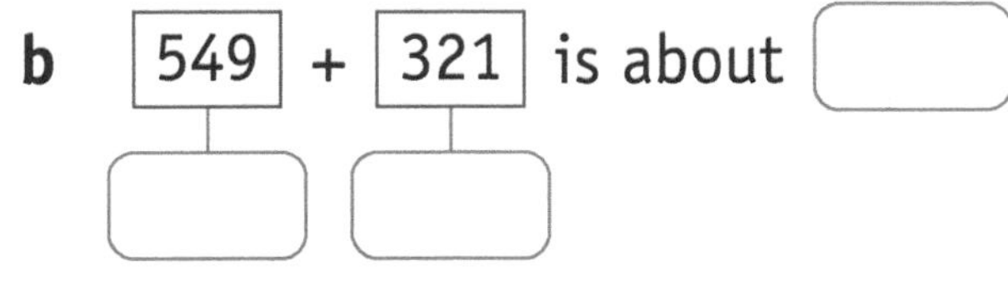

b 549 + 321 is about ☐

c 862 + 346 is about ☐

d 416 + 711 is about ☐

SUBTRACTION WITH REGROUPING

THREE-DIGIT AND FOUR-DIGIT NUMBERS

Here is an example of a four-digit subtraction problem. We need to regroup, or borrow from the tens column.

Example 1:

	Th	H	T	O
	3	7	8~~9~~	18
–	1	4	5	9
	2	3	3	9

We cannot take 9 from 8. So, we borrow 1 ten, which is the same as 10 ones. Now, we can subtract 9 from 18.

Example 2:

	Th	H	T	O
	3~~4~~	11~~2~~	9~~0~~	13
–	2	5	8	6
	1	6	1	7

Example 3:

	Th	H	T	O
	6~~7~~	11~~2~~	14~~5~~	13
–	5	8	9	7

Example 4:

	Th	H	T	O
	3	7	0~~1~~	11
–		2	0	6

Start at the ones column. Then, move to the tens column. Next, the hundreds. Finally, the thousands.

Solve these subtraction problems.

●
```
  8 9, 9 0 1 2 6
  – 3, 5 6 3
    5, 4 6 3
```

b
```
  7, 1 3 0
– 4, 2 1 9
```

a
```
  8, 2 4 9
– 2, 3 6 8
```

c
```
  6, 5 0 2
– 2, 3 6 1
```

SELF CHECK Mark how you feel		
Got it! ☐	Need help... ☐	I don't get it ☐

Check your answers
How many did you get correct? ☐

PRACTICE

1 Solve.

	Th	H	T	O
	2	8	8 ~~9~~	1 3
−	1	4	0	7
	1	4	8	6

a

	Th	H	T	O
	4	9	3	4
−	2	4	1	5

b

	Th	H	T	O
	7	0	3	2
−		1	5	3

2 Subtract.

8, 2~~3~~ 15 4
− 3, 1 9 2
5, 1 6 2

a 7, 2 6 7
− 3 4 9

b 8, 0 3 4
− 5, 0 9 3

c 5, 7 2 1
− 8 0 0

d 6, 5 0 6
− 1, 2 0 7

e 5, 8 6 2
− 1, 3 7 4

3 Solve and then check your answers with addition.

4, 7~~8~~ 9~~0~~ 13
− 1, 3 5 4
3, 4 4 9 ✓

3, 14 14 9
+ 1, 3 5 4
4, 8 0 3

a 5, 2 0 4
− 1, 3 7 3

+ 1, 3 7 3

b 8, 5 4 1
− 4 3 2

+ 4 3 2

c 9, 3 0 7
− 4, 3 5 8

+ 4, 3 5 8

d 8, 3 2 2
− 1, 7 0 3

+ 1, 7 0 3

e 4, 8 3 6
− 4 0 9

+ 4 0 9

SUBTRACTION WITH REGROUPING

FIVE-DIGIT NUMBERS

When subtracting, we sometimes need to regroup, or borrow 1 ten for 10 ones and then 1 hundred for 10 tens.

Example 1:

Here, we borrowed 1 hundred for 10 tens.

	TT	Th	H	T	O
	8	6	²~~3~~	⑬~~4~~	¹3
–	3	2	1	7	8
	5	4	1	6	5

We couldn't take 8 from 3, so we borrowed 1 ten for 10 ones.

Example 2:

	TT	Th	H	T	O
	⁶~~7~~	¹2	5	²~~3~~	¹6
–	1	5	4	2	8
	5	7	1	0	8

Example 3:

	TT	Th	H	T	O
	4	⁷~~8~~	¹²~~3~~	⁹~~0~~	¹2
–	1	0	5	6	3
	3	7	7	3	9

Example 4:

	TT	Th	H	T	O
	5	3	⁵~~6~~	¹4	5
–		2	3	7	4
					1

Solve these subtraction problems.

● 3 ³~~4~~, ¹⁰~~1~~ ¹0 6
– 3, 4 2 5
= 3 0, 6 8 1

b 5 3, 8 4 7
– 3 2, 9 8 5

a 7 3, 8 2 4
– 5, 3 2 8

c 6 5, 1 4 3
– 1 9, 0 3 7

SELF CHECK Mark how you feel		
Got it! ☐	Need help... ☐	I don't get it ☐

Check your answers
How many did you get correct? ☐

PRACTICE

1 Subtract.

Example:

	TT	Th	H	T	O
	4	⁶7̸	⁹0̸	¹3	5
−	1	4	2	4	3
	3	2	7	9	2

a

	TT	Th	H	T	O
	7	2	4	3	1
−		1	4	3	5

b

	TT	Th	H	T	O
	9	2	0	7	4
−	4	3	2	5	7

2 Subtract.

Example: 5 ⁵6̸, ¹2 ³4̸ ¹0 − 5, 7 3 5 = 5 0, 5 0 5

b 54,373 − 5,425

d 83,420 − 4,835

a 16,030 − 4,952

c 40,324 − 21,408

e 67,085 − 32,986

3 Solve and then check using addition.

Example: ¹2̸ ¹³4̸, ¹3 ⁷8̸ ¹4 − 1 4, 7 2 9 = 9, 6 5 5 ✓

Check: ¹ ¹9, 6 ¹5 5 + 1 4, 7 2 9 = 2 4, 3 8 4

a 49,340 − 15,243

\+ 15,243

b 92,731 − 24,352

\+ 24,352

4 Challenge: Fill in the missing digits.

Example: ⁶7̸ ¹4, 3 ⁷8̸ ¹2 − 2 5, 3 7 4 = 4 9, 0 0 8

a ____ − 14,275 = 38,218

b 82,310 − ____ = 38,897

REGROUPING FROM LARGER PLACE VALUES

When you are subtracting, sometimes you can't regroup, or borrow from the next place value.

Example 1:

$$\begin{array}{r} {}^{5}\cancel{6}\ {}^{9}\cancel{0}\ {}^{1}0 \\ -\quad 2\ \ 7 \\ \hline 5\ \ 7\ \ 3 \end{array}$$

We can't borrow from the tens, so move to the hundreds column.

Example 2:

$$\begin{array}{r} {}^{6}\cancel{7},\ {}^{9}\cancel{0}\ {}^{9}\cancel{0}\ {}^{1}0 \\ -\quad 2\ \ 4\ \ 3 \\ \hline 6,\ 7\ \ 5\ \ 7 \end{array}$$

Example 3:

$$\begin{array}{r} {}^{7}\cancel{8}\ {}^{9}\cancel{0},\ {}^{9}\cancel{0}\ {}^{9}\cancel{0}\ {}^{1}0 \\ -\quad 7,\ 3\ \ 2\ \ 8 \\ \hline 7\ \ 2,\ 6\ \ 7\ \ 2 \end{array}$$

Example 4:

$$\begin{array}{r} {}^{8}\cancel{9}\ {}^{9}\cancel{0}\ {}^{9}\cancel{0},\ {}^{9}\cancel{0}\ {}^{9}\cancel{0}\ {}^{1}0 \\ -\quad 1\ \ 4,\ 3\ \ 2\ \ 3 \\ \hline 8\ \ 8\ \ 5,\ 6\ \ 7\ \ 7 \end{array}$$

Example 5:

$$\begin{array}{r} {}^{5}\cancel{6}\ {}^{9}\cancel{0},\ {}^{9}\cancel{0}\ {}^{9}\cancel{0}\ {}^{1}0 \\ -\quad 3\ \ 4,\ 5\ \ 9\ \ 5 \\ \hline \end{array}$$

Solve these subtraction problems.

$$\begin{array}{r} \cancel{1}\ {}^{9}\cancel{0}\ {}^{9}\cancel{0},\ {}^{9}\cancel{0}\ {}^{1}0\ \ 0 \\ -\quad 4\ \ 3,\ 2\ \ 4\ \ 0 \\ \hline 5\ \ 6,\ 7\ \ 6\ \ 0 \end{array}$$

a

$$\begin{array}{r} 3\ \ 0,\ 0\ \ 0\ \ 0 \\ -\quad 1\ \ 3,\ 4\ \ 2\ \ 0 \\ \hline \end{array}$$

b

$$\begin{array}{r} 4,\ 0\ \ 0\ \ 0 \\ -\quad 3,\ 1\ \ 3\ \ 4 \\ \hline \end{array}$$

c

$$\begin{array}{r} 5\ \ 0\ \ 0 \\ -\quad 2\ \ 3\ \ 2 \\ \hline \end{array}$$

SELF CHECK Mark how you feel		
Got it!	Need help...	I don't get it

Check your answers

How many did you get correct?

PRACTICE

1 Solve these subtraction problems.

Example: 500,000 − 12,345 = 487,655 (regrouped: $^{4}\not5\,^{9}\not0\,^{9}\not0,\,^{9}\not0\,^{9}\not0\,^{1}0$)

a 70,000 − 2,573	**d** 40,000 − 20,302	**h** 6,000 − 253
b 5,000 − 147	**e** 200,000 − 74,003	**i** 400 − 132
c 10,000 − 3,823	**f** 28,000 − 3,436	**j** 62,000 − 13,472
	g 80,000 − 35,213	**k** 33,000 − 14,004

2 Solve these money subtraction problems.

Example: \$100.00 − \$43.65 = \$56.35 (regrouped: $\not1\,^{9}\not0\,^{9}\not0.\,^{9}\not0\,^{1}0$)

a \$50.00 − \$13.62	**c** \$80.00 − \$35.17	**f** \$360.00 − \$154.95
b \$20.00 − \$13.50	**d** \$90.00 − \$42.50	**g** \$75.00 − \$62.46
	e \$70.00 − \$25.25	**h** \$290.00 − \$187.57

ROUNDING TO ESTIMATE SUBTRACTION ANSWERS

You can use rounding to get an approximate answer that is close to the actual answer.

Example 1: Round to the nearest 10 to estimate the answer.

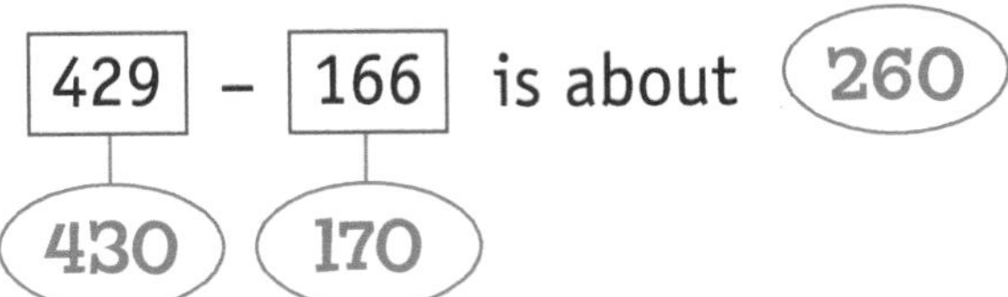

Example 2: Round to the nearest 100 to estimate the answer.

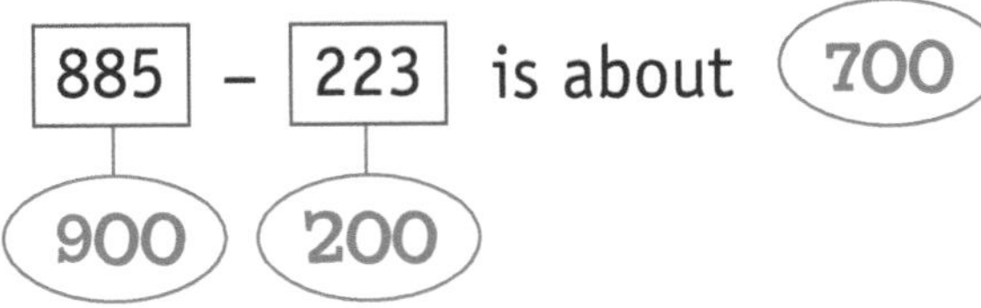

Example 3: Round to the nearest 100 to estimate the answer.

Your turn

1 Round to the nearest 10 to estimate the answer.

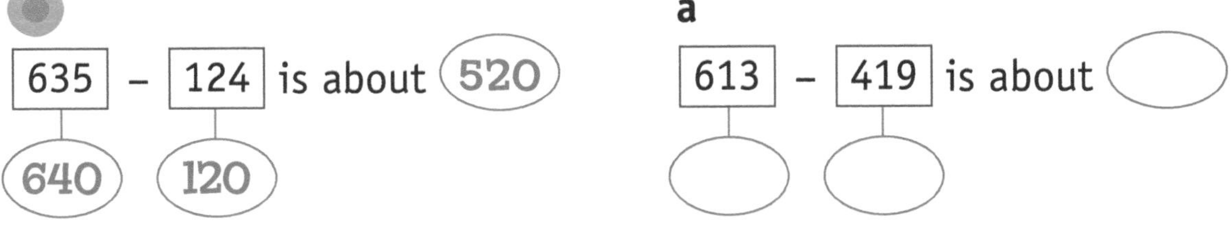

2 Round to the nearest 100 to estimate the answer.

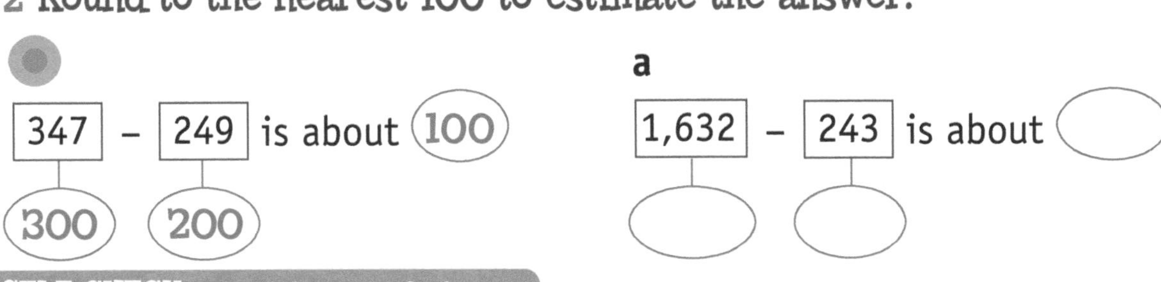

SELF CHECK Mark how you feel

Got it!	Need help...	I don't get it
☐	☐	☐

Check your answers

How many did you get correct? ☐

PRACTICE

1 Round to the nearest 10 to estimate the answers.

- 325 − 109 is about 220
  330 110

a 742 − 257 is about ____
  ____ ____

b 1,357 − 243 is about ____
  ____ ____

c 43,523 − 36,419 is about ____
  ____ ____

d 73,425 − 34,561 is about ____
  ____ ____

2 Round to the nearest 100 to estimate the answers.

- 38,427 − 26,498 is about 11,900
  38,400 26,500

a 73,582 − 21,530 is about ____
  ____ ____

b 343 − 257 is about ____
  ____ ____

c 5,984 − 3,349 is about ____
  ____ ____

SUBTRACTION REVIEW

Solve these subtraction problems.

a
```
  53
- 21
----
```

d
```
  72
- 35
----
```

g
```
  589
-  37
-----
```

j
```
  846
- 305
-----
```

b
```
  74
- 53
----
```

e
```
  81
- 43
----
```

h
```
  684
- 142
-----
```

k
```
  840
- 235
-----
```

c
```
  88
- 42
----
```

f
```
  52
- 35
----
```

i
```
  980
- 450
-----
```

l
```
  903
-  42
-----
```

Now solve these subtraction problems.

a
```
  5242
-  131
------
```

e
```
  6930
-  543
------
```

i
```
  82630
-  1410
-------
```

b
```
  4953
- 1742
------
```

f
```
  7529
- 3453
------
```

j
```
  72465
- 51323
-------
```

c
```
  972
- 340
-----
```

g
```
  54287
- 41152
-------
```

k
```
  62152
- 35983
-------
```

d
```
  3854
- 2413
------
```

h
```
  39857
- 21245
-------
```

l
```
  73154
- 42565
-------
```

Solve and then use addition to check your answers.

a
```
   57
 - 43
 ----

 +
 ----
```

b
```
  143
 - 28
 ----

 +
 ----
```

c
```
  342
- 152
 ----

 +
 ----
```

d
```
  1,532
 -  415
 ------

 +
 ------
```

e
```
  5,983
- 2,741
 ------

 +
 ------
```

f
```
  5,843
- 2,709
 ------

 +
 ------
```

g
```
  6,304
- 1,251
 ------

 +
 ------
```

h
```
  58,937
-  3,977
 -------

 +
 -------
```

i
```
  95,256
-  3,039
 -------

 +
 -------
```

j
```
  48,111
- 25,370
 -------

 +
 -------
```

k
```
  72,531
- 39,409
 -------

 +
 -------
```

l
```
  93,007
- 24,056
 -------

 +
 -------
```

REVIEW

Solve.

a $\begin{array}{r} 400 \\ -\ 32 \\ \hline \end{array}$

b $\begin{array}{r} 600 \\ -\ 143 \\ \hline \end{array}$

c $\begin{array}{r} 800 \\ -\ 768 \\ \hline \end{array}$

d $\begin{array}{r} 5000 \\ -\ 153 \\ \hline \end{array}$

e $\begin{array}{r} 7000 \\ -\ 583 \\ \hline \end{array}$

f $\begin{array}{r} 6000 \\ -\ 421 \\ \hline \\ \hline \end{array}$

g $\begin{array}{r} 3000 \\ -\ 2375 \\ \hline \end{array}$

h $\begin{array}{r} 9000 \\ -\ 4030 \\ \hline \end{array}$

i $\begin{array}{r} 4000 \\ -\ 1307 \\ \hline \end{array}$

j $\begin{array}{r} 30000 \\ -\ 3524 \\ \hline \end{array}$

k $\begin{array}{r} 50000 \\ -\ 152 \\ \hline \end{array}$

l $\begin{array}{r} 20000 \\ -\ 73 \\ \hline \end{array}$

m $\begin{array}{r} 70000 \\ -\ 5352 \\ \hline \end{array}$

n $\begin{array}{r} 60000 \\ -\ 7053 \\ \hline \end{array}$

o $\begin{array}{r} 50000 \\ -\ 8321 \\ \hline \end{array}$

p $\begin{array}{r} 30000 \\ -\ 21350 \\ \hline \end{array}$

q $\begin{array}{r} 40000 \\ -\ 15290 \\ \hline \end{array}$

r $\begin{array}{r} 76000 \\ -\ 31,304 \\ \hline \end{array}$

5 Round to the nearest 10 to estimate the answers.

a 342 – 173 is about ☐

☐ ☐

b 3,581 – 432 is about ☐

☐ ☐

c 17,437 – 1,241 is about ☐

☐ ☐

6 Round to the nearest 100 to estimate the answers.

a 436 – 132 is about ☐

☐ ☐

b 53,421 – 5,368 is about ☐

☐ ☐

PRODUCT, FACTORS, AND MULTIPLES

When you multiply numbers, the answer is called the product.

A factor is a number that you can multiply with another to give a multiple.	A multiple is the answer you get when you multiply two numbers together.

6 and 4 are factors of 24. 24 is a multiple of 6 and 4.

6 × 4 = 24 ← multiple

factors

Example 1: What are the factors of 12?

1 × 12 = 12
2 × 6 = 12
3 × 4 = 12

12

1 | 2 | 3 | 4 | 6 | 12

1, 2, 3, 4, 6, and 12 are the factors of 12.

12 is a multiple of 1, 2, 3, 4, 6, and 12.

Example 2: What are the factors of 10?

1 × _____ = 10

_____ × _____ = 10

10

1 | ___ | ___ | 10

1, _____, _____, and 10 are the factors of 10.

10 is a multiple of 1, _____, _____, and 10.

Your turn

1 Cross out the number that is NOT a factor.

- 10: 1, 2, ~~3~~, 5, 10

a 15: 1, 2, 3, 5, 15

b 20: 1, 2, 3, 4, 5, 10

2 Circle the number that is NOT a multiple.

- 10: 10, 50, 60, (25), 20

a 5: 5, 15, 30, 42, 50

b 6: 12, 18, 23, 24, 30

c 2: 1, 2, 4, 10, 20

SELF CHECK Mark how you feel		
Got it! ☐	Need help... ☐	I don't get it ☐

Check your answers

How many did you get correct? ☐

PRACTICE

1 Write the factors.

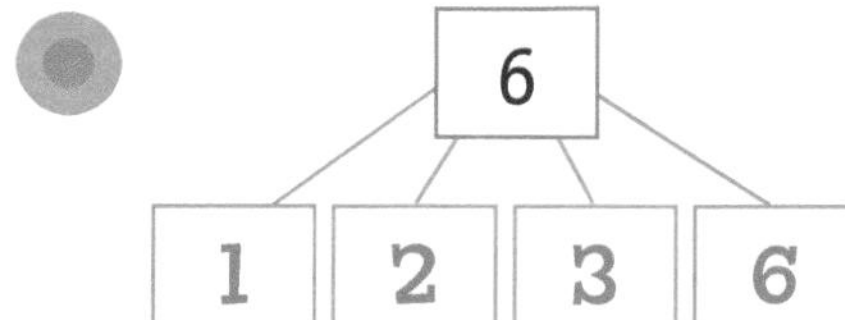

1 × 6 = 6

2 × 3 = 6

a 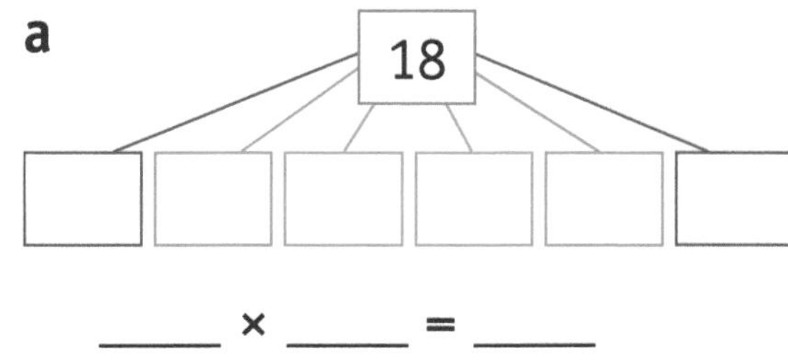

____ × ____ = ____

____ × ____ = ____

____ × ____ = ____

b 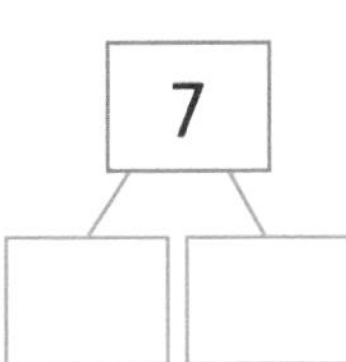

____ × ____ = ____

c 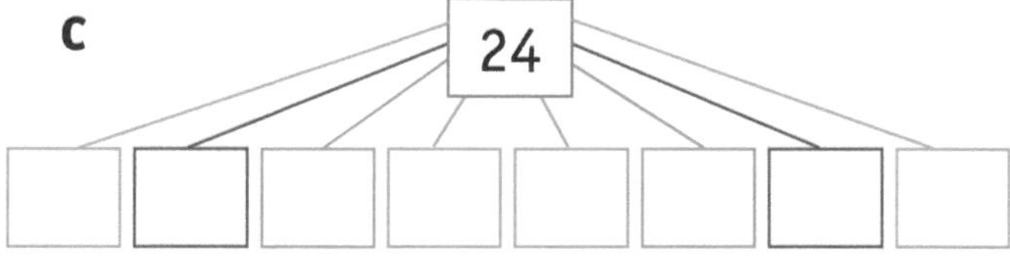

____ × ____ = ____

____ × ____ = ____

____ × ____ = ____

____ × ____ = ____

d 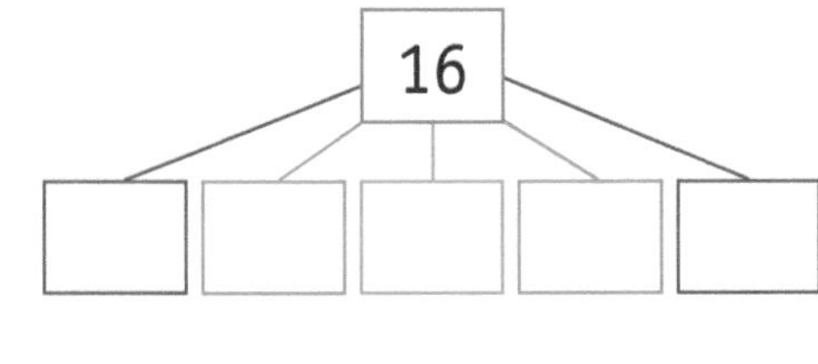

____ × ____ = ____

____ × ____ = ____

____ × ____ = ____

2 Write the products.

6 and 3 → 18

a 5 and 4 

b 8 and 7 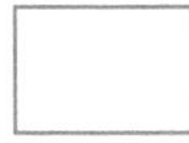

c 9 and 12 

d 11 and 12

e 9 and 8 

3 Write the next five multiples.

5: 15, 20, 25, 30, 35, 40

a 6: 36, ____, ____, ____, ____, ____

b 7: 21, ____, ____, ____, ____, ____

c 9: 27, ____, ____, ____, ____, ____

4 Write the missing numbers.

8 × 7 = 56

a 9 × ____ = 36

b ____ × 6 = 48

c 5 × 12 = ____

d 12 × ____ = 132

e 7 × ____ = 77

f ____ × 4 = 32

g 7 × ____ = 42

h 4 × ____ = 0

MULTIPLYING 2-DIGIT BY 1-DIGIT NUMBERS

Here are three different ways to multiply two-digit numbers by one-digit numbers.

Example 1: 13 × 5

Using known facts

13 × 5

10 × 5 = 50

50 + 5 + 5 + 5 (3 groups of 5)

= 65

Multiplying the tens and then the ones

13 × 5

= 5 tens + 5 threes

= 50 + 15

= 65

Using an area model

13 × 5

	10	3
5	50	15

= 50 + 15

= 65

Example 2: 23 × 4

Using known facts

23 × 4

20 × _____ = 80

80 + _____ + _____ + _____ (3 groups of 4)

= _____

Multiplying the tens and then the ones

23 × 4

= _____ tens × 4

+ _____ threes

= 80 + _____

= _____

Using an area model

23 × 4

	20	3
4	80	

= 80 + _____

= _____

Your turn

Solve using the three different methods.

32 × 8

30 × 8 = _____

_____

_____

32 × 8

3 tens × 8 + _____

_____

_____

32 × 8

	30	2
__		

_____

_____

SELF CHECK Mark how you feel

Got it!	Need help...	I don't get it

Check your answers

How many did you get correct?

PRACTICE

1 Solve using the different methods of multiplication.

63 × 5 Use known facts

60 × 5 = 300

300 + 5 + 5 + 5

= 315

63 × 5 Multiply tens then ones

6 tens × 5 + 5 threes

300 + 15 = 315

63 × 5 Use an area model

	60	3
5	300	15

300 + 15 = 315

b 67 × 8 Use known facts

______

______

= ______

67 × 8 Multiply tens then ones

______

______ = ______

67 × 8 Use an area model

	___	___
___		

______ = ______

a 34 × 5 Use known facts

______

______

= ______

34 × 5 Multiply tens then ones

______

______ = ______

34 × 5 Use an area model

	___	___
___		

______ = ______

c 41 × 3 Use known facts

______

______

= ______

41 × 3 Multiply tens then ones

______

______ = ______

41 × 3 Use an area model

	___	___
___		

______ = ______

STANDARD ALGORITHMS

We can solve multiplication problems using an algorithm.

Example 1:

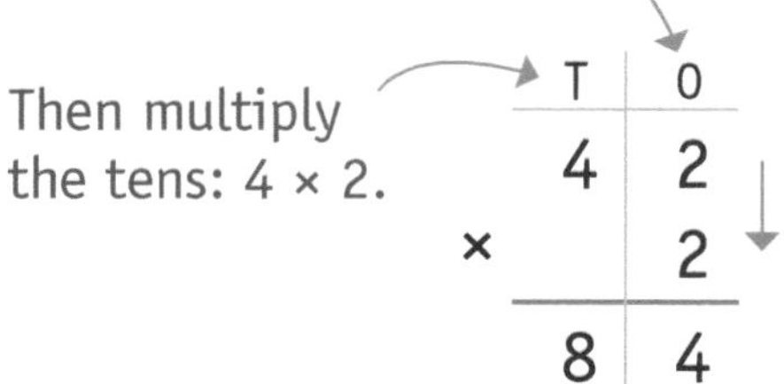

First multiply the ones: 2 × 2.

Then multiply the tens: 4 × 2.

	T	O
	4	2
×		2
	8	4

Example 2:

	H	T	O
		+1 6	3
×			5
	3	1	5

3 × 5 = 15 so carry over to the tens to add 1.

Example 3:

	H	T	O
		+4 3	8
×			6
			8

8 × 6 = 48, so carry over to the tens to add 4.

Example 4:

	H	T	O
		7	4
×			3

4 × 3 = ___, so carry over to the tens to add ___.

Solve these multiplication algorithms.

	H	T	O
		+5 4	7
×			8
	3	7	6

a

	H	T	O
		3	5
×			2

b

	H	T	O
		6	1
×			8

c

	H	T	O
		7	2
×			3

d

	H	T	O
		2	3
×			7

e

	H	T	O
		8	9
×			6

SELF CHECK Mark how you feel

Got it!	Need help...	I don't get it
☐	☐	☐

Check your answers

How many did you get correct? ☐

PRACTICE

1 Solve these multiplication problems.

● (example)

	H	T	O
		+2 2	7
×			3
		8	1

a

	H	T	O
		3	2
×			4

b

	H	T	O
		5	8
×			5

c

	H	T	O
		6	4
×			6

d

	H	T	O
		8	1
×			9

e

	H	T	O
		9	2
×			8

f

	H	T	O
		4	0
×			7

g

	H	T	O
		5	5
×			2

2 This is a student's test. Find the answers, mark the test, and write the score.

a 23 × 2 = 46 ✓

b 41 × 3 = 123

c 72 × 5 = 350

d $^{+4}$87 × 7 = 609

e $^{+4}$55 × 8 = 440

f 35 × 4 = 120

g $^{+2}$54 × 6 = 324

h 61 × 8 = 468

☐ out of 8

3 Try solving these problems with three-digit numbers.

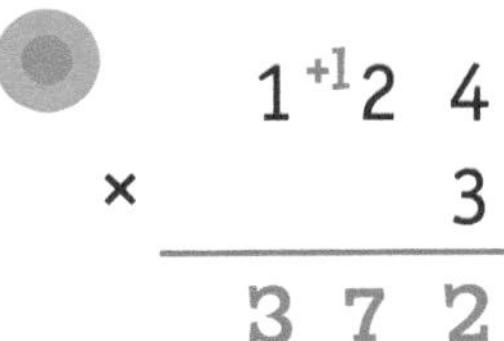

● 1 $^{+1}$2 4 × 3 = 3 7 2

a 272 × 4 =

b 329 × 5 =

c 403 × 7 =

d 516 × 6 =

e 892 × 8 =

MULTIPLYING 3-DIGIT AND 4-DIGIT NUMBERS BY 1-DIGIT NUMBERS

Here are three ways to multiply three-digit or four-digit numbers by one-digit numbers.

Example 1:

Multiplying thousands, hundreds, tens, ones

673 × 4

= (600 × 4) + (70 × 4) + (3 × 4)

= 2,400 + 280 + 12

= 2,692

Standard Algorithm

673 × 4

$$\begin{array}{r} {}^{2}6\;{}^{1}7\;\;3 \\ \times \qquad\;\; 4 \\ \hline 2,\;6\;9\;2 \end{array}$$

Area Model

673 × 4

	600	70	3
4	2,400	280	12

2,400 + 280 + 12

= 2,692

Why is it useful to learn different ways of multiplying?

Example 2:

Multiplying thousands, hundreds, tens, ones

1,432 × 5

= (______ × 5) + (______ × 5) + (30 × 5) + (2 × 5)

= ______ + ______ + 150 + 10

= 

Area Model

1,432 × 5

	1,000	400	30	2
5				

______ + ______ + ______ + ______

= ______

Standard Algorithm

1,432 × 5

$$\begin{array}{r} {}^{2}1,\;{}^{1}4\;{}^{1}3\;\;2 \\ \times \qquad\qquad\; 5 \\ \hline 0 \end{array}$$

SELF CHECK Mark how you feel		
Got it! 	Need help... 	I don't get it 

Check your answers

How many did you get correct?

Your turn

Solve.

5,382 × 4

= (5,000 × 4) + (300 × 4) + (80 × 4) + (2 × 4)

= 20,000 + 1,200 + 320 + 8

= 21,528

```
   ¹5, ³3  8  2
×             4
---------------
   2  1, 5  2  8
```

5,382 × 4

	5,000	300	80	2
4	20,000	1,200	320	8

20,000 + 1,200 + 320 + 8

= 21,528

a 631 × 4

= ____________________

= ____________________

= __________

```
   6  3  1
×        4
----------
```

631 × 4

	___	___	___
___			

____

= __________

b 742 × 8

= ____________________

= ____________________

= __________

```
   7  4  2
×        8
----------
```

742 × 8

	___	___	___
___			

= __________

SELF CHECK Mark how you feel

Got it!	Need help...	I don't get it
 ☐	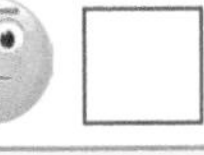 ☐	 ☐

Check your answers

How many did you get correct? ☐

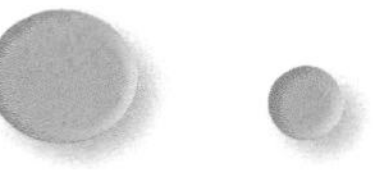

PRACTICE

1 Solve by multiplying thousands, hundreds, tens, and ones.

● 7,134 × 3 = (7,000 × 3) + (100 × 3) + (30 × 3) + (4 × 3)
= 21,000 + 300 + 90 + 12
= 21,402

a 326 × 6 = ______
= ______
= ______

b 1,526 × 5 = ______
= ______
= ______

c 439 × 7 = ______
= ______
= ______

d 5,963 × 8 = ______
= ______
= ______

2 Solve using the standard algorithm.

● $^{2}3,\ ^{1}5\ ^{2}3\ 4 \times 5 = 17{,}670$

a 615 × 4

b 1,532 × 6

c 725 × 7

d 4,936 × 8

e 503 × 7

3 Solve using the area models.

5,123 × 3

	5,000	100	20	3
3	15,000	300	60	9

15,000 + 300 + 60 + 9

= 15,369

a 732 × 4

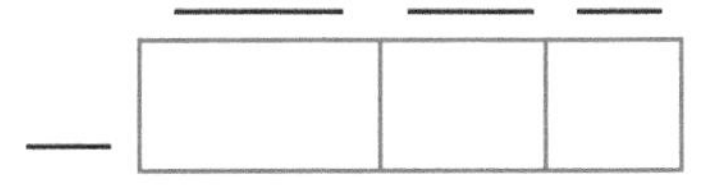

= ____

b 4,940 × 6

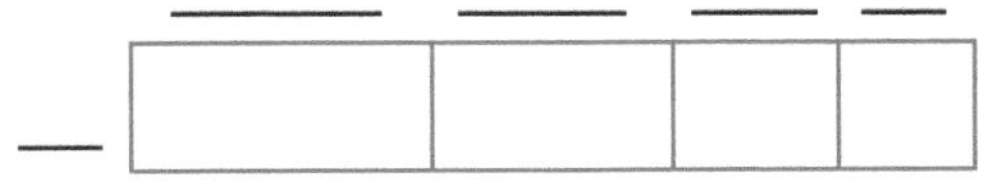

= ____

c 2,935 × 5

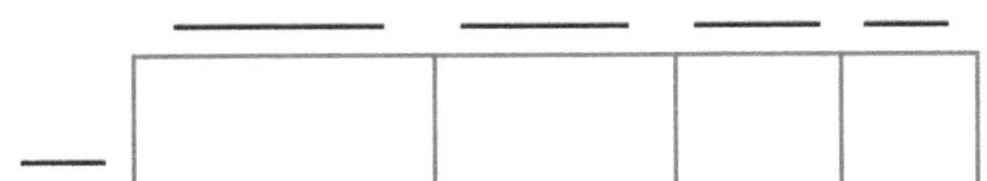

= ____

d 419 × 8

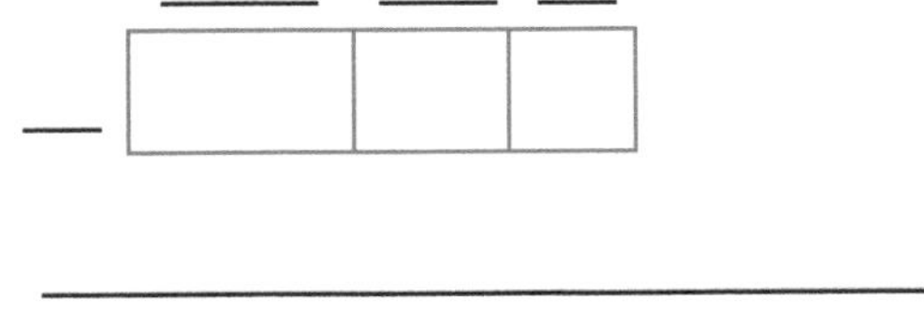

= ____

e 506 × 7

= ____

f 827 × 3

= ____

g 1,470 × 9

= ____

h 7,495 × 6

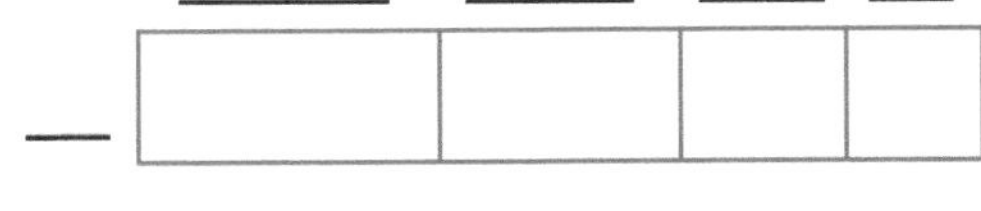

= ____

i 5,678 × 7

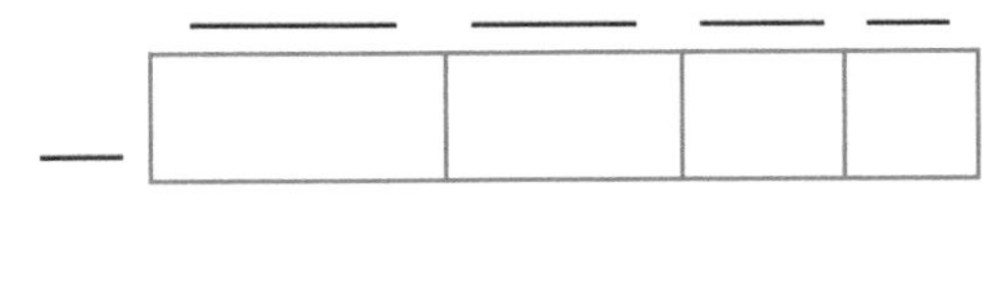

= ____

MULTIPLYING 2-DIGIT AND 3-DIGIT NUMBERS BY 2-DIGIT NUMBERS

Here are two ways of multiplying two-digit and three-digit numbers by two-digit numbers.

Example 1: 43 × 25

2-digit × 2-digit

Standard Algorithm

	Th	H	T	O
			[1]4	3
×			2	5
		2	1	5
+		8	6	0
	1	0	7	5

First, do 3 × 5. Then, do 4 × 5.

Now, write 0 in the ones.

Next, do 3 × 2, then 4 × 2.

Finally, add.

Area Model

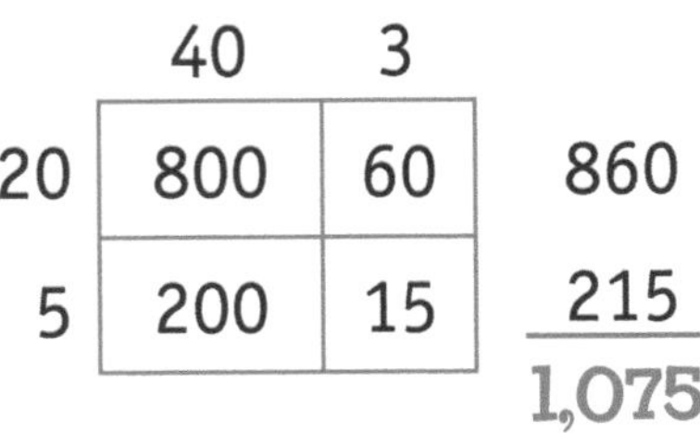

	40	3	
20	800	60	860
5	200	15	215
			1,075

860 + 215 = 1,075

Example 2: 412 × 36

3-digit × 2-digit

	TT	Th	H	T	O
			4	[1]1	2
×				3	6
		2	[1]4	7	2
+	1	2	3	6	0
	1	4	8	3	2

Steps:
2 × 6
1 × 6
4 × 6
Put 0 in the ones.
2 × 3
1 × 3
4 × 3
Add.

	400	10	2	
30	12,000	300	60	12,360
6	2,400	60	12	2,472
				14,832

12,360 + 2,472 = 14,832

Example 3: 748 × 42

	TT	Th	H	T	O
			7	[1]4	8
×				4	2
		1	4	9	6
+					0

Steps:
8 × 2
4 × 2
7 × 2
Put 0 in the ones.
8 × 4
4 × 4
7 × 4
Add.

	700	40	8	
40	28,000		320	______
2		80		______

______ + ______ = ______

SELF CHECK Mark how you feel

Got it!	Need help...	I don't get it
☐	☐	☐

Check your answers

How many did you get correct? ☐

Your turn

Complete these multiplication problems.

52 × 10

```
    5 2
×   1 0
-------
    0 0
+ 5 2 0
-------
  5 2 0
```

	50	2
10	500	20
0	0	0

520
0
520

a 64 × 13

```
    6 4
×   1 3
-------

+
-------
```

	___	___
___		
___		

b 176 × 49

```
    1 7 6
×     4 9
---------

+
---------
```

	___	___	___
___			
___			

c 843 × 70

```
    8 4 3
×     7 0
---------

+
---------
```

	___	___	___
___			
___			

SELF CHECK Mark how you feel

Got it!	Need help...	I don't get it

Check your answers
How many did you get correct?

PRACTICE

1 Solve using the standard algorithm.

Example:

	Th	H	T	O
		[1]3	[2]2	7
×			1	4
	1	3	0	8
+	3	2	7	0
	4	5	7	8

a

	Th	H	T	O
		4	2	4
×			1	5
+				

b

	Th	H	T	O
			6	9
×			2	7
+				

2 Solve using the standard algorithm.

Example:

$$\begin{array}{r} 403 \\ \times\ 32 \\ \hline 806 \\ +\ 12{,}090 \\ \hline 12{,}896 \end{array}$$

a $\begin{array}{r} 231 \\ \times\ 12 \\ \hline \\ + \\ \hline \end{array}$

b $\begin{array}{r} 72 \\ \times\ 87 \\ \hline \\ + \\ \hline \end{array}$

c $\begin{array}{r} 510 \\ \times\ 32 \\ \hline \\ + \\ \hline \end{array}$

d $\begin{array}{r} 88 \\ \times\ 43 \\ \hline \\ + \\ \hline \end{array}$

e $\begin{array}{r} 694 \\ \times\ 68 \\ \hline \\ + \\ \hline \end{array}$

f $\begin{array}{r} 594 \\ \times\ 21 \\ \hline \\ + \\ \hline \end{array}$

g $\begin{array}{r} 679 \\ \times\ 49 \\ \hline \\ + \\ \hline \end{array}$

h $\begin{array}{r} 876 \\ \times\ 69 \\ \hline \\ + \\ \hline \end{array}$

3 Solve using area models.

347 × 24

	300	40	7
20	6,000	800	140
4	1,200	160	28

$$\begin{array}{r} {}^{1}6,{}^{1}9\,4\,0 \\ +\ 1,3\,8\,8 \\ \hline 8,3\,2\,8 \end{array}$$

a 27 × 49

b 67 × 84

c 684 × 72

d 924 × 35

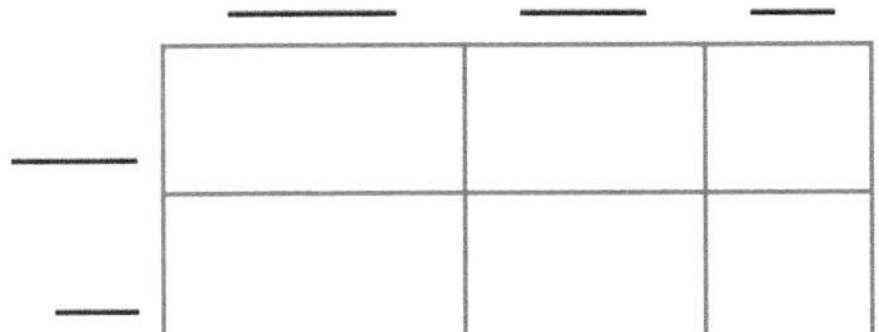

e 93 × 74

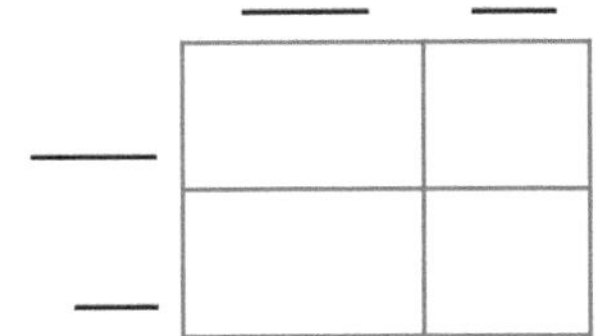

MULTIPLICATION REVIEW

Write the product of each pair of numbers.

a 6 and 9 _____

b 7 and 7 _____

c 8 and 6 _____

d 12 and 4 _____

e 8 and 9 _____

f 5 and 6 _____

Write the first six multiples of each number.

a 6: _____, _____, _____, _____, _____, _____

b 8: _____, _____, _____, _____, _____, _____

c 9: _____, _____, _____, _____, _____, _____

d 4: _____, _____, _____, _____, _____, _____

e 7: _____, _____, _____, _____, _____, _____

Write all the factors of each number.

a 36 ______________________________

b 48 ______________________________

c 15 ______________________________

d 12 ______________________________

Fill in the missing numbers.

a 11 × _____ = 110

b 6 × _____ = 24

c _____ × 8 = 72

d _____ × 12 = 48

e 7 × 8 = _____

f 12 × _____ = 60

g 3 × _____ = 27

h 6 × _____ = 36

i 9 × 9 = _____

j 4 × _____ = 20

k _____ × 7 = 63

l 8 × _____ = 32

5 Solve using the standard algorithm.

a 73×7

b 49×3

c 82×9

d 79×4

e 37×6

f 51×7

g 123×7

h 563×2

i 649×7

j 828×6

k 257×3

l 403×5

6 Solve using known facts.

 14 × 5

10 × 5 = 50

50 + 5 + 5 + 5 + 5

= 70

a 24 × 6

= ______

b 32 × 8

= ______

c 43 × 7

= ______

REVIEW

7 Solve by multiplying the tens and then multiplying the ones.

● 14 × 5

5 tens + 5 fours

50 + 20 = 70

a 78 × 9

____

__________ = _____

b 81 × 7

____

__________ = _____

c 97 × 3

____

__________ = _____

8 Solve using area models.

● 14 × 5

	10	4
5	50	20

50 + 20 = 70

a 28 × 3

	___	___
__		

__________ = _____

b 49 × 6 = ____

	___	___
__		

__________ = _____

c 54 × 7 = ____

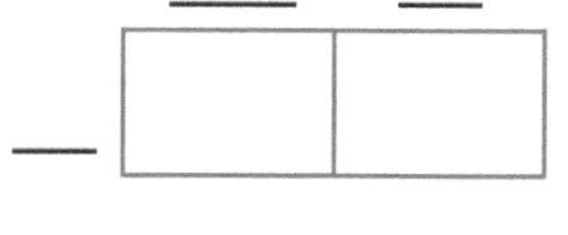

	___	___
__		

__________ = _____

9 Solve by multiplying thousands, hundreds, tens, and ones.

● 2,674 × 3 = (2,000 × 3) + (600 × 3) + (70 × 3) + (4 × 3)

= 6,000 + 1,800 + 210 + 12

= 8,022

a 362 × 4 = ____________________

= ____________________

= __________

b 4,845 × 6= ______________________

= ______________________

= ________

c 573 × 5 = ______________________

= ______________________

= ________

10 Solve using area models.

 2,674 × 3

	2,000	600	70	4
3	6,000	1,800	210	12

6,000 + 1,800 + 210 + 12

= 8,022

b 5,903 × 4

___	___	___	___	___
___				

____

= ________

a 326 × 8

___	___	___	___
___			

____

= ________

c 682 × 6

___	___	___	___
___			

____

= ________

11 Solve the following.

a $\begin{array}{r} 673 \\ \times \quad 4 \\ \hline \end{array}$

c $\begin{array}{r} 893 \\ \times \quad 5 \\ \hline \end{array}$

e $\begin{array}{r} 597 \\ \times \quad 3 \\ \hline \end{array}$

b $\begin{array}{r} 1,275 \\ \times \quad 6 \\ \hline \end{array}$

d $\begin{array}{r} 4,391 \\ \times \quad 7 \\ \hline \end{array}$

f $\begin{array}{r} 5,803 \\ \times \quad 9 \\ \hline \end{array}$

REVIEW

12 Solve using area models.

32 × 59

	30	2
50	1,500	100
9	270	18

1,600
+ 288
1,888

e 413 × 26

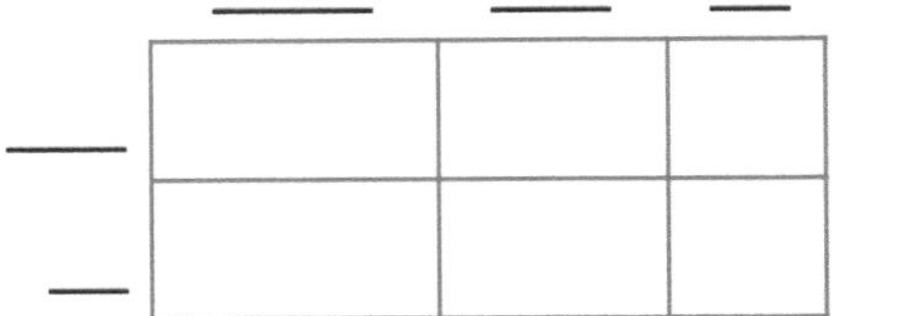

a 46 × 28

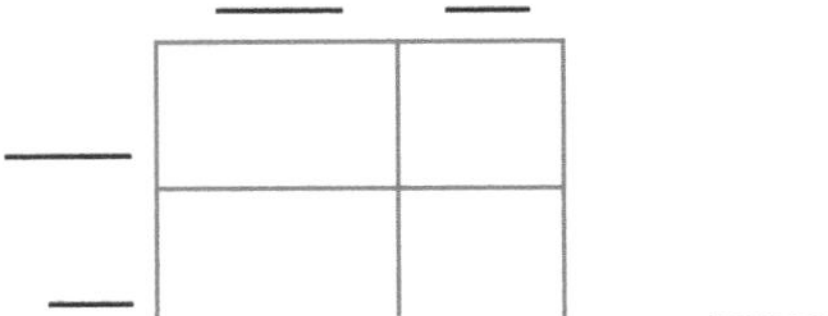

f 599 × 43

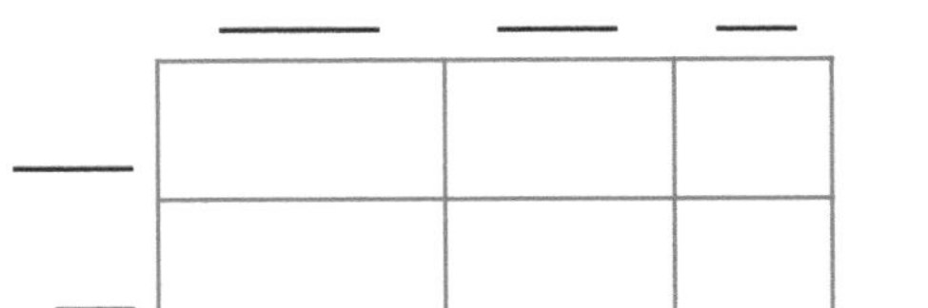

b 82 × 63

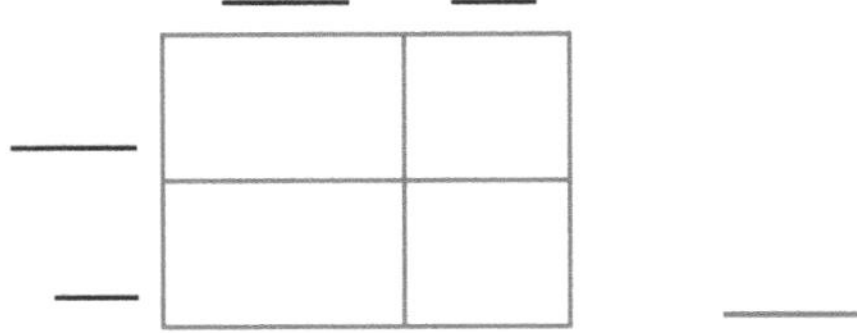

g 703 × 64

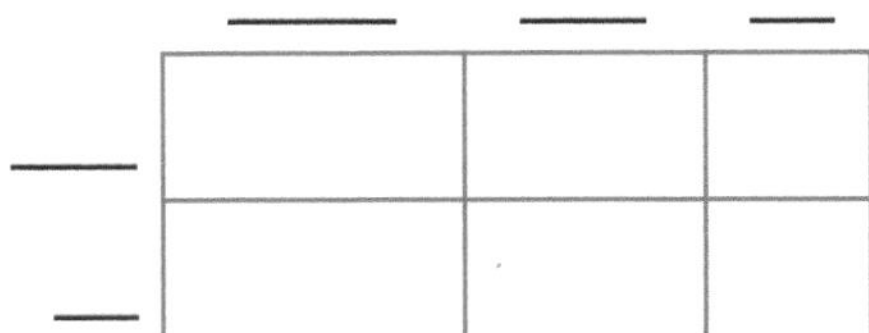

c 70 × 15

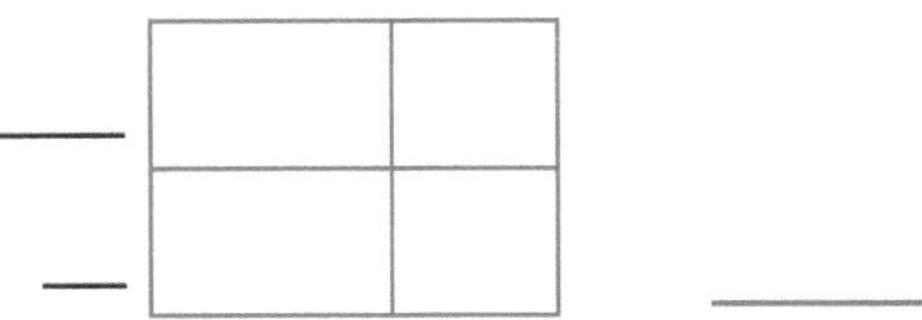

h 930 × 56

d 96 × 46

i 876 × 54

13 Solve using the standard algorithm.

a
$$\begin{array}{r} 2\ 3\ 1 \\ \times \quad 1\ 2 \\ \hline \\ + \qquad \\ \hline \end{array}$$

b
$$\begin{array}{r} 3\ 8 \\ \times \quad 9\ 5 \\ \hline \\ + \qquad \\ \hline \end{array}$$

c
$$\begin{array}{r} 9\ 5\ 9 \\ \times \quad 3\ 4 \\ \hline \\ + \qquad \\ \hline \end{array}$$

d
$$\begin{array}{r} 6\ 4 \\ \times \quad 8\ 2 \\ \hline \\ + \qquad \\ \hline \end{array}$$

e
$$\begin{array}{r} 2\ 8 \\ \times \quad 3\ 6 \\ \hline \\ + \qquad \\ \hline \end{array}$$

f
$$\begin{array}{r} 7\ 1\ 1 \\ \times \quad 4\ 9 \\ \hline \\ + \qquad \\ \hline \end{array}$$

g
$$\begin{array}{r} 2\ 0 \\ \times \quad 7\ 4 \\ \hline \\ + \qquad \\ \hline \end{array}$$

h
$$\begin{array}{r} 8\ 3\ 0 \\ \times \quad 5\ 6 \\ \hline \\ + \qquad \\ \hline \end{array}$$

i
$$\begin{array}{r} 5\ 0\ 7 \\ \times \quad 3\ 0 \\ \hline \\ + \qquad \\ \hline \end{array}$$

14 Mark as correct (✓) or incorrect (✗).

a
$$\begin{array}{r} {}^{3}2\ 5 \\ \times \quad 7 \\ \hline 1\ 7\ 5 \end{array}$$

b
$$\begin{array}{r} 8\ 4 \\ \times \quad 3 \\ \hline 2\ 4\ 2 \end{array}$$

c
$$\begin{array}{r} {}^{6}6\ 8 \\ \times \quad 8 \\ \hline 5\ 4\ 4 \end{array}$$

d
$$\begin{array}{r} {}^{2}1\ {}^{2}3\ 4 \\ \times \quad 2\ 6 \\ \hline {}^{1}\ 8\ 0\ 4 \\ +\ 2,\ 6\ 8\ 0 \\ \hline 3,\ 4\ 8\ 4 \end{array}$$

e
$$\begin{array}{r} {}^{4}5\ 5 \\ \times \quad 2\ 8 \\ \hline 4\ 0\ 0 \\ +\ 1\ 0\ 0 \\ \hline 5\ 0\ 0 \end{array}$$

f
$$\begin{array}{r} {}^{1}7\ {}^{3}2\ 7 \\ \times \quad 3\ 5 \\ \hline {}^{1}3,\ 6\ 3\ 5 \\ +\ 2\ 1,\ 8\ 1\ 0 \\ \hline 2\ 5,\ 4\ 4\ 5 \end{array}$$

g
$$\begin{array}{r} {}^{4}7\ 5 \\ \times \quad 9\ 4 \\ \hline {}^{1}\ {}^{1}2\ 8\ 0 \\ +\ 6,\ 7\ 5\ 0 \\ \hline 7,\ 0\ 3\ 0 \end{array}$$

GROUPS AND EQUAL ROWS

Grouping is sharing (or dividing) objects into groups of the same size. Equal rows have the same number of objects in each row.

Groups

Example 1:
Share 15 balls among 3 children.

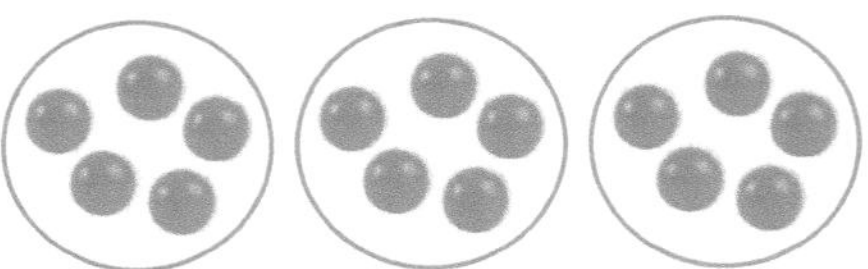

15 ÷ 3 = 5 3 groups of 5 = 15

Example 2:
Share 24 balls among 6 children.

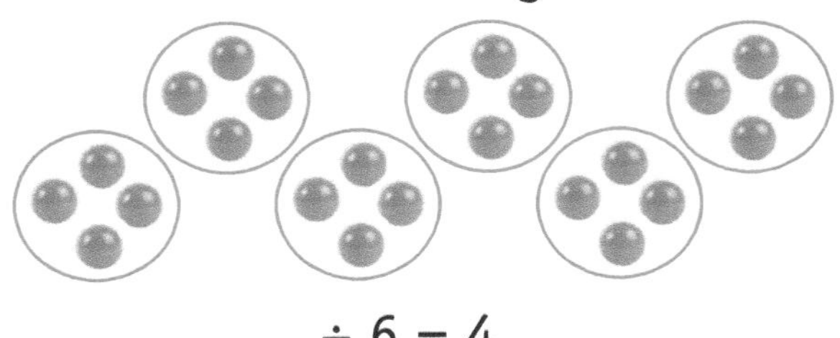

_____ ÷ 6 = 4

6 groups of _____ = _____

Equal Rows

Example 3:
Share 15 balls among 3 children.

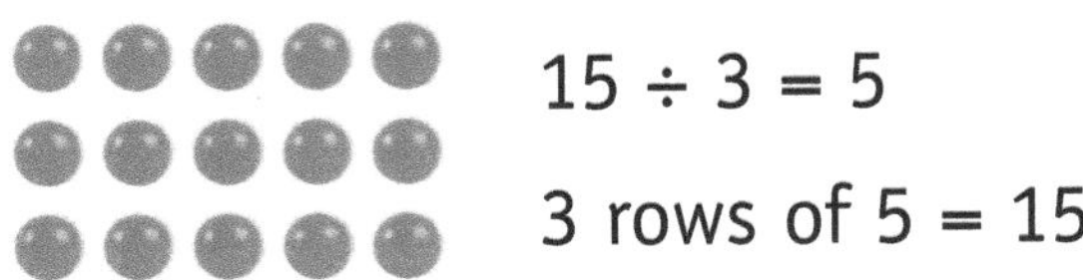

15 ÷ 3 = 5

3 rows of 5 = 15

Example 4:
Share 24 balls among 6 children.

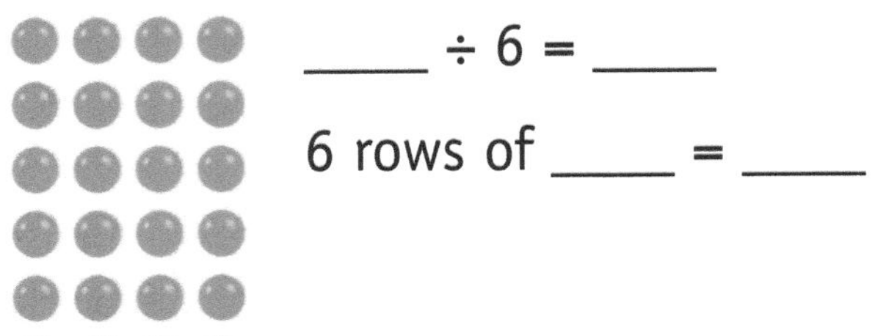

_____ ÷ 6 = _____

6 rows of _____ = _____

Your turn

1 Draw the ■, and then complete the sentence.

● Share 10 ■ among 5 children.
Each child will get 2 ■.

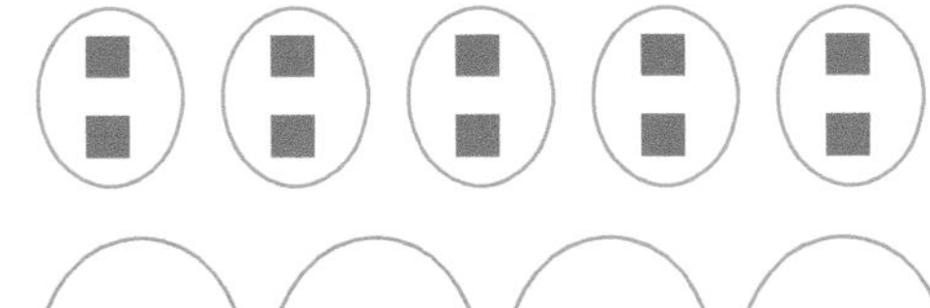

a Divide 20 ■ among 4 children.
Each child will get __ ■.

2 Draw the ● in equal rows.

● 12 ● in 3 rows

a 16 ● in 2 rows

b 9 ● in 3 rows

SELF CHECK Mark how you feel		
Got it!	Need help...	I don't get it
☐	☐	☐

Check your answers
How many did you get correct? ☐

PRACTICE

1 Make equal groups, then complete the equations.

Groups of 4 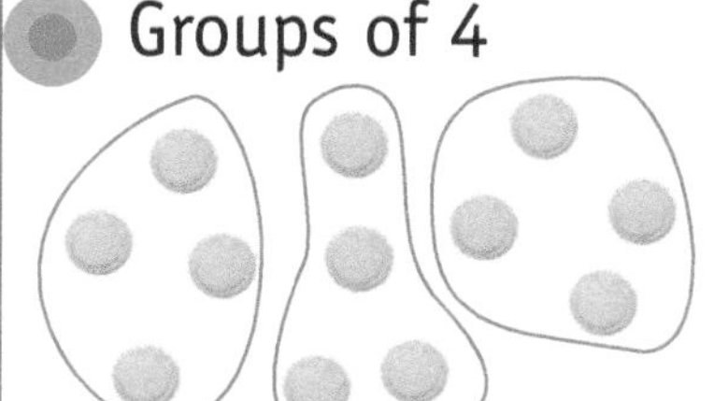 3 groups of 4 12 ÷ 3 = 4	**b** Groups of 4 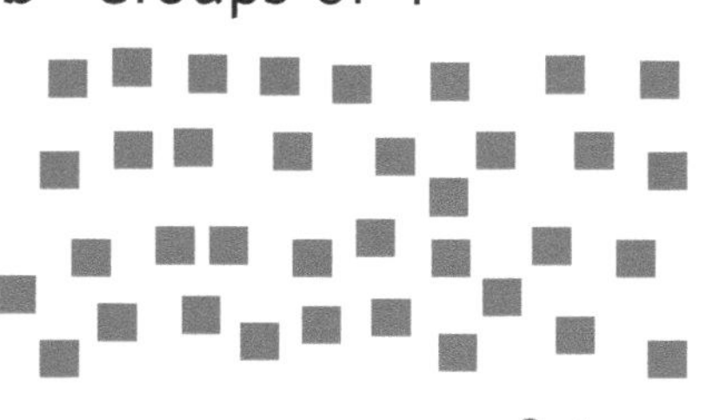 ____ groups of 4 36 ÷ ____ = 4	**d** Groups of 2 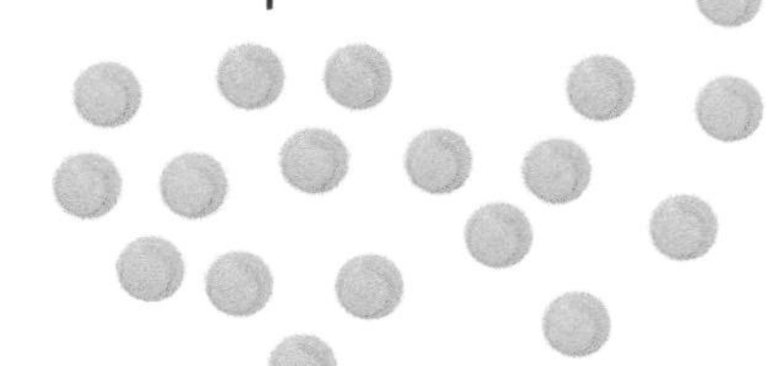 ____ groups of 2 18 ÷ ____ = 2
a Groups of 5  ____ groups of 5 10 ÷ ____ = 5	**c** Groups of 6  ____ groups of 6 24 ÷ ____ = 6	**e** Groups of 10  ____ groups of 10 20 ÷ ____ = 10

2 Draw ▲ in equal rows, then complete the equations.

10 ▲ in 2 equal rows ▲ ▲ ▲ ▲ ▲ ▲ ▲ ▲ ▲ ▲ 2 rows of 5 = 10 10 ÷ 2 = 5	**b** 40 ▲ in 5 equal rows 5 rows of ____ = 40 40 ÷ 5 = ____	**d** 12 ▲ in 6 equal rows 6 rows of ____ = 12 12 ÷ 6 = ____
a 6 ▲ in 2 equal rows 2 rows of ____ = 6 6 ÷ 2 = ____	**c** 4 ▲ in 4 equal rows 4 rows of ____ = 4 4 ÷ 4 = ____	**e** 24 ▲ in 3 equal rows 3 rows of ____ = 24 24 ÷ 3 = ____

RELATING × TO ÷

Multiplication and division are inverse operations.
This means they are the opposite of each other.

The inverse (opposite) of × is ÷, and the inverse of ÷ is ×.

4 × 3 = 12   12 ÷ 3 = 4

Example 1:

4 × 3 = 12

Number of rows — How many in each row — How many in total

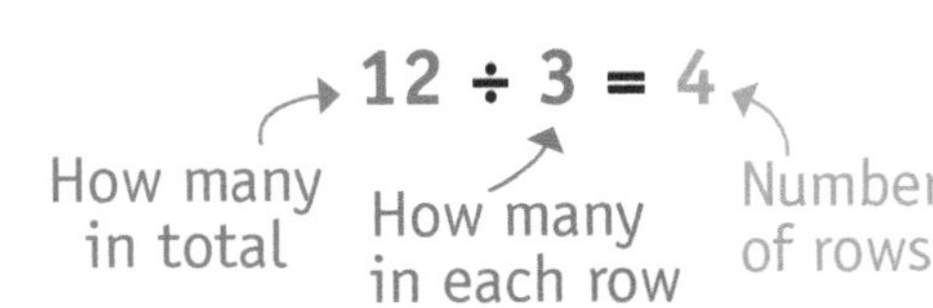

Example 2:

3 × 5 = ____

Number of rows — How many in each row — How many in total

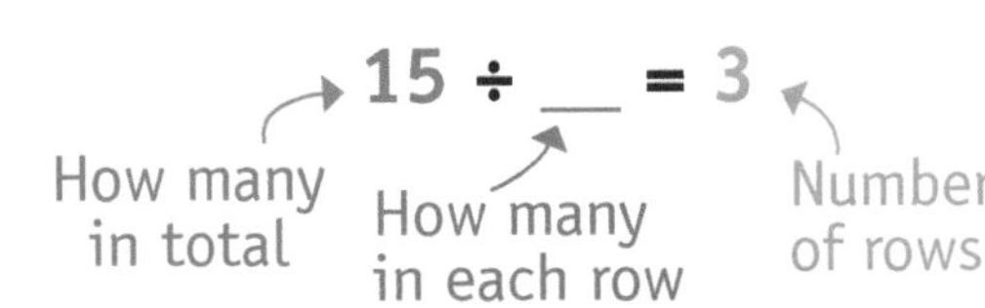

Example 3:

5 × 2 = ____   ____ ÷ ___ = 5

Your turn

Fill in the boxes.

- 6 × [8] = 48 is the inverse of 48 ÷ [8] = 6

a [ ] × 9 = 54 is the inverse of 54 ÷ 9 = [ ]

b 3 × 7 = [ ] is the inverse of [ ] ÷ 7 = 3

c 10 × 10 = [ ] is the inverse of [ ] ÷ 10 = 10

d 11 × [ ] = 121 is the inverse of 121 ÷ [ ] = 11

e 8 × [ ] = 56 is the inverse of 56 ÷ [ ] = 8

SELF CHECK Mark how you feel		
Got it!	Need help...	I don't get it
[ ]	[ ]	[ ]

Check your answers
How many did you get correct? [ ]

PRACTICE

1 Match the inverse operations.

●	8 × 3 = 24	64 ÷ 8 = 8
a	9 × 5 = 45	45 ÷ 5 = 9
b	2 × 1 = 2	24 ÷ 3 = 8
c	8 × 8 = 64	42 ÷ 7 = 6
d	6 × 7 = 42	2 ÷ 1 = 2

2 Write facts for each set of numbers.

●

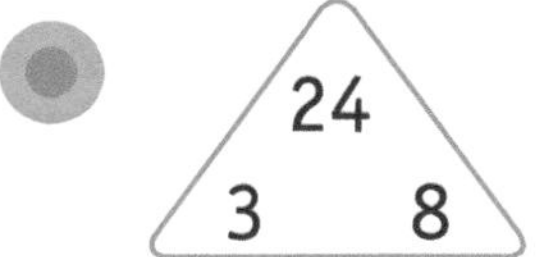

3 × 8 = 24

8 × 3 = 24

24 ÷ 8 = 3

24 ÷ 3 = 8

b

18
2 9

___ × ___ = ___

___ × ___ = ___

___ ÷ ___ = ___

___ ÷ ___ = ___

d

72
9 8

___ × ___ = ___

___ × ___ = ___

___ ÷ ___ = ___

___ ÷ ___ = ___

a

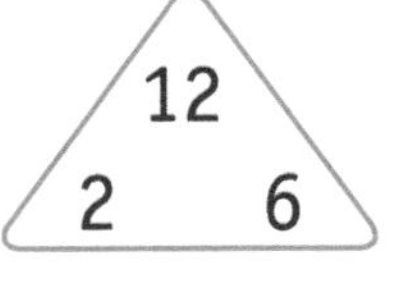

___ × ___ = ___

___ × ___ = ___

___ ÷ ___ = ___

___ ÷ ___ = ___

c

20
4 5

___ × ___ = ___

___ × ___ = ___

___ ÷ ___ = ___

___ ÷ ___ = ___

e

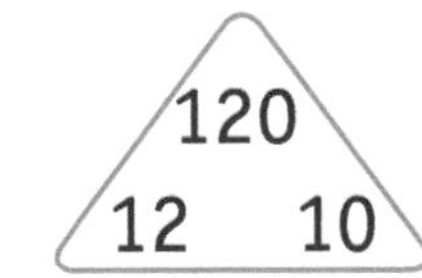

___ × ___ = ___

___ × ___ = ___

___ ÷ ___ = ___

___ ÷ ___ = ___

3 Write one multiplication fact that relates to each division problem.

● 27 ÷ 9

9 × 3

b 45 ÷ 5

____

d 28 ÷ 7

____

a 90 ÷ 9

____

c 40 ÷ 8

____

e 30 ÷ 6

____

QUOTIENT, DIVISOR, AND DIVIDEND

dividend ÷ divisor = quotient

The **dividend** is the number you are dividing.
The **divisor** is the number you are dividing by.
The **quotient** is the answer you get when you divide.

36 ÷ 12 = 3

dividend ↑ divisor ↑ quotient ↑

Example 1:
Circle the quotient.

35 ÷ 7 = (5)

Example 2:
Circle the dividend.

(32) ÷ 4 = 8

Example 3:
Circle the divisor.

326 ÷ (2) = 163

Example 4:
What is the quotient?

42 ÷ 6 = ____

1 Trace over the dividend in blue, the divisor in red, and the quotient in green.

● 10 ÷ 1 = 10 **a** 22 ÷ 2 = 11 **b** 40 ÷ 8 = 5

2 Complete the table.

	Division	Dividend	Divisor	Quotient
●	30 ÷ 5 = 6	30	5	6
a	48 ÷ 6 = 8			
b	72 ÷ 8 = 9			
c		10	5	2
d		20	10	2

Check your answers
How many did you get correct?

PRACTICE

1 Circle the quotients.

- (example) 8 ÷ 4 = (2)
- a 77 ÷ 11 = 7
- b 2 = 24 ÷ 12
- c 80 ÷ 8 = 10
- d 36 ÷ 9 = 4
- e 7 = 21 ÷ 3

2 Mark the labels that have a quotient of 4.

4 ÷ 1 ✓	24 ÷ 6	16 ÷ 4	20 ÷ 2	22 ÷ 11

24 ÷ 8	24 ÷ 4	28 ÷ 7	18 ÷ 9

3 Use red to circle the dividend and blue to circle the divisor. Then, write the quotient.

- (example) (8) ÷ (2) = 4
- a 12 ÷ 4 = _____
- b 42 ÷ 7 = _____
- c 27 ÷ 3 = _____
- d 32 ÷ 8 = _____
- e 30 ÷ 6 = _____
- f 28 ÷ 7 = _____
- g 81 ÷ 9 = _____
- h 64 ÷ 8 = _____

4 Complete the tables: **Dividend ÷ Divisor = Quotient**

	Dividend	Divisor	Quotient
(example)	12	1	12
a	27	9	
b	36	12	
c	56	8	
d	66	11	
e	49	7	
f	110	10	
g	42	6	
h	36	4	
i	25	5	
j	18	9	

	Dividend	Divisor	Quotient
k	7	7	
l	22	2	
m	33	3	
n	40	8	
o	40	4	
p	6	1	
q	9	3	
r	30	6	
s	10	1	
t	63	7	
u	60	5	

STANDARD ALGORITHM

Formal division is where division problems are written using the $\overline{)\quad}$ symbol instead of ÷.

You can use multiplication to check the answer:

4 × 5 = 20

Example 1:

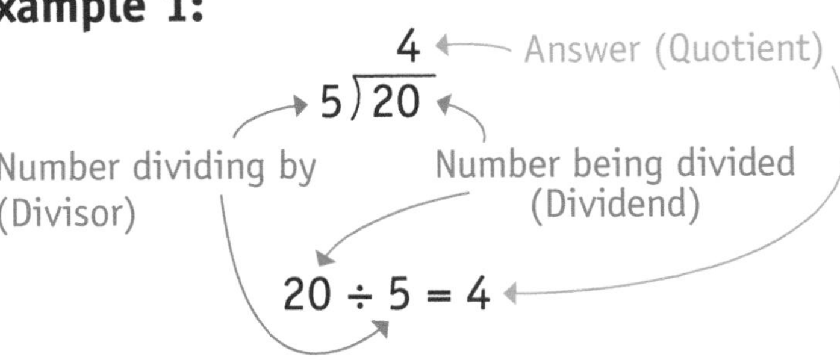

Example 2:

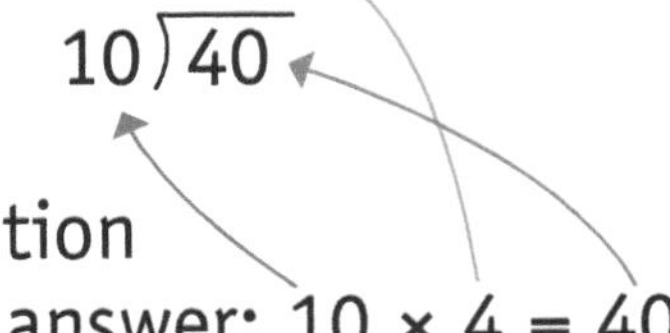

Use multiplication to check your answer: 10 × 4 = 40

Example 3:

8)24

Check using multiplication: 8 × _____ = 24

Example 4:

9)63

Check using multiplication: 9 × _____ = _____

Example 5:

8
)56

Check using multiplication: _____ × 8 = 56

Solve.

c 5)30

f 9)36

a 7)14

d 5)40

g 7)42

b 5)15

e 10)30

h 9)9

SELF CHECK Mark how you feel		
Got it!	Need help...	I don't get it

Check your answers

How many did you get correct?

PRACTICE

1 Solve. Then, check your answers with multiplication.

- (example) 3) 9, answer 3 — Check: 3 × 3 = 9
- **a** 4) 16 — Check: __ × __ = __
- **b** 2) 18 — Check: __ × __ = __
- **c** 5) 20 — Check: __ × __ = __
- **d** 6) 24 — Check: __ × __ = __
- **e** 4) 28 — Check: __ × __ = __

2 Fill in the missing numbers.

- (example) 6) 30, answer 5
- **a** __) 32, answer 4
- **b** 11) __, answer 4
- **c** 7) 56
- **d** __) 48, answer 6
- **e** 5) 50
- **f** 12) __, answer 4
- **g** 9) 72
- **h** __) 66, answer 11

3 Use the numbers in the multiplication problems to complete the division problems.

- (example) 4 × 9 = 36
  36 ÷ 9 = 4 9) 36, answer 4
- **a** 1 × 8 = 8
  ____ ÷ ____ = ____ __) __
- **b** 4 × 5 = 20
  ____ ÷ ____ = ____ __) __
- **c** 9 × 7 = 63
  ____ ÷ ____ = ____ __) __
- **d** 12 × 10 = 120
  ____ ÷ ____ = ____ __) __
- **e** 5 × 2 = 10
  ____ ÷ ____ = ____ __) __
- **f** 3 × 11 = 33
  ____ ÷ ____ = ____ __) __
- **g** 7 × 10 = 70
  ____ ÷ ____ = ____ __) __
- **h** 9 × 8 = 72
  ____ ÷ ____ = ____ __) __
- **i** 6 × 7 = 42
  ____ ÷ ____ = ____ __) __

DIFFERENT WAYS TO WRITE DIVISION

Here are three different ways of writing division.

Example 1:
Write 25 divided by 4 in three different ways.

$25 \div 4$ $\quad 4\overline{)25}$ $\quad \frac{25}{4}$

Example 2:
Write 52 divided by 3 in three different ways.

$52 \div 3$ $\quad 3\overline{)52}$ $\quad \frac{52}{3}$

Example 3:
Write 27 divided by 9 in three different ways.

$27 \div 9$ $\quad$ ___$\overline{)27}$ $\quad \frac{27}{\_\_}$

Example 4:
Write 60 divided by 10 in three different ways.

$60 \div 10$ $\quad 10\overline{)\_\_\_}$ $\quad \frac{\_\_}{10}$

Match the division problems.

- ● $23 \div 7$ — $7\overline{)23}$
- **a** $43 \div 2$
- **b** $74 \div 3$
- **c** $52 \div 4$

$4\overline{)52}$

$7\overline{)23}$

$\frac{74}{3}$

$\frac{43}{2}$

SELF CHECK Mark how you feel		
Got it!  ☐	Need help...  ☐	I don't get it   ☐

Check your answers
How many did you get correct? ☐

PRACTICE

1 Write the division problems using the $\overline{)}$ symbol.

- ● 36 ÷ 5 $5\overline{)36}$
- a 42 ÷ 6 ______
- b $\frac{93}{10}$ ______
- c 81 ÷ 9 ______
- d $\frac{63}{7}$ ______
- e $\frac{75}{25}$ ______
- f 230 ÷ 4 ______
- g $\frac{121}{11}$ ______
- h 182 ÷ 5 ______

2 Record the division problems as fractions.

- ● 26 ÷ 2 $\frac{26}{2}$
- a 53 ÷ 4 ______
- b $3\overline{)72}$ ______
- c 37 ÷ 4 ______
- d $3\overline{)82}$ ______
- e 51 ÷ 2 ______
- f $3\overline{)95}$ ______
- g $7\overline{)64}$ ______
- h 42 ÷ 6 ______

3 Write the division problems using the ÷ symbol.

- ● $\frac{53}{5}$ 53 ÷ 5
- a $3\overline{)27}$ ______
- b $\frac{47}{4}$ ______
- c $5\overline{)64}$ ______
- d $\frac{58}{4}$ ______
- e $7\overline{)83}$ ______
- f $\frac{62}{3}$ ______
- g $4\overline{)73}$ ______
- h $8\overline{)97}$ ______

4 Fill in the tables.

	Fraction	$\overline{)}$	÷
●	$\frac{57}{3}$	$3\overline{)57}$	57 ÷ 3
a		$4\overline{)61}$	
b			25 ÷ 3
c	$\frac{72}{6}$		
d	$\frac{49}{7}$		

	Fraction	$\overline{)}$	÷
e		$9\overline{)81}$	
f			74 ÷ 5
g			69 ÷ 9
h			22 ÷ 3
i		$4\overline{)16}$	

DIVISION WITH REMAINDERS

When a number cannot be divided evenly, the leftover is called the remainder.

Example 1:

17 ÷ 3 = 5 remainder 2

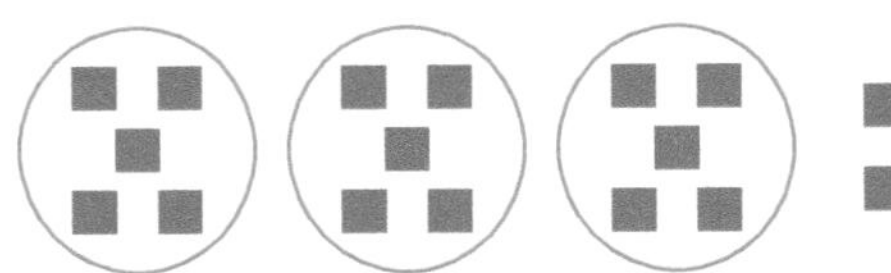

You can use multiplication to check your answer, then add the remainder at the end:

5 × 3 = 15

Add the remainder, 2:

15 + 2 = 17

Example 2: Share 23 marbles equally among 4 people.

23 ÷ 4 = 5 remainder 3

Check: 5 × 4 = 20

20 + 3 = 23

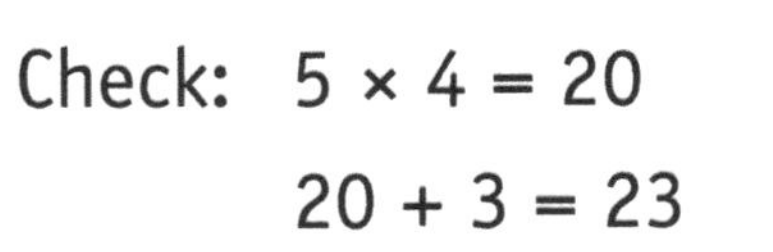

Add the remainder

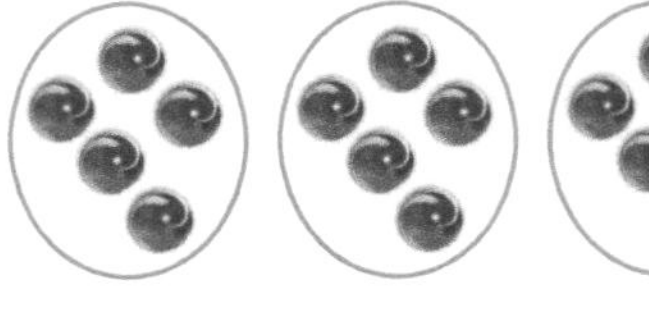
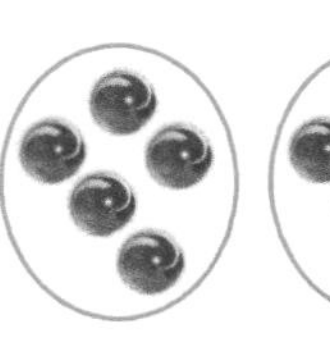
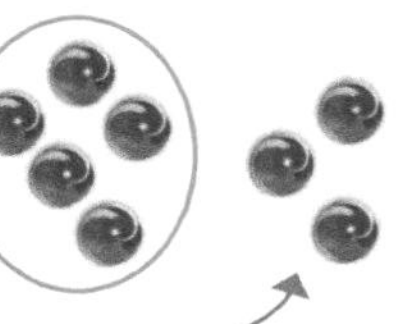

Example 3: Share 22 stars equally among 6 people.

22 ÷ 6 = __ remainder __

Check: __ × 6 = ___

___ + 4 = ___

Your turn

Solve these division problems with remainders.

- 32 ÷ 10 = 3 remainder 2

a 24 ÷ 7 = ___ remainder ___

b 44 ÷ 5 = ___ remainder ___

c 55 ÷ 9 = ___ remainder ___

Check your answers
How many did you get correct?

PRACTICE

1 Solve the following.

- 29 ÷ 3 = 9 remainder 2

a 63 ÷ 8 = ______ remainder ______

b 45 ÷ 7 = ______ remainder ______

c 75 ÷ 9 = ______ remainder ______

d 62 ÷ 8 = ______ remainder ______

e 17 ÷ 2 = ______ remainder ______

f $9\overline{)83}$ r

g $8\overline{)58}$ r

h $10\overline{)94}$ r

i $8\overline{)47}$ r

2 Use the first equation to complete each division problem.

- (6 × 3) + 2 = 20 → 20 ÷ 3 = 6 remainder 2

a (4 × 11) + 1 = 45 → 45 ÷ 11 = ______ remainder ______

b (7 × 9) + 2 = 65 → 65 ÷ 9 = ______ remainder ______

c (5 × 4) + 3 = 23 → 23 ÷ 4 = ______ remainder ______

d (9 × 7) + 5 = 68 → 68 ÷ 7 = ______ remainder ______

3 Write the equations, and then solve.

- 17 jelly beans shared among 2 people 17 ÷ 2 = 8 remainder 1

a 25 balls shared among 4 people ___ ÷ ___ = ___ remainder ___

b 70 cakes shared among 6 people ___ ÷ ___ = ___ remainder ___

c 84 balls shared among 9 people ___ ÷ ___ = ___ remainder ___

d 148 pencils shared among 12 people ___ ÷ ___ = ___ remainder ___

e 106 shirts shared among 10 people ___ ÷ ___ = ___ remainder ___

f 62 fish shared among 5 children ___ ÷ ___ = ___ remainder ___

g 29 cans shared among 6 people ___ ÷ ___ = ___ remainder ___

h 78 apples shared among 8 people ___ ÷ ___ = ___ remainder ___

DIVISION OF 2-DIGIT NUMBERS

Two-digit numbers can be divided by single-digit numbers.

Example 1:

Share 72 candies among 3 people. →	Give 20 candies to each person. →	12 candies remain. So 12 candies among 3 people is 4 each.
$3\overline{)72}$	2 tens → 2 $3\overline{)7^{1}2}$ Trade 1 ten for 10 ones	$\begin{array}{r} 24 \\ 3\overline{)7^{1}2} \end{array}$

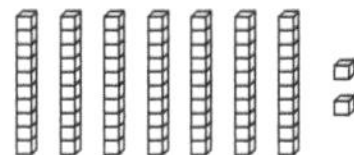

Example 2:

Share 64 balls among 4 people. →	Give __ balls to each person. →	24 balls remain. So 24 balls among 4 people is __ each.
$4\overline{)64}$	1 ten → 1 $4\overline{)6^{2}4}$ Trade 2 tens for ___ ones	$\begin{array}{r} 16 \\ 4\overline{)6^{2}4} \end{array}$

Example 3: $\begin{array}{r} 1 \\ 7\overline{)8^{1}4} \end{array}$

Example 4: $4\overline{)52}$

Example 5: $6\overline{)96}$

Solve the following.

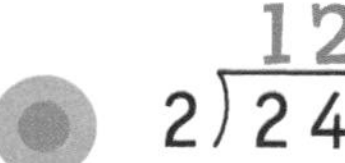

● $\begin{array}{r} 12 \\ 2\overline{)24} \end{array}$

b $4\overline{)84}$

d $4\overline{)88}$

a $3\overline{)36}$

c $6\overline{)66}$

e $3\overline{)33}$

SELF CHECK Mark how you feel

Got it!	Need help...	I don't get it
 ☐	 ☐	 ☐

Check your answers

How many did you get correct? ☐

PRACTICE

1 Solve.

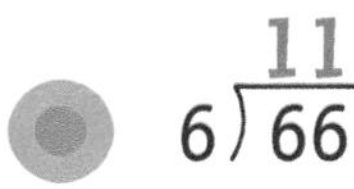

6)66 (11)	**b** 3)39	**d** 5)55	**f** 4)48
a 7)77	**c** 4)44	**e** 2)22	**g** 2)26

2 Solve these division questions. You will need to regroup.

2)5¹4 (27)	**d** 8)96	**h** 5)75	**l** 5)90
a 3)51	**e** 5)85	**i** 3)84	**m** 6)96
b 6)84	**f** 7)91	**j** 5)70	**n** 3)81
c 4)68	**g** 3)87	**k** 6)78	**o** 4)72

3 Solve. Then, multiply to check your answers.

5)8³0 (16) ✓	+3 16 × 5 = 80	**d** 6)90	× 6
a 4)76	× 4	**e** 3)96	× 3
b 3)78	× 3	**f** 5)65	× 5
c 2)74	× 2	**g** 9)99	× 9

DIVISION OF 3-DIGIT NUMBERS

Three-digit numbers can be divided by single-digit numbers.

Example 1: If I arrange 456 fish equally into 4 fish tanks, how many fish will be in each tank?

$4\overline{)4\ 5\ 6}$

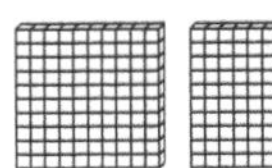
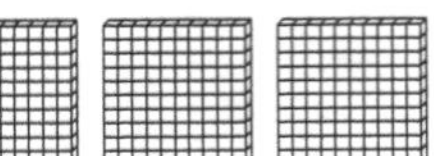
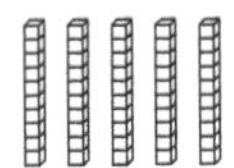

Put 100 fish in each tank. That leaves 56 fish.

$\begin{array}{r} 1 \\ 4\overline{)4\ 5\ 6} \end{array}$

Put 10 fish in each tank. That leaves 16 fish.

$\begin{array}{r} 1\ 1 \\ 4\overline{)4\ 5^{1}6} \end{array}$

16 fish into 4 tanks is 4 in each tank.

$\begin{array}{r} 1\ 1\ 4 \\ 4\overline{)4\ 5^{1}6} \end{array}$

There will be 114 fish in each tank.

Example 2:

$\begin{array}{r} 1\ 2\ 1 \\ 4\overline{)4\ 8\ 4} \end{array}$

Example 3:

$\begin{array}{r} 1\ 4\ 0 \\ 2\overline{)2\ 8\ 0} \end{array}$

Example 4:

$\begin{array}{r} 4\ 9 \\ 5\overline{)2\ 4^{4}5} \end{array}$

Example 5:

$\begin{array}{r} 5\ 1 \\ 6\overline{)3\ 0\ 6} \end{array}$

Example 6:

$2\overline{)8\ 6\ 4}$

Example 7:

$3\overline{)3\ 6\ 9}$

Example 8:

$7\overline{)3\ 6\ 4}$

Solve these division problems.

● $\begin{array}{r} 1\ 2\ 4 \\ 2\overline{)2\ 4\ 8} \end{array}$

a $3\overline{)6\ 3\ 6}$

b $2\overline{)4\ 8\ 4}$

c $5\overline{)5\ 5\ 5}$

d $4\overline{)8\ 4\ 4}$

e $2\overline{)6\ 8\ 2}$

f $3\overline{)3\ 6\ 0}$

g $4\overline{)4\ 8\ 0}$

SELF CHECK Mark how you feel		
Got it!	Need help...	I don't get it
		☐

Check your answers

How many did you get correct? ☐

PRACTICE

1 Solve the following.

- (example) $2\overline{)104}$ = 52
- d $3\overline{)963}$
- h $7\overline{)189}$
- a $7\overline{)945}$
- e $5\overline{)710}$
- i $8\overline{)448}$
- b $3\overline{)372}$
- f $9\overline{)882}$
- j $6\overline{)588}$
- c $4\overline{)636}$
- g $6\overline{)504}$
- k $9\overline{)585}$

2 Solve these division problems, and multiply to check your answers.

- (example) $5\overline{)634}$ = 126 r 4; check: 126 × 5 = 630; 630 + 4 = 634
- b $4\overline{)752}$ × 4 ___ + ___
- a $8\overline{)937}$ × 8 ___ + ___
- c $5\overline{)753}$ × 5 ___ + ___

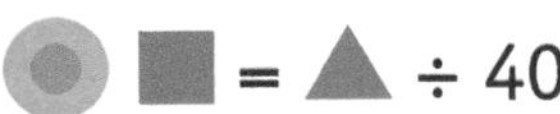

3 Use the rules to complete the tables.

(example) ■ = ▲ ÷ 40

▲	400	240	160	120	280
■	10	6	4	3	7

b ▲ = ★ ÷ 9

★	810	180	720	630	540
▲					

a ★ = ● ÷ 3

●	270	300	360	120	900
★					

c ★ = ■ ÷ 7

■	490	770	210	420	350
★					

RECORDING REMAINDERS AS FRACTIONS AND DECIMALS

The remainder from a division problem can also be written as a fraction or a decimal.

Remainder as a fraction

$4\overline{)25} = 6 \text{ r } 1$

Here, the remainder is 1.

You can write it as $\frac{1}{4}$.

$4\overline{)25} = 6\frac{1}{4}$

Remainder as a decimal

$4\overline{)25} = 6 \text{ r } 1$

$\frac{1}{4}$ as a decimal is 0.25.

$4\overline{)25} = 6.25$

Put the remainder over the number you divide by to make the fraction.

Example 1:

$4\overline{)29^{1}1} = 72 \text{ r } 3$

$= 72\frac{3}{4}$ or 72.75

Some fraction and decimal equivalents

$\frac{1}{8} = 0.125$	$\frac{2}{5} = 0.4$
$\frac{1}{5} = 0.2$	$\frac{1}{2} = 0.5$
$\frac{1}{4} = 0.25$	$\frac{2}{3} = 0.67$
$\frac{1}{3} = 0.33$	$\frac{3}{4} = 0.75$

Example 2:

$3\overline{)14^{2}9} = 49 \text{ r } 2$

$= 49\frac{2}{3}$ or 49.67

Example 3:

$4\overline{)21^{1}8} = 54 \text{ r } 2$

$= 54\frac{\ }{\ } = 54\frac{\ }{\ }$ or ____

Solve and record the remainders as fractions and decimals.

● $8\overline{)21^{5}7} = 27 \text{ r } 1$

$=$ $27\frac{1}{8}$ or 27.125

a $2\overline{)149}$

= ________ or ________

b $3\overline{)136}$

= ________ or ________

c $5\overline{)647}$

= ________ or ________

SELF CHECK Mark how you feel		
Got it! ☐	Need help... ☐	I don't get it ☐

Check your answers
How many did you get correct? ☐

PRACTICE

1 Solve and record each remainder as a fraction.

Example: $8\overline{)7\,5^{3}5}$ = 94 r 3

= 94 remainder 3 = $94\frac{3}{8}$

a $3\overline{)1\,4\,8}$

= ___ remainder ___ = ☐

b $4\overline{)4\,4\,7}$

= ___ remainder ___ = ☐

c $2\overline{)3\,4\,7}$

= ___ remainder ___ = ☐

d $4\overline{)2\,5\,4}$

= ___ remainder ___ = ☐

e $3\overline{)5\,1\,5}$

= ___ remainder ___ = ☐

2 Solve and record each remainder as a decimal. Use the table on page 92 to help you.

Example: $8\overline{)5\,5^{7}0}$ = 68 r 6

= 68 remainder 6 = 68.75

a $4\overline{)2\,1\,9}$

= _____ remainder _____ = _____

b $5\overline{)3\,1\,2}$

= _____ remainder _____ = _____

c $8\overline{)3\,4\,9}$

= _____ remainder _____ = _____

3 Fill in the table.

	Dividend	Divisor	Quotient	Remainder	Quotient and Remainder as a Fraction	Quotient and Remainder as a Decimal
Example	25	4	6	1	$6\frac{1}{4}$	6.25
a	15	2				
b	32	5				
c	57	8				
d	38	3				

DIVISION REVIEW

1 Make equal groups and complete the equations.

a Groups of 3	b Groups of 4	c Groups of 8
		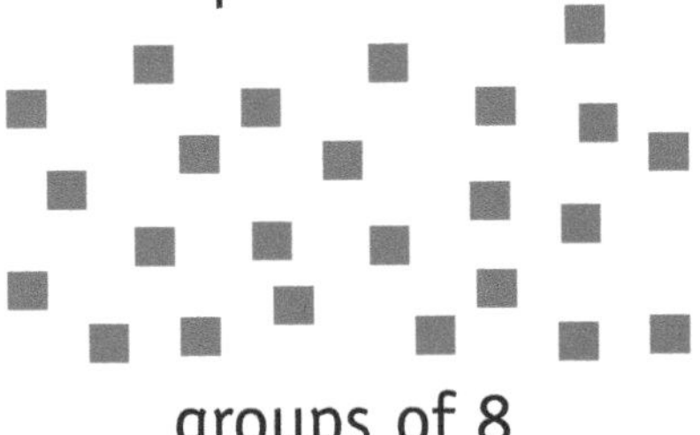
__ groups of 3	__ groups of 4	__ groups of 8
15 ÷ __ = 3	___ ÷ __ = 4	___ ÷ __ = 8

2 Draw ▲ in equal rows, then complete the equations.

a 21 ▲ in 3 equal rows	b 20 ▲ in 4 equal rows	c 12 ▲ in 2 equal rows
3 rows of __ = 21	4 rows of __ = 20	2 rows of __ = 12
21 ÷ 3 = __	20 ÷ 4 = __	12 ÷ 2 = __

3 Write an inverse equation for each problem.

a 8 × 6 = 48

____

b 9 × 8 = 72

____

c 5 × 2 = 10

____

d 4 × 7 = 28

____

e 120 ÷ 10 = 12

____

f 36 ÷ 12 = 3

____

g 64 ÷ 8 = 8

____

h 48 ÷ 12 = 4

____

i 63 ÷ 7 = 9

____

j 144 ÷ 12 = 12

____

k 7 × 1 = 7

____

l 42 ÷ 6 = 7

____

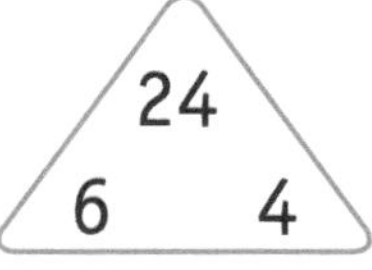
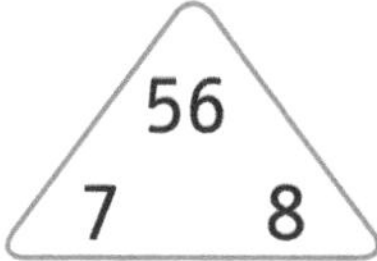

4 Write facts for each set of numbers.

a 24, 6, 4

___ × ___ = ___

___ × ___ = ___

___ ÷ ___ = ___

___ ÷ ___ = ___

b 21, 7, 3

___ × ___ = ___

___ × ___ = ___

___ ÷ ___ = ___

___ ÷ ___ = ___

c 56, 7, 8

___ × ___ = ___

___ × ___ = ___

___ ÷ ___ = ___

___ ÷ ___ = ___

5 Write one multiplication fact that relates to each division problem.

a 42 ÷ 6 ________

b 99 ÷ 11 ________

c 16 ÷ 2 ________

d 48 ÷ 8 ________

e 40 ÷ 5 ________

f 49 ÷ 7 ________

g 32 ÷ 4 ________

h 36 ÷ 6 ________

i 121 ÷ 11 ________

6 What is the quotient?

a 32 ÷ 8 ____

b 72 ÷ 9 ____

c 30 ÷ 3 ____

d 96 ÷ 12 ____

e 132 ÷ 11 ____

f 96 ÷ 8 ____

g 24 ÷ 6 ____

h 40 ÷ 4 ____

i 56 ÷ 8 ____

7 Mark the boxes that have a quotient of 12.

12 ÷ 6	18 ÷ 3	36 ÷ 3	12 ÷ 1	14 ÷ 2
24 ÷ 3	12 ÷ 4	12 ÷ 12	24 ÷ 2	24 ÷ 4

REVIEW

8 Write the division problems using the $\overline{)}$ symbol.

a $42 \div 6$ ______

b $27 \div 9$ ______

c $81 \div 9$ ______

d $127 \div 2$ ______

e $464 \div 4$ ______

f $721 \div 3$ ______

9 Record the division problems as fractions.

a $25 \div 5$ ______

b $36 \div 4$ ______

c $6\overline{)24}$ ______

d $8\overline{)72}$ ______

e $9 \div 9$ ______

f $63 \div 7$ ______

g $40 \div 4$ ______

h $8\overline{)32}$ ______

i $10 \div 2$ ______

10 Write the division problems using the ÷ symbol.

a $\frac{24}{3}$ ______

b $6\overline{)42}$ ______

c $7\overline{)49}$ ______

d $\frac{121}{11}$ ______

e $\frac{80}{8}$ ______

f $9\overline{)90}$ ______

11 Solve these division problems.

a $9\overline{)36}$

b $5\overline{)30}$

c $7\overline{)42}$

d $8\overline{)56}$

e $8\overline{)96}$

f $8\overline{)40}$

g $5\overline{)45}$

h $6\overline{)60}$

12 Solve these division problems with remainders.

a $36 \div 10 =$ _____ remainder _____

b $62 \div 6 =$ _____ remainder _____

c $24 \div 8 =$ _____ remainder _____

d $19 \div 4 =$ _____ remainder _____

e $11 \div 9 =$ _____ remainder _____

f $16 \div 3 =$ _____ remainder _____

g $23 \div 4 =$ _____ remainder _____

h $44 \div 6 =$ _____ remainder _____

i $16 \div 4 =$ _____ remainder _____

j $73 \div 8 =$ _____ remainder _____

REVIEW

13 Fill in the blank spaces.

a (7 × 2) + 1 = 15 → 15 ÷ 2 = ___ remainder ___

b (8 × 3) + 2 = 26 → 26 ÷ 3 = ___ remainder ___

c (9 × 9) + 6 = 87 → 87 ÷ 9 = ___ remainder ___

d (4 × 7) + 5 = 33 → 33 ÷ 7 = ___ remainder ___

14 Write the equations, and then solve.

a 18 jelly beans shared among 4 people ___ ÷ ___ = ___ remainder ___

b 134 pencils shared among 12 people ___ ÷ ___ = ___ remainder ___

c 109 candies shared among 10 people ___ ÷ ___ = ___ remainder ___

d 79 apples shared among 8 people ___ ÷ ___ = ___ remainder ___

e 28 cans shared among 6 people ___ ÷ ___ = ___ remainder ___

15 Solve these division problems.

a $2\overline{)62}$ d $3\overline{)63}$ g $7\overline{)91}$ j $3\overline{)87}$

b $4\overline{)48}$ e $2\overline{)86}$ h $5\overline{)85}$ k $6\overline{)96}$

c $2\overline{)48}$ f $8\overline{)96}$ i $5\overline{)75}$ l $6\overline{)84}$

16 Solve, then check your answers with multiplication.

a $5\overline{)85}$ × 5 ___

c $6\overline{)84}$ × 6 ___

b $4\overline{)80}$ × 4 ___

d $4\overline{)72}$ × 4 ___

REVIEW

17 Solve, then check your answers with multiplication. Make sure you add on the remainder.

a $5\overline{)27}$ r   × 5   + ___

b $6\overline{)94}$ r   × 6   + ___

c $9\overline{)84}$ r   × 9   + ___

d $7\overline{)68}$ r   × 7   + ___

e $3\overline{)42}$ r   × 3   + ___

f $6\overline{)49}$ r   × 6   + ___

18 Solve.

a $2\overline{)842}$

b $3\overline{)639}$

c $4\overline{)488}$

d $5\overline{)555}$

e $2\overline{)468}$

f $3\overline{)996}$

19 Solve these division problems with remainders.

a $3\overline{)964}$ r

b $8\overline{)934}$ r

c $7\overline{)836}$ r

d $4\overline{)725}$ r

e $2\overline{)687}$ r

f $5\overline{)649}$ r

20 Solve, then check your answers with multiplication.

a $5\overline{)637}$ r

× 5

\+ ____

c $8\overline{)849}$ r

× 8

\+ ____

b $4\overline{)473}$ r

× 4

\+ ____

d $7\overline{)893}$ r

× 7

\+ ____

21 Use the rules to complete the tables.

a ■ = ▲ ÷ 4

▲	16	24	32	56	88
■					

c ▲ = ■ ÷ 9

■	9	27	54	72	45
▲					

b ★ = ● ÷ 6

●	36	6	42	12	66
★					

d ⬢ = ★ ÷ 7

★	7	28	56	70	63
⬢					

22 Solve and record each remainder as a fraction.

a $4\overline{)623}$

= ____ remainder ____ = ☐

c $7\overline{)882}$

= ____ remainder ____ = ☐

b $5\overline{)532}$

= ____ remainder ____ = ☐

d $6\overline{)937}$

= ____ remainder ____ = ☐

REVIEW

e $9\overline{)863}$

= ___ remainder ___ = [ ]

f $4\overline{)775}$

= ___ remainder ___ = [ ]

g $5\overline{)416}$

= ___ remainder ___ = [ ]

h $3\overline{)328}$

= ___ remainder ___ = [ ]

i $2\overline{)694}$

= ___ remainder ___ = [ ]

j $7\overline{)852}$

= ___ remainder ___ = [ ]

k $8\overline{)514}$

= ___ remainder ___ = [ ]

l $6\overline{)291}$

= ___ remainder ___ = [ ]

23 Solve and record each remainder as a decimal.

a $2\overline{)395}$

= ___ remainder ___ = ________

b $5\overline{)784}$

= ___ remainder ___ = ________

c $4\overline{)675}$

= ___ remainder ___ = ________

d $2\overline{)563}$

= ___ remainder ___ = ________

e $4\overline{)899}$

= ___ remainder ___ = ________

f $3\overline{)373}$

= ___ remainder ___ = ________

g $8\overline{)418}$

= ___ remainder ___ = ________

h $5\overline{)324}$

= ___ remainder ___ = ________

i $5\overline{)981}$

= ___ remainder ___ = ________

k $3\overline{)454}$

= ___ remainder ___ = ________

j $4\overline{)634}$

= ___ remainder ___ = ________

l $2\overline{)121}$

= ___ remainder ___ = ________

Use multiplication to check the answers, and then mark each one as correct (✓) or incorrect (✗).

a $3\overline{)4^{1}6^{1}3}$ = 154 r 1 $\quad \times\ 3$ ______ $+$ ______

e $6\overline{)42^{1}6}$ = 72 r 4 $\quad \times\ 6$ ______ $+$ ______

b $4\overline{)25^{1}8}$ = 64 r 2 $\quad \times\ 4$ ______ $+$ ______

f $9\overline{)83^{2}5}$ = 92 r 7 $\quad \times\ 9$ ______ $+$ ______

c $7\overline{)635}$ = 90 r 3 $\quad \times\ 7$ ______ $+$ ______

g $8\overline{)74^{2}2}$ = 96 r 5 $\quad \times\ 8$ ______ $+$ ______

d $5\overline{)554}$ = 112 r 3 $\quad \times\ 5$ ______ $+$ ______

h $2\overline{)5^{1}21}$ = 260 r 1 $\quad \times\ 2$ ______ $+$ ______

COMPARING FRACTIONS

Comparing fractions means deciding which fraction is bigger and which fraction is smaller. Fraction bars make it easier to compare fractions.

1 whole									
$\frac{1}{2}$	$\frac{1}{2}$								
$\frac{1}{4}$	$\frac{1}{4}$	$\frac{1}{4}$	$\frac{1}{4}$						
$\frac{1}{8}$	$\frac{1}{8}$	$\frac{1}{8}$	$\frac{1}{8}$	$\frac{1}{8}$	$\frac{1}{8}$	$\frac{1}{8}$	$\frac{1}{8}$		
$\frac{1}{3}$	$\frac{1}{3}$	$\frac{1}{3}$							
$\frac{1}{5}$	$\frac{1}{5}$	$\frac{1}{5}$	$\frac{1}{5}$	$\frac{1}{5}$					
$\frac{1}{10}$	$\frac{1}{10}$	$\frac{1}{10}$	$\frac{1}{10}$	$\frac{1}{10}$	$\frac{1}{10}$	$\frac{1}{10}$	$\frac{1}{10}$	$\frac{1}{10}$	$\frac{1}{10}$

Example 1: Two-eighths ($\frac{2}{8}$) is equal to one-fourth ($\frac{1}{4}$).

Example 2: One-fifth ($\frac{1}{5}$) is equal to two-tenths ($\frac{2}{10}$).

Example 3: Three-fifths ($\frac{3}{5}$) is equal to _____-tenths ($\frac{}{10}$).

Example 4: Four-eighths ($\frac{4}{8}$) is equal to _____-fourths ($\frac{}{4}$).

Your turn

1 Write a smaller fraction.

● $\frac{1}{2}$ $\frac{1}{4}$ **a** $\frac{1}{3}$ ___ **b** $\frac{1}{5}$ ___ **c** $\frac{1}{4}$ ___

2 Write an equivalent (equal) fraction.

● $\frac{4}{10} = \frac{2}{5}$ **a** $\frac{2}{4} = \frac{}{2}$ **b** $\frac{1}{4} = \frac{}{8}$ **c** $\frac{4}{6} = \frac{}{3}$

SELF CHECK Mark how you feel

Got it!	Need help...	I don't get it
 ☐	 ☐	 ☐

Check your answers
How many did you get correct? ☐

PRACTICE

1 Complete each fraction. Then number the boxes to order the fractions from smallest (1) to largest (6).

a

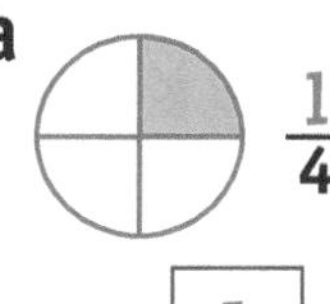 $\frac{1}{4}$ [1]

 $\frac{}{3}$ [ ]

 $\frac{}{5}$ [ ]

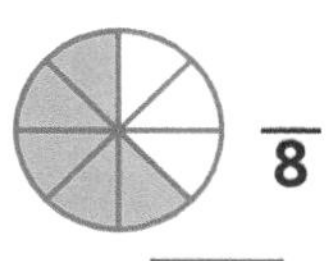 $\frac{}{8}$ [ ]

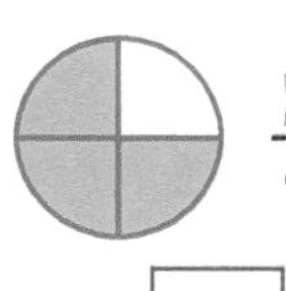 $\frac{3}{4}$ [6]

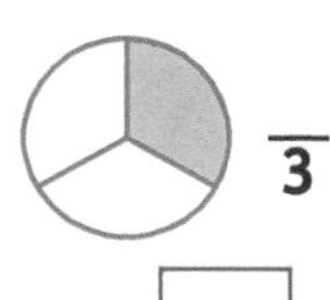 $\frac{}{3}$ [ ]

b

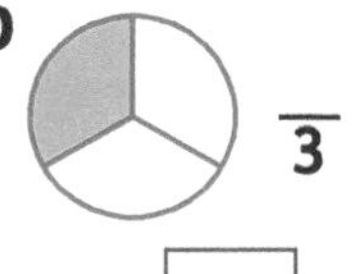 $\frac{}{3}$ [ ]

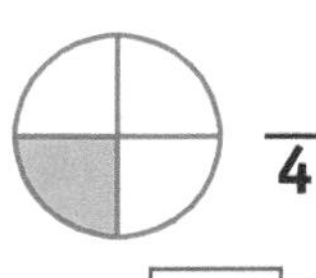 $\frac{}{4}$ [ ]

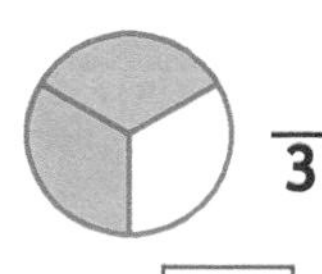 $\frac{}{3}$ [ ]

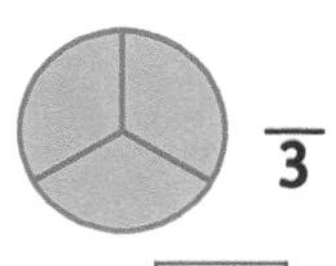 $\frac{}{3}$ [ ]

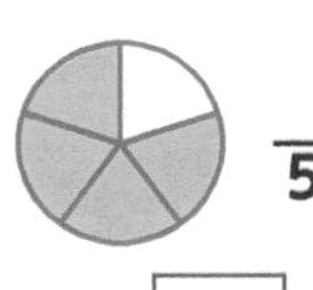 $\frac{}{5}$ [ ]

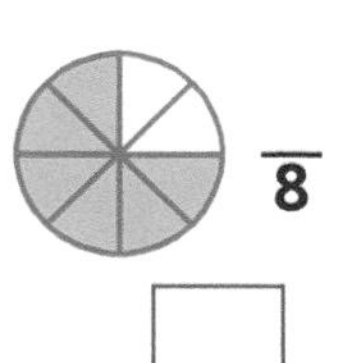 $\frac{}{8}$ [ ]

2 Draw a smaller fraction, and then write the fraction in the box.

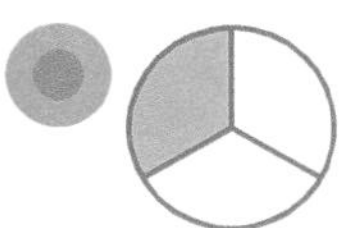

$\frac{1}{3}$ [$\frac{1}{8}$]

a 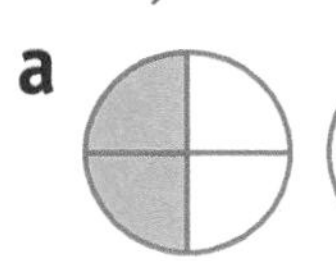 $\frac{2}{4}$ [ ]

b 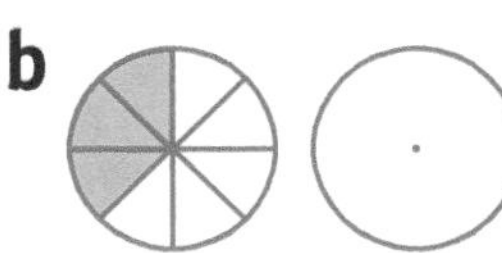 $\frac{3}{8}$ [ ]

c 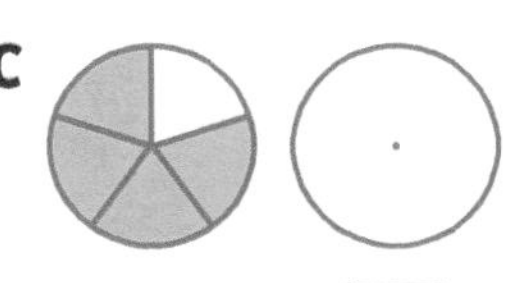 $\frac{4}{5}$ [ ]

3 Draw a larger fraction, and then write the fraction in the box.

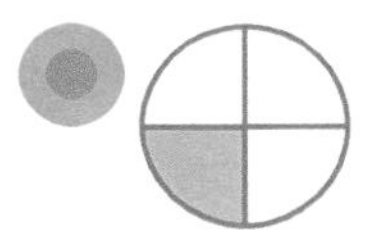

$\frac{1}{4}$ [$\frac{1}{2}$]

a 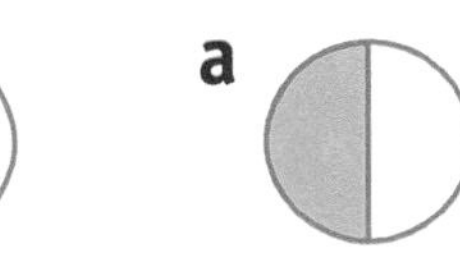

$\frac{1}{2}$ [ ]

b 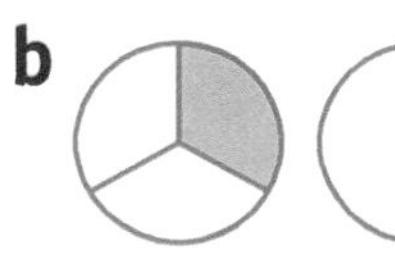

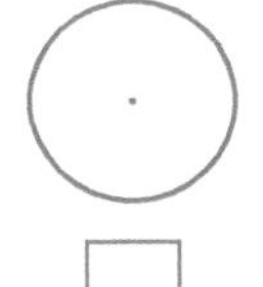

$\frac{1}{3}$ [ ]

c 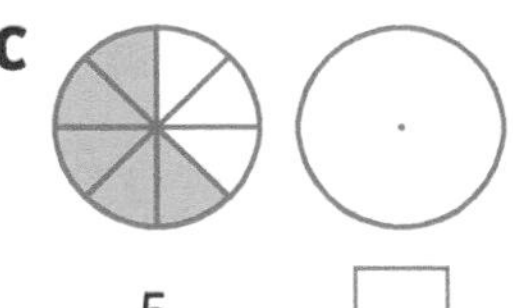 $\frac{5}{8}$ [ ]

4 Write the correct symbol: > (greater than), < (less than), or = (equal to).

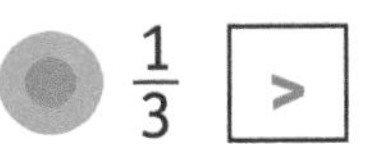

$\frac{1}{3}$ [>] $\frac{1}{4}$	**c** $\frac{7}{8}$ [ ] $\frac{3}{4}$	**f** $\frac{1}{3}$ [ ] $\frac{3}{8}$	**i** $\frac{7}{10}$ [ ] $\frac{1}{8}$
a $\frac{2}{5}$ [ ] $\frac{3}{10}$	**d** $\frac{1}{2}$ [ ] $\frac{6}{8}$	**g** $\frac{10}{10}$ [ ] $\frac{5}{5}$	**j** $\frac{8}{10}$ [ ] $\frac{7}{8}$
b $\frac{4}{10}$ [ ] $\frac{2}{5}$	**e** $\frac{6}{10}$ [ ] $\frac{3}{5}$	**h** $\frac{2}{5}$ [ ] $\frac{5}{10}$	**k** $\frac{2}{3}$ [ ] $\frac{4}{5}$

PROPER AND IMPROPER FRACTIONS

A **proper fraction** has a numerator that is smaller than the denominator.

$\frac{1}{5}$ ← The numerator is smaller. ← The denominator is larger.

These fractions are proper fractions:

$\frac{1}{5}$, $\frac{2}{3}$, $\frac{5}{10}$, $\frac{3}{5}$, $\frac{7}{8}$, $\frac{20}{100}$

An **improper fraction** has a numerator that is larger than the denominator.

$\frac{10}{8}$ ← The numerator is larger. ← The denominator is smaller.

These fractions are improper fractions:

$\frac{10}{8}$, $\frac{3}{2}$, $\frac{4}{3}$, $\frac{5}{4}$, $\frac{9}{7}$, $\frac{15}{10}$, $\frac{100}{50}$

Example 1:
Circle the improper fraction.

$\frac{1}{2}$ $\frac{3}{4}$ ($\frac{4}{3}$) $\frac{7}{12}$

Example 2:
Circle the proper fraction.

$\frac{2}{1}$ $\frac{8}{4}$ $\frac{9}{3}$ ($\frac{11}{40}$)

Example 3:
Complete to show a proper fraction. $\frac{2}{\square}$

Example 4:
Complete to show an improper fraction. $\frac{\square}{2}$

Your turn

Use green to circle the proper fractions and red to circle the improper fractions.

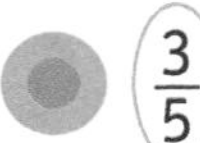

($\frac{3}{5}$) ($\frac{4}{3}$) $\frac{2}{8}$ $\frac{8}{2}$ $\frac{4}{9}$ $\frac{7}{3}$ $\frac{5}{10}$ $\frac{10}{4}$ $\frac{1}{4}$ $\frac{9}{6}$

SELF CHECK Mark how you feel		
Got it!	Need help...	I don't get it
 ☐	 ☐	 ☐

Check your answers
How many did you get correct? ☐

PRACTICE

1 Circle the proper fractions.

(example)	$\frac{1}{4}$	$\frac{5}{3}$	$\frac{2}{1}$	$\frac{6}{4}$
a	$\frac{5}{4}$	$\frac{3}{2}$	$\frac{1}{2}$	$\frac{4}{2}$
b	$\frac{2}{3}$	$\frac{4}{2}$	$\frac{10}{5}$	$\frac{8}{2}$
c	$\frac{7}{3}$	$\frac{2}{8}$	$\frac{16}{3}$	$\frac{14}{2}$
d	$\frac{21}{3}$	$\frac{16}{4}$	$\frac{12}{24}$	$\frac{13}{4}$
e	$\frac{53}{60}$	$\frac{73}{30}$	$\frac{28}{10}$	$\frac{47}{20}$

2 Cross out the improper fractions.

(example)	$\frac{1}{2}$	$\frac{3}{5}$	$\frac{5}{3}$	$\frac{1}{4}$
a	$\frac{2}{4}$	$\frac{3}{6}$	$\frac{8}{5}$	$\frac{5}{8}$
b	$\frac{1}{3}$	$\frac{3}{1}$	$\frac{2}{4}$	$\frac{10}{20}$
c	$\frac{16}{20}$	$\frac{5}{3}$	$\frac{20}{30}$	$\frac{3}{5}$
d	$\frac{16}{20}$	$\frac{14}{18}$	$\frac{81}{41}$	$\frac{24}{30}$
e	$\frac{27}{50}$	$\frac{53}{24}$	$\frac{24}{35}$	$\frac{29}{51}$

3 Write three proper fractions that match each description.

a 5 is the denominator

(example) $\frac{2}{5}$

c 10 is the denominator

b 4 is the numerator

d 3 is the denominator

4 Write three improper fractions that match each description.

a 7 is the numerator

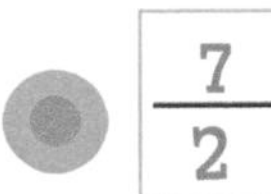

(example) $\frac{7}{2}$

d 5 is the denominator

b 3 is the denominator

e 6 is the numerator

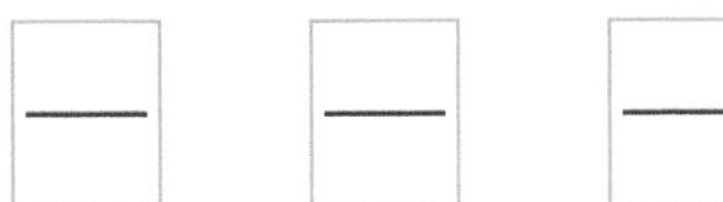

c 8 is the numerator

f 12 is the numerator

MIXED NUMBERS

A mixed number has a whole number and a proper fraction written together.

Whole number → $3\frac{1}{5}$ ← Proper fraction

↑

Mixed number

Example 1:

$3\frac{1}{5} = 3 + \frac{1}{5}$

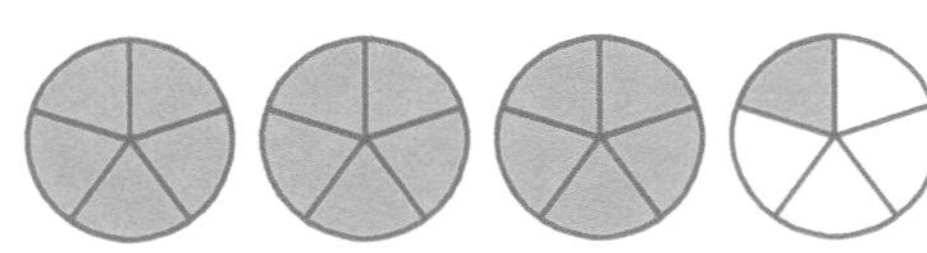

Example 2:

$1\frac{4}{6} = 1 + \frac{4}{6}$

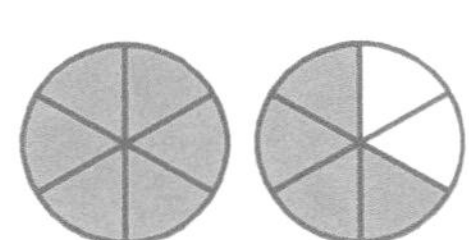

Example 3:

___ $\frac{\_}{\_}$ = ___ + $\frac{\_}{\_}$

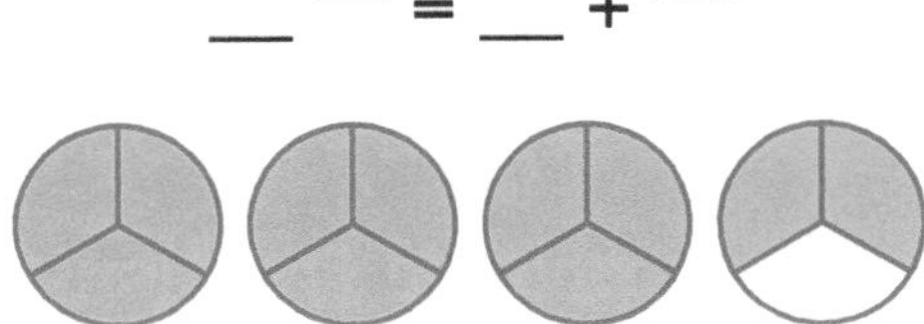

Example 4:

2 $\frac{\_}{\_}$ = ___ + $\frac{\_}{\_}$

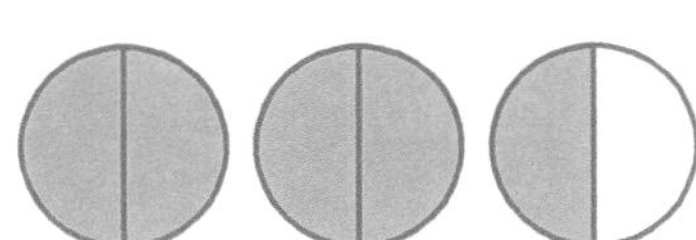

Your turn

Color the shapes to show the mixed numbers.

$2\frac{1}{4}$ 

a $3\frac{2}{3}$ 

b $6\frac{1}{2}$ 

c $1\frac{5}{10}$ 

SELF CHECK Mark how you feel		
Got it! ☐	Need help... ☐	I don't get it ☐

Check your answers

How many did you get correct? ☐

PRACTICE

1 Color the shapes to show the mixed numbers.

$2\frac{2}{3}$ of the circles 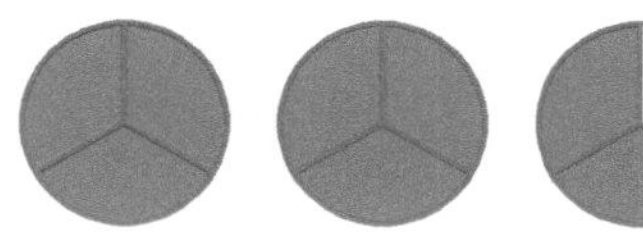 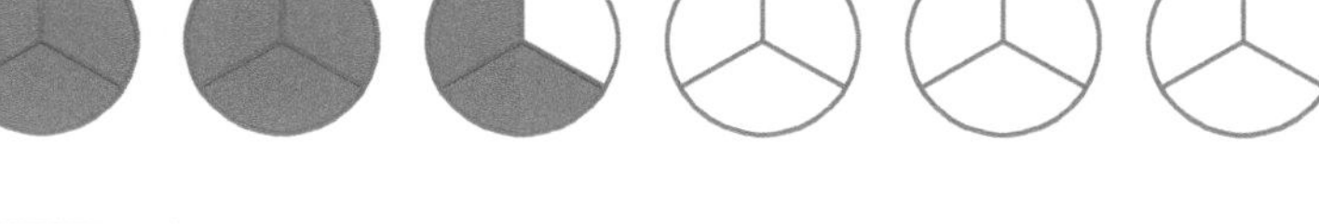

a $4\frac{3}{4}$ of the squares 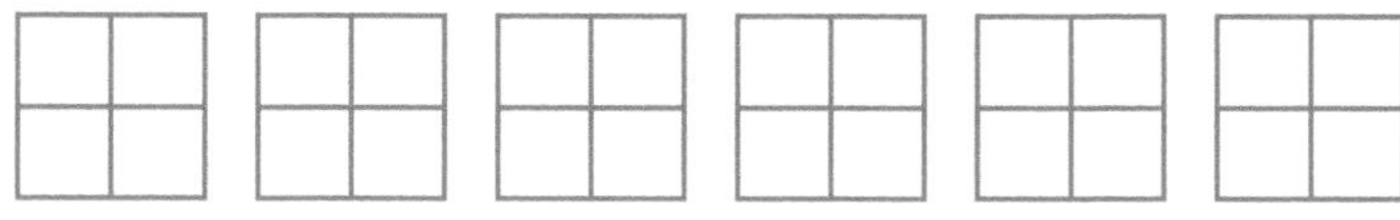

b $5\frac{1}{2}$ of the triangles 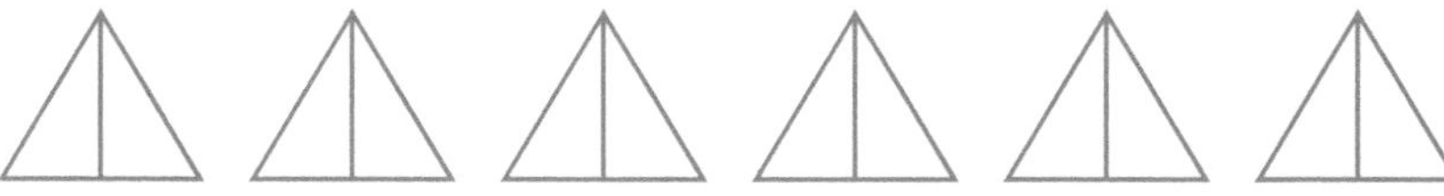

c $3\frac{4}{5}$ of the rectangles 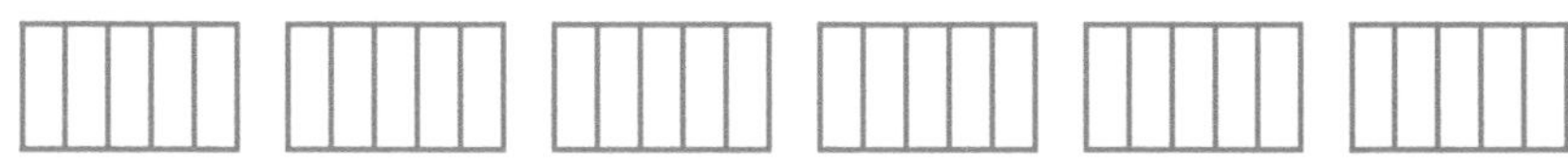

2 Write the mixed numbers to show how many shapes are colored orange.

$2\frac{4}{6}$ of the hexagons are orange.

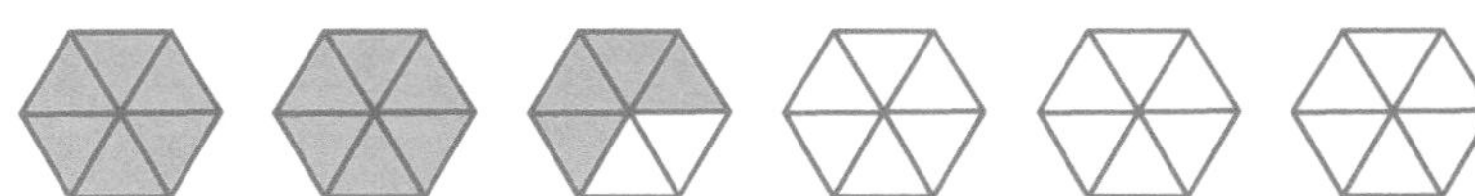

a ☐ of the pentagons are orange.

b ☐ of the octagons are orange.

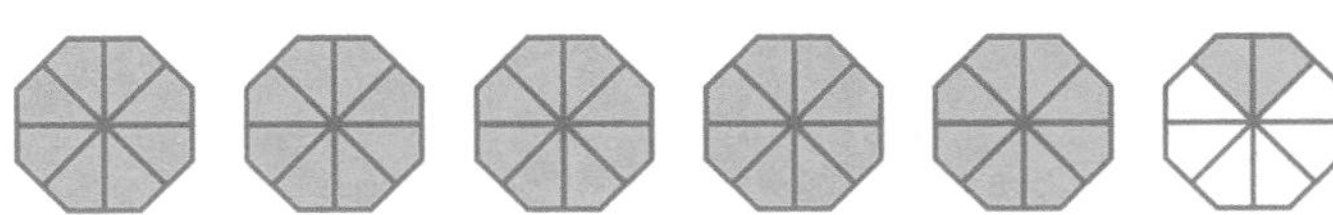

c ☐ of the triangles are orange.

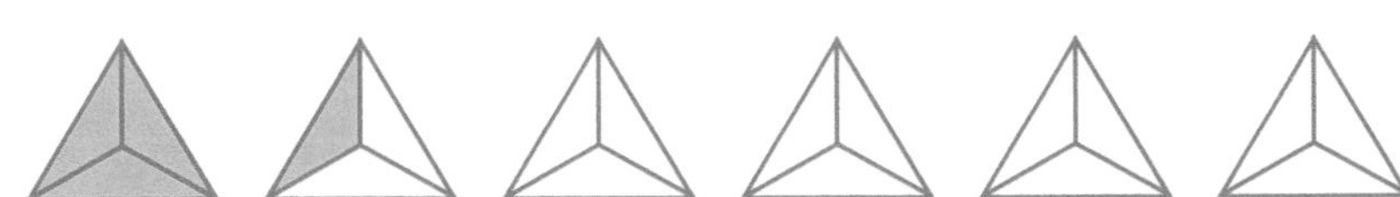

IMPROPER FRACTIONS AND MIXED NUMBERS

You can write mixed numbers as improper fractions.

Mixed number → $3\frac{1}{4}$ $\frac{13}{4}$ ← Improper fraction

Change a mixed number to an improper fraction

Example 1: $4\frac{3}{5} = \frac{23}{5}$

Step 1: Multiply the denominator (5) by the whole number (4): $5 \times 4 = 20$

Step 2: Add the answer to the numerator (3): $20 + 3 = 23$. Keep the same denominator, 5.

Example 2: $3\frac{2}{3} = \frac{\_\_}{3}$

$3 \times 3 + 2 =$ ____

Change an improper fraction to a mixed number

Example 3: $\frac{23}{5} = 4\frac{3}{5}$

Find out how many wholes there are in $\frac{23}{5}$. How many times can 5 go into 23?

$23 \div 5 = 4$ remainder 3

Write the 3 remainder as the numerator. Keep the same denominator, 5.

Example 4: $\frac{29}{3} = \_\_\frac{\_\_}{3}$

$29 \div 3 =$ __ remainder __

Complete the table.

	Diagram	Improper Fraction	Mixed Number
●		$\frac{10}{3}$	$3\frac{1}{3}$
a		$\frac{\_\_}{4}$	$\_\_\frac{\_\_}{\_\_}$
b		$\frac{\_\_}{8}$	$\_\_\frac{\_\_}{\_\_}$
c		$\frac{\_\_}{2}$	$\_\_\frac{\_\_}{\_\_}$

SELF CHECK Mark how you feel

Got it!	Need help...	I don't get it

Check your answers
How many did you get correct?

PRACTICE

1 Change these mixed numbers to improper fractions.

- Example: $2\frac{3}{4} = \frac{11}{4}$
- a $3\frac{1}{2} = \_$
- b $2\frac{4}{6} = \_$
- c $3\frac{2}{3} = \_$
- d $1\frac{3}{4} = \_$
- e $5\frac{2}{3} = \_$
- f $6\frac{1}{2} = \_$
- g $4\frac{1}{2} = \_$
- h $2\frac{2}{5} = \_$

2 Change these improper fractions to mixed numbers.

- Example: $\frac{5}{4} = 1\frac{1}{4}$
- a $\frac{10}{3} = \_\_$
- b $\frac{7}{5} = \_\_$
- c $\frac{5}{3} = \_\_$
- d $\frac{9}{2} = \_\_$
- e $\frac{6}{4} = \_\_$
- f $\frac{12}{10} = \_\_$
- g $\frac{21}{4} = \_\_$
- h $\frac{32}{3} = \_\_$

3 Circle the mixed number that matches each improper fraction.

Example	$\frac{12}{5}$	$2\frac{3}{5}$	$2\frac{2}{5}$ (circled)	$1\frac{1}{5}$
a	$\frac{25}{7}$	$3\frac{4}{7}$	$3\frac{7}{4}$	$1\frac{25}{7}$
b	$\frac{50}{9}$	$5\frac{5}{9}$	$5\frac{4}{5}$	$5\frac{1}{9}$
c	$\frac{35}{10}$	$3\frac{1}{10}$	$3\frac{5}{10}$	$3\frac{4}{10}$
d	$\frac{67}{8}$	$8\frac{3}{8}$	$8\frac{7}{8}$	$9\frac{3}{8}$
e	$\frac{45}{6}$	$7\frac{3}{6}$	$5\frac{3}{6}$	$6\frac{5}{6}$

4 Circle the improper fraction that matches each mixed number.

Example	$2\frac{3}{4}$	$\frac{15}{4}$	$\frac{11}{4}$ (circled)	$\frac{12}{4}$
a	$3\frac{3}{5}$	$\frac{18}{5}$	$\frac{17}{5}$	$\frac{19}{5}$
b	$4\frac{7}{8}$	$\frac{36}{8}$	$\frac{37}{8}$	$\frac{39}{8}$
c	$6\frac{2}{3}$	$\frac{21}{3}$	$\frac{20}{3}$	$\frac{22}{3}$
d	$1\frac{3}{9}$	$\frac{12}{9}$	$\frac{15}{9}$	$\frac{13}{9}$
e	$5\frac{4}{7}$	$\frac{39}{7}$	$\frac{40}{7}$	$\frac{35}{7}$
f	$7\frac{1}{5}$	$\frac{30}{5}$	$\frac{35}{5}$	$\frac{36}{5}$
g	$2\frac{5}{8}$	$\frac{25}{8}$	$\frac{21}{8}$	$\frac{19}{8}$

ADD AND SUBTRACT FRACTIONS WITH THE SAME DENOMINATOR

Look at the denominators. If the denominators are the same, you can add or subtract the numerators to find the answer.

Adding fractions

Example 1: $\frac{2}{4} + \frac{1}{4}$

First look at the denominators. The denominators are both 4.

You can add the numerators:
2 + 1 = 3

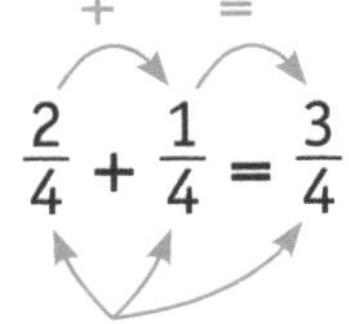

$\frac{2}{4} + \frac{1}{4} = \frac{3}{4}$

The denominators are the same.

Example 2: $\frac{3}{5} + \frac{1}{5} = \frac{\quad}{5}$

Example 3: $\frac{2}{8} + \frac{3}{8} = \frac{\quad}{8}$

Subtracting fractions

Example 4: $\frac{5}{12} - \frac{2}{12}$

First look at the denominators. The denominators are both 12.

You can subtract the numerators:
5 − 2 = 3

$\frac{5}{12} - \frac{2}{12} = \frac{3}{12}$

The denominators are the same.

Example 5: $\frac{8}{10} - \frac{3}{10} = \frac{\quad}{10}$

Example 6: $\frac{4}{5} - \frac{2}{5} = \frac{\quad}{5}$

Solve these addition and subtraction problems.

- ● $\frac{7}{10} - \frac{3}{10} = \frac{4}{10}$
- **a** $\frac{5}{8} - \frac{2}{8} = \frac{\quad}{8}$
- **b** $\frac{5}{6} - \frac{1}{6} = \frac{\quad}{6}$
- **c** $\frac{3}{5} + \frac{1}{5} = \frac{\quad}{5}$
- **d** $\frac{3}{8} + \frac{4}{8} = \frac{\quad}{8}$
- **e** $\frac{2}{4} + \frac{2}{4} = \frac{\quad}{4}$

SELF CHECK Mark how you feel

Got it!	Need help...	I don't get it
 	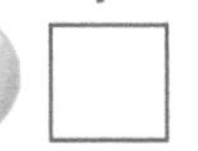	 

Check your answers

How many did you get correct?

PRACTICE

1 Solve these addition problems.

- $\frac{1}{4} + \frac{1}{4} = \frac{2}{4}$
- a $\frac{1}{3} + \frac{1}{3} =$ —
- b $\frac{4}{8} + \frac{1}{8} =$ —
- c $\frac{3}{8} + \frac{2}{8} =$ —
- d $\frac{3}{10} + \frac{2}{10} =$ —
- e $\frac{1}{2} + \frac{1}{2} =$ —
- f $\frac{7}{10} + \frac{1}{10} =$ —
- g $\frac{2}{5} + \frac{2}{5} =$ —
- h $\frac{3}{6} + \frac{1}{6} =$ —
- i $\frac{2}{10} + \frac{7}{10} =$ —
- j $\frac{5}{8} + \frac{2}{8} =$ —
- k $\frac{6}{10} + \frac{2}{10} =$ —

2 Solve these subtraction problems.

- $\frac{5}{12} - \frac{1}{12} = \frac{4}{12}$
- a $\frac{7}{10} - \frac{3}{10} =$ —
- b $\frac{7}{8} - \frac{4}{8} =$ —
- c $\frac{5}{8} - \frac{1}{8} =$ —
- d $\frac{7}{10} - \frac{2}{10} =$ —
- e $\frac{2}{3} - \frac{1}{3} =$ —
- f $\frac{2}{4} - \frac{1}{4} =$ —
- g $\frac{3}{8} - \frac{1}{8} =$ —
- h $\frac{4}{5} - \frac{2}{5} =$ —
- i $\frac{9}{10} - \frac{3}{10} =$ —
- j $\frac{6}{8} - \frac{2}{8} =$ —
- k $\frac{11}{12} - \frac{7}{12} =$ —

3 Match each problem to the correct answer..

$\frac{5}{8} - \frac{2}{8}$	$= \frac{3}{4}$
a $\frac{6}{10} + \frac{1}{10}$	$= \frac{7}{8}$
b $\frac{5}{8} + \frac{2}{8}$	$= \frac{3}{8}$
c $\frac{3}{4} - \frac{1}{4}$	$= \frac{1}{10}$
d $\frac{9}{10} - \frac{8}{10}$	$= \frac{2}{4}$
e $\frac{1}{4} + \frac{2}{4}$	$= \frac{7}{10}$

FRACTIONS REVIEW

1 Add these fractions.

a $\frac{1}{4} + \frac{2}{4} = \underline{\quad}$ b $\frac{3}{5} + \frac{1}{5} = \underline{\quad}$ c $\frac{3}{8} + \frac{2}{8} = \underline{\quad}$ d $\frac{2}{6} + \frac{1}{6} = \underline{\quad}$

2 Subtract these fractions.

a $\frac{7}{8} - \frac{2}{8} = \underline{\quad}$ b $\frac{3}{5} - \frac{2}{5} = \underline{\quad}$ c $\frac{6}{8} - \frac{1}{8} = \underline{\quad}$ d $\frac{9}{10} - \frac{4}{10} = \underline{\quad}$

3 Write the equivalent fractions.

a $\frac{3}{4} = \frac{\quad}{8}$ d $\frac{4}{10} = \frac{\quad}{5}$ g $\frac{2}{10} = \frac{\quad}{5}$ j $\frac{2}{4} = \frac{\quad}{2}$ m $\frac{4}{5} = \frac{\quad}{10}$

b $\frac{1}{2} = \frac{\quad}{10}$ e $\frac{2}{8} = \frac{\quad}{4}$ h $\frac{4}{8} = \frac{\quad}{2}$ k $\frac{4}{4} = \frac{\quad}{8}$ n $\frac{1}{2} = \frac{\quad}{8}$

c $\frac{1}{4} = \frac{\quad}{16}$ f $\frac{3}{5} = \frac{\quad}{10}$ i $\frac{2}{5} = \frac{\quad}{10}$ l $\frac{1}{5} = \frac{\quad}{10}$ o $\frac{1}{2} = \frac{\quad}{10}$

4 Circle the improper fractions.

a $\frac{2}{3}$ $\frac{3}{2}$ $\frac{1}{3}$ c $\frac{1}{3}$ $\frac{2}{3}$ $\frac{4}{3}$ e $\frac{1}{2}$ $\frac{2}{3}$ $\frac{3}{2}$ g $\frac{22}{26}$ $\frac{45}{30}$ $\frac{32}{50}$

b $\frac{1}{4}$ $\frac{1}{2}$ $\frac{4}{2}$ d $\frac{1}{5}$ $\frac{5}{1}$ $\frac{5}{10}$ f $\frac{3}{8}$ $\frac{5}{4}$ $\frac{8}{10}$ h $\frac{15}{30}$ $\frac{51}{30}$ $\frac{20}{25}$

5 Color the circles to show the mixed numbers.

a $2\frac{1}{2}$ 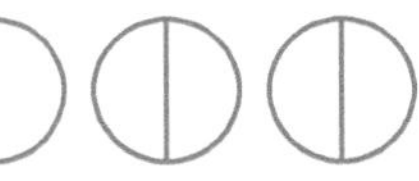   c $4\frac{3}{4}$ 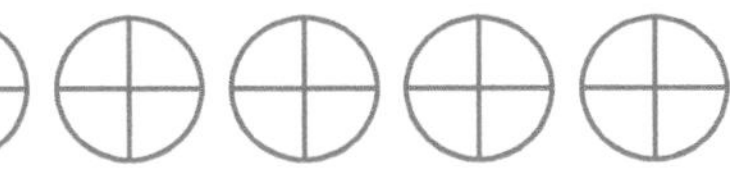

b $3\frac{1}{3}$ d $1\frac{5}{8}$ 

6 Write the mixed numbers.

a ______ of the circles are colored.

b ______ of the circles are colored.

c ______ of the circles are colored.

d ______ of the circles are colored.

7 Change these mixed numbers to improper fractions.

a $3\frac{1}{3} = \frac{}{}$ c $1\frac{5}{8} = \frac{}{}$ e $10\frac{1}{2} = \frac{}{}$ g $2\frac{4}{7} = \frac{}{}$

b $2\frac{3}{6} = \frac{}{}$ d $4\frac{1}{3} = \frac{}{}$ f $7\frac{3}{8} = \frac{}{}$ h $2\frac{1}{4} = \frac{}{}$

8 Change these improper fractions to mixed numbers.

a $\frac{10}{4} =$ ___ — c $\frac{21}{5} =$ ___ — e $\frac{64}{9} =$ ___ — g $\frac{49}{5} =$ ___ —

b $\frac{15}{7} =$ ___ — d $\frac{32}{10} =$ ___ — f $\frac{32}{3} =$ ___ — h $\frac{17}{2} =$ ___ —

WRITING DECIMALS

You can write fractions in decimal form.

The 0 in the ones place means there are no whole numbers.

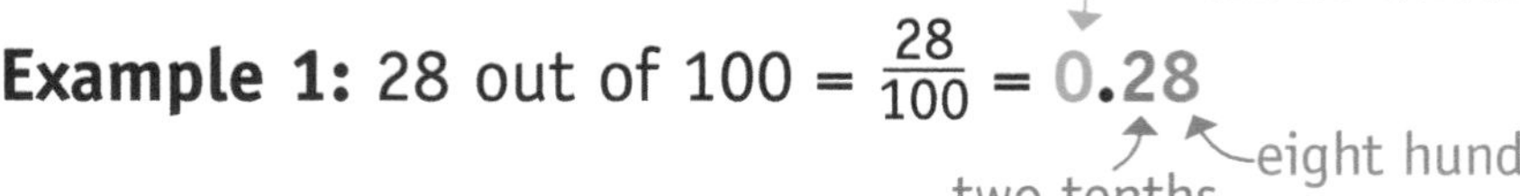

Example 1: 28 out of 100 = $\frac{28}{100}$ = 0.28

two tenths — eight hundredths

The 1 in the ones place means there is 1 whole number.

Example 2: 143 out of 100 = $\frac{143}{100}$ = 1.43

four tenths — three hundredths

Example 3: 62 out of 100 = $\frac{\quad}{100}$ = __ . __ __

Example 4: 259 out of 100 = $\frac{\quad}{100}$ = __ . __ __

Your turn

Complete the table.

	Fraction	Decimal	Out of 100
●	$\frac{78}{100}$	0.78	78 out of 100
a		0.32	___ out of ___
b	$\frac{57}{100}$		___ out of ___
c		0.93	___ out of ___
d			22 out of 100
e	$\frac{138}{100}$		___ out of ___
f			365 out of 100

SELF CHECK Mark how you feel

Got it! ☐ Need help... ☐ I don't get it ☐

Check your answers
How many did you get correct? ☐

PRACTICE

1 Use blue to circle the whole numbers and red to circle the decimal parts.

- ● 24.63
- a 124.35
- b 20.34
- c 82.10
- d 64.39
- e 913.26
- f 1.34
- g 52.45
- h 142.53
- i 106.50

2 Write the numbers in the place value table below.

- ● 9 ones, 33 hundredths
- a 1 ten, 3 ones, 78 hundredths
- b 4 tens, 6 ones, 24 hundredths
- c 5 tens, 1 one, 3 hundredths
- d 3 tens, 8 hundredths

	Tens	Ones	.	Tenths	Hundredths
●		9	.	3	3
a			.		
b			.		
c			.		
d			.		

3 Write these decimals in place value words.

- ● 7.65 7 ones + 6 tenths + 5 hundredths
- a 8.23 ____________________
- b 4.05 ____________________
- c 0.76 ____________________

4 Write the decimals from least to greatest.

- ● 2.35, 4.73, 1.29, 5.63, 1.07 1.07, 1.29, 2.35, 4.73, 5.63
- a 2.17, 7.12, 2.71, 1.27, 7.21 ____________________
- b 3.03, 3.30, 0.33, 0.30, 3.31 ____________________
- c 8.15, 1.85, 1.8, 8.51, 5.18 ____________________
- d 6.37, 7.63, 6.73, 3.76, 3.67 ____________________

RELATING TENTHS TO HUNDREDTHS

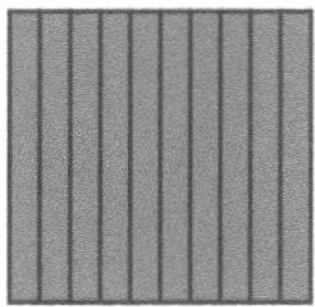

This square is cut into tenths. It has 10 equal parts.
Each tenth is $0.10 = \frac{1}{10}$.

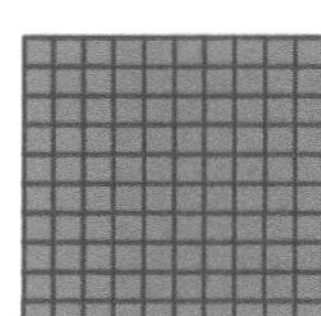

This square is cut into hundredths.
It has 100 equal parts.
Each hundredth is $\frac{1}{100} = 0.01$.

Example 1:

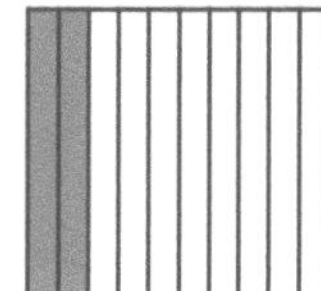

This square shows 2 tenths.
$\frac{2}{10} = 0.20$

Example 2:

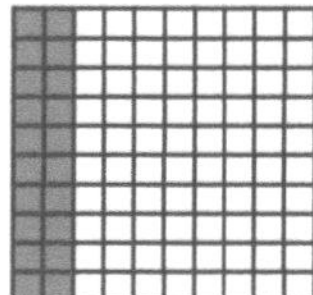

This square shows 20 hundredths.
$\frac{20}{100} = 0.20$

Example 3:

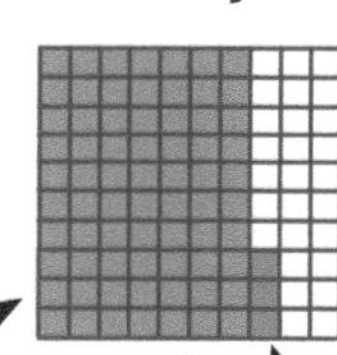

This square shows 73 hundredths.
$\frac{73}{100} = 0.73$

Example 4:

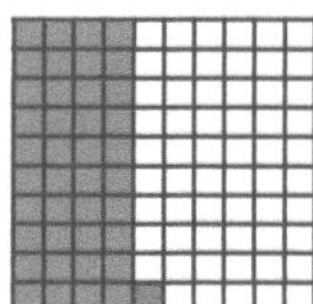

This square shows 41 hundredths.
$\frac{41}{100} = 0.41$

Example 5:

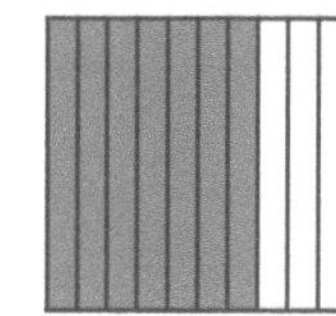

This square shows __ tenths.
$\frac{\ }{10}$ = 0.____

Example 6:

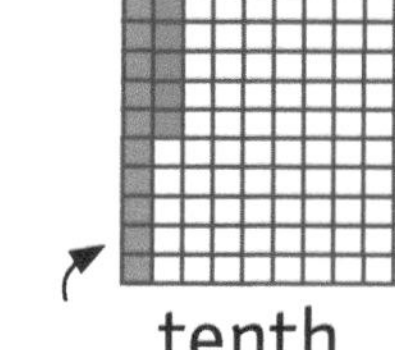

This square shows ____ hundredths.
$\frac{\ }{100}$ = 0.____

Your turn

What fraction is colored?

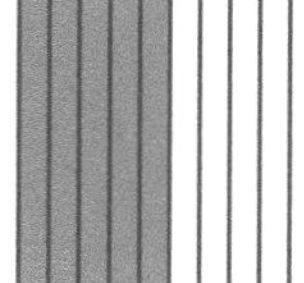

$\frac{5}{10}$ = 0.50

a

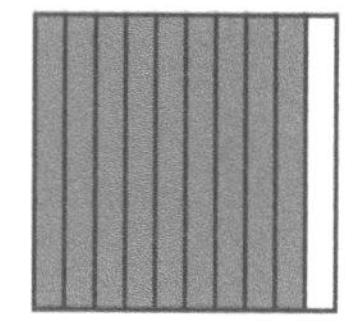

$\frac{\ }{10}$ = _____

b

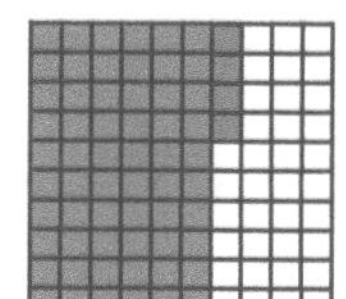

$\frac{\ }{100}$ = ______

c

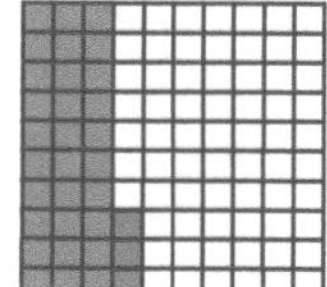

$\frac{\ }{100}$ = ______

SELF CHECK Mark how you feel		
Got it!	Need help...	I don't get it
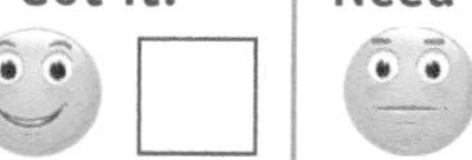		

Check your answers
How many did you get correct?

PRACTICE

1 Color the decimals. Use blue for tenths and red for hundredths.

● 0.63

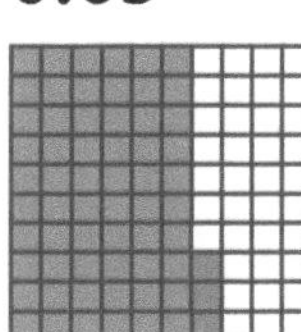

a 0.40

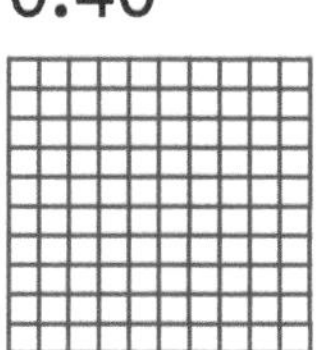

b 0.98

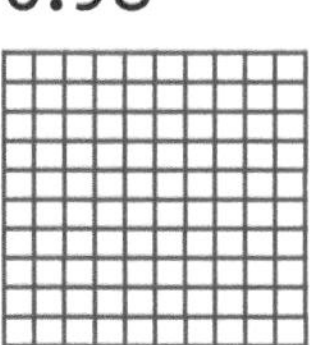

c 0.03

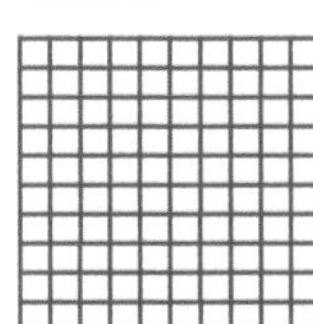

2 Write the decimals.

● 0.24

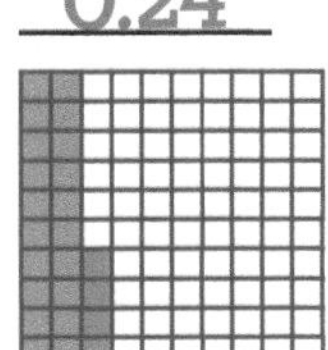

a ______

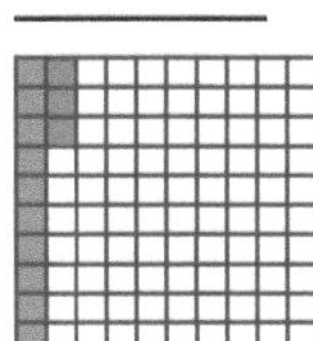

b ______

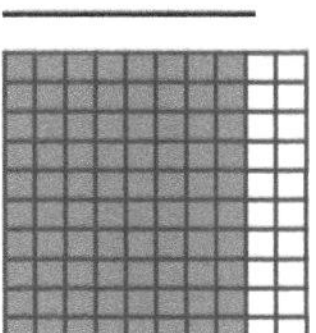

c ______

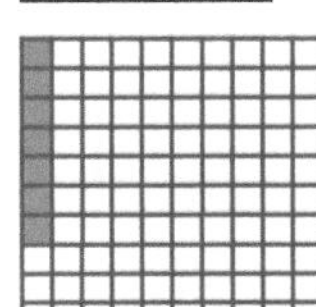

3 Complete the table.

	Words	Diagram	Fraction	Decimal
●	seventy-five hundredths		$\frac{75}{100}$	0.75
a			$\frac{60}{100}$	
b				0.42
c	ninety-three hundredths			
d				0.01
e	eighteen hundredths			

DECIMALS AND FRACTIONS IN WORDS

A decimal is a fraction with a denominator that is 10 or a power of 10, such as 100, 1,000 or 10,000.

Example 1: 0.27 = zero and twenty-seven hundredths

= $\frac{27}{100}$ = twenty-seven hundredths

Example 2: 3.45 = three and forty-five hundredths

= $\frac{345}{100}$ = three hundred and forty-five hundredths

Example 3:

82.69 = ____________-_____ and __________ __________

= $\frac{\quad}{100}$ = _______ thousand, _____ hundred, and _______-_____ hundredths

Example 4:

0.99 = _____ and ______ ______

= $\frac{\quad}{100}$ = ___________-______ hundredths

Your turn

Complete the table.

	Fraction	Fraction in words	Decimal
●	$\frac{92}{100}$	ninety-two hundredths	0.92
a	$\frac{84}{100}$		
b			0.36
c		one hundred and thirty-nine hundredths	

SELF CHECK Mark how you feel

Got it! ☐ Need help... ☐ I don't get it ☐

Check your answers

How many did you get correct? ☐

PRACTICE

1 Write these decimals in words.

- 3.05 three and five hundredths
- a 2.94 ______
- b 0.82 ______
- c 8.93 ______
- d 1.37 ______
- e 2.40 ______
- f 10.73 ______
- g 20.02 ______
- h 0.16 ______
- i 29.06 ______
- j 43.44 ______

2 Write as fractions.

- twelve out of 100 $\frac{12}{100}$
- a six out of 100 ______
- b twenty-three out of 100 ______
- c forty-two out of 100 ______
- d eighty-nine out of 100 ______
- e one hundred two out of 100 ______
- f seven hundred twelve out of 100 ______
- g nine hundred sixty-three out of 100 ______
- h eight hundred ninety out of 100 ______
- i seven hundred one out of 100 ______
- j five hundred forty-seven out of 100 ______
- k eight hundred out of 100 ______
- l three hundred twenty out of 100 ______

THOUSANDTHS

The third decimal place is thousandths.
There are 1,000 thousandths in 1 whole.

Example 1:

2.451 has:
2 ones
4 tenths
5 hundredths
1 thousandth

Example 2:

86.873 has:
8 tens
6 ones
8 tenths
7 hundredths
3 thousandths

Example 3:

8.296 has:
_____ ones
_____ tenths
_____ hundredths
_____ thousandths

Example 4:

47.609 has:
_____ tens
_____ ones
_____ tenths
_____ hundredths
_____ thousandths

1 one = 10 tenths
= 100 hundredths
= 1,000 thousandths

Your turn

Write the missing numbers.

- 6.924 6 ones, 9 tenths, 2 hundredths, 4 thousandths
- **a** 7.382 __ ones, __ tenths, __ hundredths, __ thousandths
- **b** 5.410 __ ones, __ tenths, __ hundredth, __ thousandths
- **c** 9.734 __ ones, __ tenths, __ hundredths, __ thousandths
- **d** 8.532 __ ones, __ tenths, __ hundredths, __ thousandths
- **e** 6.593 __ ones, __ tenths, __ hundredths, __ thousandths
- **f** 7.113 __ ones, __ tenth, __ hundredth, __ thousandths

SELF CHECK Mark how you feel

Got it!	Need help...	I don't get it
☐	☐	☐

Check your answers
How many did you get correct? ☐

PRACTICE

1 Write the digit in each place in 6.842.

- ● tenths place 8
- **a** ones place ____
- **b** thousandths place ____
- **c** hundredths place ____

2 Write the digit in each place in 3.079.

- ● tenths place 0
- **a** thousandths place ____
- **b** ones place ____
- **c** hundredths place ____

3 Write the numbers. Include the decimal point.

● 7 in the thousandths place,
2 in the ones place,
4 in the tenths place, and
6 in the hundredths place

2.467

a 8 in the ones place,
9 in the hundredths place,
6 in the tenths place, and
1 in the thousandths place

____

b 5 in the thousandths place,
8 in the hundredths place,
4 in the ones place, and
3 in the tenths place

____

c 7 in the tenths place,
6 in the ones place,
2 in the thousandths place,
and 0 in the hundredths place

____

4 Write in decimal form.

- ● 3,674 thousandths = 3.674
- **a** 1,672 thousandths = ________
- **b** 5,381 thousandths = ________
- **c** 9,035 thousandths = ________
- **d** 8,354 thousandths = ________
- **e** 7,438 thousandths = ________
- **f** 1,085 thousandths = ________
- **g** 1,006 thousandths = ________
- **h** 6,952 thousandths = ________
- **i** 2,010 thousandths = ________
- **j** 2,340 thousandths = ________
- **k** 5,000 thousandths = ________
- **l** 6,100 thousandths = ________
- **m** 7,467 thousandths = ________

PLACE VALUE

Place value is the value of each digit in a number.
It means how much the digit is worth.

Example 1:
Complete the place value chart for 64.832.

6 tens, 4 ones, 8 tenths, 3 hundredths, 2 thousandths

64.832

Tens	Ones	.	Tenths	Hundredths	Thousandths	Ten Thousandths
6	4	.	8	3	2	

Example 2: Write 32.5194 in the place value chart.

Tens	Ones	.	Tenths	Hundredths	Thousandths	Ten Thousandths
		.				

Example 3: Write 14.3109 in the place value chart.

Tens	Ones	.	Tenths	Hundredths	Thousandths	Ten Thousandths
		.				

Your turn

1 Use orange to trace over the thousandths place.

● 24.927 **a** 62.493 **b** 25.620 **c** 7.358

2 Use red to trace over the hundredths place.

● 3.845 **a** 1.246 **b** 29.368 **c** 84.721

3 Use blue to trace over the tenths place.

● 26.429 **a** 32.739 **b** 1.435 **c** 0.583

4 Use green to trace over the ones place.

● 3.246 **a** 73.282 **b** 1.122 **c** 40.475

5 Use yellow to trace over the tens place.

● 32.473 **a** 10.650 **b** 74.009 **c** 21.436

SELF CHECK Mark how you feel

Got it!	Need help...	I don't get it
 ☐	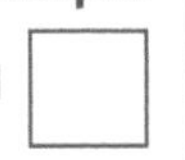 ☐	 ☐

Check your answers
How many did you get correct? ☐

PRACTICE

1 What is the place value of the 5?

- 25.2368 ones
- a 63.7454 ______
- b 54.2790 ______
- c 1.3527 ______
- d 4.5796 ______
- e 43.5391 ______
- f 12.2053 ______
- g 2.6521 ______
- h 14.5263 ______
- i 53.2104 ______
- j 13.0506 ______
- k 73.8045 ______

2 Trace the tens in yellow, ones in green, tenths in blue, hundredths in red, thousandths in orange, and ten thousandths in purple.

- 35.3782
- a 21.350
- b 71.4583
- c 0.359
- d 54.9252
- e 99.9999
- f 64.381
- g 82.563
- h 0.5034
- i 17.32
- j 53.1
- k 80.0019

3 Complete the table.

	Decimal	Tens	Ones	.	Tenths	Hundredths	Thousandths	Ten Thousandths
	20.8351	2	0	.	8	3	5	1
a	43.246							
b	74.9783							
c	87.903							
d	95.0902							
e	16.10							
f		2	4	.	6	4	9	
g		3	0	.	2	5	8	7
h		6	1	.	0	8	2	
i		5	3	.	9	4	2	
j		6	0	.	4	3	6	5

DECOMPOSING DECIMALS

A decimal is made up of parts. These parts can be whole numbers and fractions of whole numbers.

$$2.39 = 2\frac{39}{100}$$

This mixed number is made up of 2 wholes + $\frac{3}{10}$ + $\frac{9}{100}$.
It can be written as 2 + $\frac{39}{100}$.

Example 1:

$6.876 = 6\frac{876}{1,000}$

$= 6 \text{ wholes} + \frac{8}{10} + \frac{7}{100} + \frac{6}{1,000}$

$= 6 + \frac{876}{1,000}$

Example 2:

$2.493 = 2\frac{493}{1,000}$

$=$ ___ wholes $+ \frac{}{10} + \frac{}{100} + \frac{}{1,000}$

$= 2 + \frac{}{1,000}$

Example 3:

$5.457 = 5\frac{}{1,000}$

$=$ ___ wholes $+ \frac{}{10} + \frac{}{100} + \frac{}{1,000}$

$=$ ___ $+ \frac{}{1,000}$

There are many different ways to write numbers.

Complete the fractions.

● 1.32 $= 1\frac{32}{100} = 1 + \frac{3}{10} + \frac{2}{100}$

a 2.27 $= 2\frac{27}{100} = 2 + \frac{}{10} + \frac{}{100}$

b 8.327 $= 8\frac{327}{1,000} = 8 + \frac{}{10} + \frac{}{100} + \frac{}{1,000}$

c 7.43 $= 7\frac{}{100} = 7 + \frac{}{10} + \frac{}{100}$

d 4.103 $= 4\frac{}{1,000} =$ ___ $+ \frac{}{10} + \frac{}{100} + \frac{}{1,000}$

SELF CHECK Mark how you feel

Got it!	Need help...	I don't get it
☐	☐	☐

Check your answers

How many did you get correct? ☐

PRACTICE

Complete the table.

	Decimal	Mixed Number	Wholes	Tenths	Hundredths	Thousandths
	5.213	$5\frac{213}{1,000}$	5	$\frac{2}{10}$	$\frac{1}{100}$	$\frac{3}{1,000}$
a			4	$\frac{1}{10}$	$\frac{7}{100}$	$\frac{5}{1,000}$
b	6.157					
c			1	$\frac{4}{10}$	$\frac{9}{100}$	$\frac{3}{1,000}$
d		$8\frac{459}{1,000}$				
e			3	$\frac{2}{10}$	$\frac{3}{100}$	$\frac{7}{1,000}$
f	7.368					
g			9	$\frac{9}{10}$	$\frac{4}{100}$	$\frac{5}{1,000}$

Complete the table.

	Decimal	Mixed Number	Wholes	Thousandths
	1.453	$1\frac{453}{1,000}$	1	$\frac{453}{1,000}$
a			5	$\frac{324}{1,000}$
b	6.173			
c			4	$\frac{159}{1,000}$
d		$3\frac{438}{1,000}$		
e			6	$\frac{805}{1,000}$
f	7.590			
g			9	$\frac{720}{1,000}$

DECIMALS REVIEW

1 Use blue to circle the whole numbers and red to circle the decimals.

a 24.20 **b** 63.58 **c** 0.30 **d** 58.37 **e** 70.59

2 Write the numbers in the place value table below.

a 3 tens, 5 ones, 6 tenths, 5 hundredths, 1 thousandth

b 8 ones, 6 hundredths, 5 tenths, 2 thousandths

c 9 thousandths, 6 tens, 3 hundredths, 9 ones, 8 tenths

d 5 tenths, 7 tens, 6 ones, 8 hundredths, 6 thousandths

e 1 tenth, 6 thousandths, 5 hundredths, 9 ones, 3 tens

f 1 ten, 4 tenths, 9 hundredths, 7 thousandths

	Tens	Ones	.	Tenths	Hundredths	Thousandths
a						
b						
c						
d						
e						
f						

3 Write the decimals from greatest to least.

a 3.42, 2.43, 4.32, 2.34, 3.24 ______________________

b 1.473, 1.734, 3.174, 4.371, 7.317 ______________________

c 5.968, 8.695, 5.698, 8.965, 6.895 ______________________

d 9.034, 4.093, 3.904, 9.34, 9.304 ______________________

e 5.243, 3.781, 9.501, 3.331, 9.529 ______________________

4 Write these decimals with place value words.

a 8.234 _____ ones + _____ tenths + _____ hundredths _____ + thousandths

b 5.40 ________________________________

c 24.07 ________________________________

d 51.78 ________________________________

e 4.738 ________________________________

f 24.825 ________________________________

5 Write the decimals.

a _______

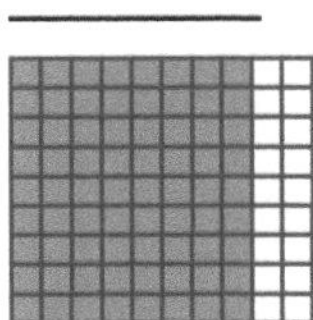

c _______

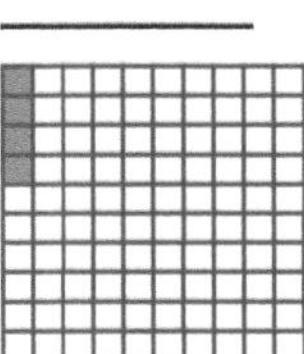

e _______

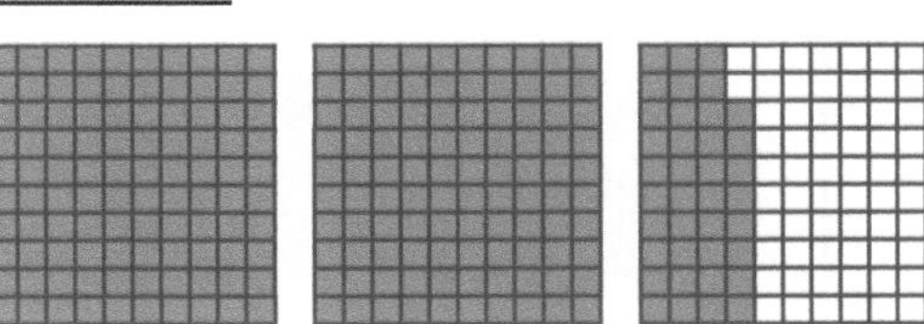

b _______

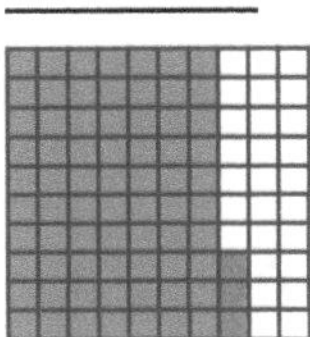

d _______

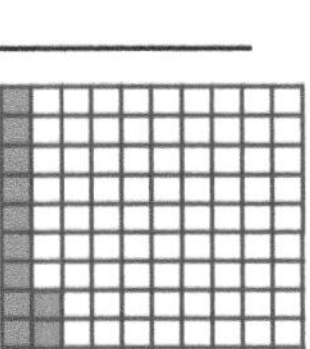

f _______

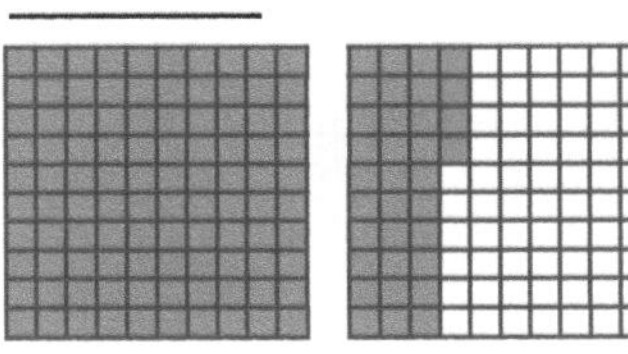

6 Color the decimals. Use blue for tenths and red for hundredths.

a 0.51

c 0.90

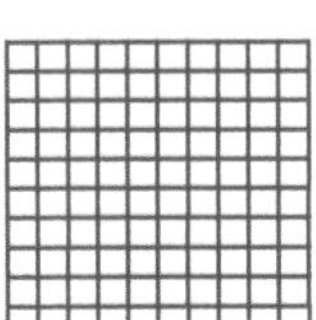

e 1.03

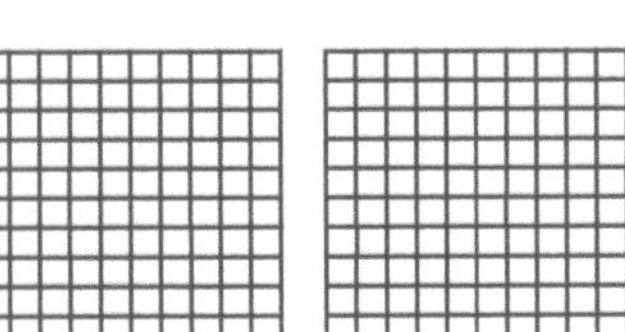

b 0.38

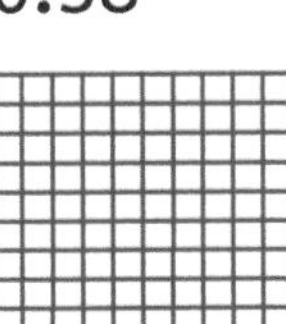

d 0.06

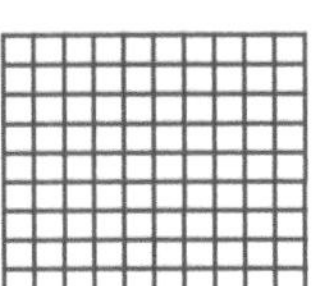

f 2.57

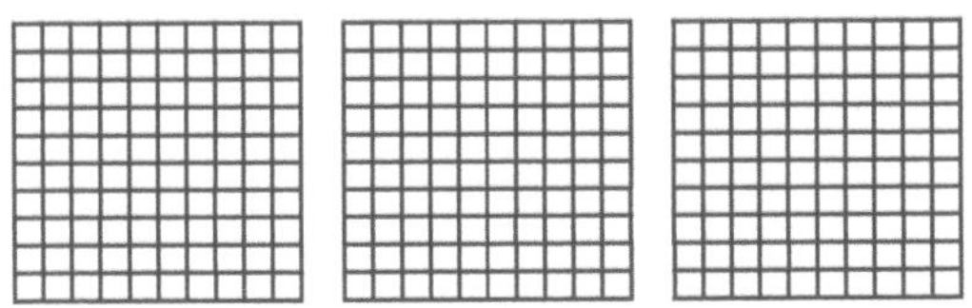

REVIEW

7 Fill in the table.

	Fraction	Fraction in words	Decimal
a	$\frac{29}{100}$		
b	$\frac{38}{100}$		
c		one hundred ninety-seven hundredths	
d			2.54
e			6.348
f		two hundred forty-one thousandths	
g			6.846
h	$\frac{483}{100}$		

8 Write these decimals in words.

a 6.593 ______________________________

b 0.742 ______________________________

c 3.561 ______________________________

d 0.803 ______________________________

e 2.41 ______________________________

9 Write the digit in each place in 35.609.

a ones place _____

b thousandths place _____

c tens place _____

d hundredths place _____

e tenths place _____

10 Write the digit in each place in 46.837.

a tens place _____

b thousandths place _____

c ones place _____

d hundredths place _____

e tenths place _____

11 Write the digit in each place in 2.498.

a tenths place _____

b ones place _____

c hundredths place _____

d thousandths place _____

12 Write the numbers. Include the decimal points.

a 8 in the thousandths place,
3 in the ones place,
7 in the tenths place,
6 in the hundredths place

____

b 9 in the ones place,
7 in the hundredths place,
1 in the tenths place,
6 in the tens place,
8 in the thousandths place

____

c 3 in the hundredths place,
5 in the tens place,
2 in the ones place,
4 in the thousandths place,
8 in the tenths place

____

d 7 in the thousandths place,
8 in the tens place,
0 in the ones place,
9 in the tenths place,
2 in the hundredths place

____

e 0 in the tenths place,
6 in the tens place,
4 in the ones place,
5 in the thousandths place,
8 in the hundredths place

____

REVIEW

13 Write in decimal form.

a 5,935 thousandths = ________

b 6,710 thousandths = ________

c 8,423 thousandths = ________

d 2,872 thousandths = ________

e 4,731 thousandths = ________

f 6,481 thousandths = ________

g 3,700 thousandths = ________

h 5,490 thousandths = ________

i 4,907 thousandths = ________

j 8,034 thousandths = ________

14 Write in decimal form.

a two tenths = ________

b 375 hundredths = ________

c 147 hundredths = ________

d nine-tenths = ________

e 733 hundredths = ________

f six tenths = ________

g 843 hundredths = ________

h 125 hundredths = ________

15 Complete the table.

	Decimal	Tens	Ones	.	Tenths	Hundredths	Thousandths
a	15.723						
b	74.978						
c	73.098						
d	3.432						
e	5.24						
f	6.13						
g	8.354						
h	91.407						
i	70.320						
j	90.004						

16 Write the missing numbers.

a $2\frac{63}{100}$ = ____ + $\frac{\quad}{10}$ + $\frac{\quad}{100}$

b $7\frac{30}{100}$ = ____ + $\frac{\quad}{10}$ + $\frac{\quad}{100}$

c $1\frac{17}{100}$ = ____ + $\frac{\quad}{10}$ + $\frac{\quad}{100}$

d $5\frac{8}{100}$ = ____ + $\frac{\quad}{10}$ + $\frac{\quad}{100}$

17 Write the missing numbers.

a $6\frac{28}{100}$ = ____ + $\frac{\quad}{100}$

b $8\frac{48}{100}$ = ____ + $\frac{\quad}{100}$

c $4\frac{3}{100}$ = ____ + $\frac{\quad}{100}$

d $3\frac{50}{100}$ = ____ + $\frac{\quad}{100}$

18 Write the missing numbers.

a $2\frac{624}{1,000}$ = 2 + $\frac{\quad}{10}$ + $\frac{\quad}{100}$ + $\frac{\quad}{1,000}$

b $8\frac{183}{1,000}$ = 8 + $\frac{\quad}{10}$ + $\frac{\quad}{100}$ + $\frac{\quad}{1,000}$

c $9\frac{759}{1,000}$ = ____ + $\frac{\quad}{10}$ + $\frac{\quad}{100}$ + $\frac{\quad}{1,000}$

d $4\frac{923}{1,000}$ = ____ + $\frac{\quad}{10}$ + $\frac{\quad}{100}$ + $\frac{\quad}{1,000}$

e $15\frac{409}{1,000}$ = ____ + $\frac{\quad}{10}$ + $\frac{\quad}{100}$ + $\frac{\quad}{1,000}$

f $10\frac{790}{1,000}$ = ____ + $\frac{\quad}{10}$ + $\frac{\quad}{100}$ + $\frac{\quad}{1,000}$

19 Write the missing numbers.

a $3\frac{729}{1,000}$ = ____ + $\frac{\quad}{1,000}$

b $8\frac{430}{1,000}$ = ____ + $\frac{\quad}{1,000}$

c $5\frac{745}{1,000}$ = ____ + $\frac{\quad}{1,000}$

d $14\frac{657}{1,000}$ = ____ + $\frac{\quad}{1,000}$

e $20\frac{130}{1,000}$ = ____ + $\frac{\quad}{1,000}$

f $39\frac{429}{1,000}$ = ____ + $\frac{\quad}{1,000}$

NUMBER PATTERNS

A number pattern is a series of numbers that follows a rule. The rule tells you what to do with each number to make the pattern.

Example 1:

24, 26, 28, 30, 32, 34, 36 ...

Rule: Add 2

Example 2:

3, 12, 48, 192, 768, 3072 ...

Rule: Multiply by 4

Example 3:

97, 94, 91, 88, 85, 82, 79 ...

Rule: Subtract 3

Example 4:

128, 64, 32, 16, 8, 4, 2, 1

Rule: Divide by 2

Example 5:

73, 76, 79, 82, 85, 88, 91 ...

Rule: ______________

Example 6:

187, 181, 175, 169, 163, 157 ...

Rule: ______________

Use the rule to continue the pattern.

- 128, 132, 136, 140, 144 — Rule: + 4

a 8, ____, ____, ____, ____ — Rule: × 2

b 144, ____, ____, ____, ____ — Rule: Subtract 12

c 96, ____, ____, ____, ____ — Rule: Divide by 2

d 67, ____, ____, ____, ____ — Rule: Add 6

e 6, ____, ____, ____, ____ — Rule: Multiply by 3

SELF CHECK Mark how you feel		
Got it! ☐	Need help... ☐	I don't get it ☐

Check your answers

How many did you get correct? ☐

1 Complete the table.

	Rule	Number Pattern
●	+ 6	3, 9, 15, 21, 27, 33
a	÷ 2	4,000, ____, ____, ____, ____, ____
b	+ 2	2,000, ____, ____, ____, ____, ____
c	+ 3	185, ____, ____, ____, ____, ____
d	+ 8	1,009, ____, ____, ____, ____, ____

2 Write the rule for each pattern.

● 8, 15, 22, 29, 36, 43 Rule: + 7

a 129, 126, 123, 120, 117 Rule: ____

b 7, 14, 28, 56, 112, 224 Rule: ____

c 5, 25, 125, 625, 3,125 Rule: ____

d 10, 21, 32, 43, 54, 65 Rule: ____

e 6, 36, 216, 1,296, 7,776 Rule: ____

f 48, 24, 12, 6, 3 Rule: ____

3 Use the rules to continue these two-step patterns.

● 10, 12, 18, 36, 90, 252, 738 Rule: – 6, × 3

a 5, 8, ____, ____, ____, ____, ____ Rule: – 1, × 2

b 4, 7, ____, ____, ____, ____, ____ Rule: × 2, – 1

c 260, 132, ____, ____, ____, ____, ____ Rule: ÷ 2, + 2

d 20, 26, ____, ____, ____, ____, ____ Rule: – 7, × 2

4 Continue each pattern, and write the rule.

● 6, 12, 18, 24, 30, 36 Rule: + 6

a 81, 72, 63, ______, ______, ______ Rule: ______

b 4, 20, 100, ______, ______, ______ Rule: ______

c 73, 69, 65, ______, ______, ______ Rule: ______

5 Write the equation that describes each pattern.

● Rule: A + B = C

A	B	C
3	5	8
4	6	10
5	7	12
24	21	45

a Rule: ______________

●	■	▲
11	4	7
12	6	6
13	4	9
14	10	4

b Rule: ______________

D	E	F
2	3	6
4	2	8
5	3	15
9	6	54

c Rule: ______________

▲	■	★
10	2	5
3	1	3
8	4	2
24	3	8

d Rule: ______________

G	H	I
30	3	10
36	9	4
72	8	9
66	11	6

e Rule: ______________

X	⬢	A
6	15	9
12	27	15
15	29	14
20	52	32

PATTERN GRIDS

You can use tables to show patterns.
The rows of numbers are related by a rule.

Example 1:

Rule: ● = ■ + 6

■	2	3	4	5	6
●	8	9	10	11	12

● = ■ + 6
● = 2 + 6
● = 8

Example 2:

Rule: ▲ = ★ × 4

★	8	10	12	14	16
▲	32	40	48	56	64

▲ = ★ × 4
▲ = 8 × 4
▲ = 32

Example 3:

■ = ▲ ÷ 3

▲	36	33		27	
■	12		10		8

Example 4:

● = ⬢ − 5

⬢	93	95	97		101
●	88	90		94	

Your turn

Complete the pattern grids.

■ = ▲ × 3

▲	3	5	7	9	11
■	9	15	21	27	33

b ▲ = ⬢ − 5

⬢	5	10	15	20	25
▲					

a ▲ = ● × 4

●	2	4	6	8	10
▲					

c ● = ▲ ÷ 2

▲	6	12	18	24	30
●					

SELF CHECK Mark how you feel

Got it!	Need help...	I don't get it
 ☐	 ☐	 ☐

Check your answers
How many did you get correct? ☐

PRACTICE

1 Complete the pattern grids.

● B = A + 7

A	11	13	15	17	19	21	23
B	18	20	22	24	26	28	30

a D = 28 – C

C	16	14	12	10	8	4	2
D							

2 Write the rule for each pattern grid.

● Rule: ● = ▲ × 3

▲	3	5	7	9	11	13	15
●	9	15	21	27	33	39	45

b Rule: ______________

C	1	2	3	4	5	6	7
K	11	22	33	44	55	66	77

a Rule: ______________

B	4	8	12	16	20	24	28
D	1	2	3	4	5	6	7

c Rule: ______________

■	3	6	9	12	15	18	21
▲	1	2	3	4	5	6	7

3 Use the rules to continue these two-step patterns.

● 3, 15, 63, 255, 1,023, 4,095 Rule: Multiply by 4, plus 3

a 1, 16, ______, ______, ______, ______ Rule: Add 7, multiply by 2

b 14, 16, ______, ______, ______, ______ Rule: Subtract 6, multiply by 2

c 8, 20, ______, ______, ______, ______ Rule: Minus 3, times 4

4 Complete the following.

●

Rule	3	4	7	8	12	11
+ 5	8	9	12	13	17	16
× 2	6	8	14	16	24	22

b

Rule	25	5	65	10	60	20
÷ 5						
+ 8						

a

Rule	27	18	3	9	12	63
÷ 3						
+ 7						

c

Rule	7	8	10	11	13	9
+ 12						
– 7						

EQUIVALENT EXPRESSIONS

Expressions that are equal to each other are called equivalent expressions. One side of the expression equals the other.

SCAN to watch video

Example 1:

34 + 2 = 20 + 16

Both sides equal 36.

Example 2:

38 − 22 = 20 − 4

Both sides equal 16.

Example 3:

3 × 4 = 12 × 1

Both sides equal 12.

Example 4:

20 − 13 = 21 ÷ 3

Both sides equal 7.

Example 5:

56 ÷ 7 = 2 × 4

Both sides equal ____.

Example 6:

2 × 9 = 10 + 8

Both sides equal ____.

Equivalent means "equal in value."

Your turn

Complete these equivalent expressions.

- 24 + [4] = 20 + 8
- **a** 8 + 4 = [ ] − 8
- **b** 7 × 3 = [ ] × 7
- **c** 50 − 25 = [ ] + 5
- **d** 36 ÷ 3 = [ ] × 3
- **e** 5 × 4 = [ ] ÷ 5
- **f** 35 − 5 = [ ] + 5
- **g** 36 + 4 = [ ] − 10
- **h** 4 × 4 = 2 × [ ]
- **i** 40 + 2 = [ ] + 6

SELF CHECK Mark how you feel

Got it!	Need help...	I don't get it

Check your answers
How many did you get correct? [ ]

PRACTICE

1 Fill in the boxes to make equivalent expressions.

- Example: $7 \times 8 = \boxed{60} - 4$
- **a** $120 \div 10 = \square \times 3$
- **b** $8 \times 6 = 32 + \square$
- **c** $64 \div 8 = 24 \div \square$
- **d** $\square \times 9 = 30 + 6$
- **e** $\square + 10 = 4 \times 11$
- **f** $56 \div \square = 20 - 12$
- **g** $132 \div 12 = 20 - \square$
- **h** $3 \times \square = 80 - 50$
- **i** $5 + \square = 108 \div 12$
- **j** $144 \div 12 = \square - 8$
- **k** $169 \div 13 = 8 + \square$

2 Write an equivalent expression for each problem.

- Example: $24 \div 2 =$ <u>6 × 2</u>
- **a** $3 \times 6 =$ ________
- **b** $12 + 3 =$ ________
- **c** $50 \div 5 =$ ________
- **d** $8 \times 8 =$ ________
- **e** $20 - 13 =$ ________
- **f** $72 \div 9 =$ ________
- **g** $4 \times 4 =$ ________
- **h** $30 - 27 =$ ________
- **i** $6 + 4 =$ ________
- **j** $24 \div 3 =$ ________
- **k** $5 \times 5 =$ ________

3 Fill in the boxes to make equivalent expressions.

- **a** $30 - \square$ | 9×3
- **b** 2×9 | $40 - \square$
- **c** $\square + 45$ | 9×10
- **d** $4 \times \square$ | 6×2
- **e** $110 \div 11$ | $5 \times \square$
- **f** $50 - 15$ | $7 \times \square$
- **g** $24 + 32$ | $30 + \square$

EQUATIONS AND PATTERNS WITH FRACTIONS AND DECIMALS

These equations and patterns look like other equations and patterns you have seen and solved before, but they include fractions and decimals.

SCAN to watch video

Equations with fractions

Example 1:

$\frac{1}{4} \times 12 = 3$

(Read $\frac{1}{4}$ of 12,

Solve $\frac{1}{4} \times 12$)

Equations with decimals

Example 2:

$7 \times 1.1 = 7.7$

Solve: $1.1 \times 7 = 7.7$

Patterns with fractions

Example 3:

$\frac{1}{4}, \frac{1}{2}, \frac{3}{4}, 1$

Rule: Add $\frac{1}{4}$

Patterns with decimals

Example 4:

2.2, 2.0, 1.8, 1.6, 1.4

Rule: Subtract 0.2

Example 5:

$\frac{3}{4} \times 20 =$ ______

Example 6:

3.8, 4.1, 4.4, 4.7, 5.0

Rule: ____________

Your turn

Complete the following.

$\frac{2}{5} \times 20$

$= 20 \div 5 \times 2$

$= 8$

$24 \div \frac{3}{4}$

$= \frac{24}{1} \times \frac{4}{3}$ (Flip and multiply)

$= \frac{96}{3} = 32$

a $8 \times$ ______ $= 8.8$

b $\frac{2}{3} \times 18$

= ____________

= ______

c $12 \div \frac{3}{4}$

= ____________

= ______ = ______

d $1.2 \times 3 =$ ______

SELF CHECK Mark how you feel

Got it!	Need help...	I don't get it
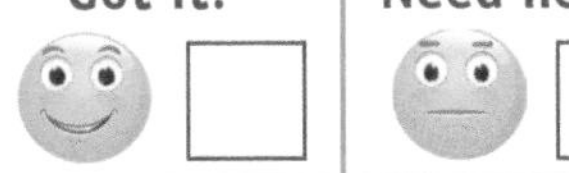		

Check your answers

How many did you get correct?

PRACTICE

1 Write the missing numbers.

- 1.2 × __3__ = 3.6
- a ______ × 3 = 9.6
- b 4 × ______ = 4.8
- c 3.2 – 0.8 = ______
- d 7 × ______ = 7.7
- e 8.8 ÷ ______ = 2.2
- f 4.8 – ______ = 3.3
- g 3.4 × ______ = 6.8
- h 3 × ______ = 6.6
- i ______ × 1.1 = 3.3
- j 6 × 0.8 = ______
- k 0.9 × ______ = 7.2
- l 7 × ______ = 6.3
- m 4.1 × ______ = 8.2
- n 2 × ______ = 8.2

2 Complete these multiplication problems.

- $\frac{2}{3} \times 12 =$ __8__
- a $\frac{1}{4} \times 16 =$ ______
- b $\frac{2}{3} \times 24 =$ ______
- c $\frac{3}{8} \times 16 =$ ______
- d $\frac{2}{5} \times 15 =$ ______
- e $\frac{3}{8} \times 32 =$ ______
- f $\frac{2}{4} \times 24 =$ ______
- g $\frac{1}{8} \times 32 =$ ______
- h $\frac{1}{3}$ of 3 = ______
- i $\frac{2}{3} \times 27 =$ ______
- j $\frac{2}{9} \times 36 =$ ______
- k $\frac{3}{4}$ of 12 = ______

3 Complete these division problems.

- $8 \div \frac{1}{4} = \frac{8}{1} \times \frac{4}{1}$
  (Flip and multiply) $= \frac{32}{1} =$ __32__
- a $2 \div \frac{2}{3} =$ ______
  = ____ = ____
- b $6 \div \frac{1}{2} =$ ______
  = ____ = ____
- c $4 \div \frac{1}{5} =$ ______
  = ____ = ____
- d $4 \div \frac{2}{3} =$ ______
  = ____ = ____
- e $5 \div \frac{1}{2} =$ ______
  = ____ = ____

4 Write the next three terms in these number patterns.

- 1.4, 1.5, 1.6, __1.7__, __1.8__, __1.9__
- a 2.7, 2.4, 2.1, ____, ____, ____
- b 2.9, 3.1, 3.3, ____, ____, ____
- c 0.4, 0.6, 0.8, ____, ____, ____
- d 1.9, 2.1, 2.3, ____, ____, ____
- e 6.1, 5.7, 5.3, ____, ____, ____
- f 10.6, 10.2, 9.8, ____, ____, ____
- g 8.8, 8.5, 8.2, ____, ____, ____

PATTERNS AND ALGEBRA REVIEW

1 Use the rules to continue the patterns.

a 6, ______, ______, ______, ______ Rule: × 3

b 102, ______, ______, ______, ______ Rule: + 2

c 1,250, ______, ______, ______, ______ Rule: ÷ 5

d 91, ______, ______, ______, ______ Rule: – 6

2 Write the rule for each pattern.

a 9, 16, 23, 30, 37 Rule: ______

b 128, 125, 122, 119, 116 Rule: ______

c 16, 32, 64, 128, 256 Rule: ______

d 68, 64, 60, 56, 52 Rule: ______

Use the rules to continue these two-step patterns.

a 4, 6, ______, ______, ______, ______, ______ Rule: – 1, × 2

b 369, 126, ______, ______, ______, ______, ______ Rule: ÷ 3, + 3

c 1, 6, ______, ______, ______, ______, ______ Rule: × 2, + 4

Write the equation that describes each pattern.

a Rule: ____________

A	B	C
7	4	28
5	9	45
10	3	30
24	2	48

b Rule: ____________

▲	●	■
29	10	19
34	17	17
18	9	9
50	25	25

c Rule: ____________

D	E	F
7	70	10
7	49	7
7	56	8
7	63	9

REVIEW

5 Complete the pattern grids.

a ⬢ = ▲ × 5

▲	9	7	5	3	1	0
⬢						

b B = A × 4

A	3	8	11	15	20	22
B						

c

Rule	60	50	25	10	15
÷ 5					
+ 9					

d

Rule	5	7	9	11	6
× 7					
− 4					

6 Complete these equivalent expressions.

a $24 \div 4 = \square \times 2$

b $56 \div 8 = 20 - \square$

c $132 \div 11 = \square \times 1$

d $12 + 9 = 3 \times \square$

e $110 \div 11 = 50 - \square$

f $\square \times 3 = 36 - 12$

7 Write equivalent expressions.

a $24 \div 3 =$ __________

b $55 \div 5 =$ __________

c $30 - 13 =$ __________

d $72 \div 8 =$ __________

e $60 + 10 =$ __________

f $8 + 4 =$ __________

8 Complete the following equations.

a $\frac{3}{5} \times 20 =$ ________
= ________

b $\frac{2}{3} \times 24 =$ ________
= ________

c $\frac{4}{5} \times 25 =$ ________
= ________

d $12 \div \frac{1}{4} =$ ________
= ________

e $24 \div \frac{1}{4} =$ ________
= ________

f $2 \div \frac{2}{3} =$ ________
= ________

9 Fill in the missing numbers.

a 1.1 × ______ = 6.6

b 3 × ______ = 3.6

c 0.8 × ______ = 7.2

d 1.2 × ______ = 9.6

e ______ × 1.4 = 2.8

f 6 × 0.8 = ______

10 Write the next three terms in each number sequence.

a 1.9, 2.2, 2.5, ____, ____, ____

b 10.6, 10.2, 9.8, ____, ____, ____

c 3, 5.5, 8, ____, ____, ____

d 1.2, 2.2, 3.2, ____, ____, ____

e 4, 5.5, 7, ____, ____, ____

f 8.7, 7.6, 6.5, ____, ____, ____

METERS AND FEET

A meter (m) is a unit of measurement used to measure big things. There are 100 cm in 1 meter.

Cars and scooters can be measured in meters.

1 m | 100 cm

A foot (ft.) is also used to measure big things. There are 12 inches in 1 foot.

Boats and homes can be measured in feet.

1 ft. | 12 in.

Examples: Color the boxes next to the items. Use blue for items less than 1 meter and red for items more than 1 meter.

a ■ a train

b ☐ a fingernail

c ☐ a bridge

d ☐ a tricycle

e ☐ a laptop

f ☐ a road

Your turn

List five things in each column.

More than 1 ft.	Less than 1 ft.
a big dog	a pencil

SELF CHECK Mark how you feel

Got it!	Need help...	I don't get it
☐	☐	☐

Check your answers

How many did you get correct? ☐

PRACTICE

1 Circle the items that would be measured in meters instead of centimeters.

2 Circle the items that would be measured in feet instead of inches.

3 Use a ruler to measure things around you. List items that are about 1 foot (12 in.) long.

____

____

____

____

____

CENTIMETERS AND INCHES

A centimeter (cm) is a unit of measurement used to measure smaller things. There are 100 centimeters in 1 meter.

0 CM 1 2 3 4 5 6 7 8 9 10 11 12 13 14 15

This is 1 cm

Inches (in.) can also be used to measure smaller things. There are 12 inches in 1 foot.

INCH 1 2 3 4 5 6

This is 1 in.

Examples: Mark the items you would measure in centimeters or inches.

a ☑ a shoe		**c** ☐ a pen		**e** ☐ a toy car	
b ☐ a bed		**d** ☐ a bus		**f** ☐ a backpack	

Start at 0 when you measure with a ruler.

INCH 1 2 3 4 5 6

This crayon is 3 in. long.

Your turn

Use a ruler to measure the lengths of the crayons.

__7__ cm

a ______ cm

b ______ cm

SELF CHECK Mark how you feel

Got it! ☐ Need help... ☐ I don't get it ☐

Check your answers

How many did you get correct? ☐

PRACTICE

1 Draw lines of these lengths.

- 13 cm ________________________________

a 4 cm

b 8 cm

c 10 cm

d 2 cm

2 Measure the lines, and write the lengths.

- 4 in. ________________________

a ______ ______

b ______ __________________

c ______ ____________

d ______ ______________________________

3 Measure each pencil, and write each length.

- 10 cm

a ______

b ______

c ______

4 Use the pencils in Question 3 to answer the following questions.

a What color is the shortest pencil? ______________

b What color is the longest pencil? ______________

c Write the colors of the pencils in order from longest to shortest.

____

MILLIMETERS AND QUARTER-INCHES

Millimeters (mm) are used to measure very small lengths.

There are 10 millimeters in 1 centimeter.

The small marks on the ruler are millimeters.

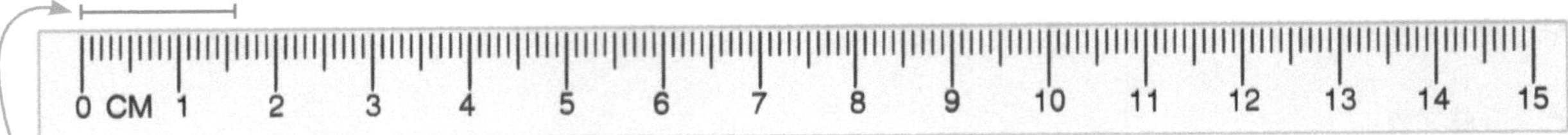

This is 16 mm.

Quarter-inches can also be used to measure very small lengths.

INCH 1 2 3 4 5 6

This is $1\frac{1}{4}$ in.

Example: Write the lengths marked on the ruler.

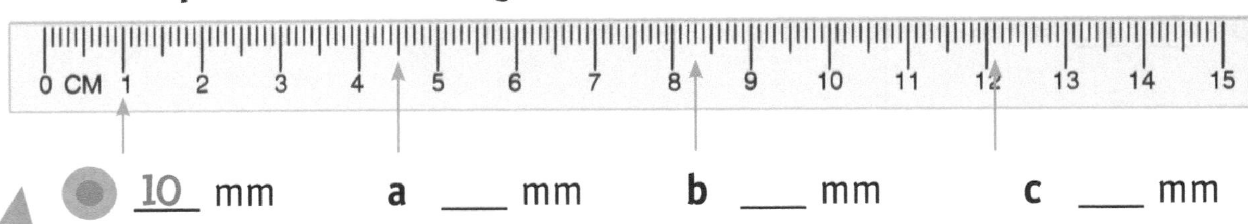

10 mm   **a** ___ mm   **b** ___ mm   **c** ___ mm

Your turn

1 Write the lengths marked on the ruler.

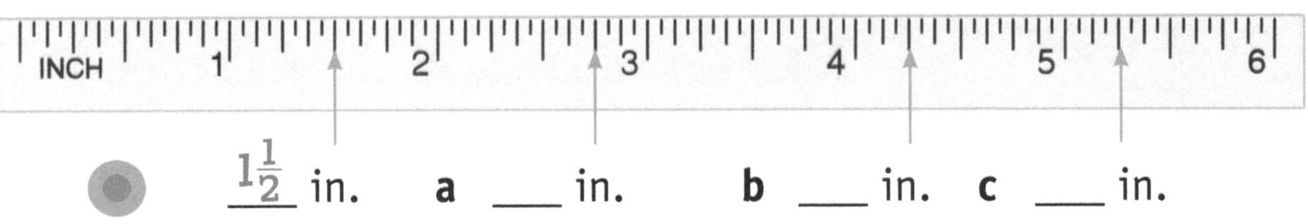

$1\frac{1}{2}$ in.   **a** ___ in.   **b** ___ in.   **c** ___ in.

2 Mark these lengths on the ruler.

7 mm   **a** 19 mm   **b** 58 mm   **c** 110 mm

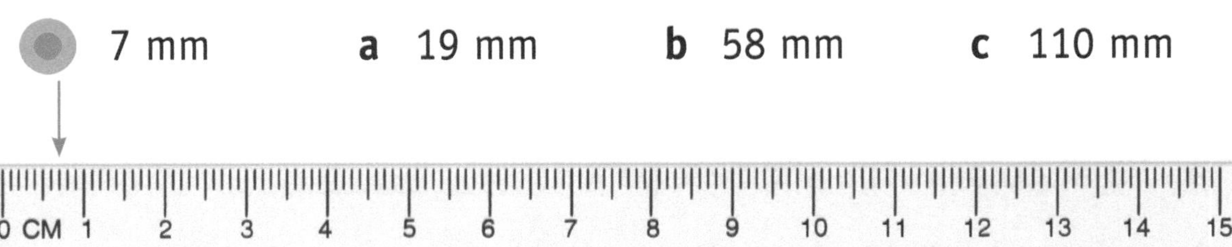

Check your answers

How many did you get correct?

PRACTICE

1 Name four things that would be measured in millimeters or quarter-inches.

- an ant ______

2 Measure and write the lengths in millimeters.

- 72 mm ______
- a ______
- b ______
- c ______
- d ______

3 Write the lengths in Question 2 from shortest to longest.

13 mm ______

4 Measure and write the lengths in inches.

- $2\frac{3}{4}$ in. ______
- a ______
- b ______
- c ______
- d ______

5 Write the lengths from Question 4 from shortest to longest.

______

CONVERTING MEASUREMENTS

Sometimes, we need to convert measurements to larger or smaller units. There are 10 millimeters in 1 centimeter and 100 centimeters in 1 meter. There are 12 inches in 1 foot.

SCAN to watch video

Multiply to convert a larger unit to a smaller unit.

4 m × 100 (number of cm in a m) = 400 cm

8 cm × 10 (number of mm in a cm) = 80 mm

3 ft. × 12 (number of in. in a ft.) = 36 in.

Divide to convert a smaller unit to a larger unit.

400 cm ÷ 100 (number of cm in a m) = 4 m

80 mm ÷ 10 (number of mm in a cm) = 8 cm

36 in. ÷ 12 (number of in. in a ft.) = 3 ft.

Example: Convert these measurements.

a 5 m = 500 cm

b 48 in. = ______ ft.

c 60 mm = ______ cm

d 6 ft. = ______ in.

e 120 cm = ______ mm

f 16 m = ______ cm

g 20 ft. = ______ in.

h 96 in. = ______ ft.

Your turn

Complete these unit conversions.

a	cm to m
250	2.5
400	
350	
680	
1,200	

b	ft. to in.
$4\frac{1}{2}$	54
8	
$3\frac{1}{2}$	
12	
$1\frac{1}{2}$	

SELF CHECK Mark how you feel		
Got it! ☐	Need help... ☐	I don't get it ☐

Check your answers

How many did you get correct? ☐

PRACTICE

1 Convert these measurements.

- 2 ft. = 24 in.
- **a** 6 ft. = ______ in.
- **b** 12 in. = ______ ft.
- **c** 10 ft. = ______ in.
- **d** 60 in. = ______ ft.
- **e** $1\frac{1}{2}$ ft. = ______ in.
- **f** 36 in. = ______ ft.
- **g** 30 in. = ______ ft.

2 Convert these measurements.

- 50 mm = 5 cm
- **a** 3 m = ______ cm
- **b** 5 cm = ______ mm
- **c** 120 mm = ______ cm
- **d** 40 mm = ______ cm
- **e** 100 mm = ______ cm
- **f** 800 cm = ______ m
- **g** 170 mm = ______ cm

3 Are these measurement conversions correct? Write Yes or No.

- 30 mm = 3 cm Yes
- **a** 5 ft. = 50 in. ______
- **b** 190 mm = 19 cm ______
- **c** 24 in. = 2 ft. ______
- **d** 300 cm = 3 m ______
- **e** 200 mm = 2 cm ______
- **f** 4 ft. = 48 in. ______
- **g** 5 mm = 50 cm ______
- **h** 40 in. = 4 ft. ______
- **i** 60 mm = 6 cm ______

4 Complete these unit conversions.

a mm to cm	
30	3
60	
130	
280	
1,490	

b ft. to in.	
5	60
8	
$2\frac{1}{2}$	
11	
$5\frac{1}{2}$	

c in. to ft.	
42	$3\frac{1}{2}$
72	
66	
24	
78	

d m to cm	
8	800
24	
56	
740	
153	

KILOMETERS AND MILES

Long distances are measured in miles (mi.) or kilometers (km). One mile is 5,280 feet. One kilometer is equal to 1,000 meters.

The length of this road would be measured in kilometers or miles.

Examples:
Mark the items you would measure in kilometers or miles.

- **a** ☑ the distance to the next town
- **b** ☐ the length of a hair ribbon
- **c** ☐ the distance to Canada from Australia
- **d** ☐ the distance you would walk in one day
- **e** ☐ the distance around your house
- **f** ☐ the distance from New York to Chicago

Your turn

1 Write these lengths in meters or feet.

	5 km	5,000 m	
a	7 km	________	m
b	2 mi.	________	ft.
c	14 km	________	m
d	4 mi.	________	ft.
e	315 km	________	m

2 Write these lengths in kilometers or miles.

	6,000 m	6 km	
a	9,000 m	________	km
b	5,280 ft.	________	mi.
c	34,000 m	________	km
d	10,560 ft.	________	mi.
e	537,000 m	________	km

SELF CHECK Mark how you feel

Got it!	Need help...	I don't get it
☐	☐	☐

Check your answers
How many did you get correct? ☐

1 Name five things that would be measured using kilometers or miles.

a river ______________________ ______________________

______________________ ______________________

______________________ ______________________

2 Write these lengths in meters or feet.

- 2 km = 2,000 meters
- a 5 km = ________ meters
- b 2 mi. = ________ feet
- c 1 km = ________ meters
- d 3 mi. = ________ feet
- e 1 mi. = ________ feet
- f 8 km = ________ meters
- g 22 km = ________ meters

3 Complete each row in the table.

	m	km
	4,000 m	4 km
a	6,250 m	
b		2 km
c	3,500 m	
d		4.5 km
e	53,000 m	

PERIMETER

Perimeter (P) is the distance around a 2D shape.

Perimeter = 2 cm + 4 cm + 2 cm + 4 cm

P = 12 cm

The perimeter (P) of the rectangle is 12 cm.

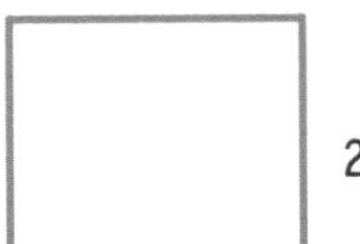

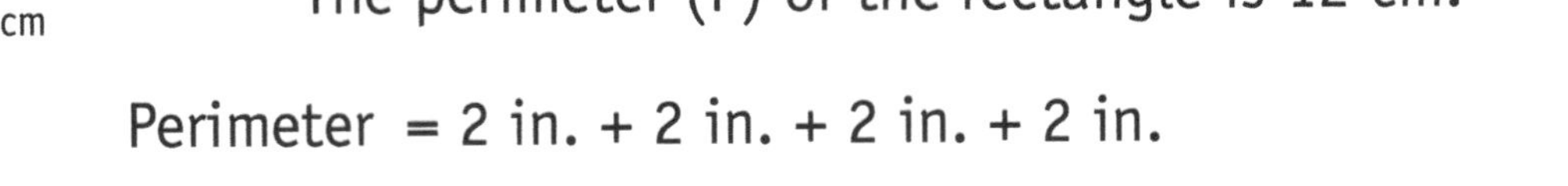

Perimeter = 2 in. + 2 in. + 2 in. + 2 in.

P = 8 in.

The perimeter (P) of the square is 8 in.

Examples: Find the perimeter.

a (3 m, 1 m)

P = 1 m + 3 m + 1 m + 3 m

= 8 m

b

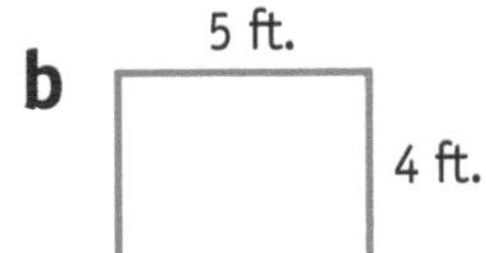

P = 5 ft. + 4 ft. + 5 ft. + 4 ft.

= _____ ft.

Calculate the perimeters.

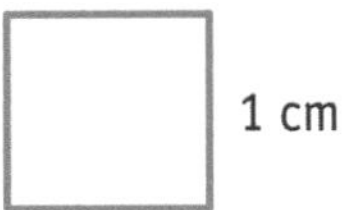

P = 1 + 1 + 1 + 1

= 4 cm

a (5 in., 1 in.)

P = _____ + _____ + _____ + _____

= _____ in.

b

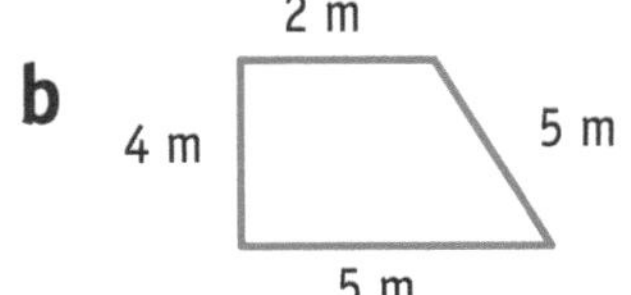

P = _____ + _____ + _____ + _____

= _____ m

SELF CHECK Mark how you feel		
Got it!	Need help...	I don't get it

Check your answers

How many did you get correct?

PRACTICE

Calculate the perimeters of these shapes.

6 m

P = 6 m + 6 m + 6 m + 6 m

= 24 m

a 3 in. 2 in.

P = ______________________

= __________

b 7 cm 2 cm 3 cm 8 cm

P = ______________________

= __________

c

P = ______________________

= __________

d

P = ______________________

= __________

e

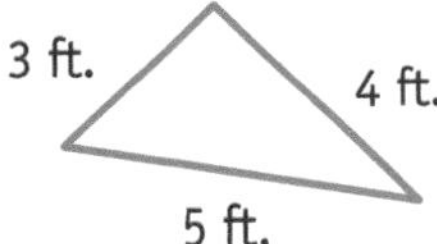

P = ______________________

= __________

f

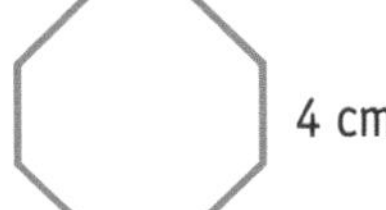

P = ______________________

= __________

Draw three different shapes with a perimeter of 24 units.

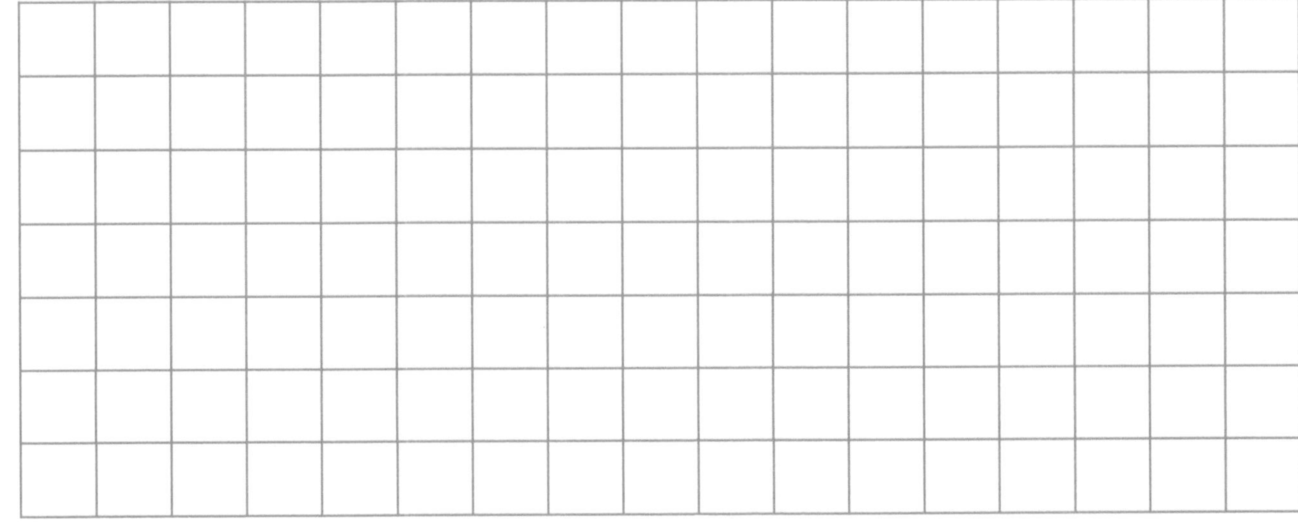

Use this diagram to answer the following questions. Each centimeter on the diagram represents 1 meter in the flower center.

Flower Center Scale: 1 cm = 1 m

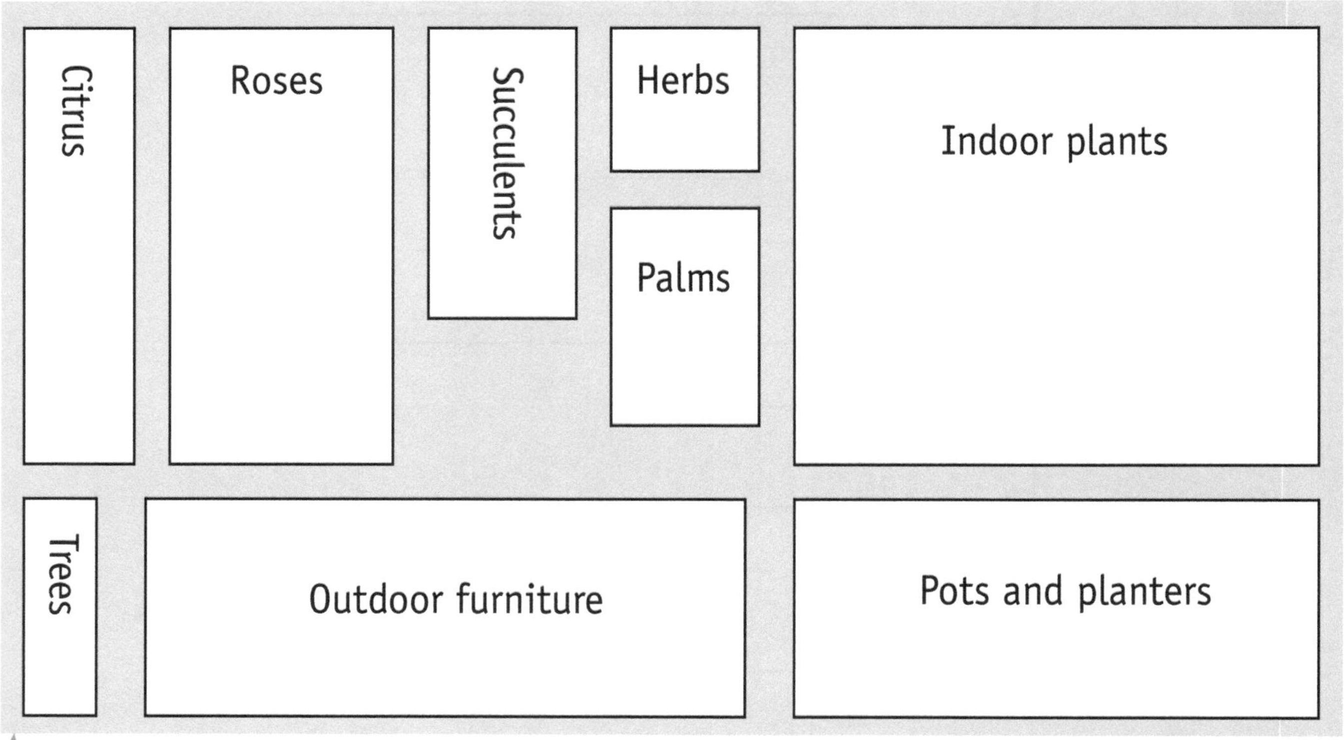

3 Peter wants to fence some of the enclosures. How much fencing will these enclosures require?

- Palms 10 m
- **a** Indoor plants ______
- **b** Pots and planters ______
- **c** Roses ______

4 Did Peter order enough fencing for these enclosures? Write Yes or No.

- Citrus: 15 m Yes
- **a** Succulents: 10 m ______
- **b** Herbs: 8 m ______
- **c** Outdoor furniture: 22 m ______
- **d** Trees: 6 m ______

5 Order the perimeters from smallest (1) to largest (8).

☐ Citrus	☐ Outdoor furniture	☐ Indoor plants
☐ Succulents	1 Trees	☐ Pots and planters
1 Herbs	☐ Palms	☐ Roses

6 Complete the tables for rectangles with these dimensions.

	Height	Width	Perimeter
●	22 cm	13 cm	70 cm
a		5 ft.	18 ft.
b	7 mm	8 mm	
c	8 in.		32 in.

	Height	Width	Perimeter
d	3 in.	6 in.	
e	2 m	2 m	
f	32 ft.		100 ft.
g		2 mm	38 mm

7 Find the perimeter of each shape.

●

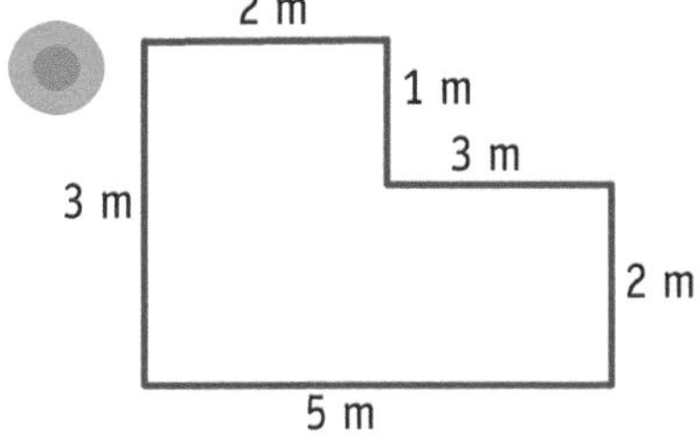

P = 2 + 1 + 3 + 2 + 5 + 3 m

= 16 m

a

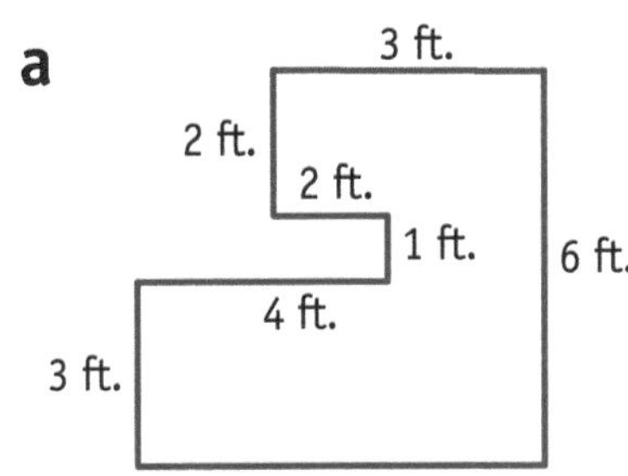

P = ______________________

= __________

b

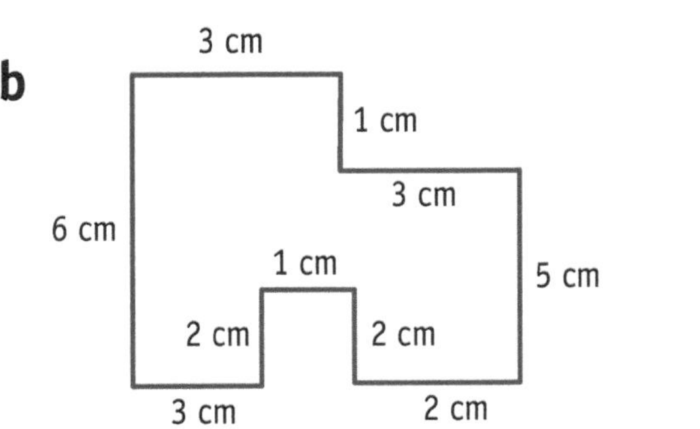

P = ______________________

= __________

c

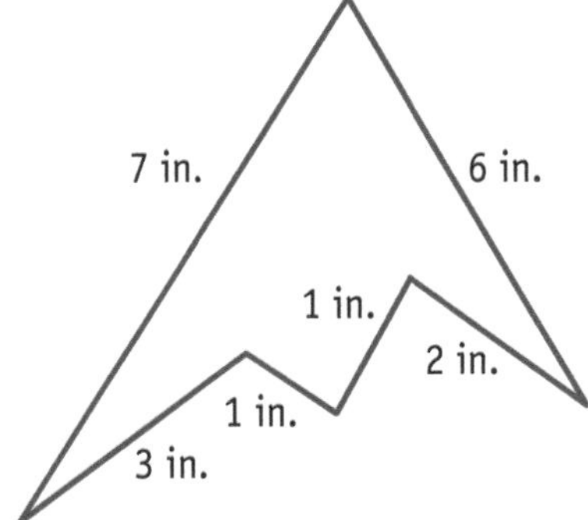

P = ______________________

= __________

d

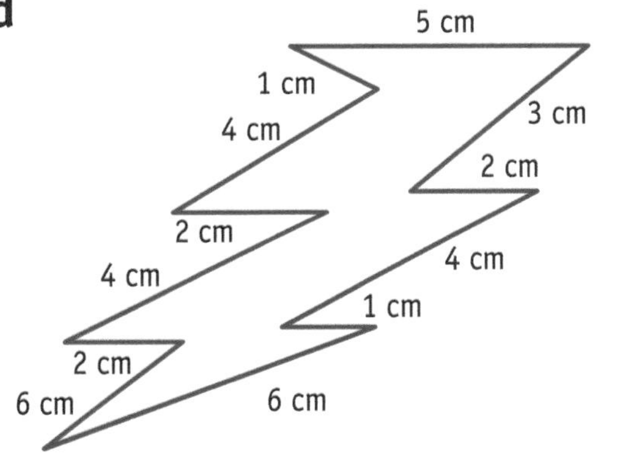

P = ______________________

= __________

LENGTH REVIEW

1 Measure and write the lengths of the lines in centimeters.

a _____ cm ____

b _____ cm ____

c _____ cm _________

d _____ cm ___________________________________

2 Write the lengths in Question 1 in order from shortest to longest.

____

3 Draw lines of these lengths.

a 4 in.

b 3 in.

c 6 in.

d $5\frac{1}{2}$ in.

e $3\frac{3}{4}$ in.

f $4\frac{1}{4}$ in.

4 Would these things be measured in mm or cm? Write the units to complete the measurements.

a pencil length: 10 ______

b pin length: 4 ______

c computer keyboard key width: 9 ______

d mobile phone length: 15 ______

e thickness of a fingernail: 1 ______

f length of an ant: 2 ______

5 Write the lengths marked on the ruler.

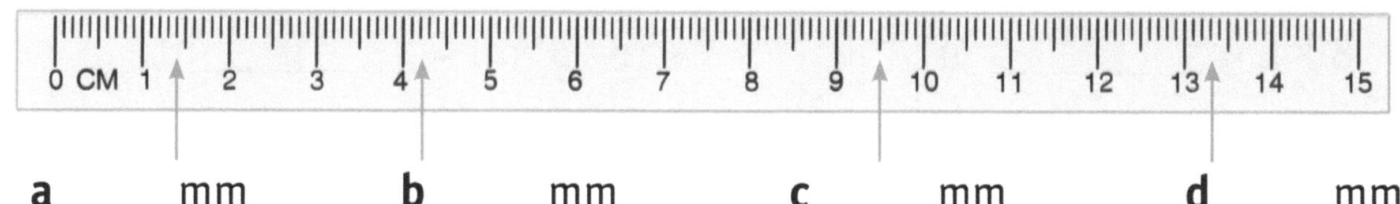

a ___ mm **b** ___ mm **c** ___ mm **d** ___ mm

6 Mark these measurements on the ruler.

a 2 in. **b** $3\frac{3}{4}$ in. **c** 5 in. **d** $5\frac{1}{2}$ in.

INCH 1 2 3 4 5 6

7 Circle the answer that is the best estimate.

a	length of a glue stick	4 in.	4 ft.	4 mi.
b	width of a road	6 m	6 mm	6 cm
c	length of a train	300 in.	300 ft.	300 mi.
d	length of a pinhead	1 cm	1 mm	1 m
e	length of a candy bar	6 in.	6 ft.	6 mi.

8 Convert these measurements.

a 70 mm = ______ cm

b 4 cm = ______ mm

c 20 m = ______ cm

d 100 cm = ______ m

e 6 m = ______ cm

f 136 mm = ______ cm

g 2 ft. = ______ in.

h 48 in. = ______ ft.

i 60 in. = ______ ft.

j 3 ft. = ______ in.

k $2\frac{1}{2}$ ft. = ______ in.

l 42 in. = ______ ft.

REVIEW

9 Write how many meters or feet.

a 6 km = __________ m

b 8 km = __________ m

c 17 km = __________ m

d 1 mi. = __________ ft.

e 3 mi. = __________ ft.

f 2 mi. = __________ ft.

10 Write how many kilometers or miles.

a 7,000 m = ________ km

b 11,000 m = ________ km

c 2,000 m = ________ km

d 10,560 ft. = ________ mi.

e 5,280 ft. = ________ mi.

11 Find the perimeter of each shape.

a

3 ft.

P = __________________________

= _________

b

6 cm

2 cm

P = __________________________

= _________

c

4 cm

2.5 cm

1.5 cm

6 cm

P = __________________________

= _________

d

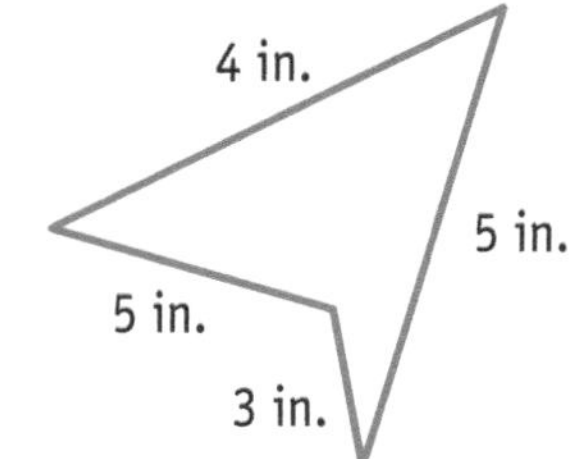

P = __________________________

= _________

e

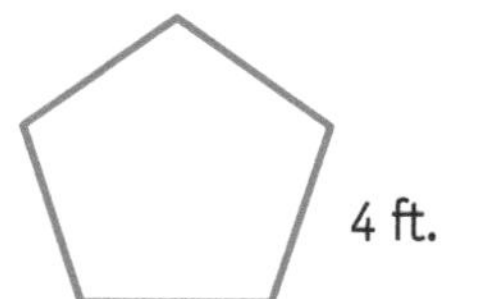

P = __________________________

= _________

f

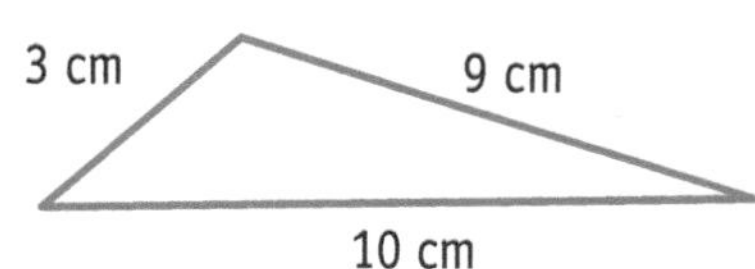

P = __________________________

= _________

12 Draw three different shapes with a perimeter of 18 units.

13 Complete the tables for rectangles with these dimensions.

	Height	Width	Perimeter
a		9	40
b	8	6	
c		14	60
d		8	36
e	9		44

	Height	Width	Perimeter
f	66		156
g	7	28	
h		15	74
i	9		38
j	16	35	

14 Find the perimeter of each shape.

a

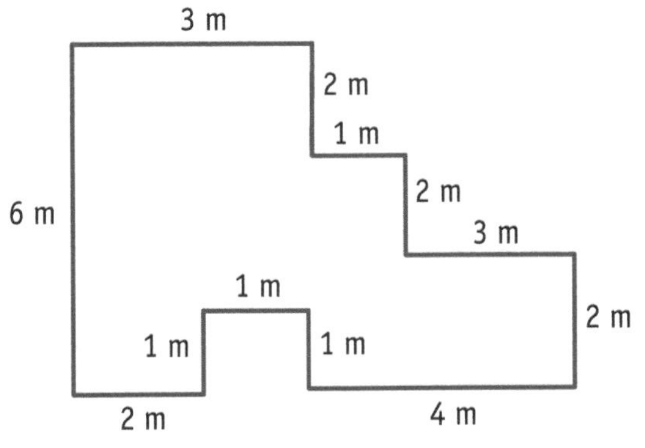

P = ____________________

= __________

b

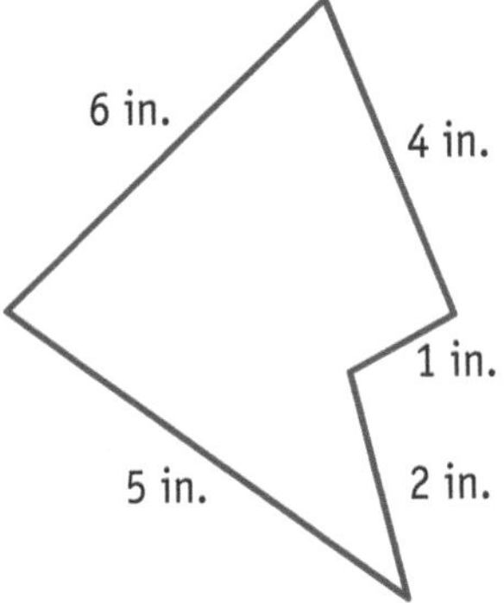

P = ____________________

= __________

ANGLES

An angle is made by measuring the amount of turn between the two arms. The two arms meet at a point (vertex).

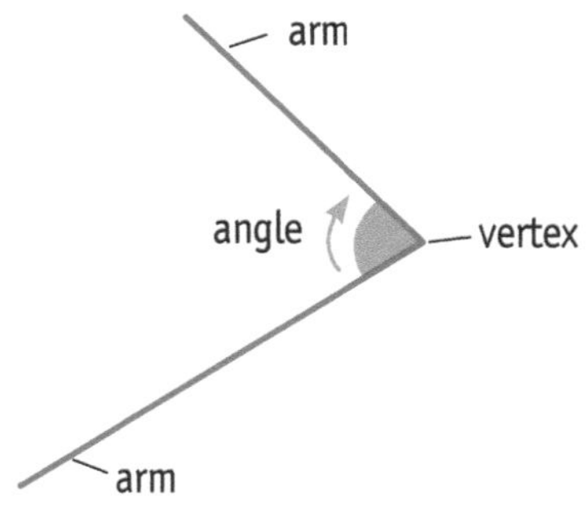

One arm of an angle can be shorter than the other.

Examples:
Use red to trace the arms, use blue to show the angle, and draw a green circle on the vertex.

a

b

c

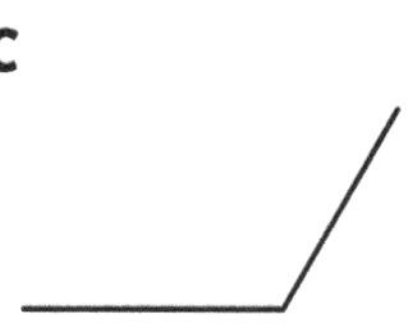

d

Your turn

Make each line into an angle by drawing another arm in red. Use blue to show the angle you made, and draw a green circle on the vertex.

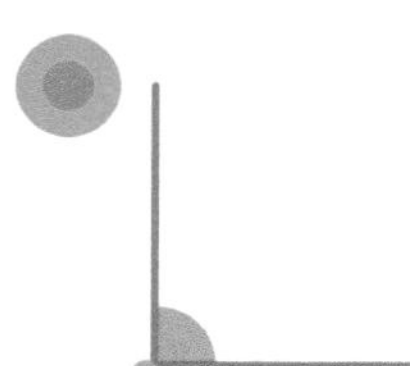

b

d

f

a

c

e

g

Check your answers
How many did you get correct?

PRACTICE

Draw four objects around you that have angles in them.

Use red to trace the arms, use blue to show the angle, and draw a green circle on the vertex. Then, number the angles to order them from smallest (1) to largest (5).

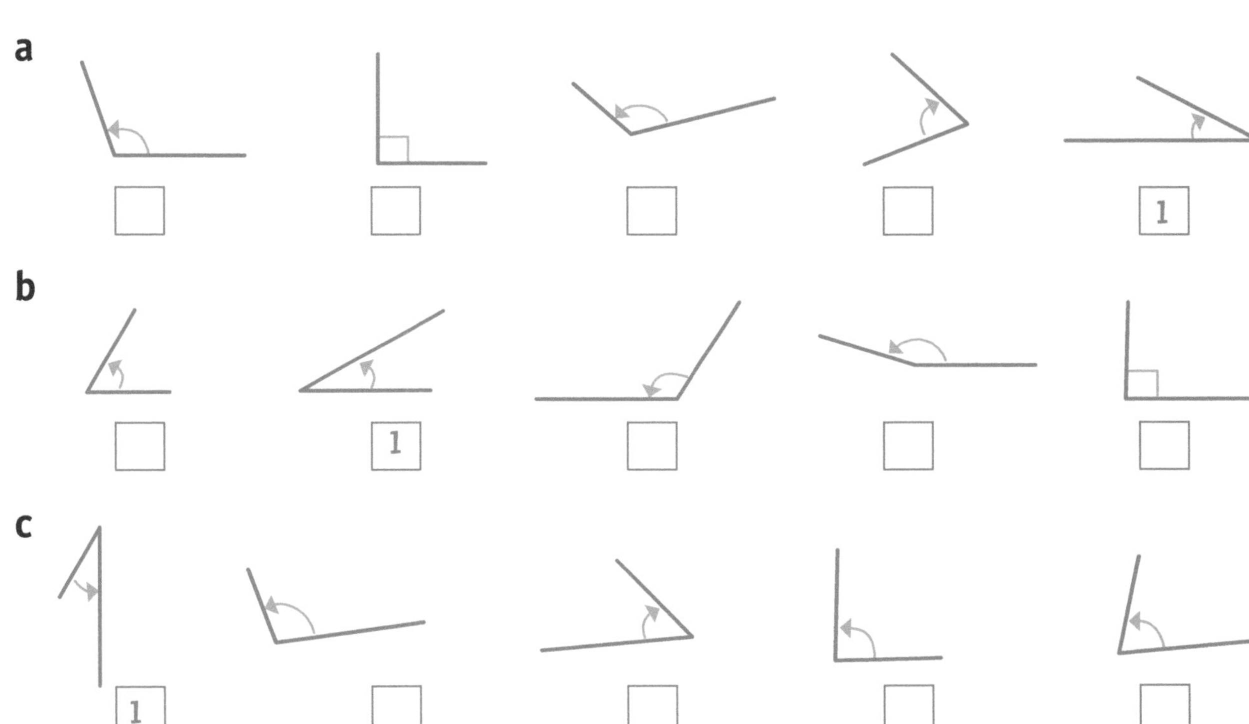

Circle the angles in the picture.

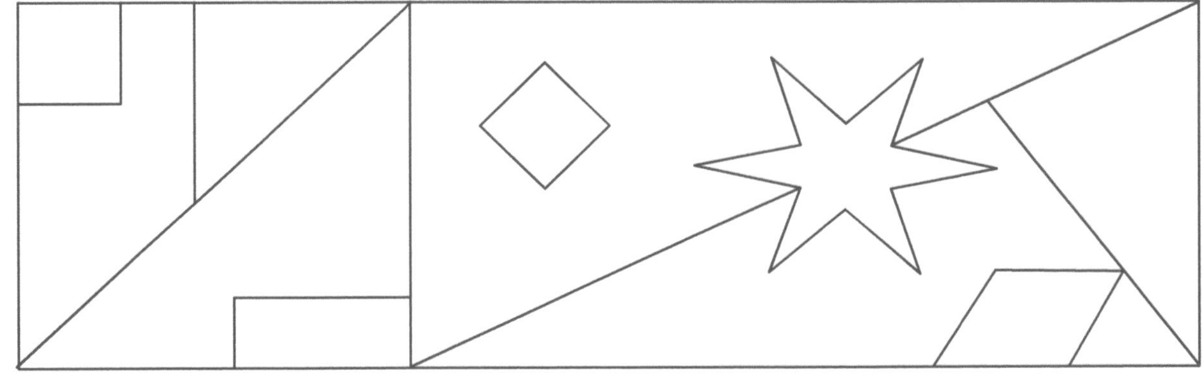

RIGHT ANGLES

A quarter turn is called a right angle.
A right angle measures 90 degrees.

° is the symbol for degrees.
So 90 degrees is written 90°.

This corner symbol shows the angle is 90°.

These angles are 90°.

Examples: Are these angles right angles?
Use a corner of a piece of paper to test them.
Draw the corner symbol in the right angles and cross out the angles that are not right.

The corner of a piece of paper fits perfectly, so this is a right angle.

a

c

e

b

d

f

Your turn

Draw another arm to make a right angle.
Mark the right angle with the corner symbol.

a

b

c

SELF CHECK Mark how you feel		
Got it!	Need help...	I don't get it

Check your answers
How many did you get correct?

PRACTICE

Draw two angles in each box that match the description.

Smaller than 90°	90°	Larger than 90°

List five things around you that have right angles.

picture frame

____

Label the angles as equal to (=), less than (<), or greater than (>) a right angle.

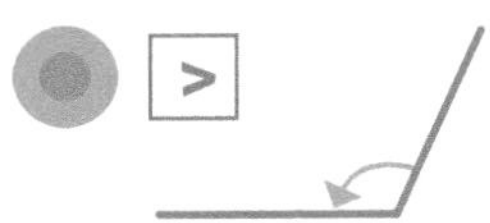

>

b

d 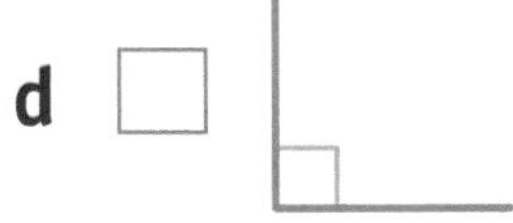

f 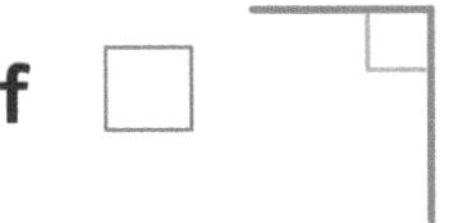

a

c 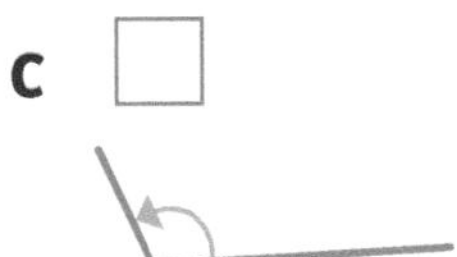

e 

g 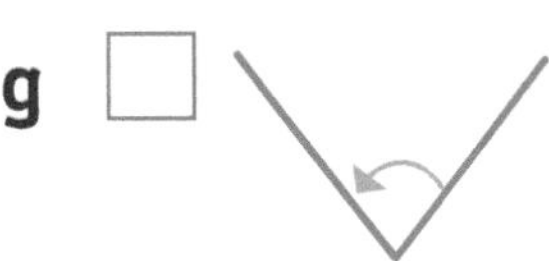

4 Trace over the right angles in each shape.

b 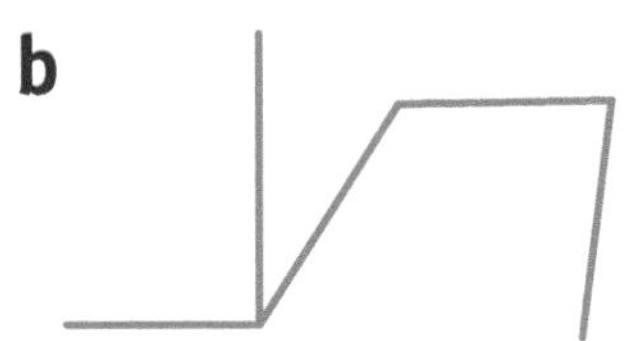

d 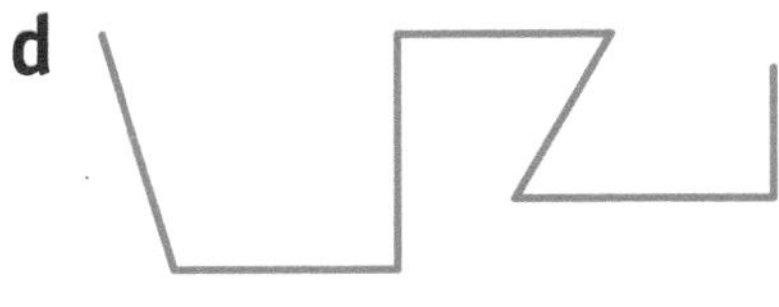

a 

c 

e

ACUTE AND OBTUSE ANGLES

Acute angles are less than 90°. You may remember them as narrow angles.

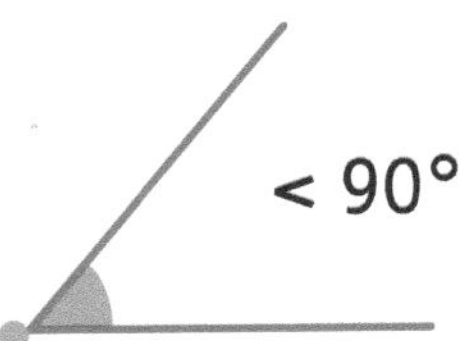

Obtuse angles are more than 90°. You may remember them as wide angles.

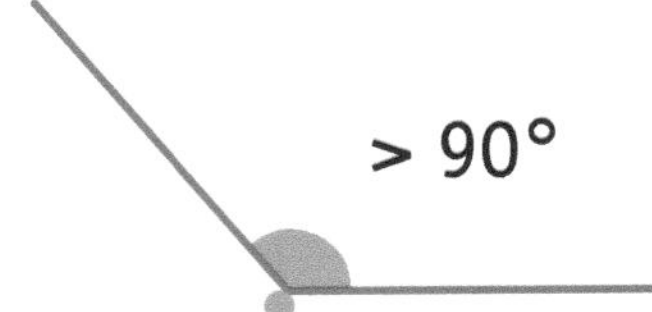

Examples:
Circle the acute angles in orange and the obtuse angles in green.

a 
c 
e 
g 
i 

b 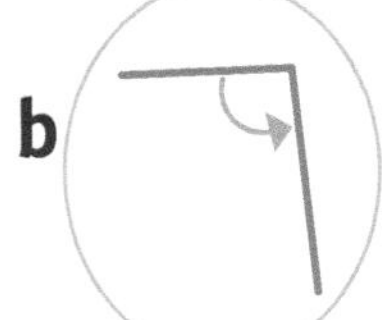
d 
f 
h 

1 Draw another line to turn each line into an acute angle.

c  
a 
d 
b 
e 

2 Draw another line to turn each line into an obtuse angle.

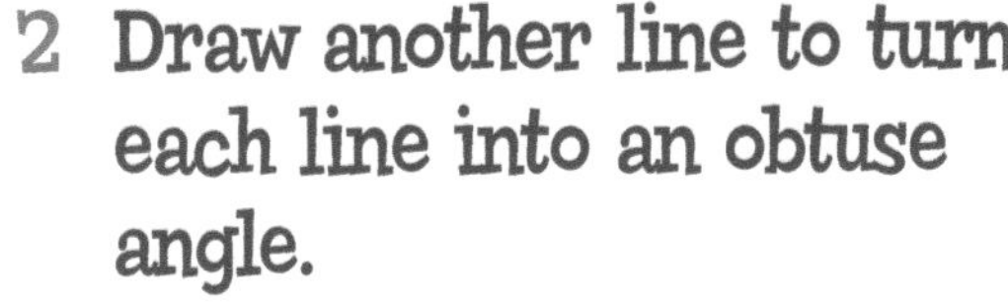
c
a 
d 
b 
e 

SELF CHECK Mark how you feel

Got it!	Need help...	I don't get it

Check your answers
How many did you get correct?

1 We name angles using three letters.

Put the letter at the vertex in the middle, and use ∠ for the angle sign.

A, B, C — Name: ∠ABC or ∠CBA Type: Acute

c C, A, T — Name: ____________ Type: ____________

a Name: ____________ Type: ____________

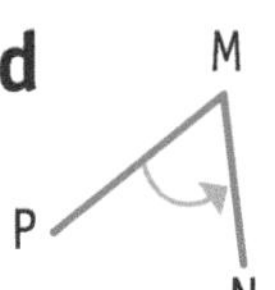

d Name: ____________ Type: ____________

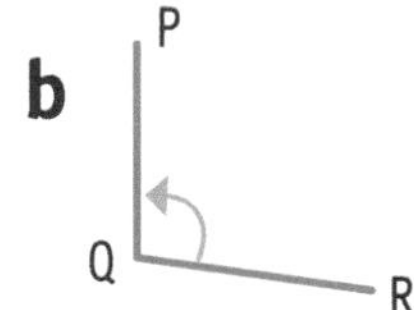

b Name: ____________ Type: ____________

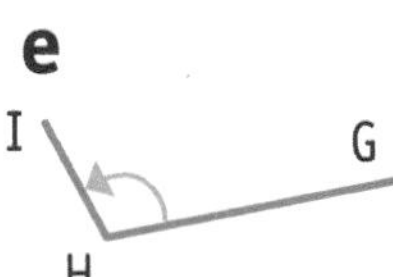

e Name: ____________ Type: ____________

2 Order these angles from narrowest (1) to widest (5).

a

 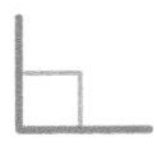   

   1 

b

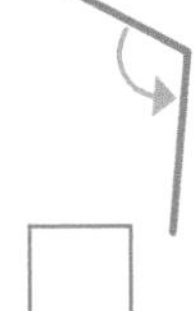   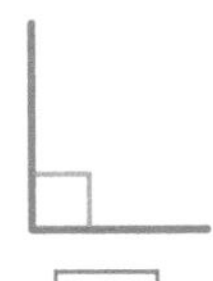

☐ 1 ☐ ☐ ☐

c

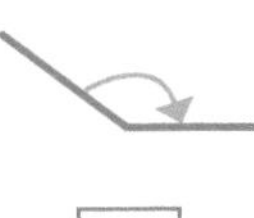    

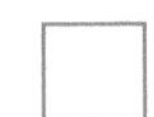    

3 Shade the acute angles orange and the obtuse angles green.

a 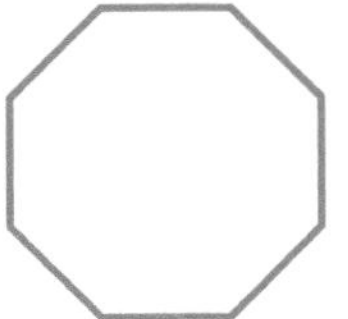

b 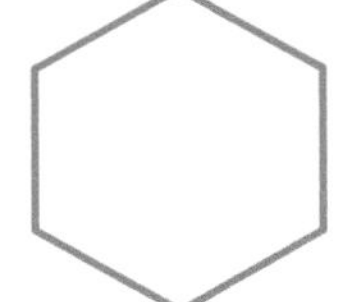

c 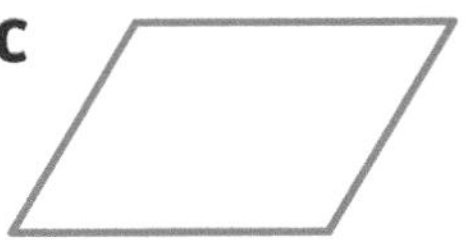

d 

STRAIGHT, REFLEX, AND REVOLUTION ANGLES

Straight angles	Reflex angles	Revolution (full turn)
Always 180°	Between 180° and 360°	Always 360°
Looks like a straight line.	The arrow on the outside shows it is a reflex angle.	The two arms are together.

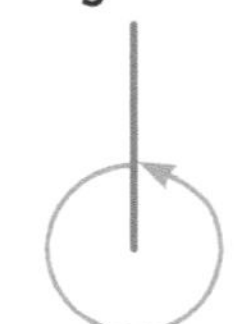

Examples: Write Reflex, Straight, or Revolution for each angle.

a Revolution  b ________  c ________  d ________ 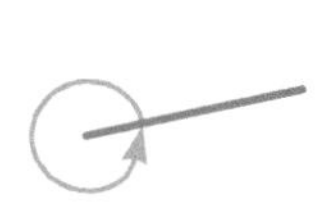

Your turn

1 Mark in the angle to show straight angles.

a 

b 

2 Mark in the angle to show revolutions.

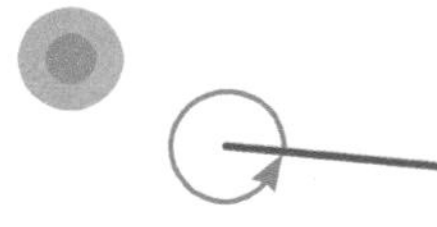

a 

b 

3 Mark in the angle to show reflex angles.

a 

b 

SELF CHECK Mark how you feel

Got it!	Need help...	I don't get it

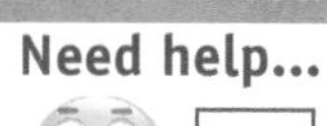

Check your answers

How many did you get correct?

PRACTICE

Use yellow to circle the reflex angles, use red to circle the straight angles, and use purple to circle the revolutions.

b

d

f

a

c

e

g

Draw two of each type of angle.

Straight Angles	Revolutions	Reflex Angles

Write the letter of the angle that matches each type.

a right angle ______

b reflex angle ______

c acute angle ______

d obtuse angle ______

e straight angle ______

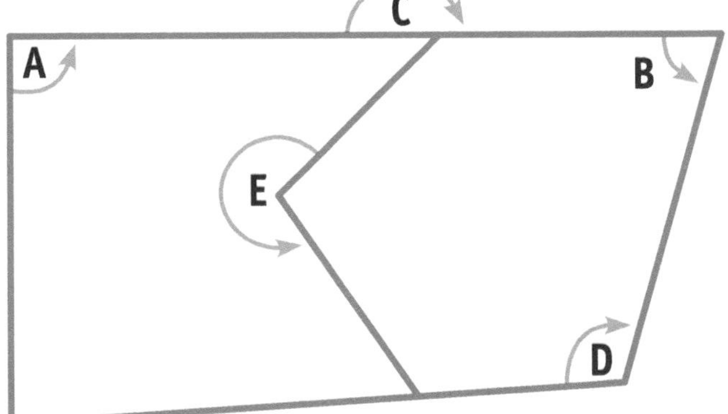

Find three more acute angles in the shape in Question 3. Label them F, G, and H.

Find three more obtuse angles in the shape in Question 3. Label them I, J, and K.

USING A PROTRACTOR

A protractor is used to measure or draw angles.
It measures the amount of turn.

SCAN to watch video

How to measure an angle

1 Put the lower arm of the angle on the base line.

2 Put the vertex of the angle at the center point.

3 Find 0° on the lower arm to determine whether to use the inside or outside scale.

4 Read the scale.

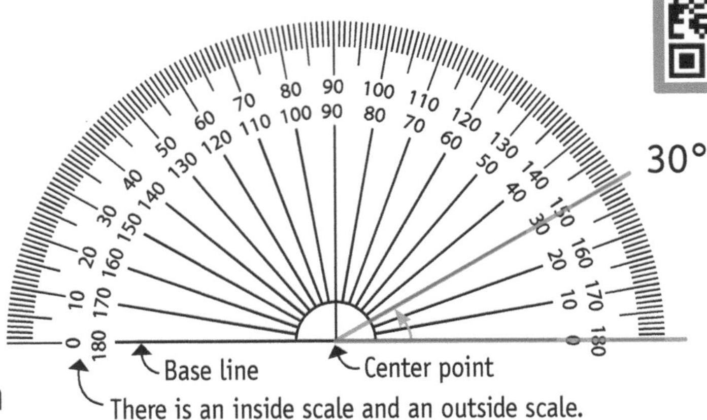

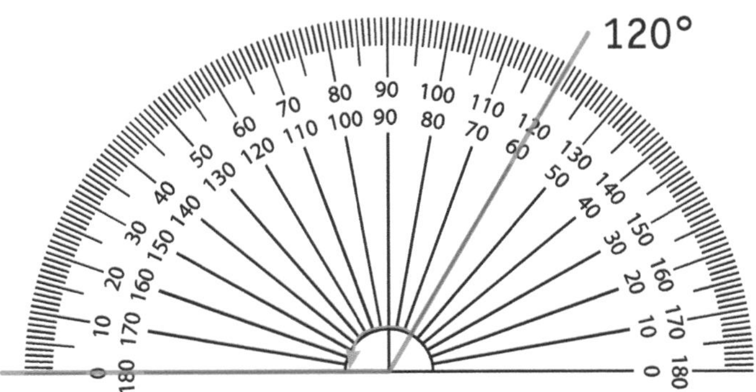

Example:

Label the protractor above with these features.

a Inside numbers

b Base line

c Center point

d Outside numbers

Your turn

Should you use the inside numbers (I) or the outside numbers (O) to measure these angles?

● O

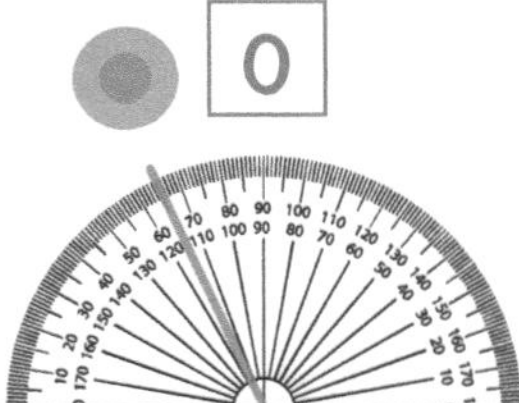

a ☐

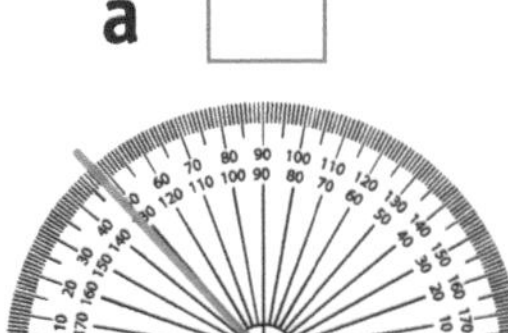

b ☐

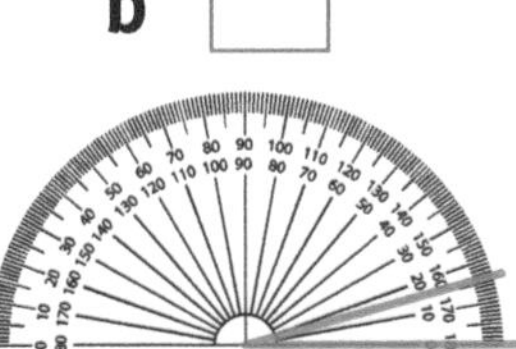

SELF CHECK	Mark how you feel	
Got it! ☐	Need help... ☐	I don't get it ☐

Check your answers
How many did you get correct? ☐

PRACTICE

1 Write the size of each angle.

40°

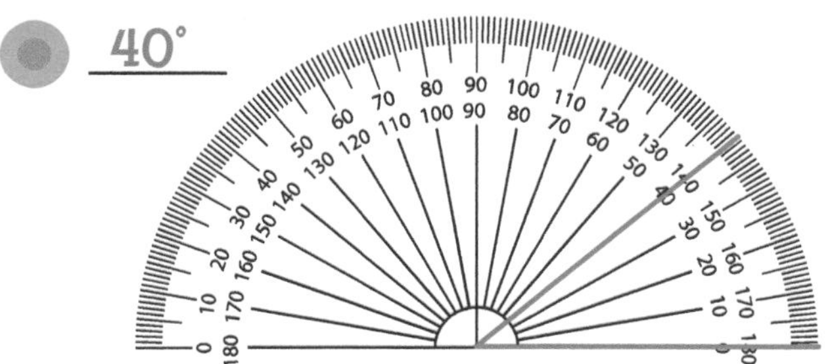

c ______

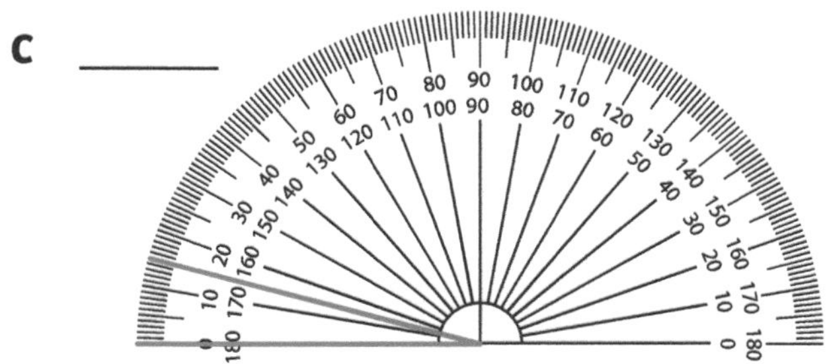

a ______

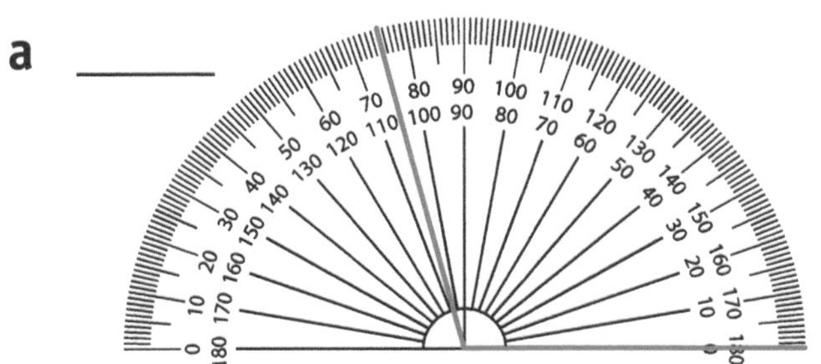

d ______

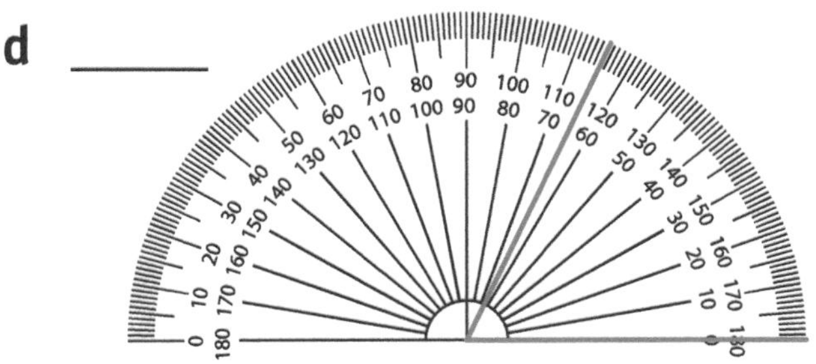

b ______

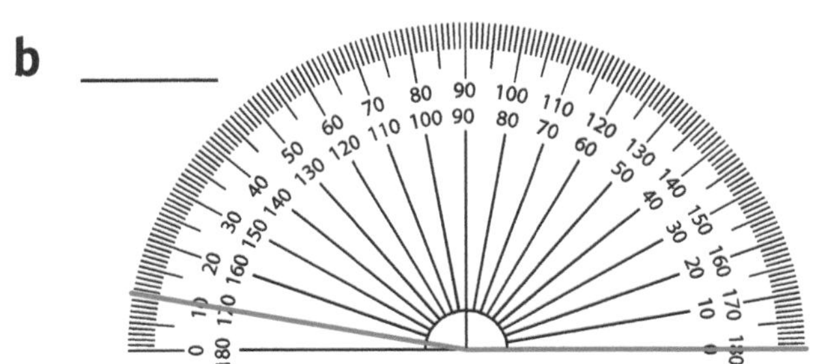

e ______

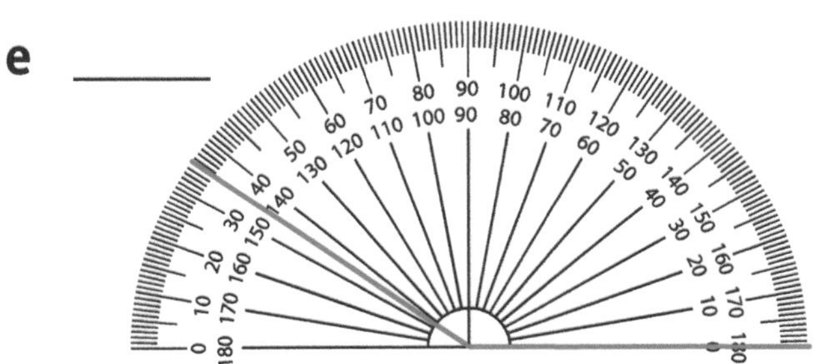

2 Measure these angles using a protractor.

50°

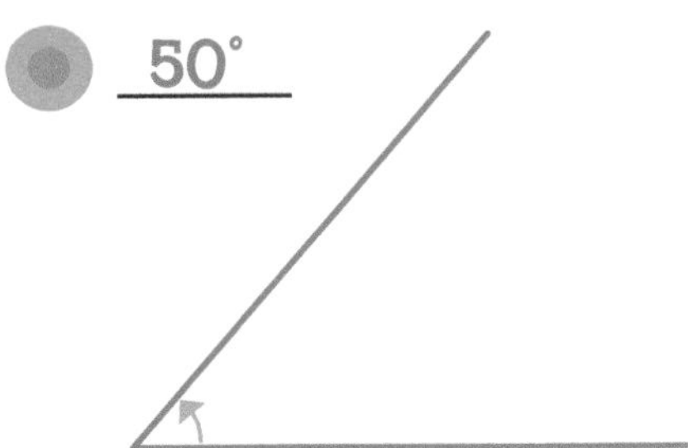

b ______

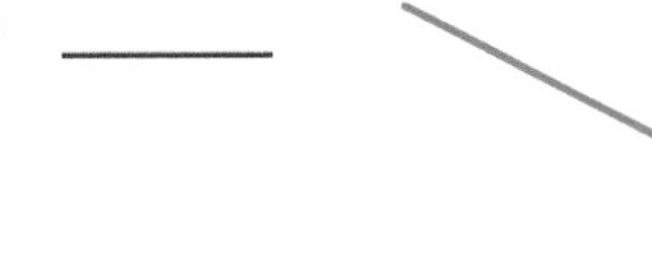

a ______

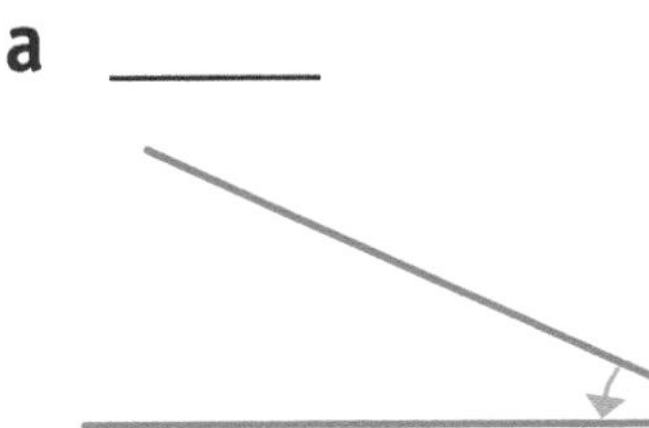

c ______

d ______

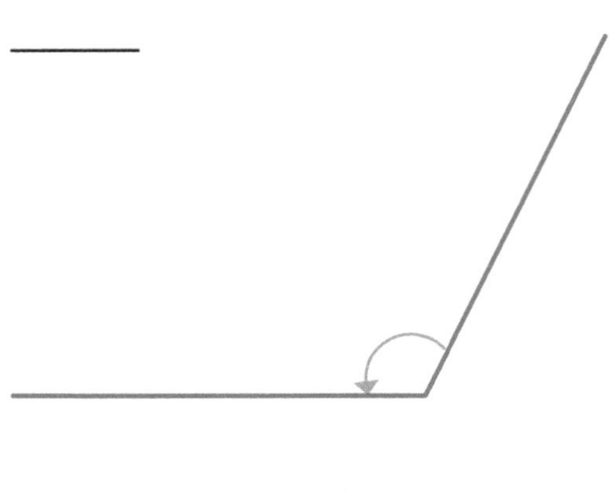

f ______

e ______

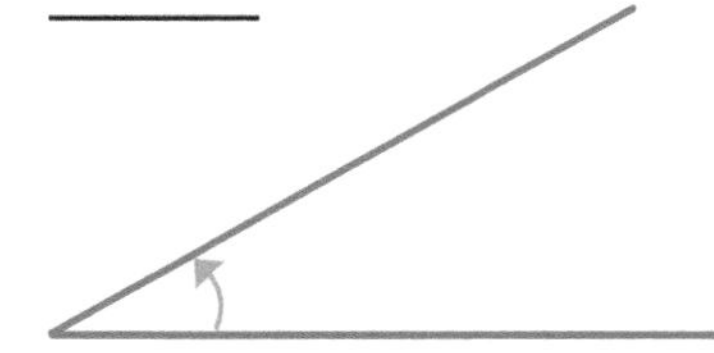

g ______

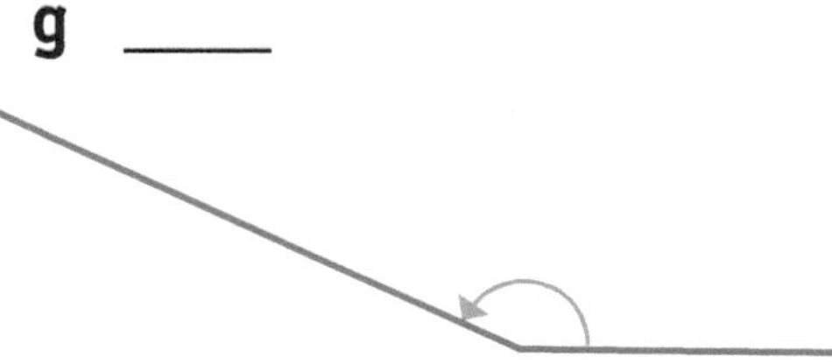

3 Use a protractor to draw angles of the given sizes.

 10°

b 105°

d 170°

a 60°

c 20°

e 26°

ANGLE SUM OF A TRIANGLE

The three angles in any triangle always add up to 180°.

Equilateral triangle

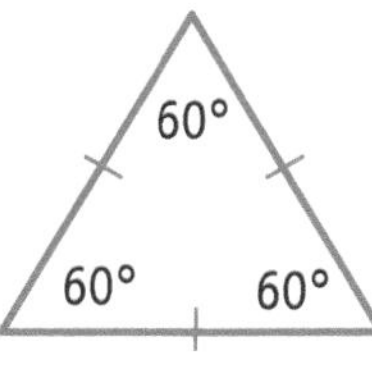

60° + 60° + 60° = 180°

Right triangle

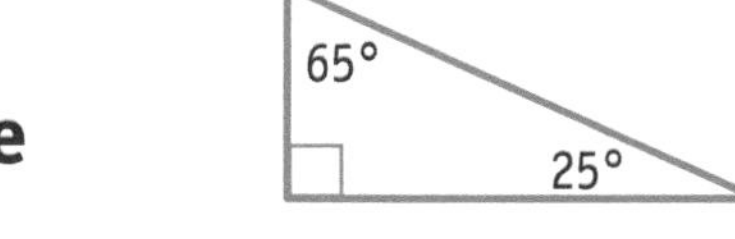

65° + 25° + 90° = 180°

Isosceles triangle

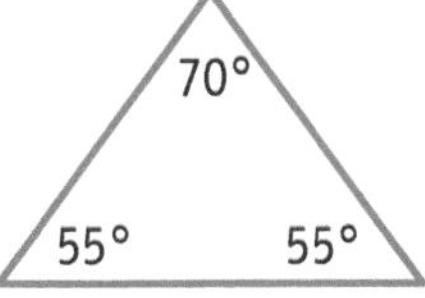

70° + 55° + 55° = 180°

Scalene triangle

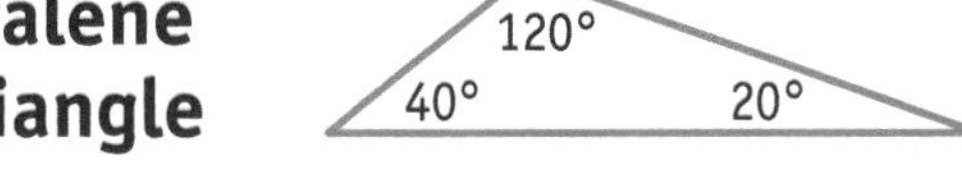

120° + 40° + 20° = 180°

Examples: Write the type of triangle.

a scalene

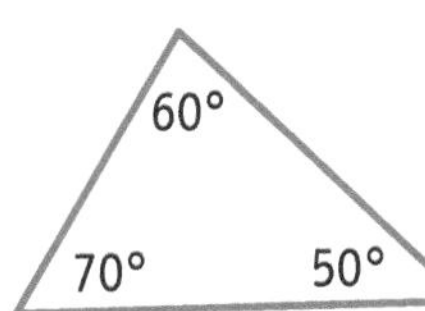

b ____________

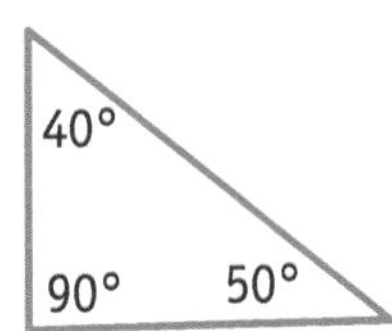

c ____________

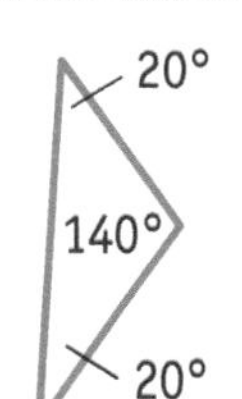

d ____________

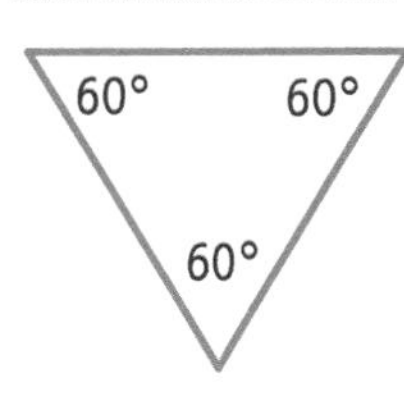

Your turn

Write the size of the missing angles.

● 60°

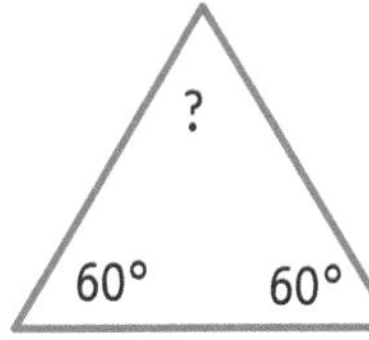

a ____________

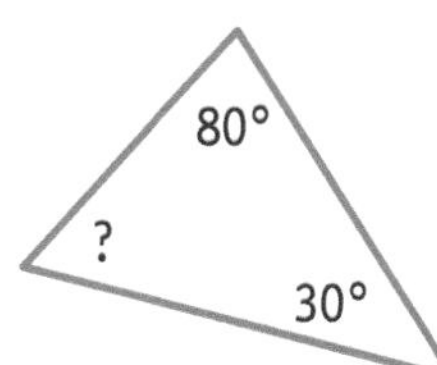

b ____________

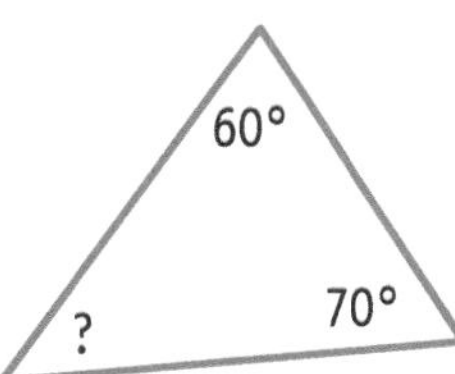

c ____________

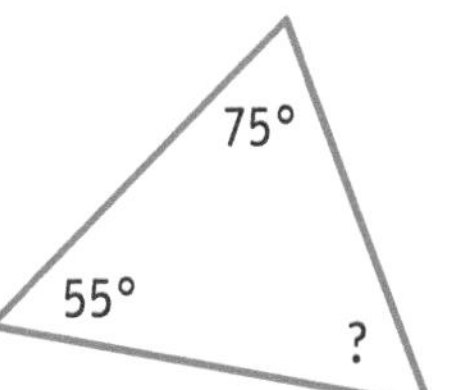

SELF CHECK Mark how you feel		
Got it!  	Need help... 	I don't get it

Check your answers

How many did you get correct?

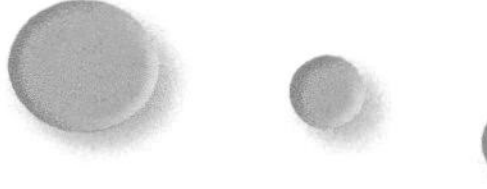

1 Find the size of each missing angle, and then write the triangle type.

● (example)

x, 60°, 60°

x = 60°

equilateral

b

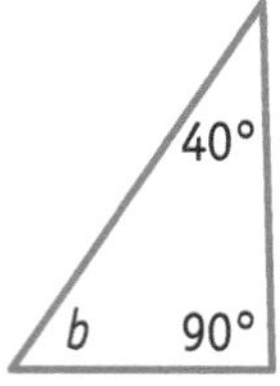

b = ______

____

d

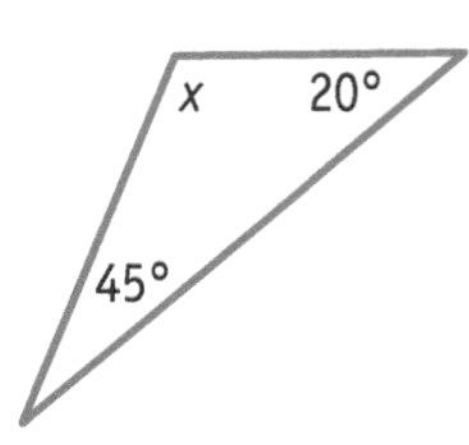

x = ______

____

a

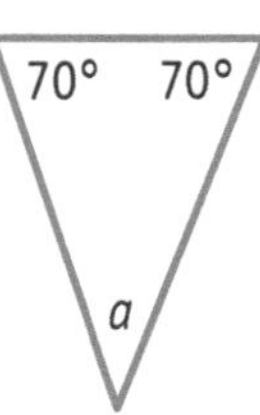

a = ______

____

c

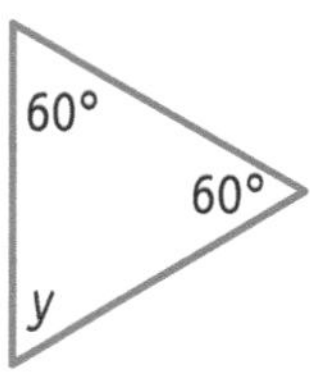

y = ______

____

e

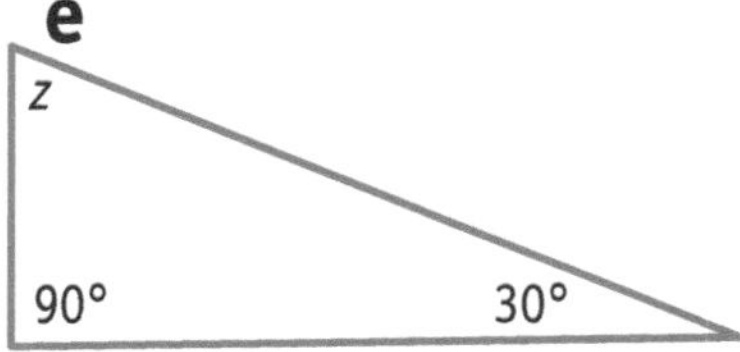

z = ______

____

2 A student found the angle sizes of these triangles. Write the total on the line inside each triangle. Mark the box if the student is incorrect.

● ☒

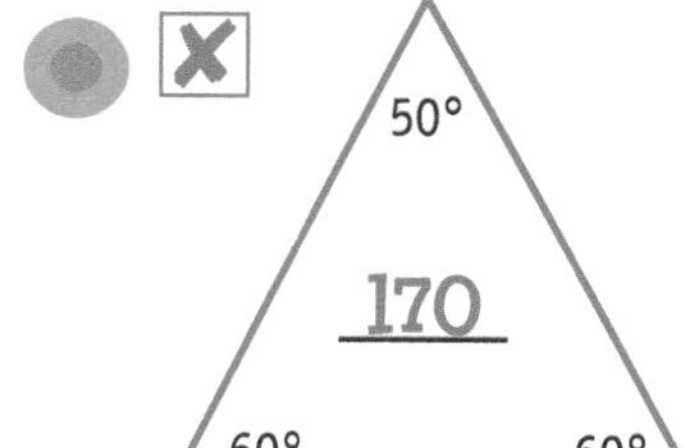

b ☐

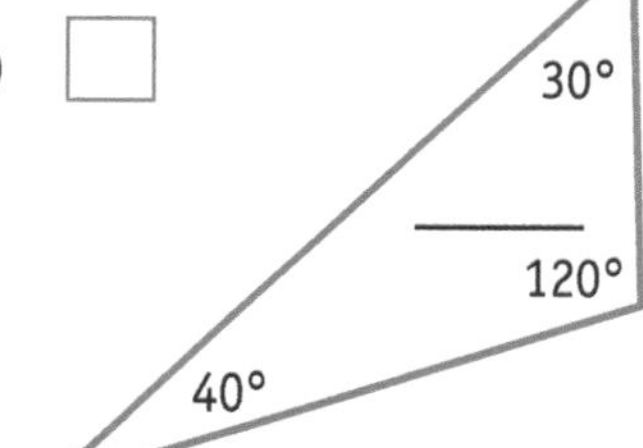

d ☐

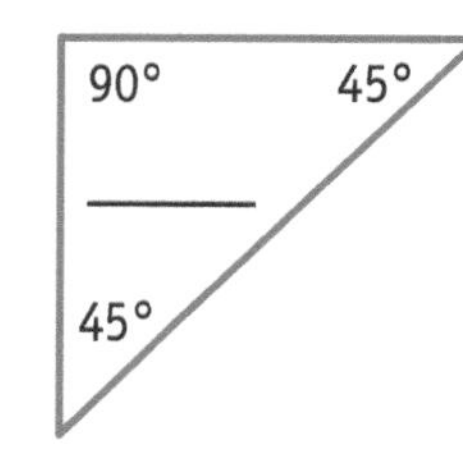

a ☐

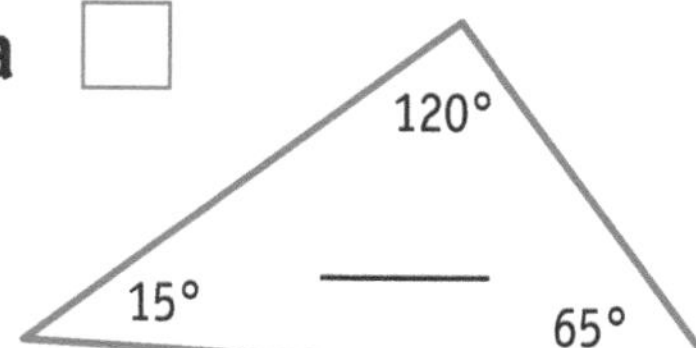

c ☐

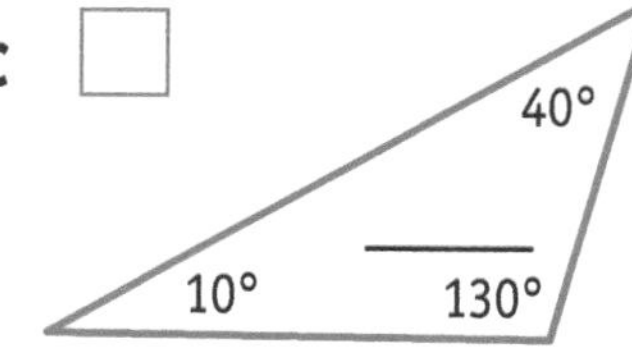

e ☐

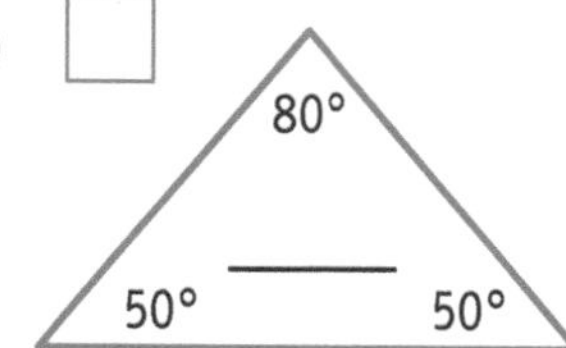

ANGLE SUM OF QUADRILATERALS

The four angles in any quadrilateral always add up to 360°.

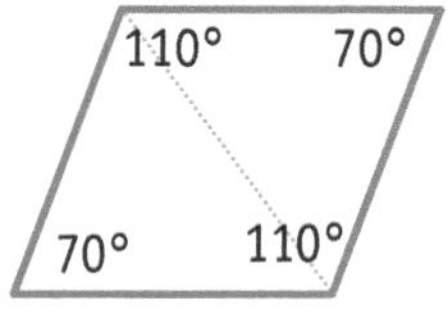

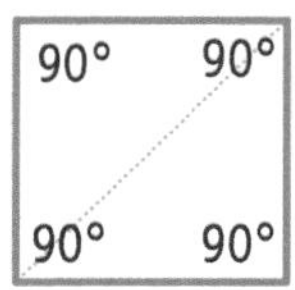

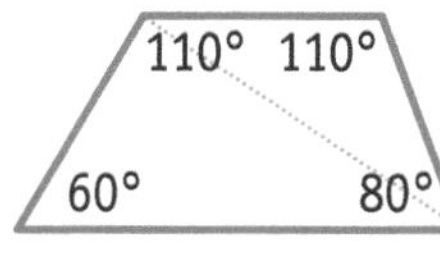

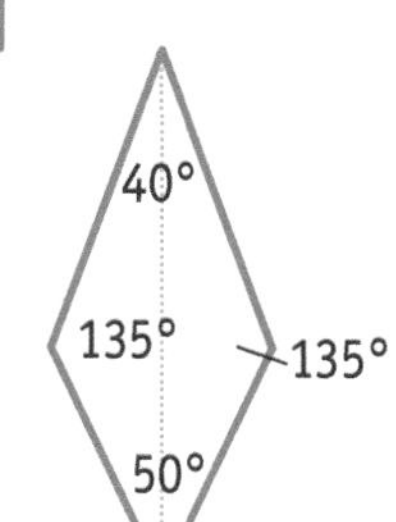

Each quadrilateral is made up of two triangles. 180° + 180° = 360°

Examples: Divide each quadrilateral into two triangles.

a

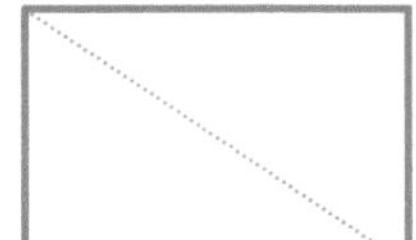

b

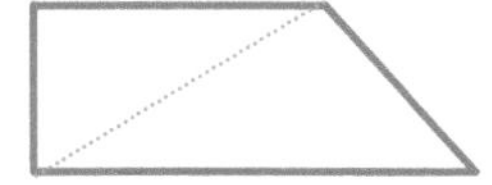

c

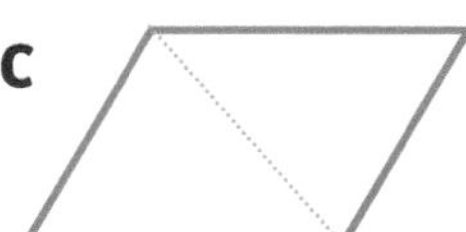

d

Your turn Find the size of the missing angle in each quadrilateral.

x = 50°

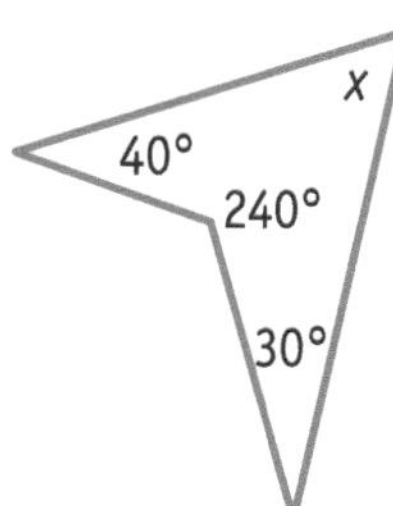

a a = ______

45°
90°
90°

b b = ______

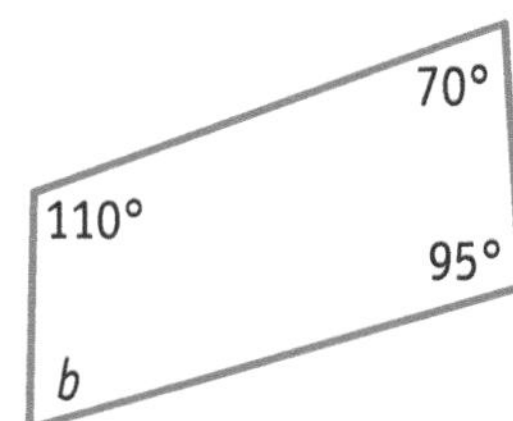

c c = ______

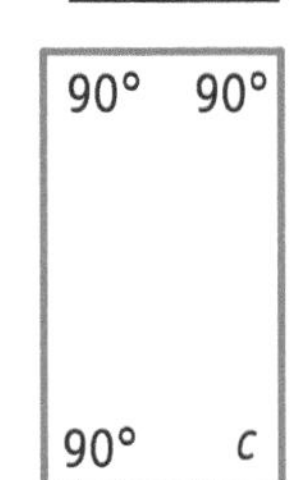

d d = ______

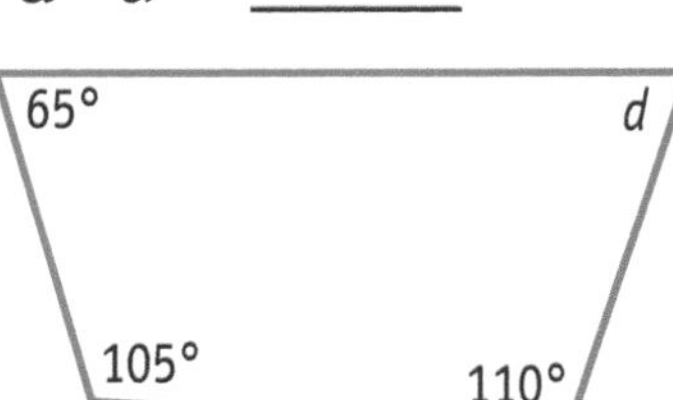

e e = ______

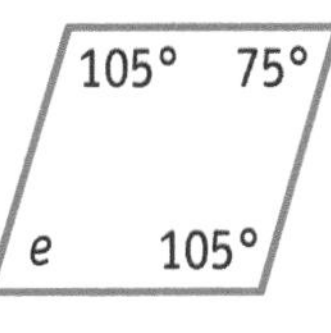

SELF CHECK Mark how you feel		
Got it!	Need help...	I don't get it

Check your answers

How many did you get correct?

PRACTICE

Find the sizes of the missing angles.

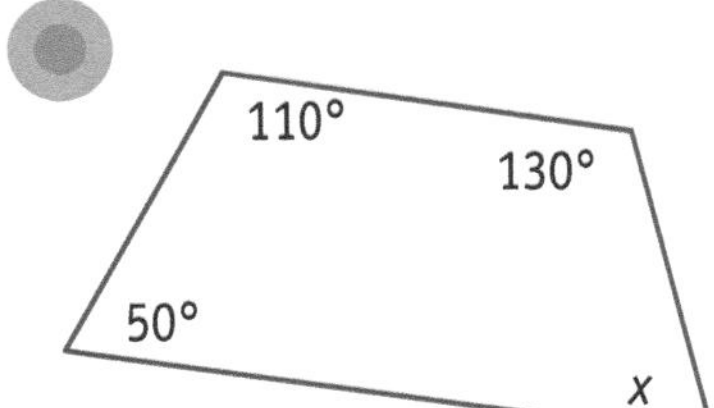

x = 70°

d

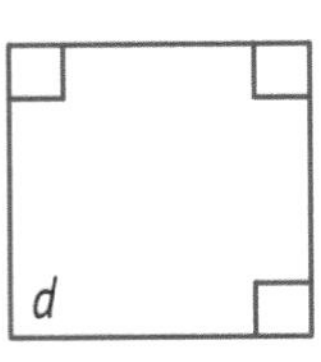

d = ______

h

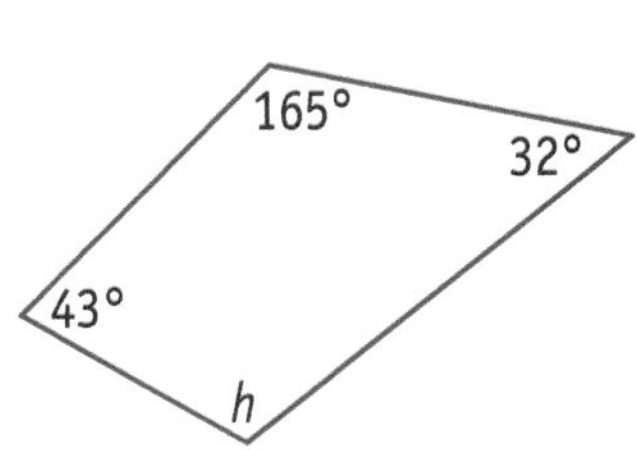

h = ______

a

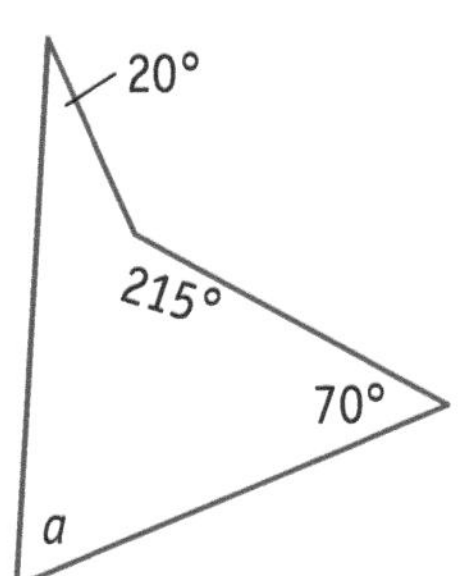

a = ______

e

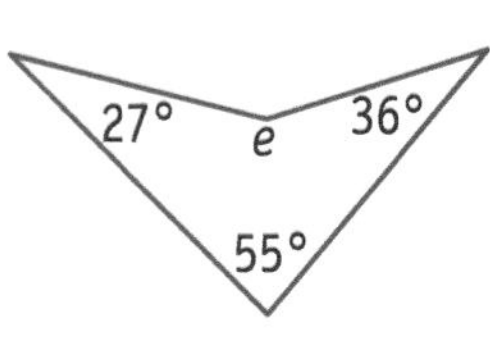

e = ______

i

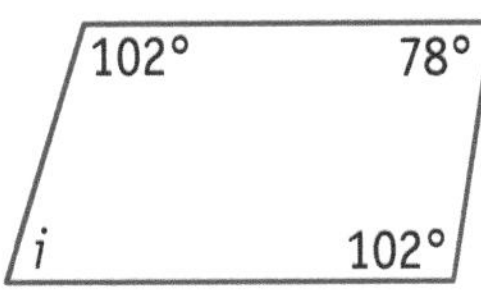

i = ______

b

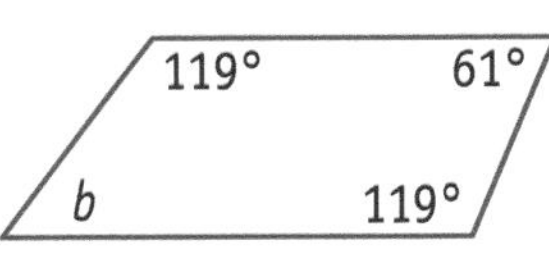

b = ______

f

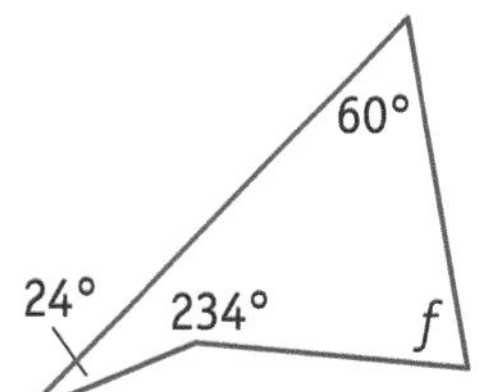

f = ______

j

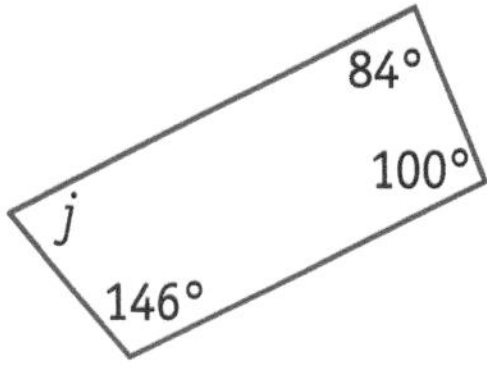

j = ______

c

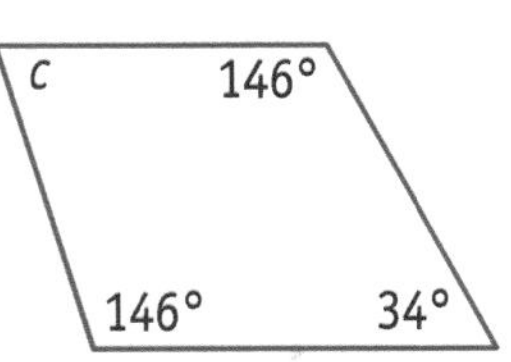

c = ______

g

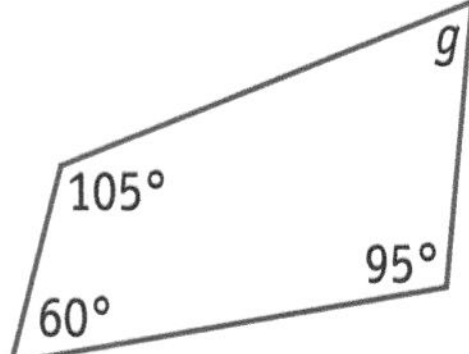

g = ______

k

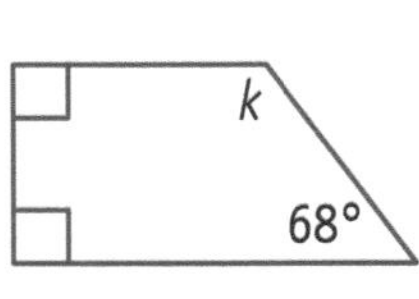

k = ______

ANGLES REVIEW

1 Use these words to complete the statements: ninety, arms, right, turn.

a An angle is made by measuring the amount of ________ between the two ________.

b A quarter turn is called a ________ angle. It measures ________ degrees.

2 Trace over the arms in red and the angle made in blue, and draw a green circle on the vertex.

a 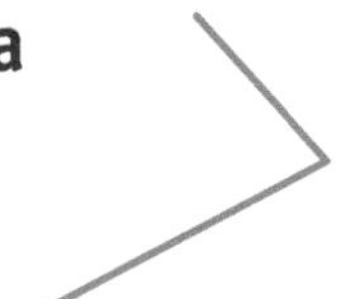

b 

c 

d 

3 Draw another line to turn each ray into a right angle.

a 

b 

c 

d 

4 Trace over the right angles in each shape.

a 

c 

e 

b 

d 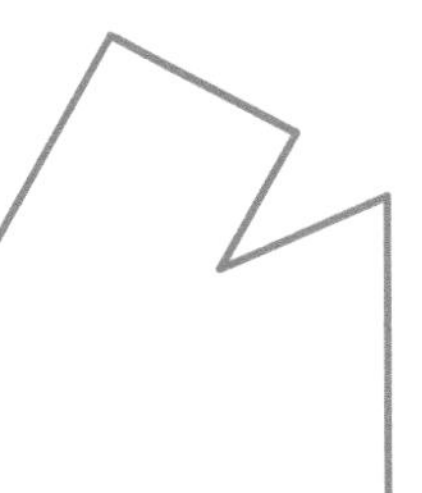

f 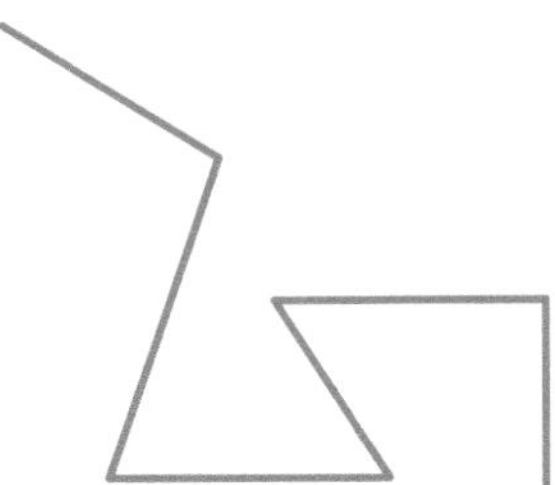

REVIEW

5 Draw three of each type of angle.

Acute angles	Obtuse angles

6 Name and label each angle.

a A B C

Name: ____________

Type: __________

b

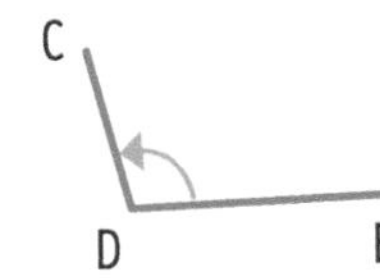

Name: ____________

Type: __________

c P R Q

Name: ____________

Type: __________

d

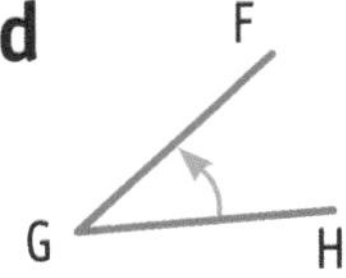

Name: ____________

Type: __________

e S T U

Name: ____________

Type: __________

f V W X

Name: ____________

Type: __________

7 Use orange to circle the acute angles, green to circle the obtuse angles, red to circle the reflex angles, blue to circle the straight angles, and yellow to circle the revolutions.

a

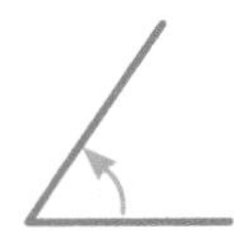

c

e

g

b

d

f

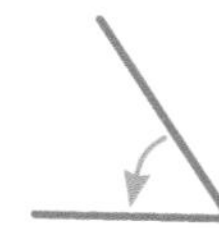

h

8 Write the letter of the angle that matches each type.

a reflex angle ______

b obtuse angle ______

c acute angle ______

d straight angle ______

e right angle ______

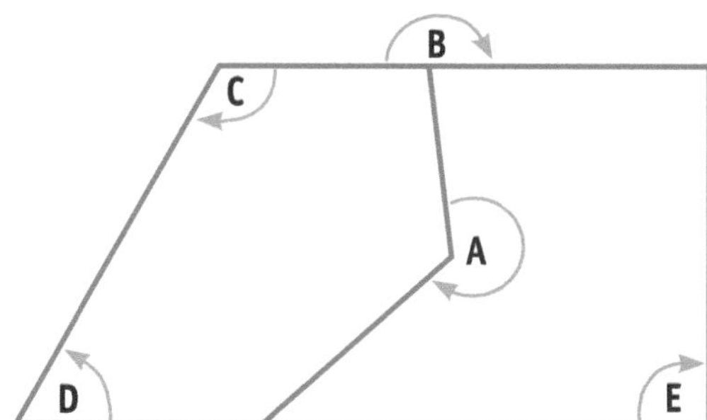

9 Find two more acute angles in the shape in Question 8. Label them F and G.

10 Find three more obtuse angles in the shape in Question 8. Label them H, I, and J.

11 Draw another right angle in the shape in Question 8. Label it K.

12 Write the size of these angles.

a ______

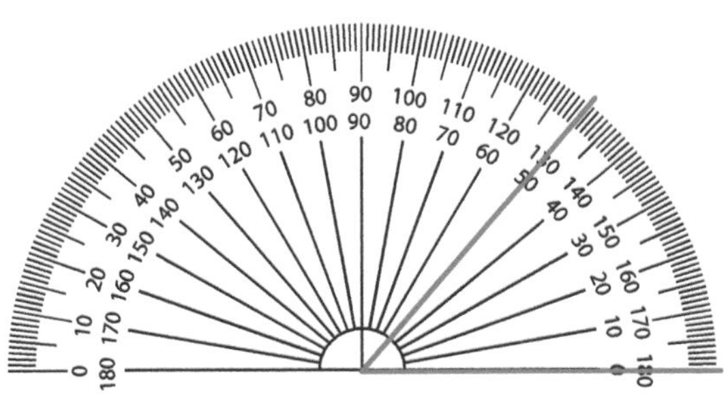

c ______

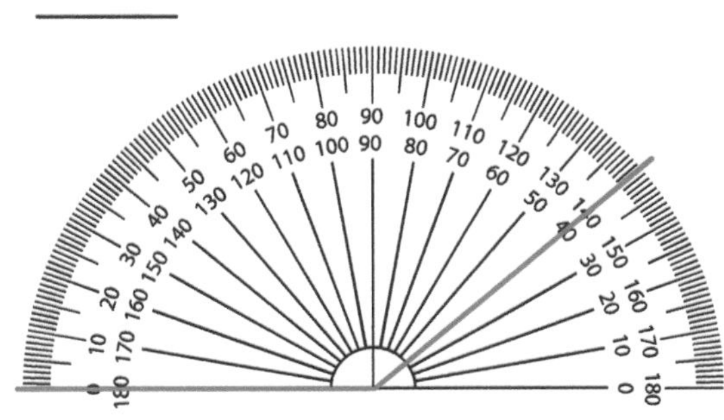

b ______

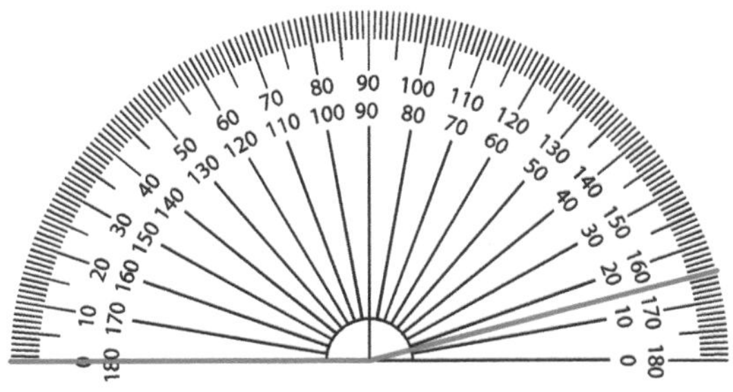

d ______

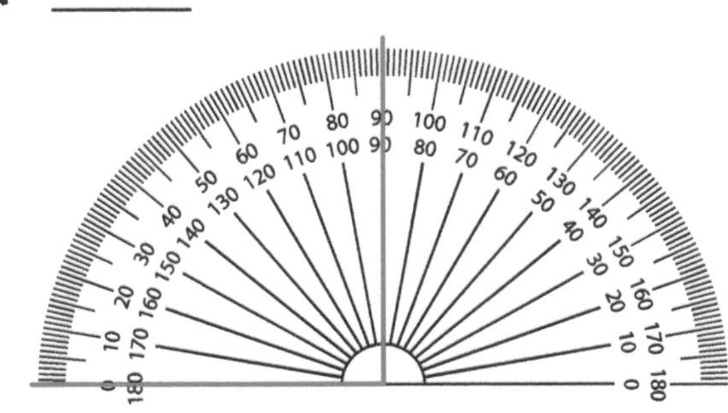

REVIEW

13 Measure these angles using a protractor.

a ______

b ______

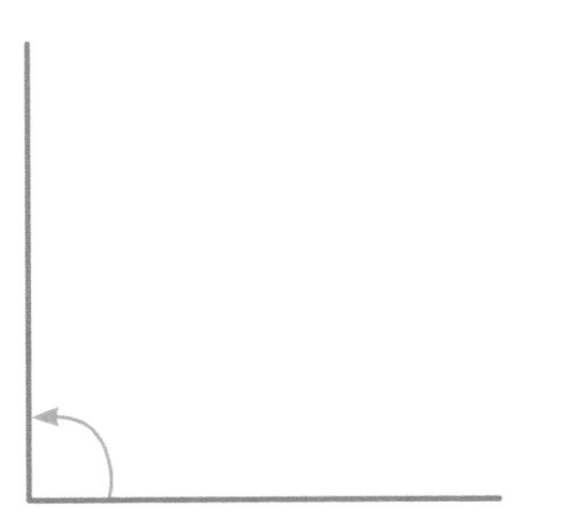

c ______

d ______

e ______

14 Use a protractor to draw angles of the given sizes.

a 15°

c 133°

e 122°

b 72°

d 243°

f 84°

15 Find the size of each missing angle, and then write the triangle type.

a

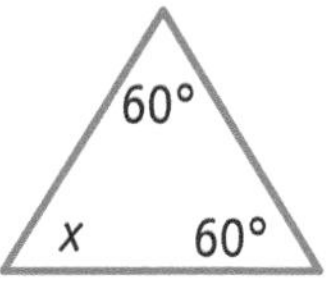

$x =$ ______

____

c

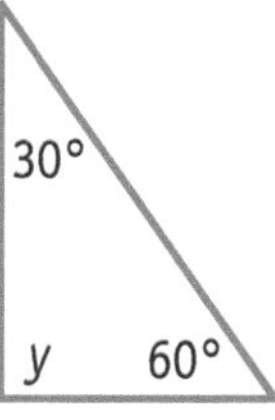

$y =$ ______

____

e

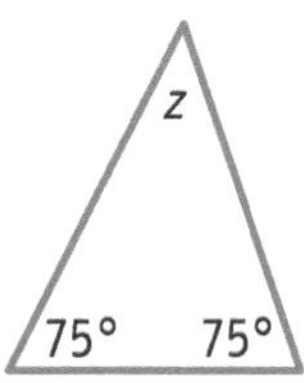

$z =$ ______

____

b

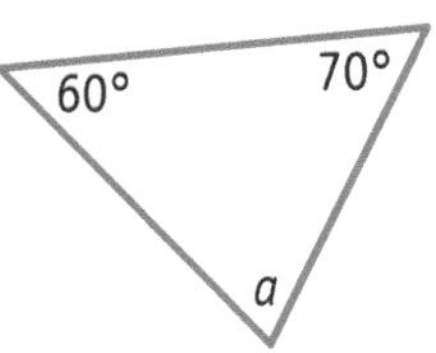

$a =$ ______

____

d

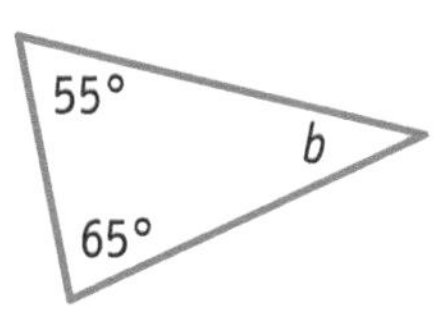

$b =$ ______

____

f

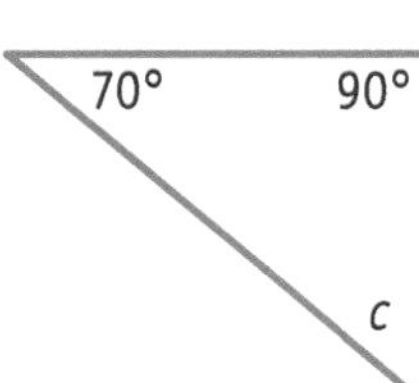

$c =$ ______

____

16 Find the sizes of the missing angles in these quadrilaterals.

a

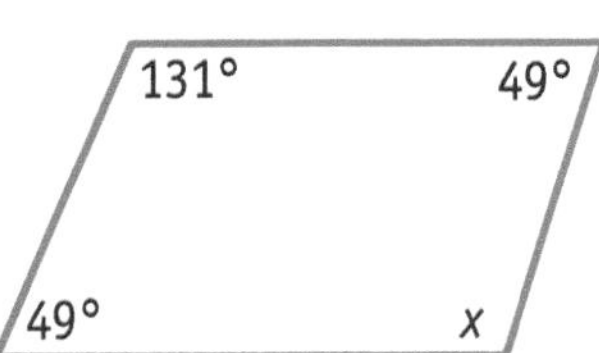

$x =$ ______

c

$b =$ ______

e

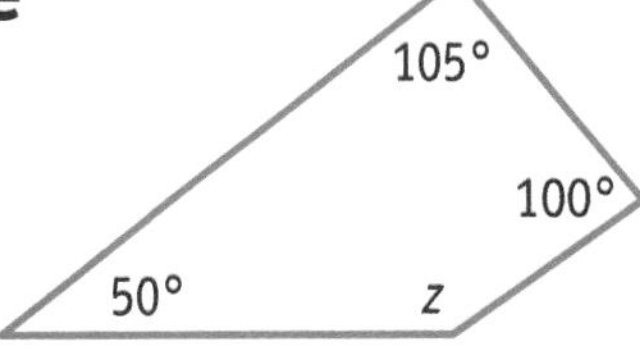

$z =$ ______

b

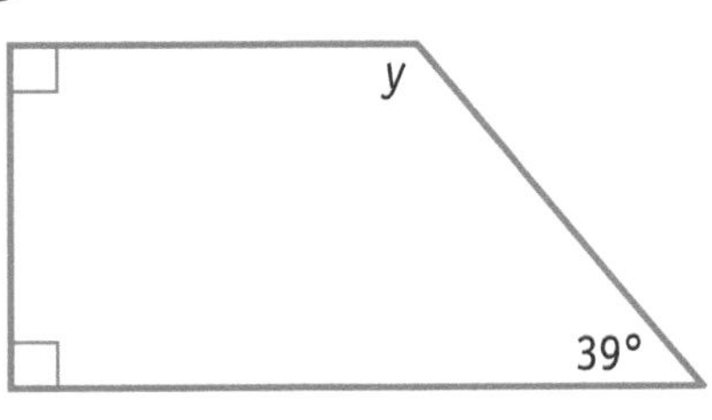

$y =$ ______

d

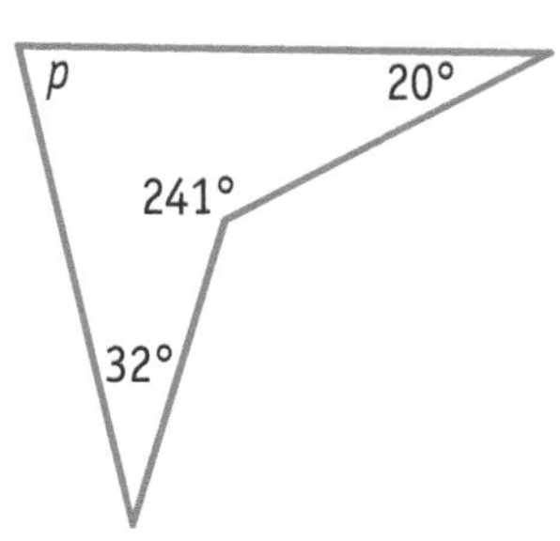

$p =$ ______

f

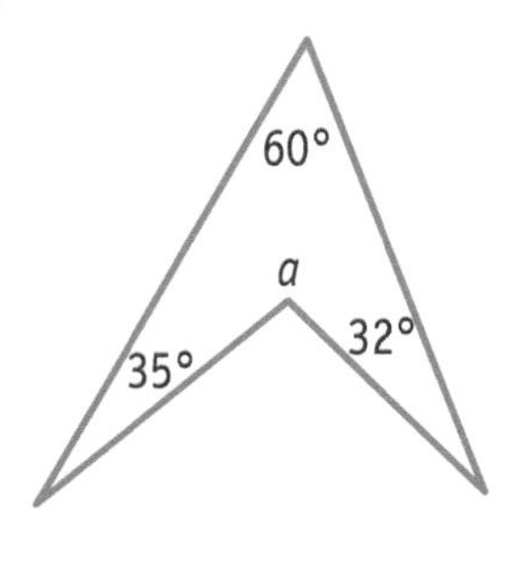

$a =$ ______

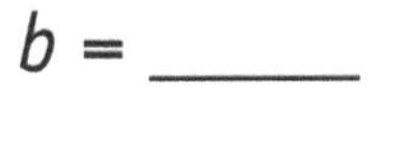

SHAPES

Flat shapes (polygons) have two dimensions: length and width. Some shapes are named by the number of sides and angles they have.

triangle:
3 angles,
3 sides

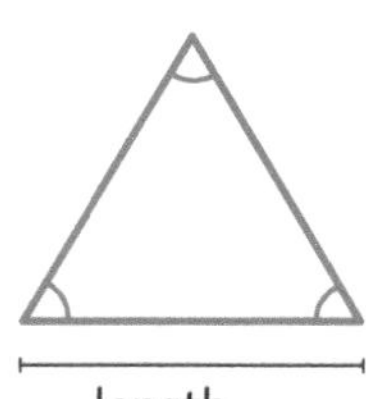

hexagon:
6 sides,
6 angles

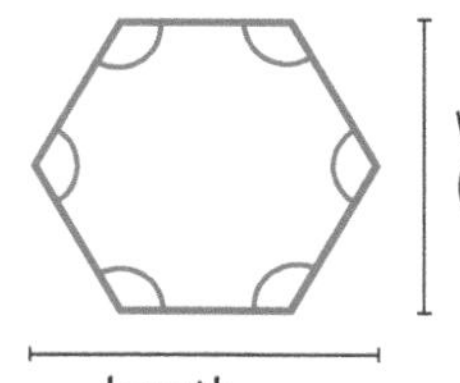

Regular polygons have angles and sides that are all the same size.

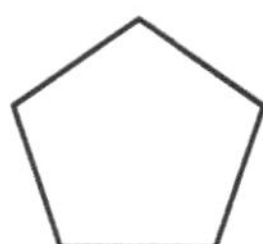

regular pentagon

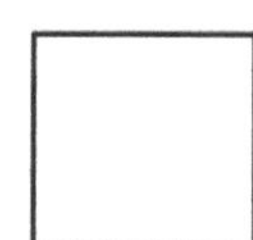

square (regular quadrilateral)

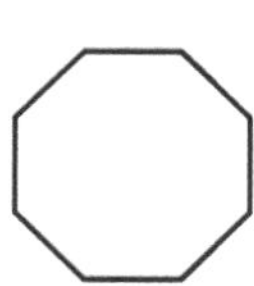

regular octagon

Irregular polygons have sides and angles of different sizes.

irregular pentagon

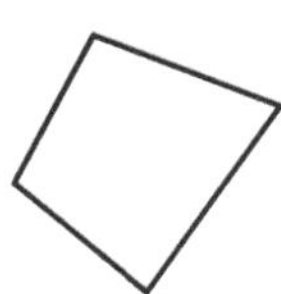

irregular quadrilateral

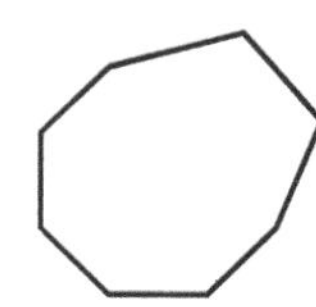

irregular octagon

Examples: Color the regular polygons red and the irregular polygons blue.

a  **b**  **c**  **d**  **e**  **f**

Your turn

Write the names of the polygons from the Examples.

a square ____________ d ____________

b ____________ e ____________

c ____________ f ____________

SELF CHECK Mark how you feel		
Got it! ☐	Need help... ☐	I don't get it ☐

Check your answers
How many did you get correct? ☐

PRACTICE

1 Trace the regular polygons with red and the irregular polygons with blue. Then write the name of each shape.

● irregular pentagon

a ______

b ______

c ______

d ______

e ______

2 Complete the chart.

	Polygon	Name	Letters that help identify polygon	Angles	Sides
●		quadrilateral	quad	4	4
a					
b					
c					
d		heptagon			
e					
f		nonagon			
g		decagon			

TYPES OF LINES

Many shapes have lines that are vertical, horizontal, parallel, and perpendicular.

Vertical lines go up and down.

Horizontal lines go left to right.

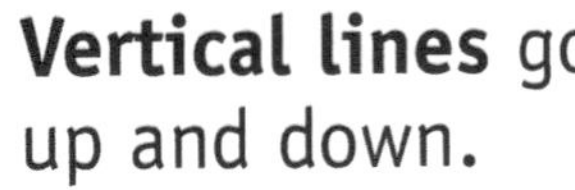

Parallel lines never meet and are equal distances apart.

Perpendicular lines meet at right angles.

This parallelogram has two sets of parallel lines.

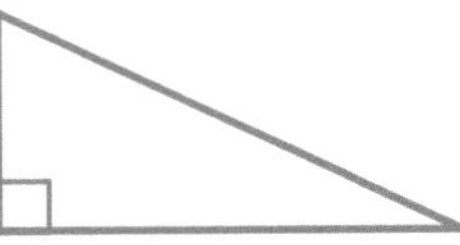

This right triangle has two lines that meet at right angles.

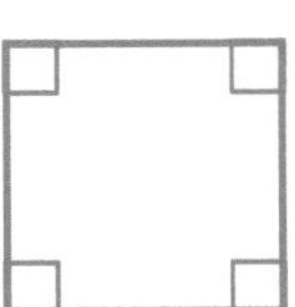

All lines of this square meet at right angles.

Examples:
Label the lines as vertical, horizontal, parallel, or perpendicular.

a parallel

b ____________________

c ____________________

d ____________________

Your turn

Trace the vertical lines with blue, horizontal lines with orange, parallel lines with green, and perpendicular lines with purple.

b

d

f

h

a

c

e

g

i

SELF CHECK Mark how you feel

Got it!	Need help...	I don't get it

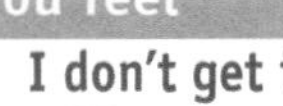

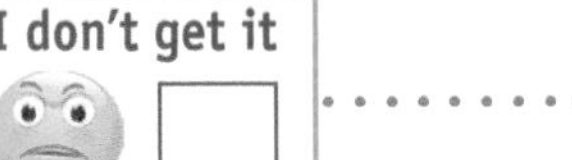

Check your answers
How many did you get correct?

PRACTICE

Draw two examples of each type of line.

Horizontal	Parallel	Perpendicular	Vertical

List five things that have parallel lines.

train tracks

Trace over the lines that match the line type.

a perpendicular

b parallel

c horizontal

d vertical

TRIANGLES

Triangles have 3 sides and 3 angles.
There are four different types of triangles.

Equilateral

- All sides the same length
- All angles the same size
- Regular triangle

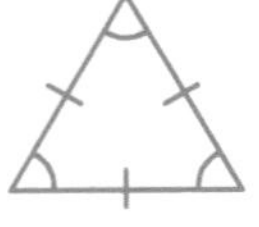

Isosceles

- Two sides the same length
- Two angles the same size
- Irregular triangle

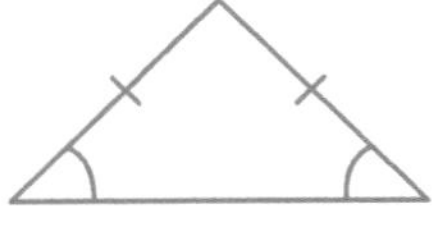

Right

- One right angle
- Irregular triangle

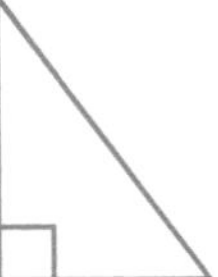

Scalene

- All sides different lengths
- All angles different sizes
- Irregular triangle

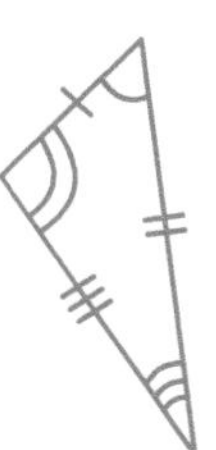

Examples: Trace the regular triangles in red.

a 

b 

c 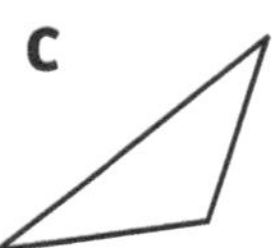

d 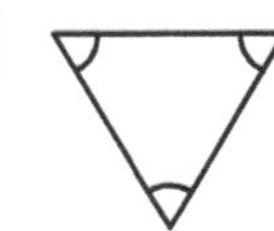

e 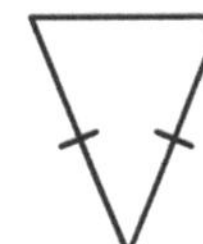

Trace the equilateral triangles in red, isosceles triangles in blue, scalene triangles in yellow, and right triangles in green.

b 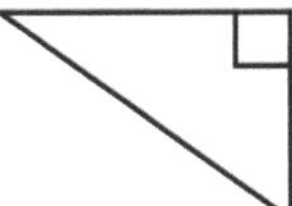

d 

f 

a 

c 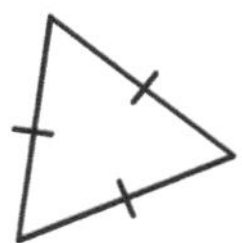

e 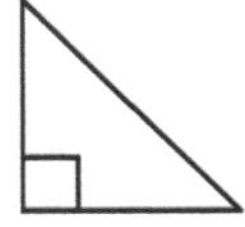

g 

SELF CHECK Mark how you feel		
Got it! 	Need help... 	I don't get it 

Check your answers
How many did you get correct?

PRACTICE

1 Measure the sides and angles of each triangle, and then label it.

isosceles

d  ______________

a  ______________

e ______________

b 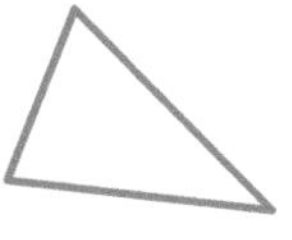 ______________

f  ______________

c  ______________

g  ______________

2 Draw two of each type of triangle.

Isosceles triangles	Equilateral triangles
Scalene triangles	Right triangles

3 Write a definition for each triangle.

a isosceles triangle ______________________________

____

b equilateral triangle ______________________________

____

c scalene triangle ______________________________

____

d right triangle ______________________________

____

QUADRILATERALS

Quadrilaterals have four straight sides and four corners.

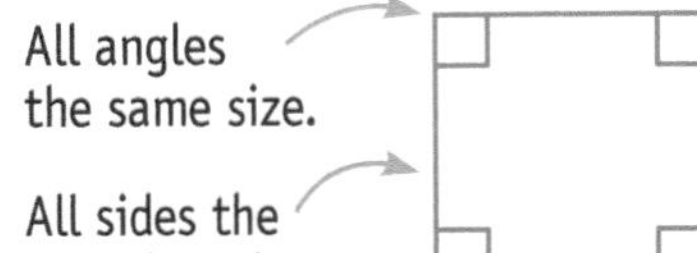

The square is the only regular quadrilateral.

Irregular quadrilaterals

Rectangle

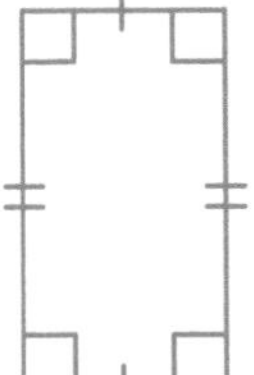

- Opposite sides equal in length
- All angles 90°

Rhombus

- All sides equal in length
- Two pairs of parallel sides
- Opposite angles equal in size

Parallelogram

- Opposite sides equal in length
- Two pairs of parallel sides
- Opposite angles equal in size

Kite

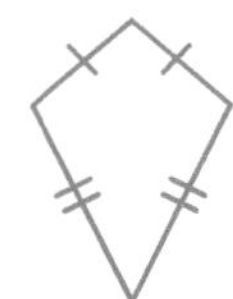

- Two pairs of sides the same length
- No parallel sides

Trapezoid

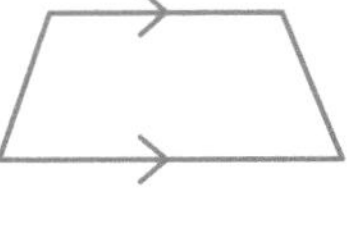

- One pair of parallel sides

Examples:
Label each quadrilateral as regular or irregular.

a irregular

b  ______________

c 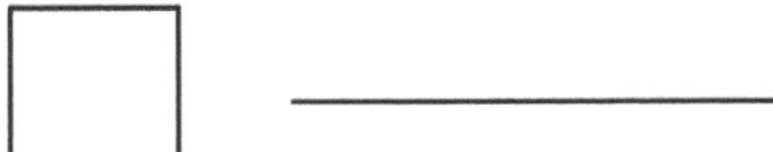 ______________

d ______________

Your turn

Name each quadrilateral in the Examples above.

a trapezoid

b ______________

c ______________

d ______________

SELF CHECK Mark how you feel		
Got it! 	Need help... 	I don't get it 

Check your answers
How many did you get correct?

PRACTICE

Trace the squares with red, the rectangles with blue, rhombuses with green, parallelograms with yellow, trapezoids with orange, and kites with brown.

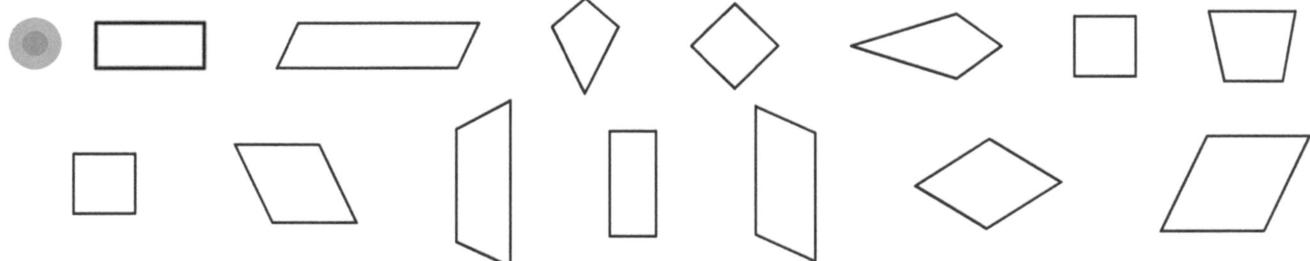

Write a definition for each quadrilateral, and then draw an example.

	Definition	Diagram
a	square	
b	rectangle	
c	kite	

	Definition	Diagram
d	rhombus	
e	parallelogram	
f	trapezoid	

Trace the parallel lines with purple and the perpendicular lines with red.

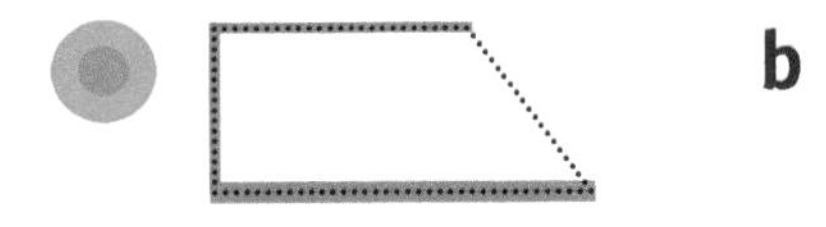

b

d

f

a

c

e

g

POLYGONS

Polygons are named for the number of sides they have.

Remember, regular polygons have sides of equal lengths and angles of equal sizes.

Irregular polygons have the same number of sides and angles, but the lengths and sizes are not equal.

Pentagon	Hexagon	Heptagon
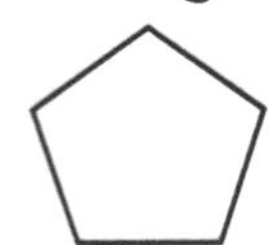	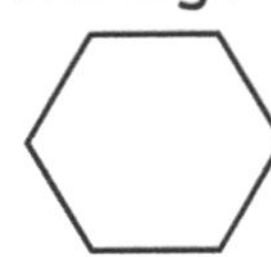	
5 straight sides 5 equal angles 5 corners	6 straight sides 6 equal angles 6 corners	7 straight sides 7 equal angles 7 corners

Octagon	Nonagon	Decagon	Dodecagon
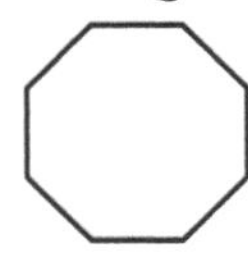	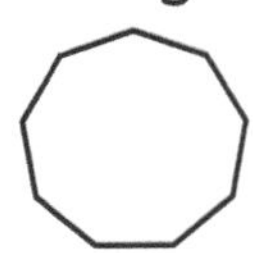		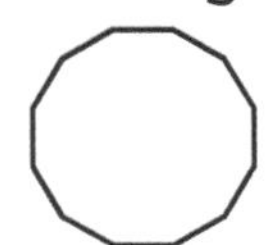
8 straight sides 8 equal angles 8 corners	9 straight sides 9 equal angles 9 corners	10 straight sides 10 equal angles 10 corners	12 straight sides 12 equal angles 12 corners

Examples: Trace the dotted lines to complete the shapes and then label them.

a  regular ________ octagon ________

b  ________ ________

c  ________ ________

d ________ ________

Your turn

Trace over the regular polygons in red and the irregular polygons in blue. Then, write the number of sides.

● 8 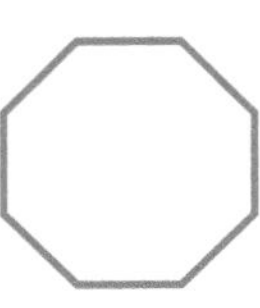

a ___ 

b ___ 

c ___ 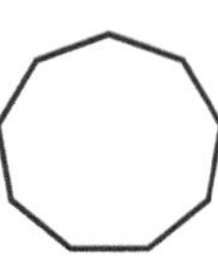

d ___ 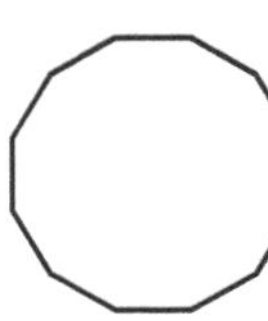

SELF CHECK Mark how you feel		
Got it!	Need help...	I don't get it
 ☐	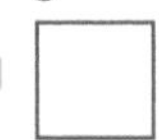 ☐	☐

Check your answers
How many did you get correct? ☐

PRACTICE

1. Draw two polygons that match each description.

Irregular decagons	Irregular octagons
Irregular pentagons	Irregular hexagons
Irregular dodecagons	Irregular nonagons
Irregular heptagons	Irregular quadrilaterals

2. Color the regular pentagons purple and the regular hexagons blue. Put an X on the irregular pentagons, and put a checkmark on the irregular hexagons.

a  b  c 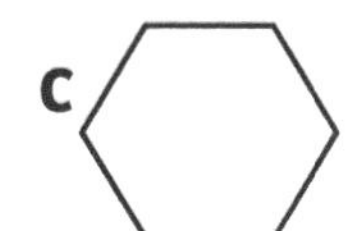 d 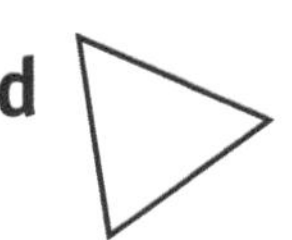 e  f 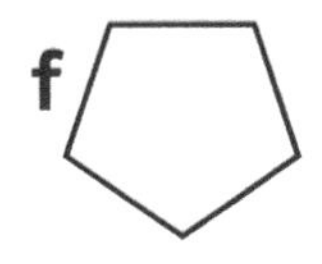 g

3. Color the regular heptagons orange and the regular octagons yellow. Put an X on the irregular heptagons, and put a checkmark on the irregular octagons.

a 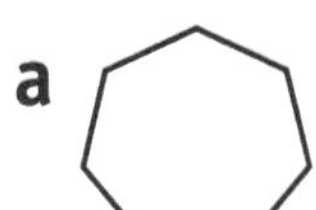 b  c  d 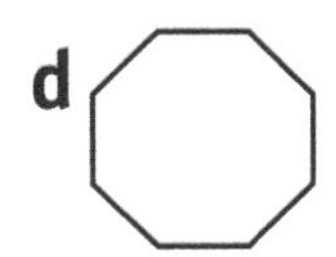 e 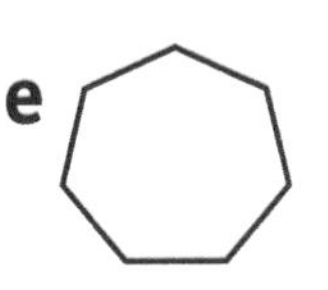 f 

4. Color the regular nonagons red, the regular decagons green, and the regular dodecagons blue. Put an X on the irregular nonagons, put a checkmark on the irregular decagons, and circle the irregular dodecagons.

a   b 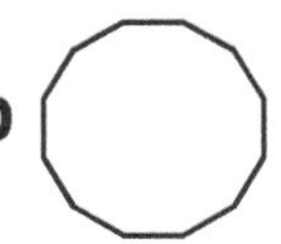 c  d  e  f 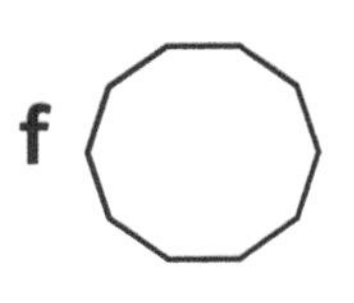 g 

SYMMETRY

Symmetry is when one half of a shape is a reflection of the other half.

This building is symmetrical because both halves fit on top of each other exactly.

A line of symmetry is always dotted.

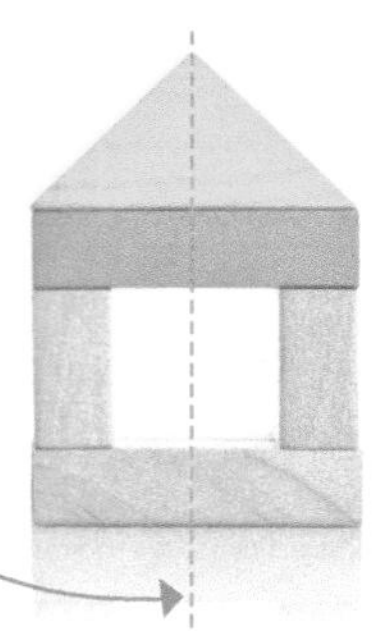

This building is not symmetrical because the two sides are not the same size.

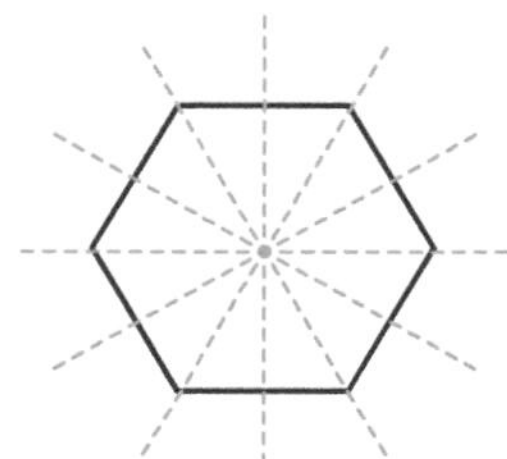

This hexagon has 6 lines of symmetry.

Examples: Circle the shapes that are symmetrical and cross out the shapes that are not symmetrical.

a

b

c

d

e

Your turn

Draw the lines of symmetry.

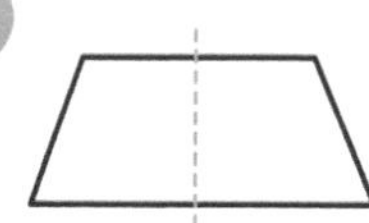

a

b

c

SELF CHECK Mark how you feel

Got it!	Need help...	I don't get it

Check your answers

How many did you get correct?

PRACTICE

Draw five letters that are symmetrical. Draw in the lines of symmetry.

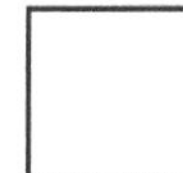

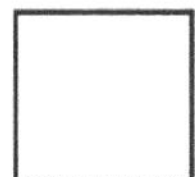
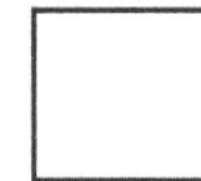

Write your name in block letters.
Draw in any lines of symmetry on the letters.

Use these shapes to answer the following questions.

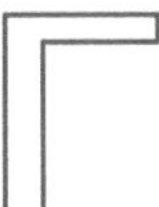

a Draw any lines of symmetry on the shapes above.

b Put a checkmark on the shapes that are symmetrical.

c Put an X on the shapes that are not symmetrical.

d Circle the shapes that have more than one line of symmetry.

4 Complete the other half of each picture along its axis of symmetry.

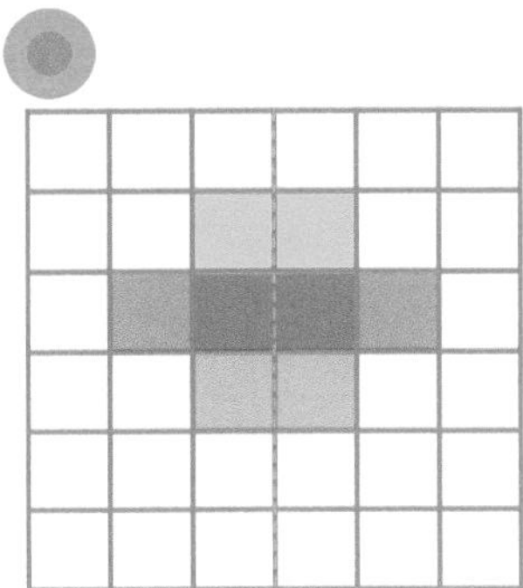

a

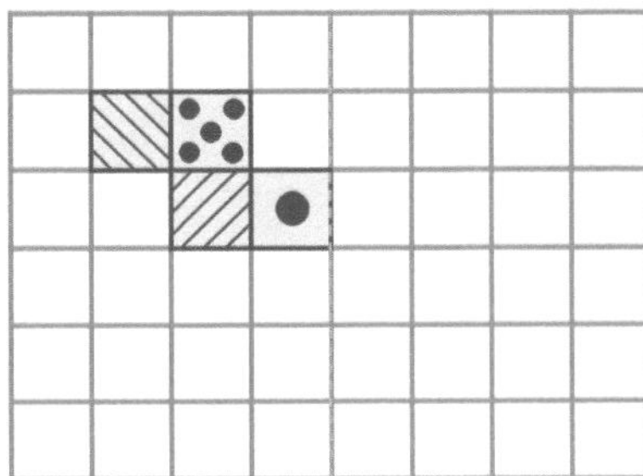

b

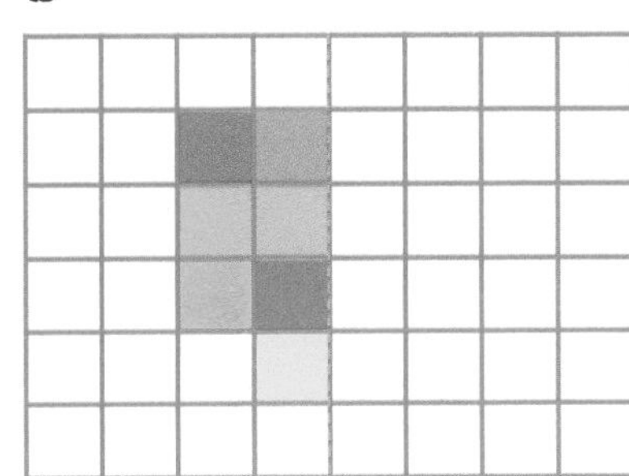

SHAPES REVIEW

1 Label each shape with its name, and note whether it is regular or irregular.

a ______ ______

b ______ ______

c ______ ______

d ______ ______

e ______ ______

f ______ ______

g ______ ______

h ______ ______

i ______ ______

j ______ ______

k 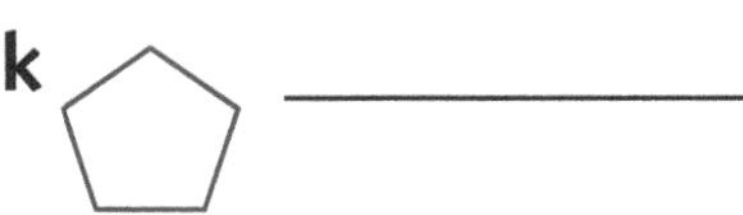

l 

m 

n 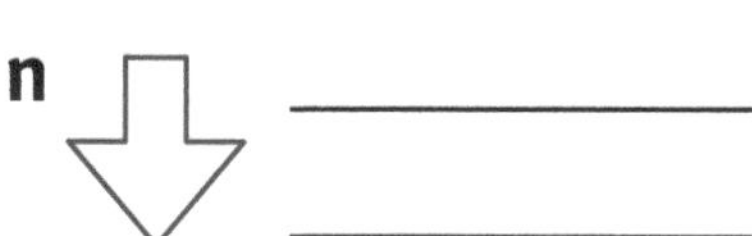

o 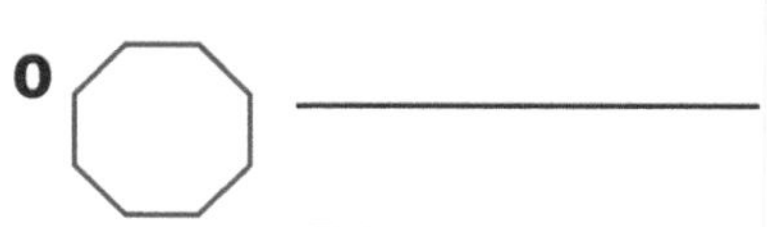

2 Label the lines as vertical, horizontal, parallel, or perpendicular.

a ______

b ______

c ______

d ______

e ______

f  ______

g 

h ______

i ______

j ______

3 Draw two examples of each type of line.

Vertical	Perpendicular	Parallel	Horizontal

4 Label the type of triangle for each shape.

a 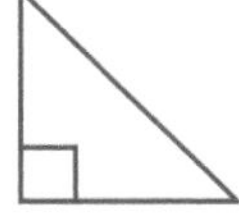 ____________

c 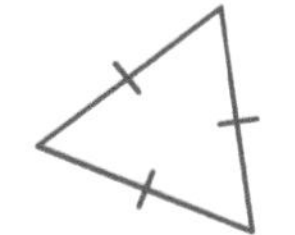 ____________

b  ____________

d 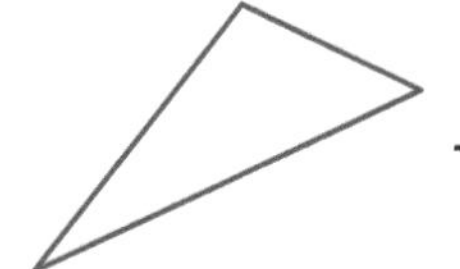 ____________

5 Match each description to the correct type of triangle.

- Two sides the same length
- All sides different lengths
- Two angles the same size

- Equilateral triangle
- Isosceles triangle
- Scalene triangle
- Right triangle

- One right angle
- All sides the same length
- All angles different sizes
- All angles the same size

REVIEW

6 Write the name of each quadrilateral.

a ______________ d ______________

b ______________ e ______________

c ______________ f ______________

7 Use the quadrilaterals in Question 6 to answer the questions.

a Which quadrilaterals have parallel lines? ________

b Which quadrilaterals have perpendicular lines? ________

8 Write the number of sides each polygon has.

a octagon _____

b nonagon_____

c irregular heptagon _____

d dodecagon _____

e irregular decagon _____

f quadrilateral _____

g pentagon _____

h irregular hexagon _____

i heptagon _____

j triangle _____

9 Complete the sentence.

Symmetry is when one ______ of a shape is a ______________ of the other half.

Write three numbers that are symmetrical.

a ______ b ______ c ______

Draw in the lines of symmetry.

a 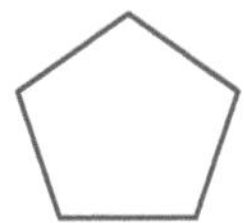 b 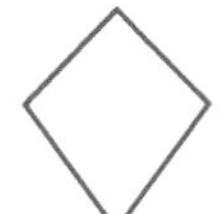 c 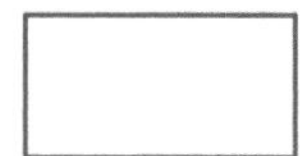 d 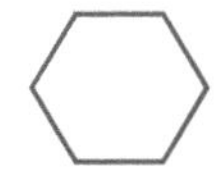 e 

12 Complete the other half of each picture along its axis of symmetry.

a

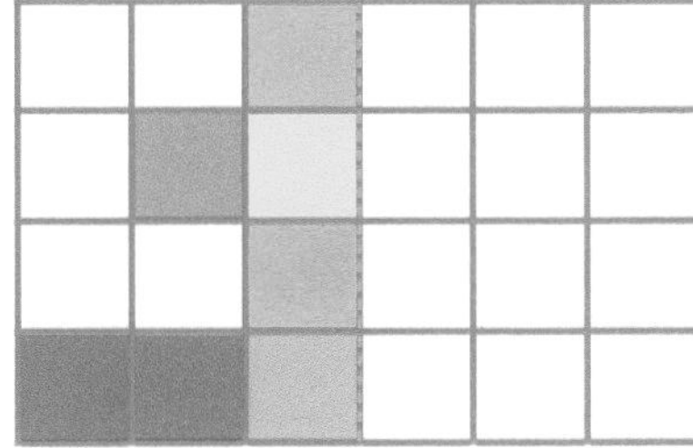

b

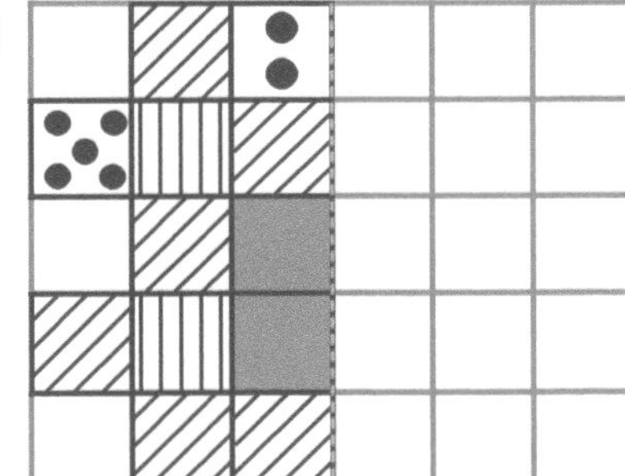

c

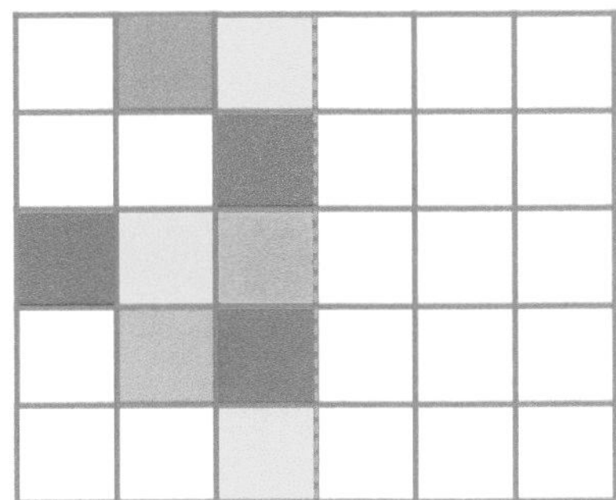

SQUARE CENTIMETERS AND INCHES

When measuring small areas, we use square centimeters (cm^2) or square inches ($in.^2$).

one square centimeter

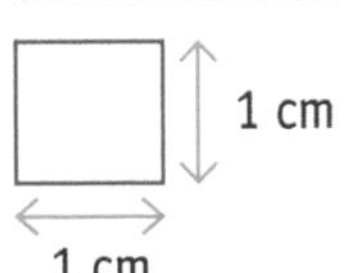

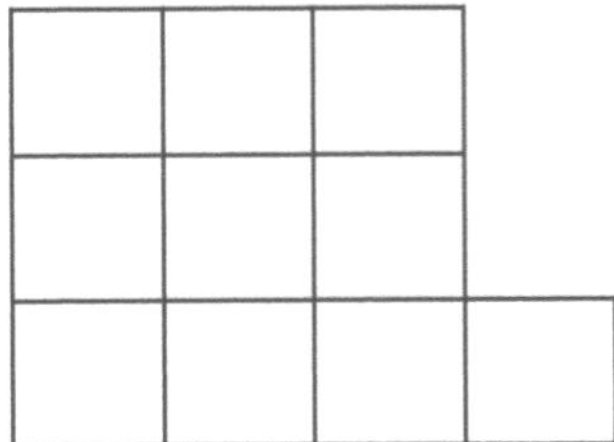

There are 10 square centimeters in this shape.

Area = $10\ cm^2$

one square inch

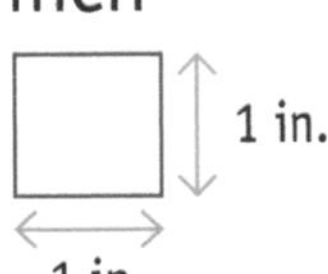

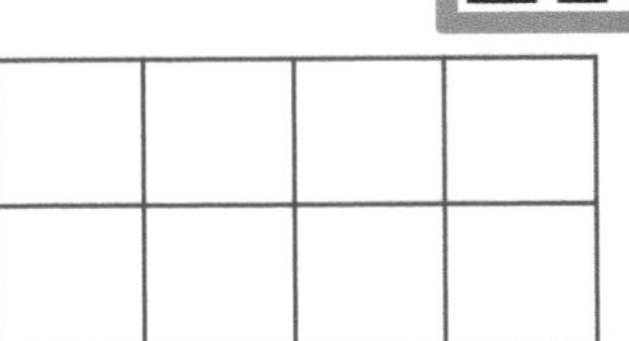

There are 8 square inches in this shape.

Area = $8\ in.^2$

Examples: Find the area of each shape by counting the square inches.

a Area = 6 $in.^2$

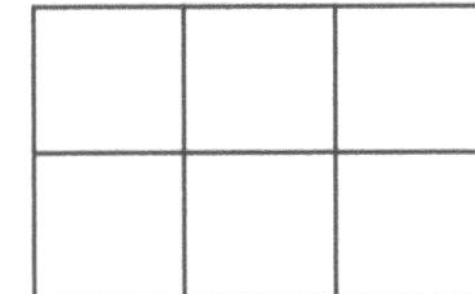

b Area = ______ $in.^2$

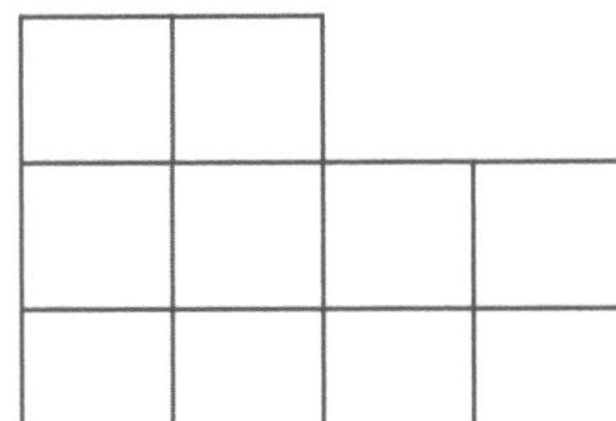

c Area = ______ $in.^2$

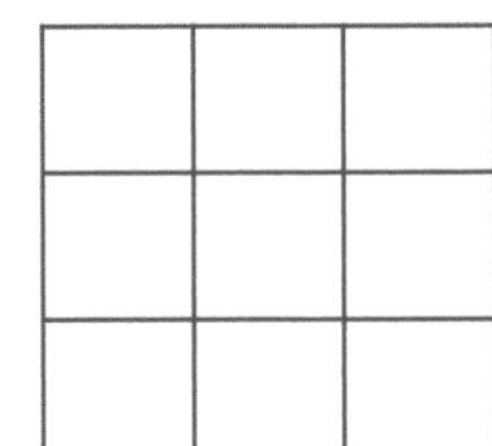

Your turn

Calculate the area of each shape, and record your answer.

☐ = $1\ cm^2$

A = $24\ cm^2$

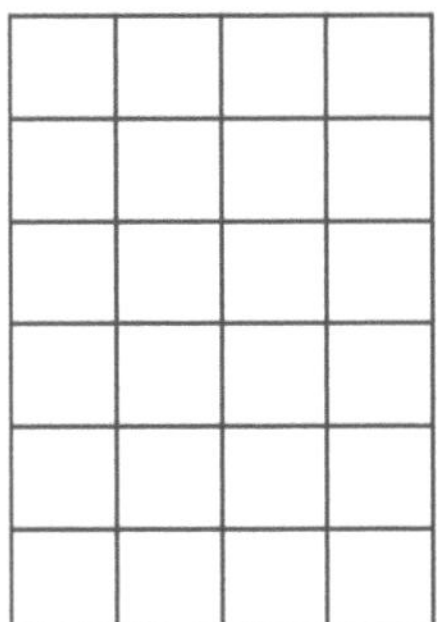

a A = ______

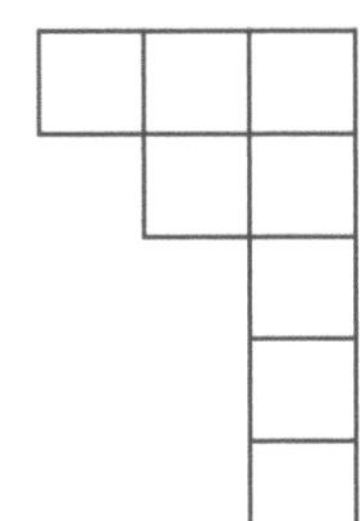

b A = ______

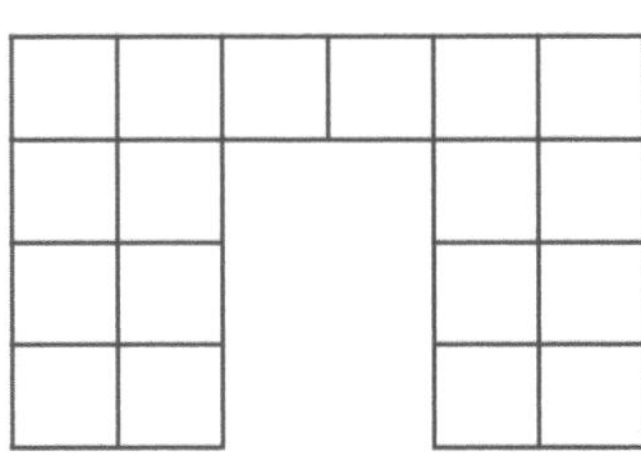

SELF CHECK Mark how you feel

Got it!	Need help...	I don't get it
☐	☐	☐

Check your answers

How many did you get correct? ☐

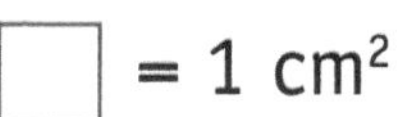

What is the area of each colored shape? ☐ = 1 cm² ◸ = $\frac{1}{2}$ cm²

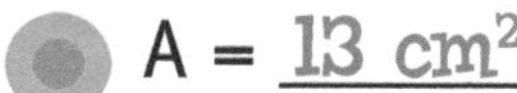

● A = 13 cm²

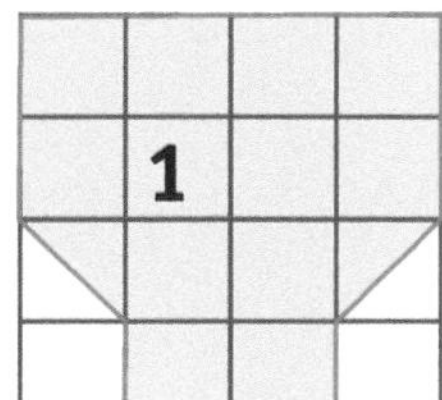

b A = ______

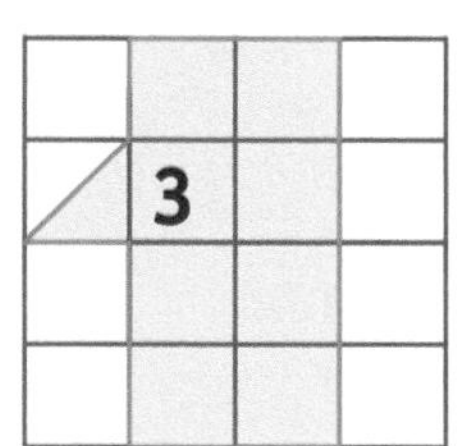

d A = ______

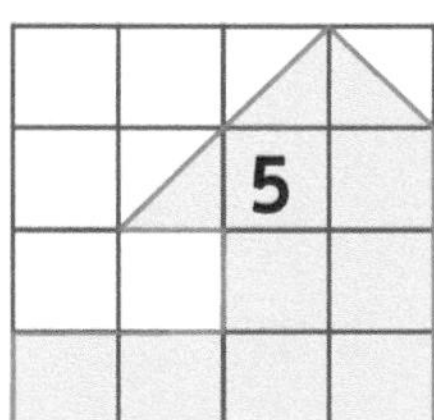

f A = ______

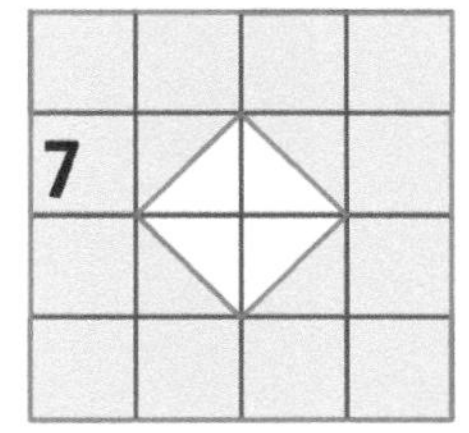

a A = ______

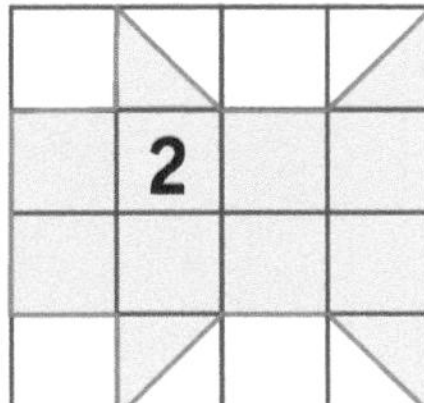

c A = ______

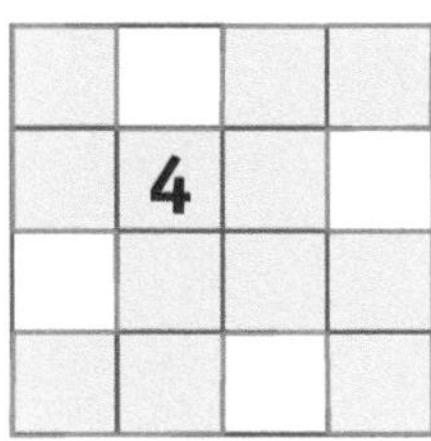

e A = ______

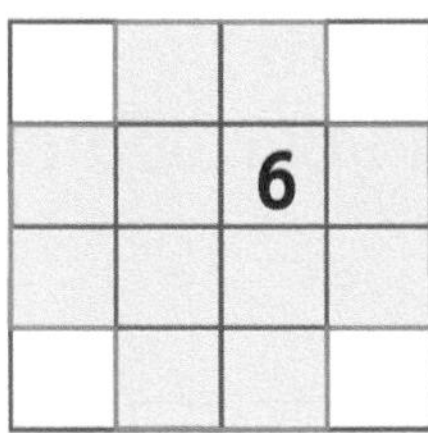

g A = ______

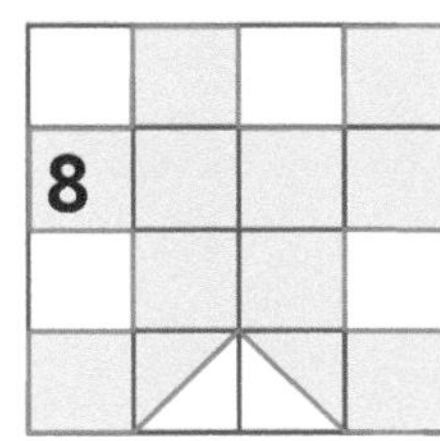

2 Use the shapes in Question 1 to answer the following questions.

● Which shape has the smallest area? 3

a Which shape has the largest area? ______

b Which two shapes have the same area? ______ and ______

c What is the difference in area between Shape 6 and Shape 3? ______

d Shape ______ is 3 cm² larger in area than Shape 8.

e Shape ______ is $\frac{1}{2}$ cm² smaller in area than Shape 2.

f Shape 1 is ______ cm² larger in area than Shape 3.

Draw five different shapes that have an area of 8 sq. in. ☐ = 1 in.²

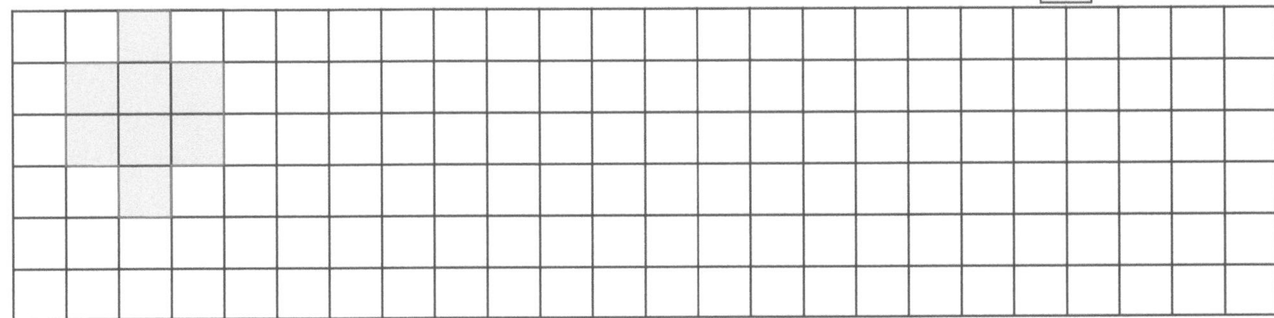

SQUARE METERS AND FEET

Square meters (m^2) and square feet ($ft.^2$) are used to measure larger areas.

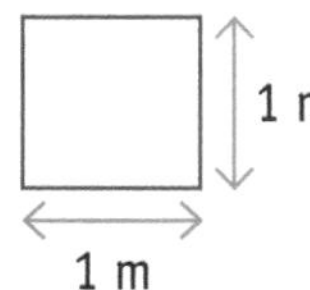

This is 1 square meter.

Area = 1 meter × 1 meter
= 1 m^2

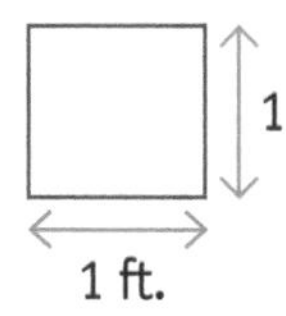

This is 1 square foot.

Area = 1 foot × 1 foot
= 1 $ft.^2$

You would use square feet or square meters to measure the board in your classroom and your bedroom floor.

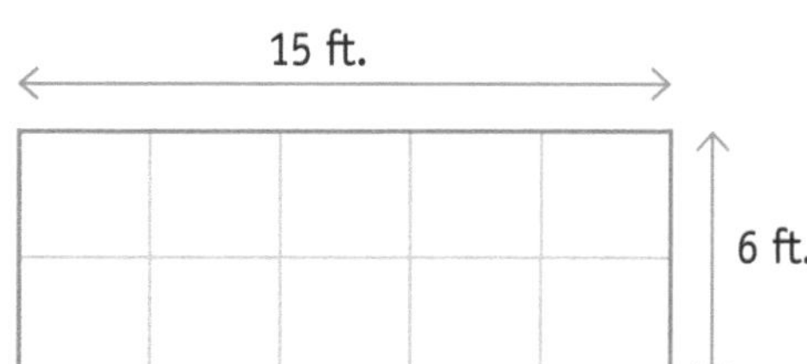

The area of the board is 90 $ft.^2$

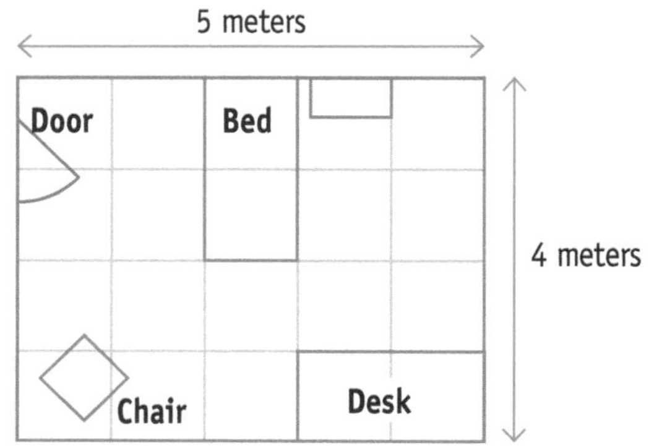

The area of the bedroom floor is 20 m^2.

Examples: Calculate the area. 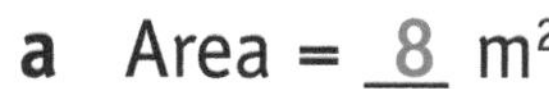 = 1 m^2

a Area = 8 m^2

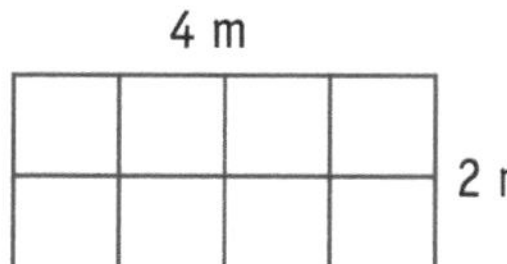

b Area = __ m^2

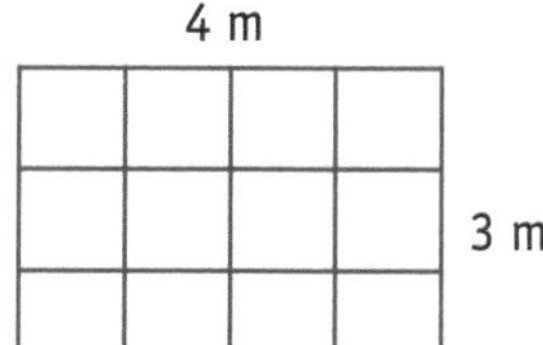

c Area = __ m^2

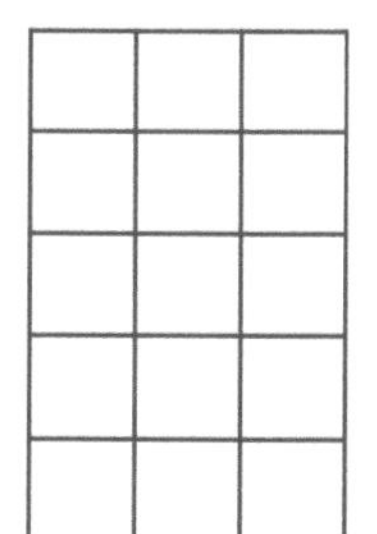

Your turn

Calculate the area in square feet.

A = 5 $ft.^2$

a A = ________

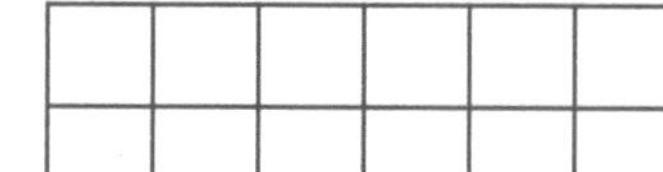

b A = ________

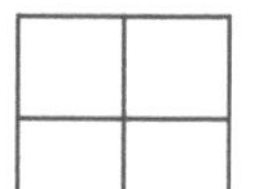

SELF CHECK Mark how you feel

Got it!	Need help...	I don't get it

Check your answers

How many did you get correct?

PRACTICE

Circle the items that would be measured using square meters or square feet instead of square centimeters or square inches.

    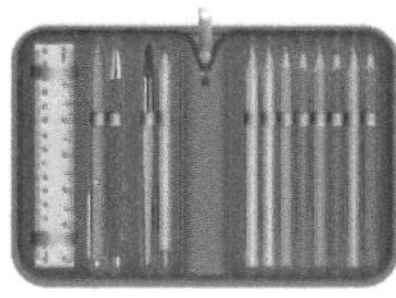  

2 Draw objects that are the given sizes on the grid. Each square is 1 square foot.

- 12 sq. ft.
- **a** 4 sq. ft.
- **b** 6 sq. ft.
- **c** 11 sq. ft.

Jay wants to lay flooring in each room. How much of each product will he need to buy?

1 square equals 1 meter

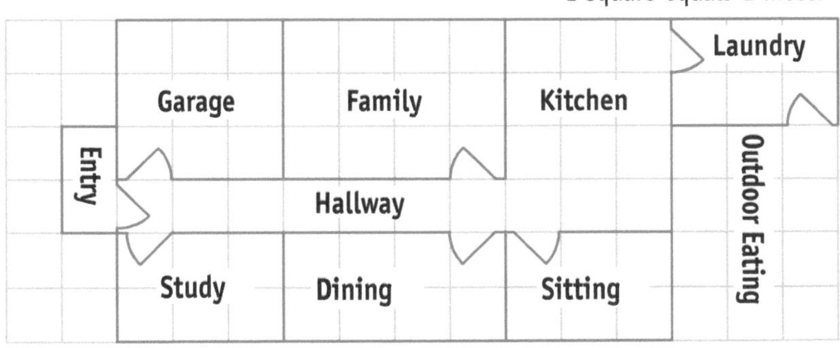

- Carpet for the study $\underline{6\ m^2}$
- **a** Carpet for the family room _____
- **b** Tiles for the kitchen, laundry, and sitting area _____
- **c** Tiles for the outdoor eating area _____

- **d** Vinyl for the garage _____
- **e** Tiles for the entry _____

Jay buys 7 m^2 of tiles for the dining room. Will he have enough?

____

SQUARE KILOMETERS AND MILES

Very large areas are measured in square miles or square kilometers.

National parks can be measured using square miles or square kilometers.

Cities can be measured in square miles or square kilometers.

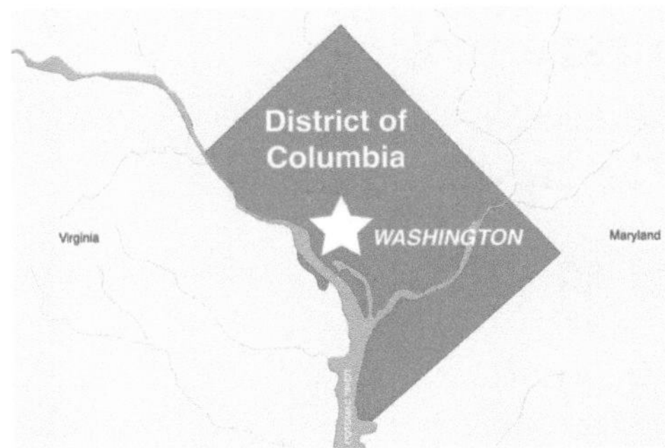

Examples:
Mark the places you would measure in square miles or square kilometers.

- **a** ☑ a country
- **b** ☐ the Amazon Rainforest
- **c** ☐ a football field
- **d** ☐ the Great Barrier Reef
- **e** ☐ a soccer field
- **f** ☐ a basketball court

Name five things you would measure in square miles or square kilometers.

A town ____________________

____

____

____

____

SELF CHECK Mark how you feel

Got it!	Need help...	I don't get it
 ☐	 ☐	 ☐

Check your answers

How many did you get correct? ☐

PRACTICE

1 Find the area (A) of each shape.

A = 11 sq. mi.

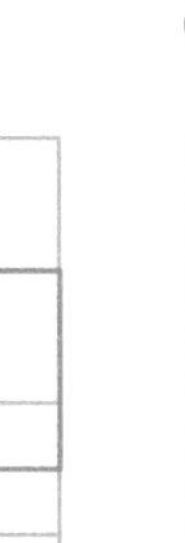

a A = ___ km²

b A = ___ sq. mi.

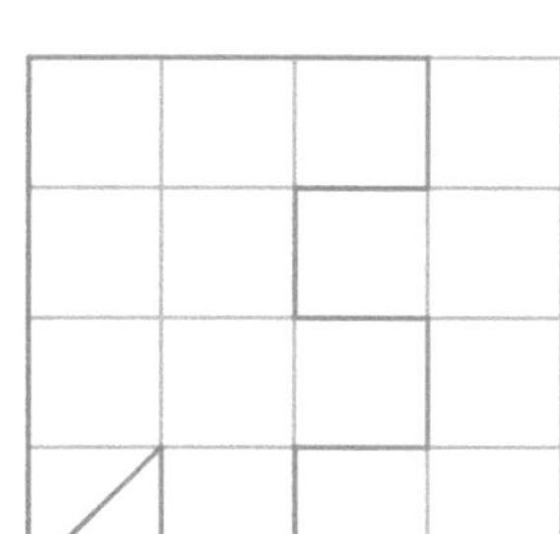

c A = ___ km²

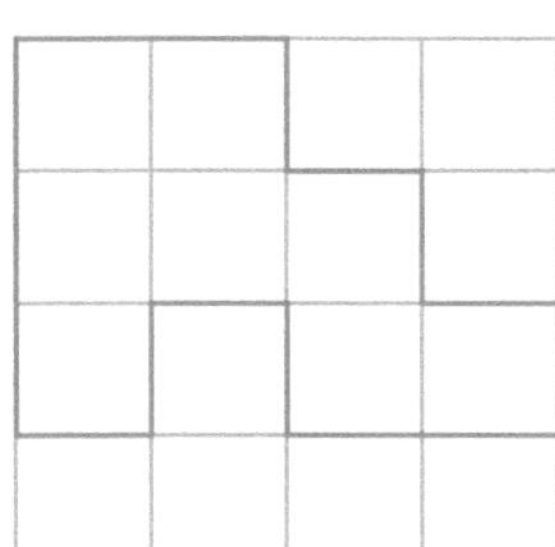

d A = ___ sq. mi.

e A = ___ km²

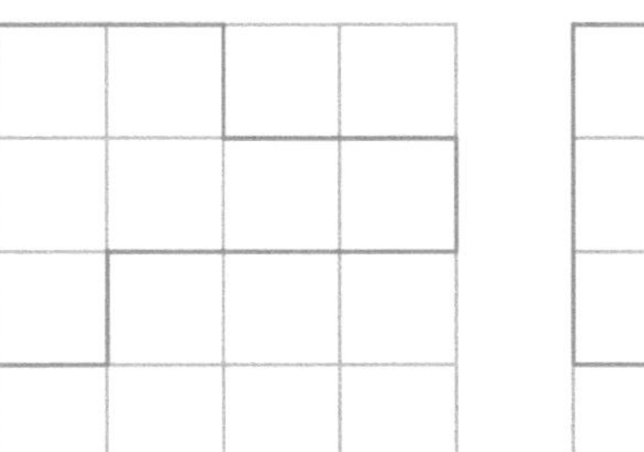

f A = ___ sq. mi.

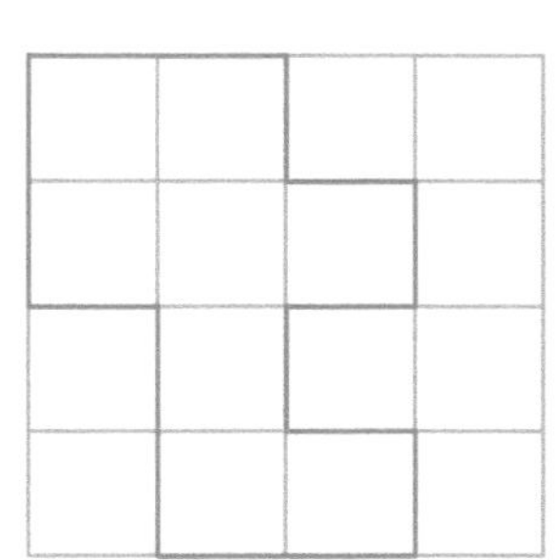

g A = ___ km²

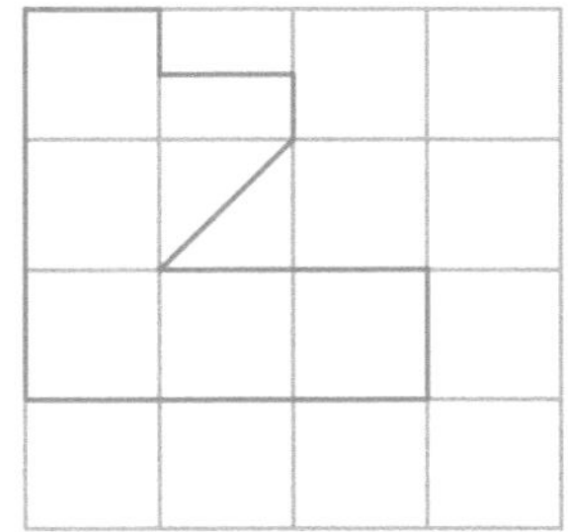

2 Use the map to answer the following questions.

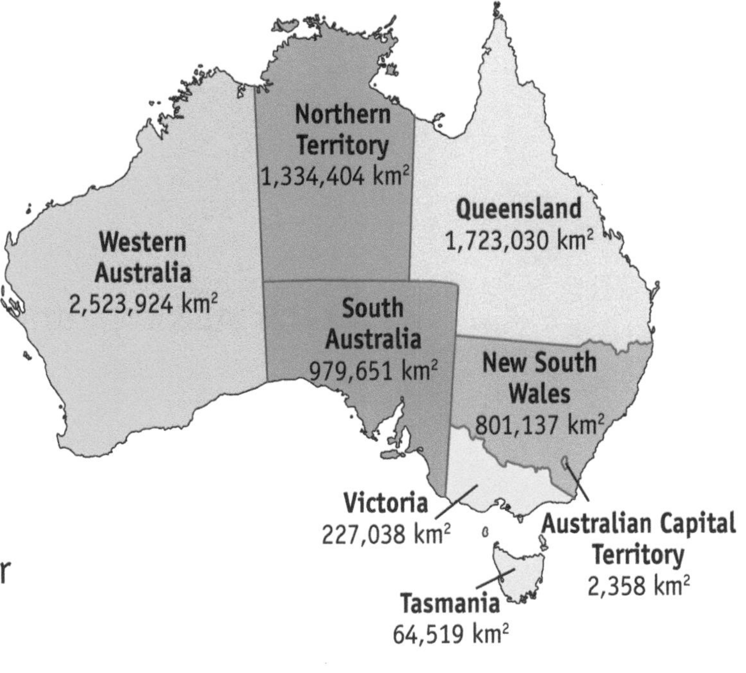

a Which state or territory has the smallest area?

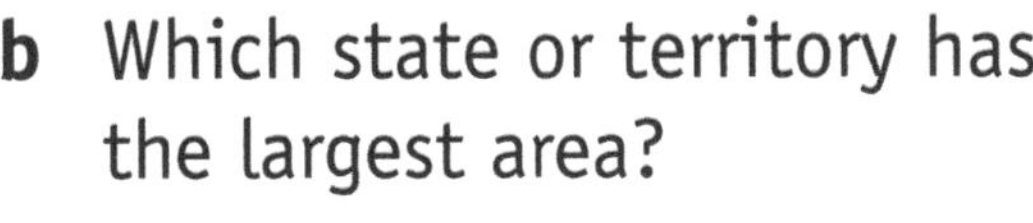

b Which state or territory has the largest area?

____

c Which state or territory is larger in area than Queensland?

____

AREA – USING MULTIPLICATION

You can use multiplication to calculate the area of squares and rectangles.

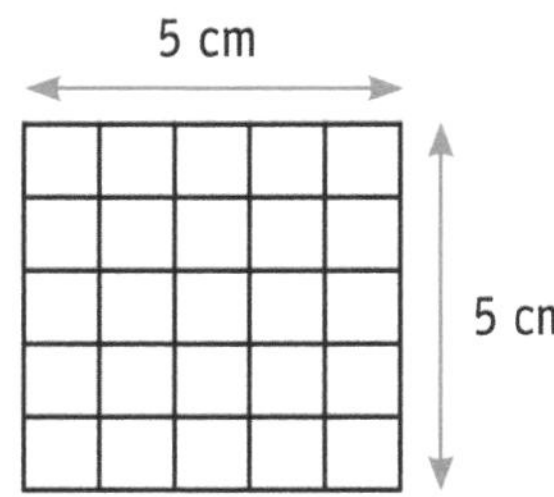

Area = length × width
= 5 cm × 5 cm
= 25 cm^2

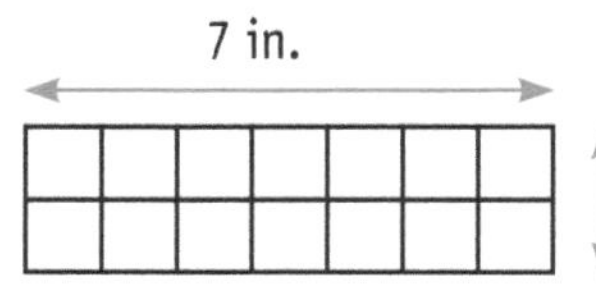

Area = length × width
= 2 in. × 7 in.
= 14 in.^{2}

Examples: Fill in the gaps.

a Area = length × width
= 2 cm × 4 cm
= 8 cm^2

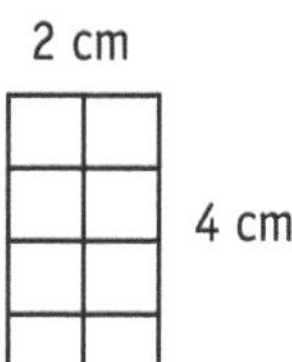

b Area = ________ × width
= 3 in. × ______
= ___ sq. in.

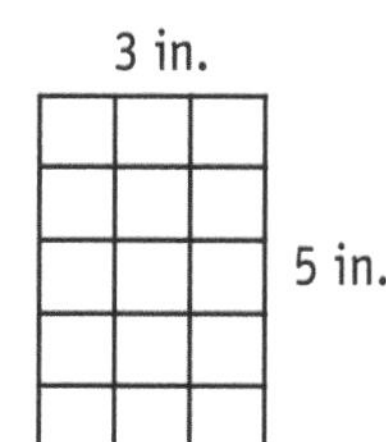

Your turn

Write the missing information.

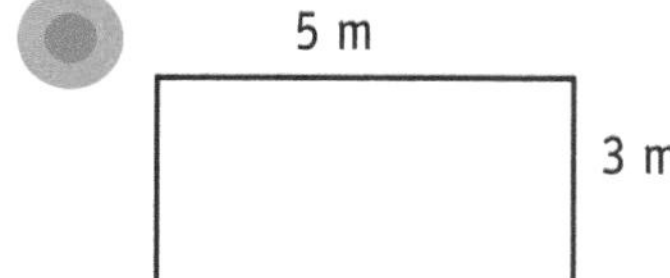

Area = length × width
= 5 m × 3 m
= 15 m^2

a

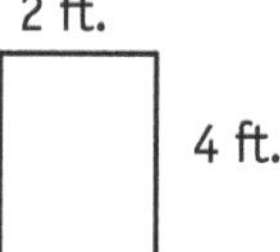

Area = ________ × ________
= _____ × _____
= ___ ft.^{2}

SELF CHECK Mark how you feel

Got it!	Need help...	I don't get it
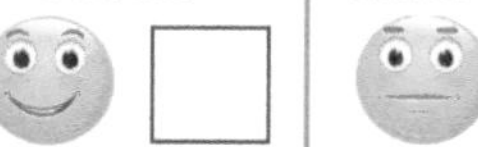 		

Check your answers

How many did you get correct?

PRACTICE

1 Calculate the areas using multiplication.

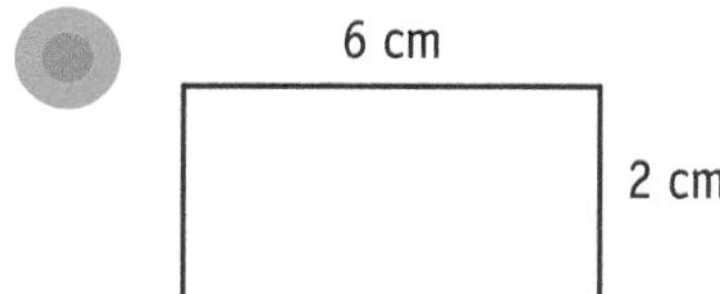

(Example) Rectangle: 6 cm by 2 cm

Area = length × width
= 6 cm × 2 cm
= 12 cm^2

a Rectangle: 5 ft. by 4 ft.

Area = ______ × ______
= ______ × ______
= ______ sq. ft.

b Rectangle: 6 m by 1 m

Area = ______ × ______
= ______ × ______
= ______ m^2

c Rectangle: 4 in. by 3 in.

Area = ______ × ______
= ______ × ______
= ______ in.^{2}

2 Calculate the areas using multiplication.

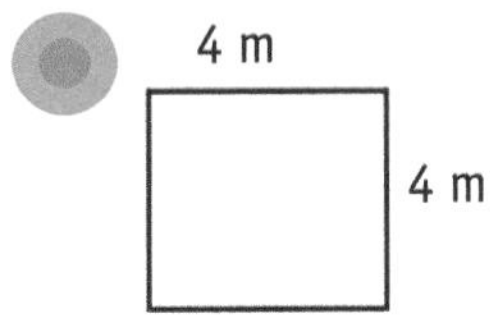

(Example) Square: 4 m by 4 m

A = l × w
= 4 m × 4 m
= 16 m^2

a Square: 7 in. by 7 in.

A = ______ × ______
= ______ × ______
= ______ in.^{2}

b Rectangle: 3 cm by 6 cm

A = ______ × ______
= ______ × ______
= ______ cm^2

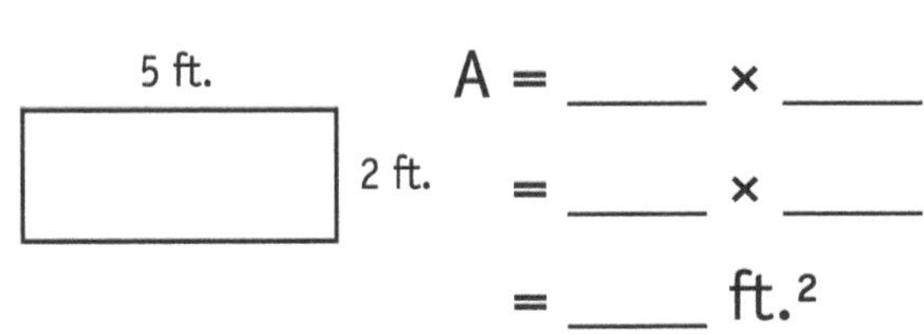

c Rectangle: 5 ft. by 2 ft.

A = ______ × ______
= ______ × ______
= ______ ft.^{2}

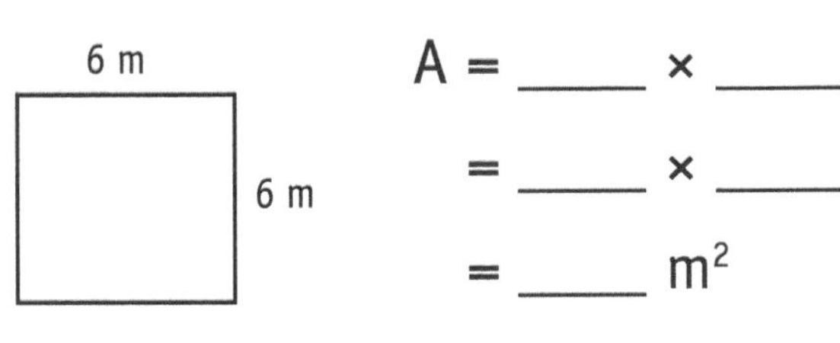

d Square: 6 m by 6 m

A = ______ × ______
= ______ × ______
= ______ m^2

e Square: 1 in. by 1 in.

A = ______ × ______
= ______ × ______
= ______ in.^{2}

PERIMETER

The distance around the outside of a shape is the perimeter (P). To find the perimeter, add the lengths of all the sides.

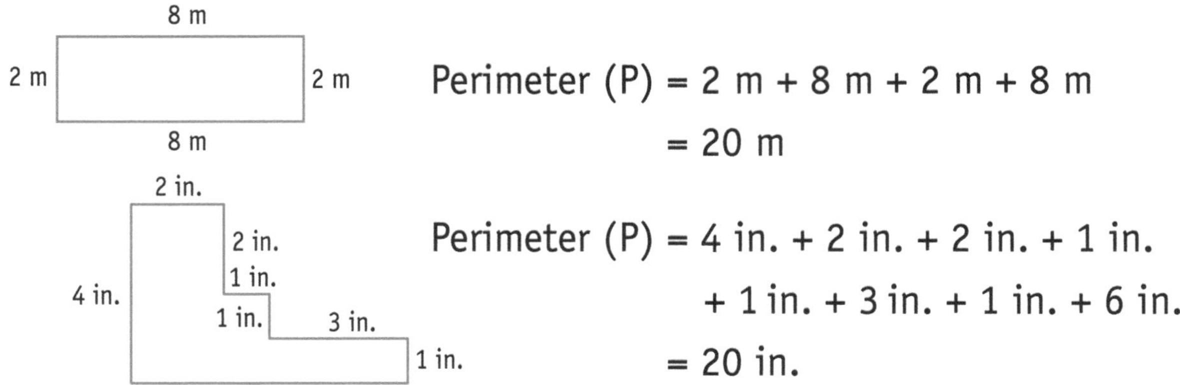

Perimeter (P) = 2 m + 8 m + 2 m + 8 m
= 20 m

Perimeter (P) = 4 in. + 2 in. + 2 in. + 1 in.
+ 1 in. + 3 in. + 1 in. + 6 in.
= 20 in.

Examples: Calculate the perimeter.

a

2 cm, 2 cm, 1 cm, 1 cm, 4 cm, 1 cm, 3 cm, 4 cm

P = 4 cm + 2 cm + 2 cm + 1 cm
+ 1 cm + 1 cm + 3 cm + 4 cm
= 18 cm

b

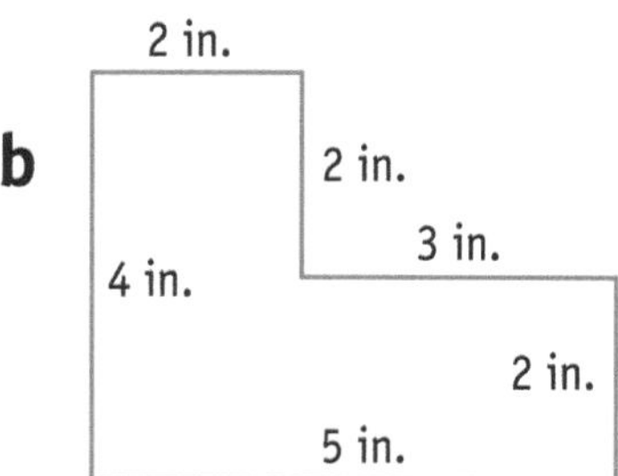

P = 4 in. + 2 in. + 2 in.
+ 3 in. + 2 in. + 5 in.
= ____ in.

Your turn

Find the perimeter.

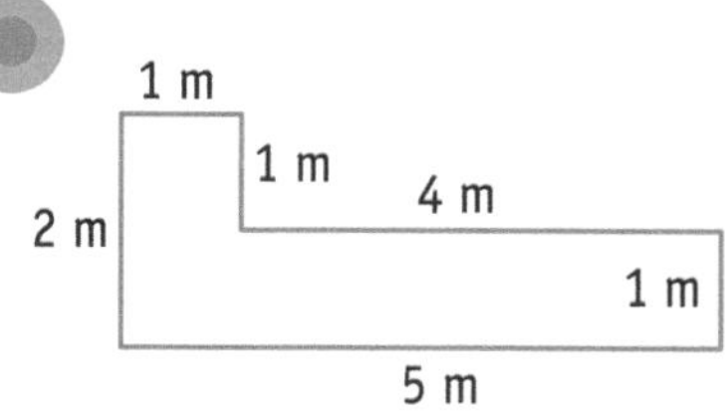

P = 2 + 1 + 1 + 4 + 1 + 5
= 14 m

a

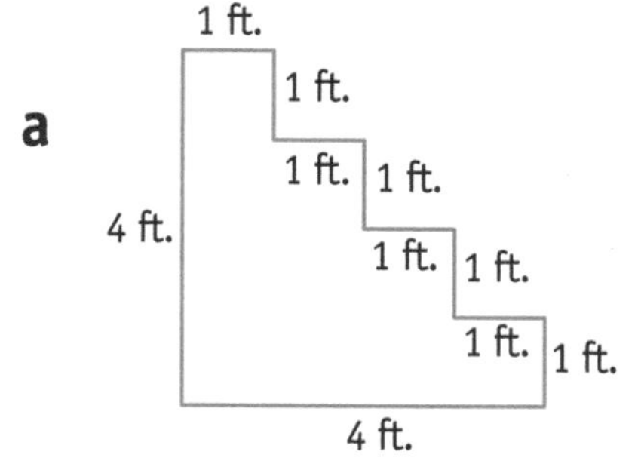

P = __ + __ + __ + __ + __
+ __ + __ + __ + __ + __
= ____ ft.

SELF CHECK Mark how you feel		
Got it!	Need help...	I don't get it

Check your answers
How many did you get correct?

PRACTICE

1 Calculate the perimeters.

2 m

P = 2 + 2 + 2 + 2

= 8 m

a

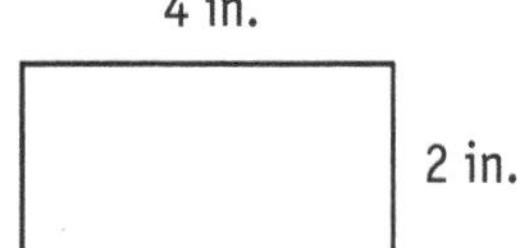

P = ___ + ___ + ___ + ___

= ___ in.

b

2 cm
1 cm
1 cm
4 cm

P = ___ + ___ + ___ + ___

= ___ cm

c

P = ___ + ___ + ___ + ___ + ___

= ___ ft.

d

3 cm
1.5 cm

P = ___ + ___ + ___ + ___

= ___ cm

e

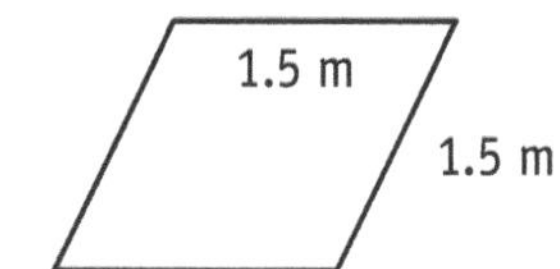

P = ___ + ___ + ___ + ___

= ___ m

f

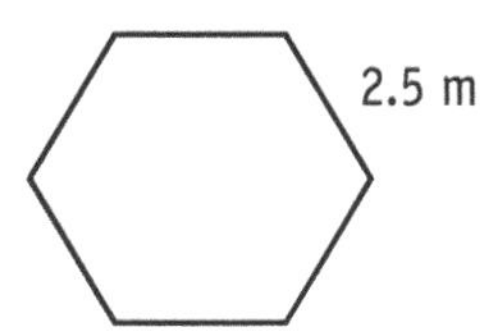

P = ___ + ___ + ___ + ___ + ___ + ___

= ___ m

g

2 in.
2 in.
1 in.
1 in.
3 in.
1 in.
5 in.
6 in.
1 in.
6 in.

P = ___ + ___ + ___ + ___ + ___ +

___ + ___ + ___ + ___ + ___

= ___ in.

h

7 ft.
1 ft.
1 ft.
4 ft.
3 ft.
3 ft.
3 ft.
3 ft.
4 ft.
1 ft.
3 ft.
1 ft.

P = ___ + ___ + ___ + ___ + ___ + ___

\+ ___ + ___ + ___ + ___ + ___ + ___

= ___ ft.

AREA REVIEW

1 What is the area of each colored shape? □ = 1 cm^2

a A = _______ b A = _______ c A = _______ d A = _______

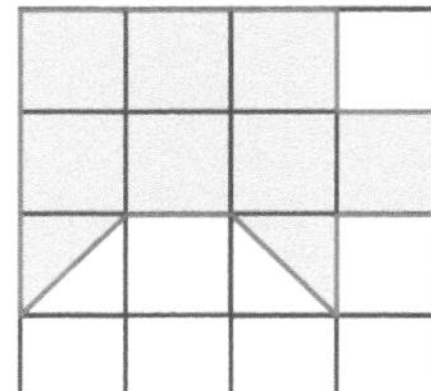
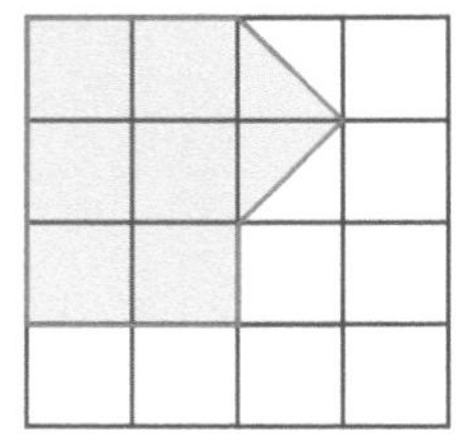
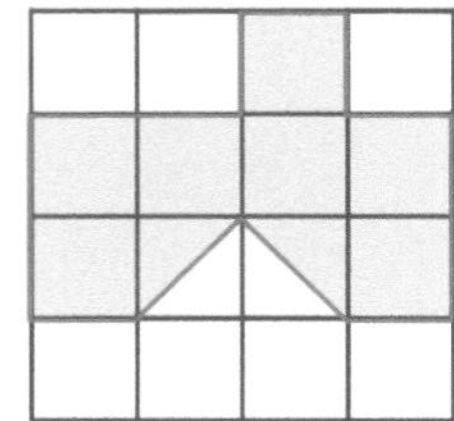
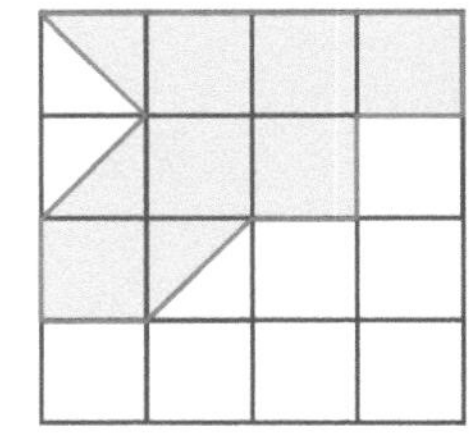

2 Draw five different shapes that have an area of 12 sq. in. □ = 1 $in.^2$

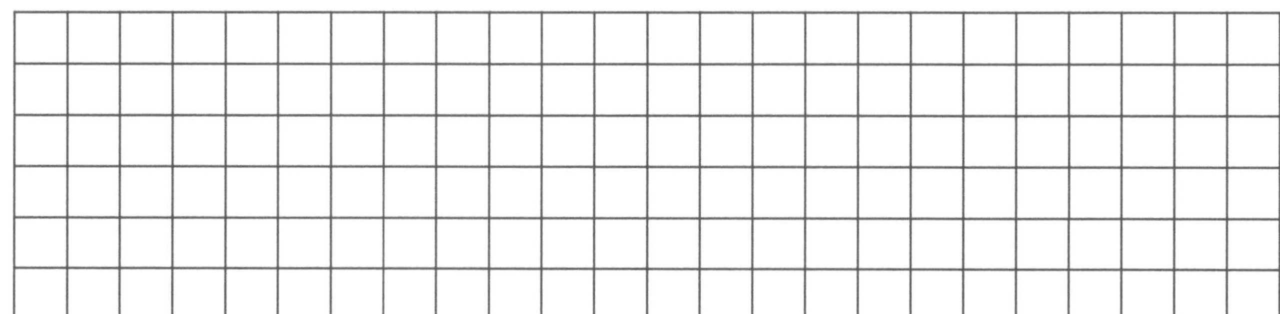

3 Mark the things you would measure using square inches or square centimeters.

a □ sticky note
b □ backyard
c □ envelope
d □ book cover
e □ large desktop
f □ garage door
g □ phone case
h □ watch face

4 If □ = 1 m^2, find the area (A) of each shape.

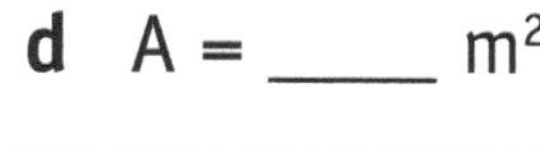

a A = _____ m^2 b A = _____ m^2 c A = _____ m^2 d A = _____ m^2

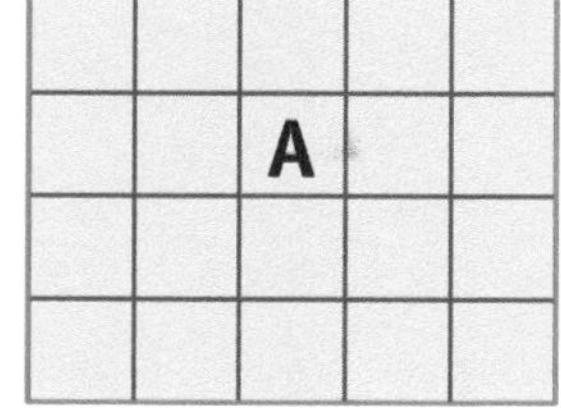

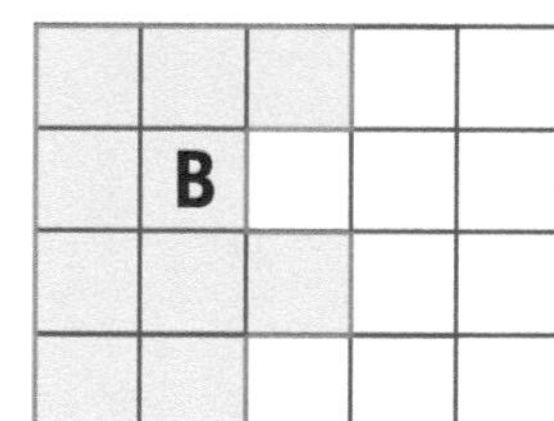

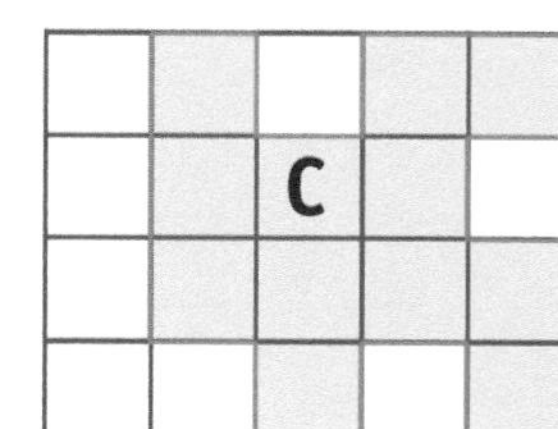

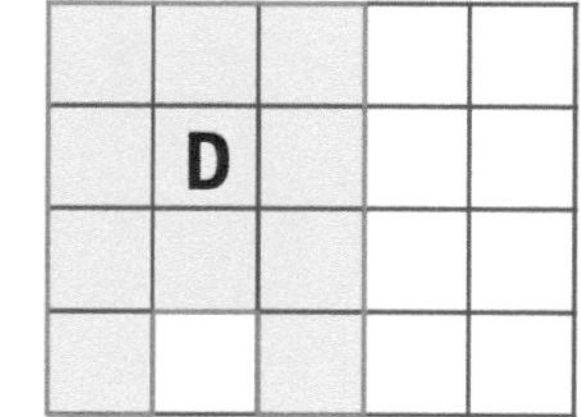

e A = _____ m^2 **f** A = _____ m^2 **g** A = _____ m^2 **h** A = _____ m^2

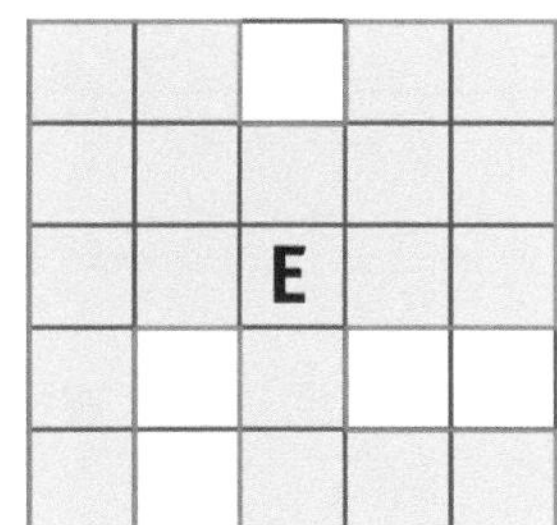

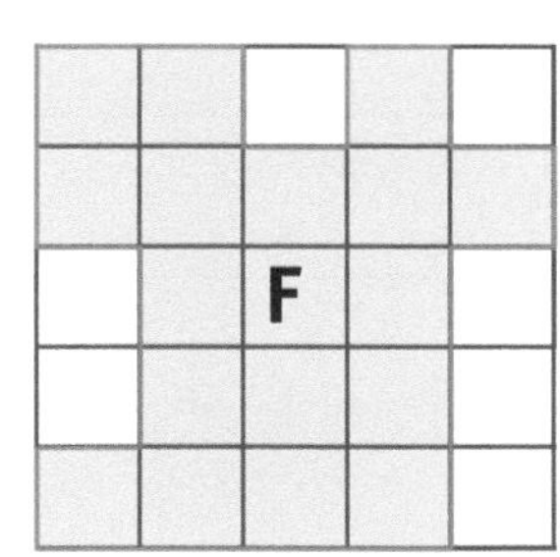

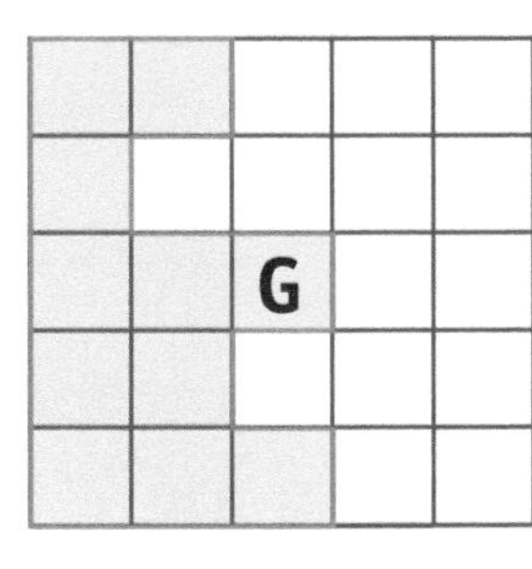

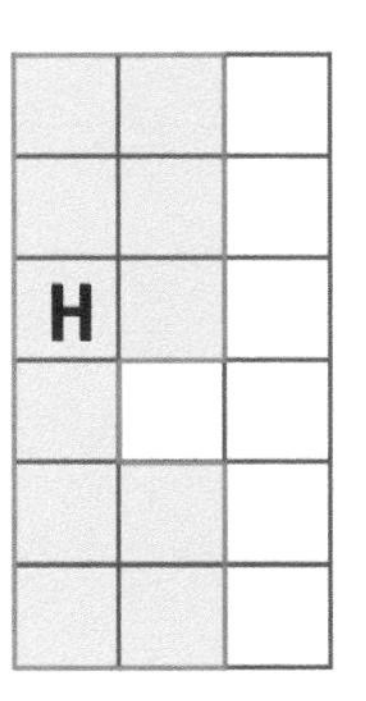

5 Use the shapes in Question 4 to answer the following questions.

a Which shapes have an area of 11 m^2? _________

b Which shapes have an area larger than 12 m^2? _________

c Which shapes have an area of 20 m^2? _________

d Which shape has an area of 18 m^2? _________

e What is the difference in area between Shape E and Shape B? _________

6 How many square feet of tiles will Christian need for these spaces?

☐ = 1 $ft.^2$

a Pool (floor only) _________

b Kitchen _________

c Barbecue area _________

d Family room _________

e Hallway _________

f Bedroom _________

g Office _________

h Entry _________

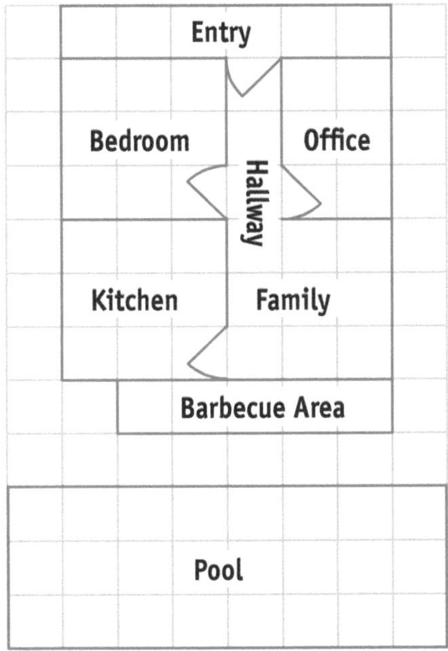

7 How many square feet of tiles altogether does Christian need?

____

REVIEW

8 Name five things measured using square kilometers or square miles.

___

___

9 Look at this map of Arizona. What is the difference in area between the following counties in km^2?

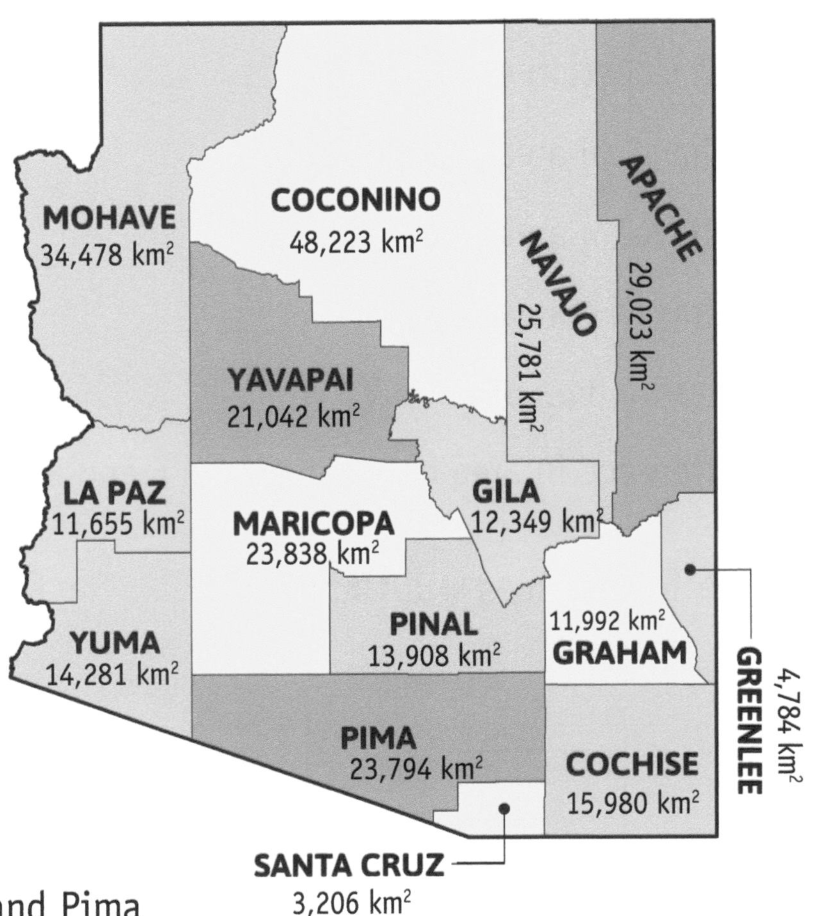

a Coconino and Pima

___

b Mohave and Apache

___

c Yuma and Santa Cruz

___

d Maricopa and Greenlee ___

Calculate the areas using multiplication.

a

1 m

1 m

Area = ________ × ________

= ________ × ________

= ________ m^2

b

7 in.

1 in.

Area = ________ × ________

= ________ × ________

= ________ in.²

c

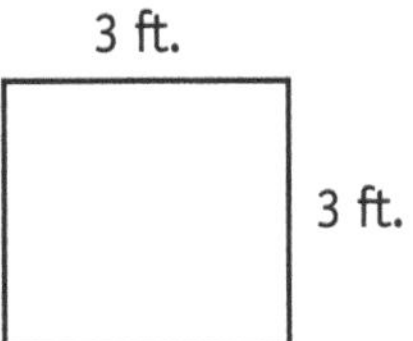

Area = ________ × ________

= ________ × ________

= ________ ft.²

d

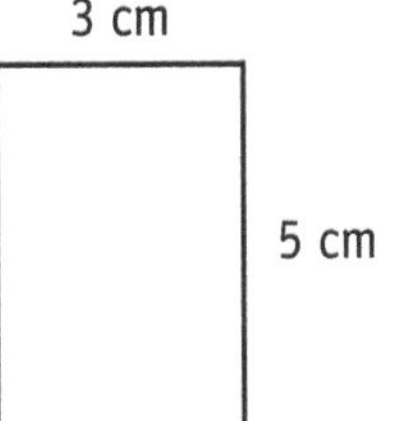

Area = ________ × ________

= ________ × ________

= ________ cm^2

e

8 ft.

2 ft.

A = ________ × ________

= ________ × ________

= ________ ft.²

f

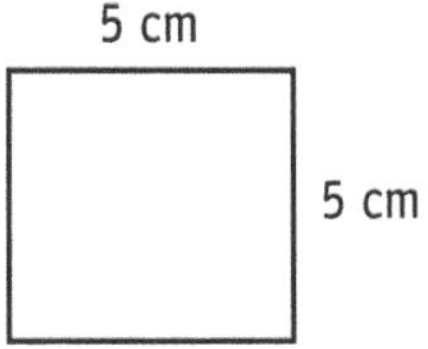

A = ________ × ________

= ________ × ________

= ________ cm^2

g

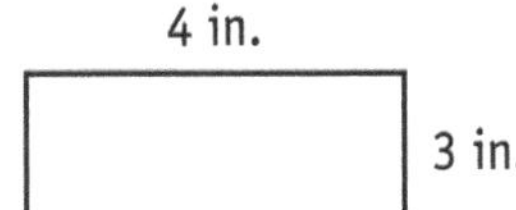

A = ________ × ________

= ________ × ________

= ________ in.²

h

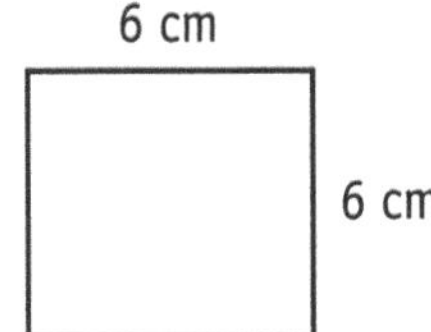

A = ________ × ________

= ________ × ________

= ________ cm^2

REVIEW

Calculate the perimeters.

a

3 m

5 m

P = ____________________

= ________ m

b

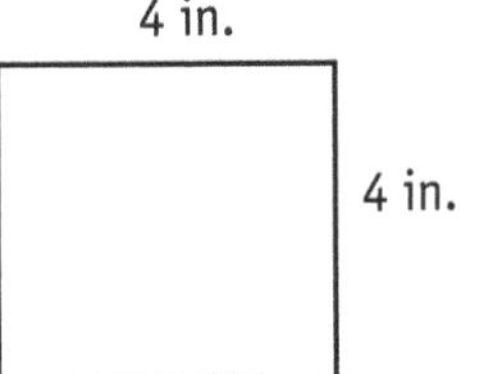

P = ____________________

= ________ in.

c

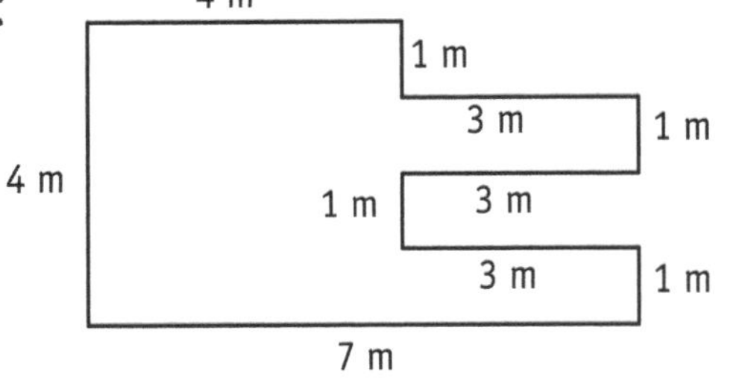

P = ____________________

____

= ________ m

d

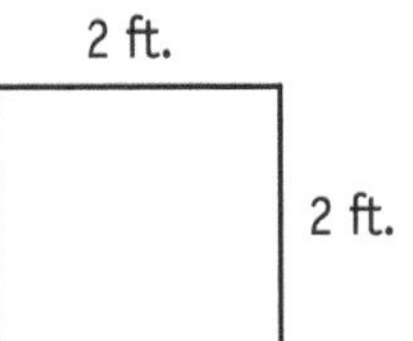

P = ____________________

= ________ ft.

e

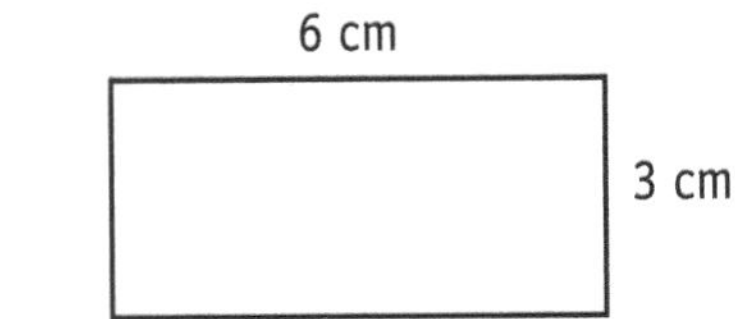

P = ____________________

= ________ cm

f

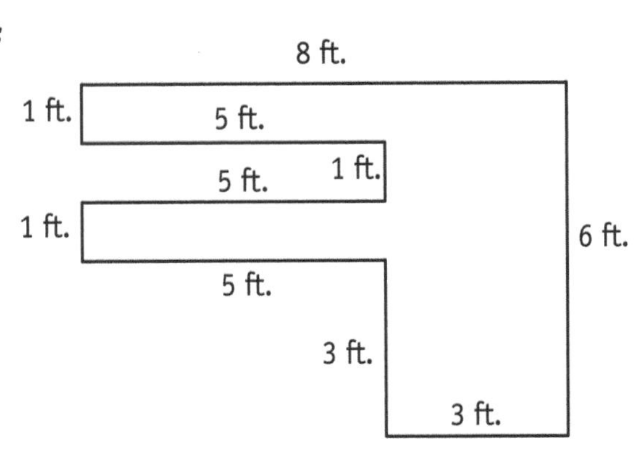

P = ____________________

____

= ________ ft.

g

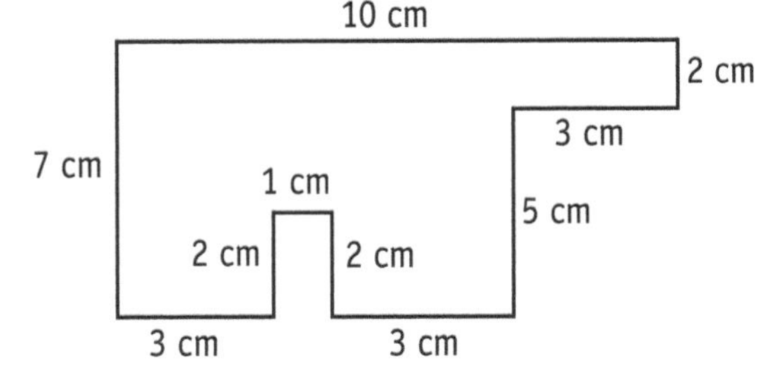

P = ____________________

____

= ________ cm

VOLUME

Volume is the amount of space an object takes up.
Volume is measured in cubic units.
The symbol for volume is V.

This is one cubic centimeter, 1 cm^3. 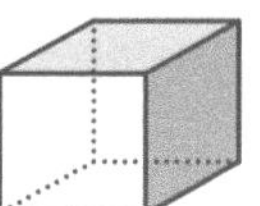

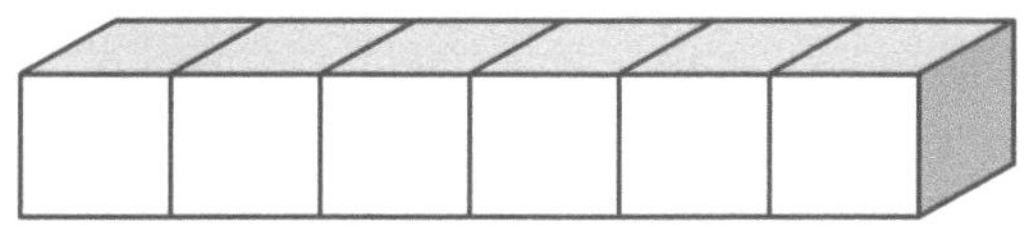

This object is made from 6 one-centimeter cubes. It has a volume of 6 cm^3.

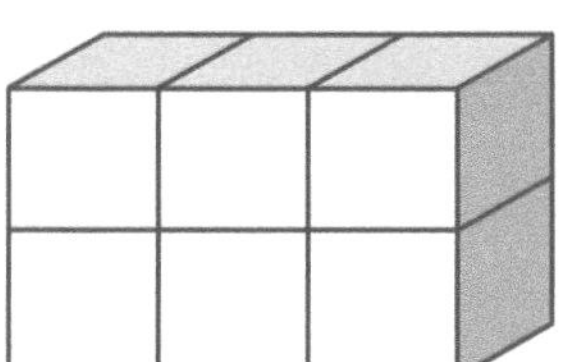

This object is also made from 6 one-centimeter cubes It has a volume of 6 cm^3.

Examples: What is the volume? 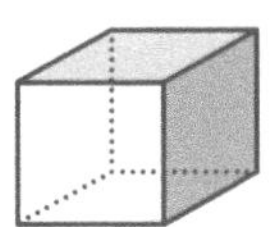 = 1 cubic inch (cu. in.)

a

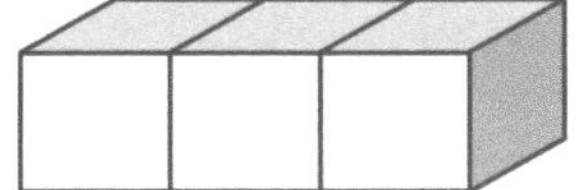

V = ________ cubic inches

= ________ cu. in.

b

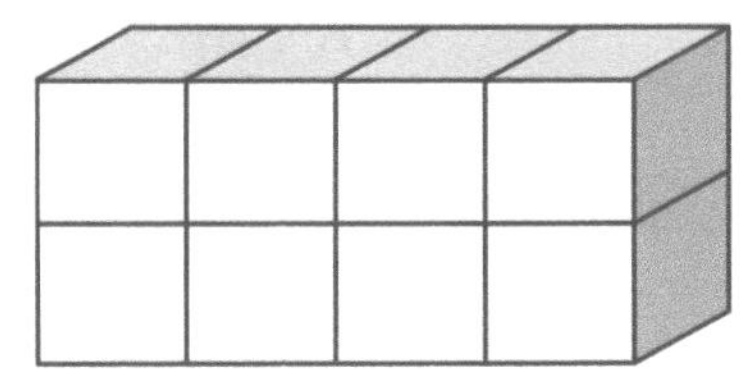

V = ________ cubic inches

= ________ cu. in.

Your turn

What is the volume of each object?

6 cm^3

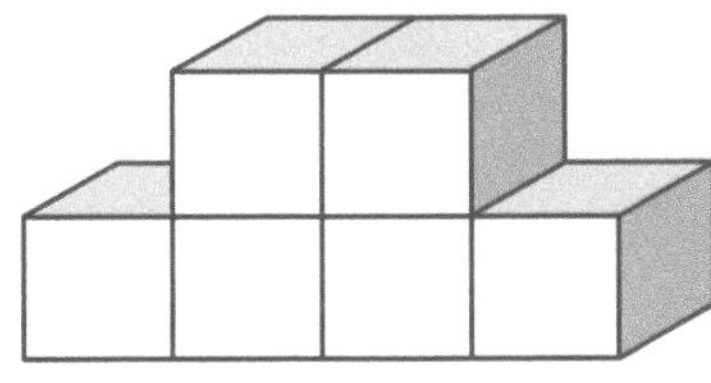

a ______ cu. in.

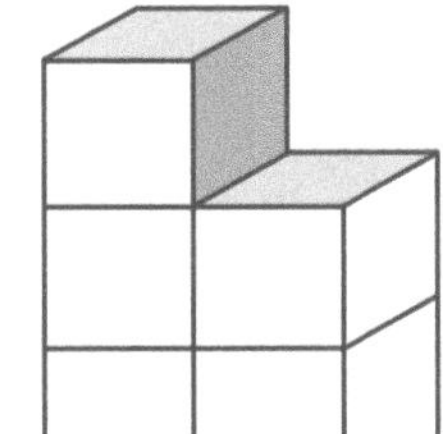
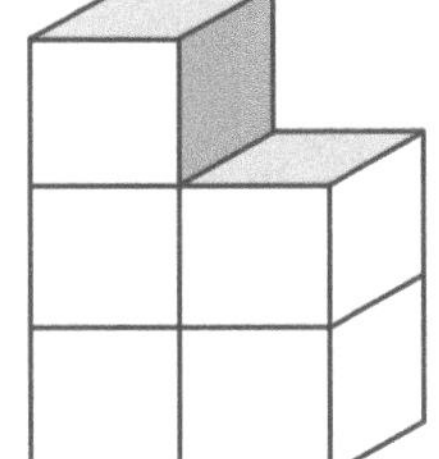

b ______ cm^3

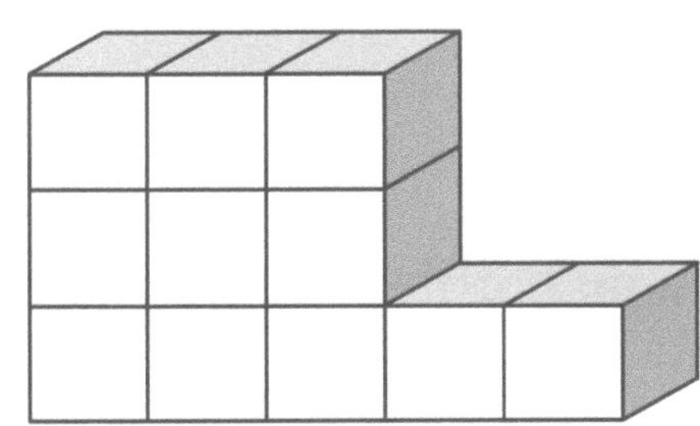

SELF CHECK Mark how you feel

Got it!	Need help...	I don't get it

Check your answers
How many did you get correct?

PRACTICE

1 What is the volume? Circle the correct answer.

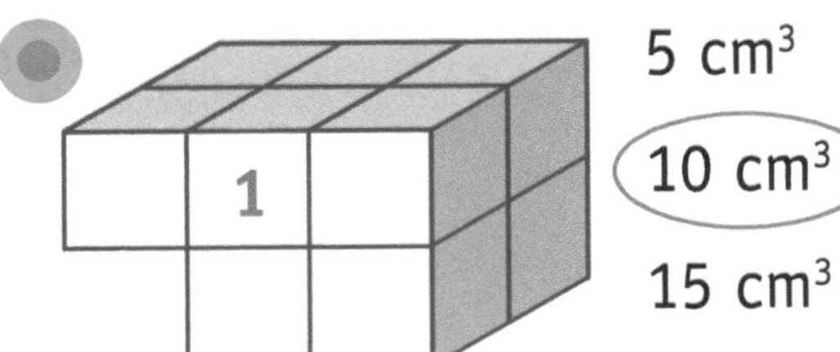

5 cm^3
10 cm^3
15 cm^3

a

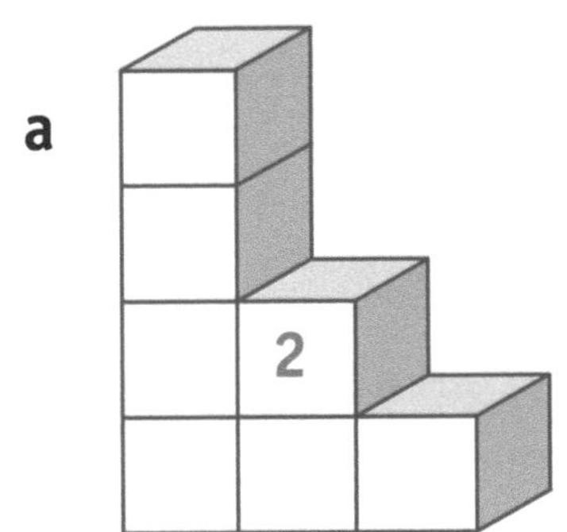

5 cu. in.
6 cu. in.
7 cu. in.

b

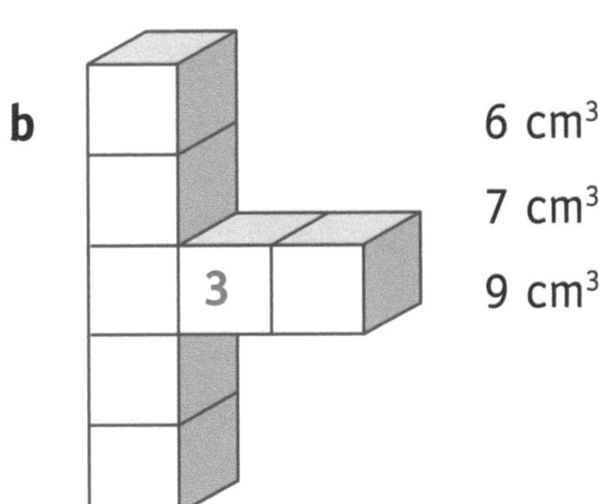

6 cm^3
7 cm^3
9 cm^3

c

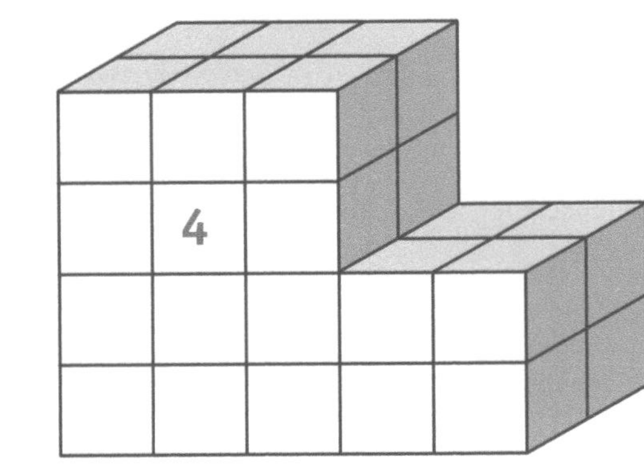

16 cu. in. 20 cu. in. 32 cu. in.

d

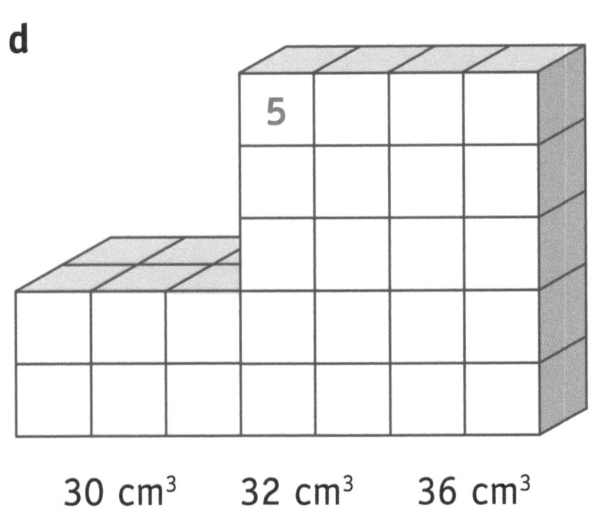

30 cm^3 32 cm^3 36 cm^3

2 What is the difference in volume between:

a objects 1 and 3? ________

b objects 5 and 1? ________

3 Which object has the greater volume, object 2 or object 4?

____

CAPACITY

Capacity is the amount of liquid a container can hold.

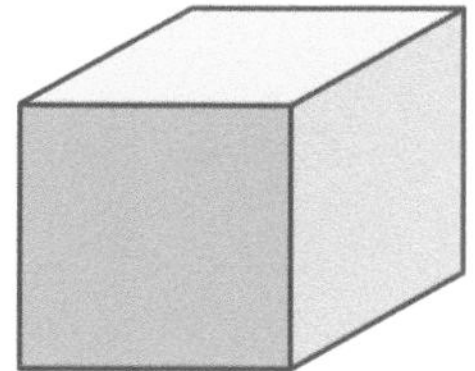

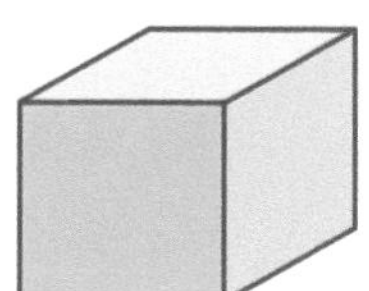

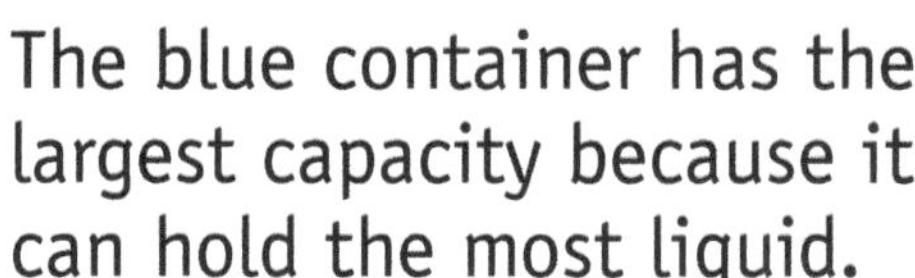

The blue container has the largest capacity because it can hold the most liquid.

The green container has the smallest capacity because it can hold the least liquid.

Glass A

Glass B

Glass A has more water in it than Glass B. But Glass B can hold more water than Glass A, so it has a larger capacity.

Examples: Circle the container with the greater capacity.

a

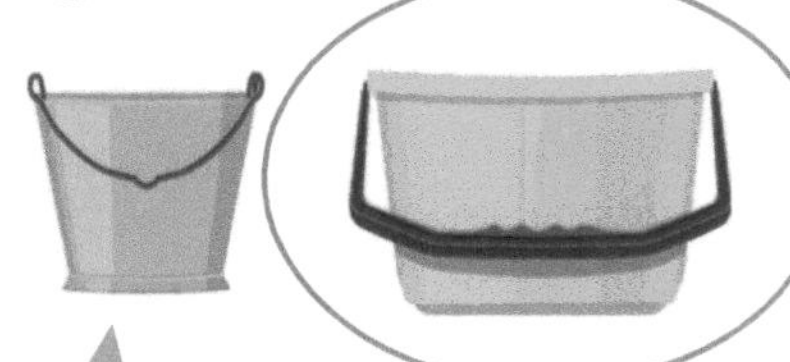

b

c

Your turn

Draw a similar object with a smaller capacity.

a

b

SELF CHECK Mark how you feel		
Got it!	Need help...	I don't get it
 ☐	 ☐	 ☐

Check your answers

How many did you get correct? ☐

PRACTICE

1 Number the containers to order them from largest capacity (5) to smallest capacity (1).

5 

a

b

c

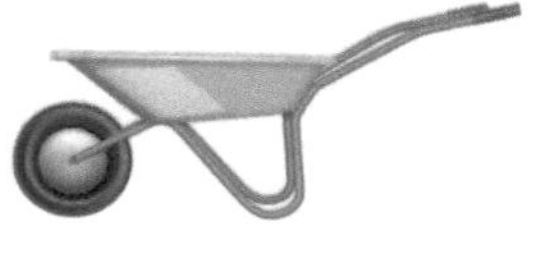

2 What is the total capacity of each set of containers?

 10 L

a ________

b ________

c ________

2 L 5 L 2 L 5 L

d ________

e ________

LITERS AND GALLONS

Liters (L) and gallons (gal.) are used to measure liquids.

1 liter = 1,000 millimeters (mL)

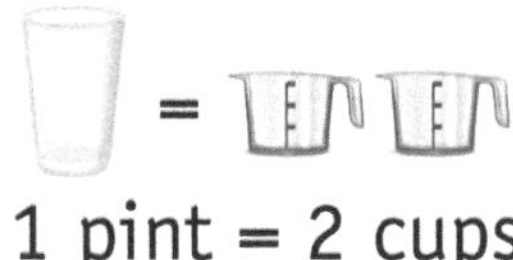

1 pint = 2 cups

1 quart = 2 pints = 4 cups

1 gallon = 4 quarts = 8 pints = 16 cups

Examples: How many liters or gallons can each container hold?

a 2 L **b** ___ gal. **c** ___ L **d** ___ gal.

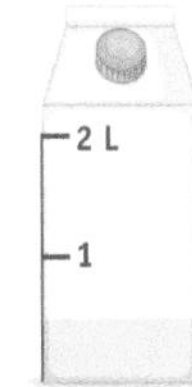

Your turn

Write the equivalent measurements.

2 L = 2,000 mL

a 6 pints = ________ cups

b 9,000 mL = ________ L

c 3 quarts = ______ pints

d 8 liters = ________ mL

e 12 cups = _______ pints

f 500 L = ________ mL

g 2 quarts = _______ cups

SELF CHECK Mark how you feel		
Got it! ☐	Need help... ☐	I don't get it ☐

Check your answers
How many did you get correct? ☐

PRACTICE

Write the equivalent measurements.

- 7 liters 7,000 mL

a 4,000 mL = ________ L

b 8 cups = ________ pints

c 15 L = ________ mL

d 2 gal. = ________ quarts

e 2 gal. = ________ pints

List five containers that would hold less than 1 gallon.

juice box ____________________

List five containers that would hold at least 1 liter.

bucket ____________________

What is the total capacity of each group of containers?

- 6 L

a _____ gal.

b _____ L

Color each container to show 2 liters.

a

b

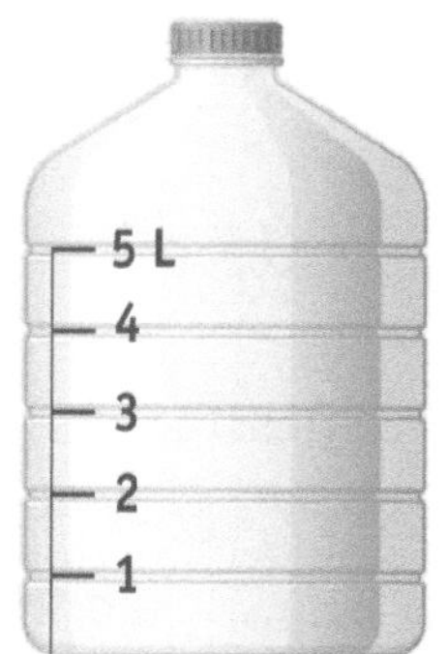

c

6 What amount of liquid is in each container?

3 gal. | b _____ gal. | d _____ gal. | f _____ gal.

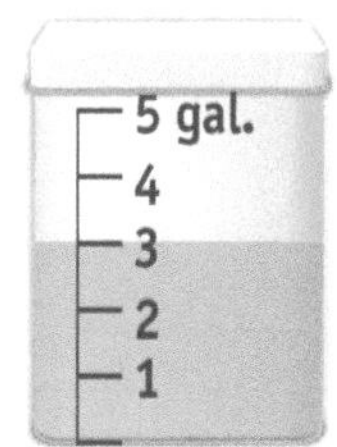

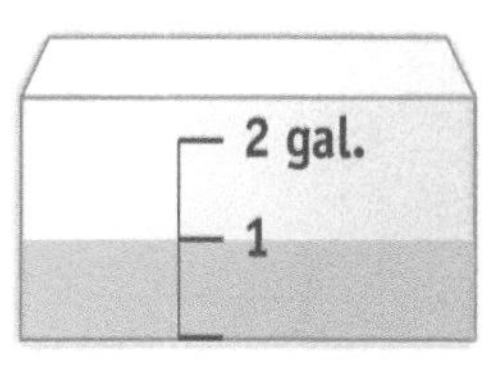

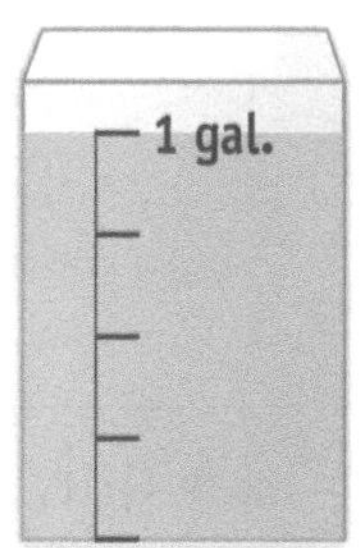

a _____ gal. | c _____ gal. | e _____ gal. | g _____ gal.

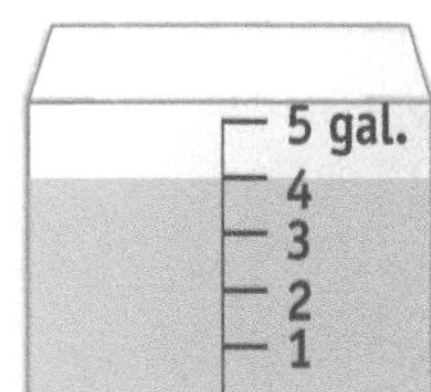

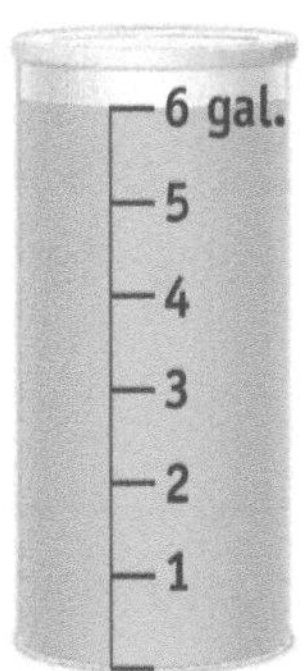

7 Color the pitchers to show the amounts.

Pitcher 1: 3 L

a Pitcher 2: 1 L

b Pitcher 3: 4 L

c Pitcher 4: 5 L

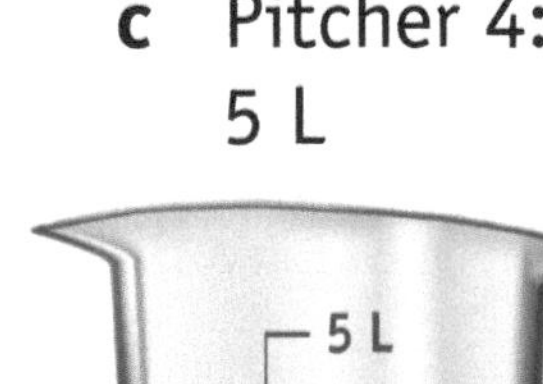

8 Use the pitchers in Question 7 to answer the following questions.

a Which pitcher has the most liquid in it? _________

b Which pitcher has the least liquid in it? _________

c Which pitcher has the greatest capacity? _________

d Which pitcher has the least capacity? _________

9 Match the containers to the correct amounts.

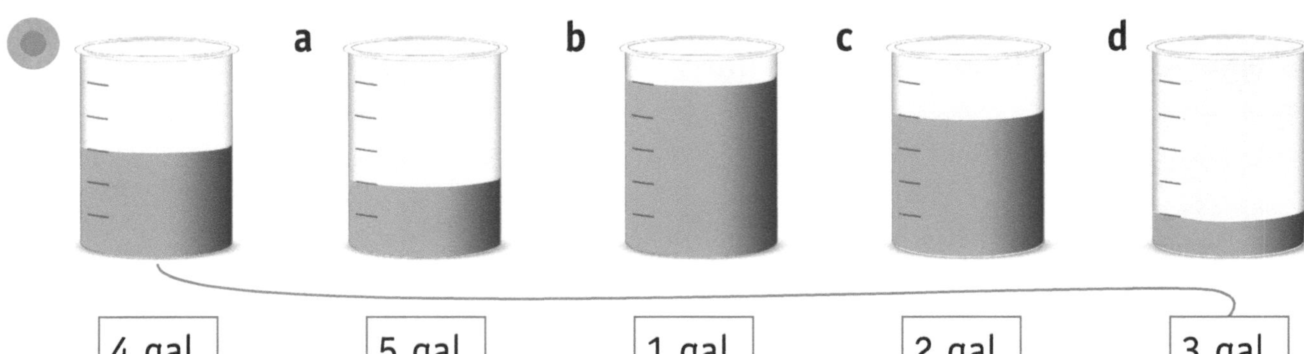

4 gal. | 5 gal. | 1 gal. | 2 gal. | 3 gal.

10 Solve. Show your work.

● Allan drinks 3 liters of water each weekday and 2 liters each day of the weekend. How much does he drink in one week?	3 L × 5 days = 15 L 2 L × 2 days = 4 L 15 L + 4 L = 19 L
a Tony has a container that holds 1 liter. How many containers can Tony fill from a bucket that holds 20 liters?	
b A bucket holds 5 gallons. How many buckets of water will it take to fill a 150 gal. fish tank?	
c Roslynn squeezes 8 oranges to make 1 liter of juice. How many oranges will she need to make 6 liters of juice?	
d Janice's juice stand has these pitchers with juice left over. If Janice had 16 gal. of juice to begin with, how much juice did she sell? 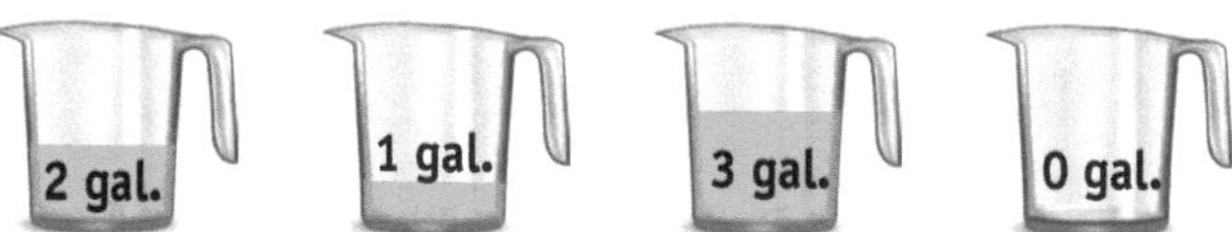	

MILLILITERS AND FLUID OUNCES

We use milliliters (mL) and fluid ounces (fl oz) to measure smaller amounts of liquid. There are 1,000 mL in 1 liter. There are 8 fl oz in 1 cup.

SCAN to watch video

1,000 mL = 1 liter
750 mL = $\frac{3}{4}$ liter
500 mL = $\frac{1}{2}$ liter
250 mL = $\frac{1}{4}$ liter

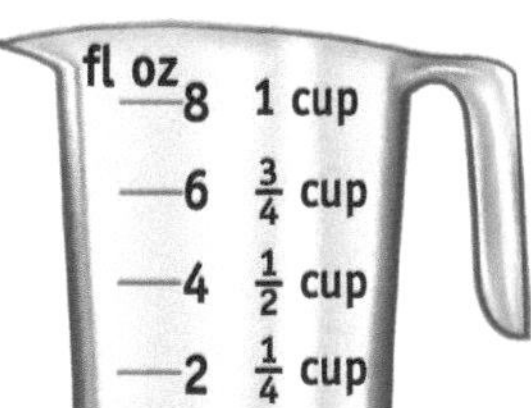

8 fl oz = 1 cup
6 fl oz = $\frac{3}{4}$ cup
4 fl oz = $\frac{1}{2}$ cup
2 fl oz = $\frac{1}{4}$ cup

Examples: Color the containers to show the measurements.

a $\frac{1}{4}$ liter

b 1 liter

c $\frac{1}{2}$ cup

d $\frac{3}{4}$ cup

Your turn

Color the containers to show the measurements.
Hint: Each mark shows 100 mL or 2 fl oz.

300 mL

b 400 mL

d 4 fl oz

a 250 mL

c 6 fl oz

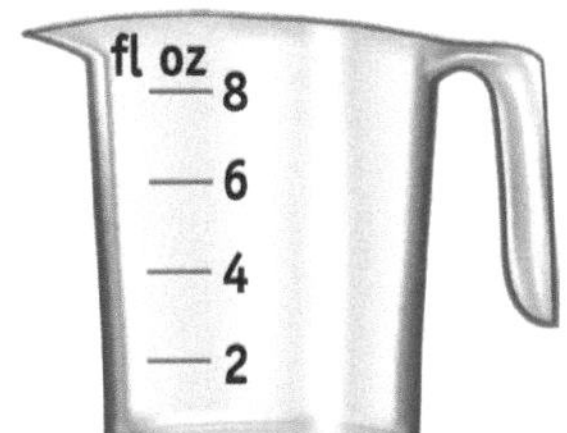

e 8 fl oz

SELF CHECK Mark how you feel

Got it!	Need help...	I don't get it

Check your answers
How many did you get correct?

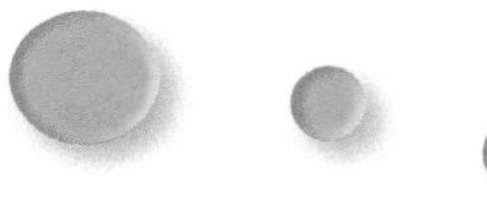

PRACTICE

1 Circle the items you would measure in milliliters or fluid ounces.

- a glass of milk (circled)
- **a** a large carton of milk
- **b** a dose of medicine
- **c** drops in an eyedropper
- **d** water in a spa
- **e** gas in a boat
- **f** a cup of coffee
- **g** juice in a juice box

2 Write as liters or cups.

- 2,500 mL = $2\frac{1}{2}$ L
- **a** 1,000 mL = _______ L
- **b** 16 fl oz = _______ c
- **c** 9,750 mL = _______ L
- **d** 12 fl oz = _______ c
- **e** 8,500 mL = _______ L
- **f** 24 fl oz = _______ c
- **g** 10,000 mL = _______ L
- **h** 20 fl oz = _______ c

3 Write as milliliters or fluid ounces.

- 7 L = 7,000 mL
- **a** 4 L = _________ mL
- **b** $3\frac{1}{4}$ c = _________ fl oz
- **c** $3\frac{1}{2}$ L = _________ mL
- **d** $1\frac{1}{4}$ c = _________ fl oz
- **e** $1\frac{3}{4}$ L = _________ mL
- **f** 3 c = _________ fl oz
- **g** $6\frac{3}{4}$ L = _________ mL
- **h** $5\frac{1}{2}$ c = _________ fl oz

4 Color the containers to show the measurements.

150 mL

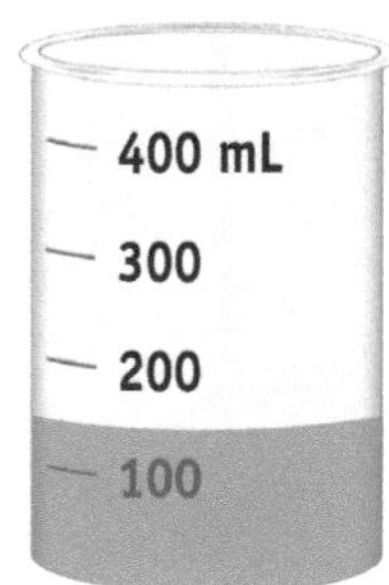

a 500 mL

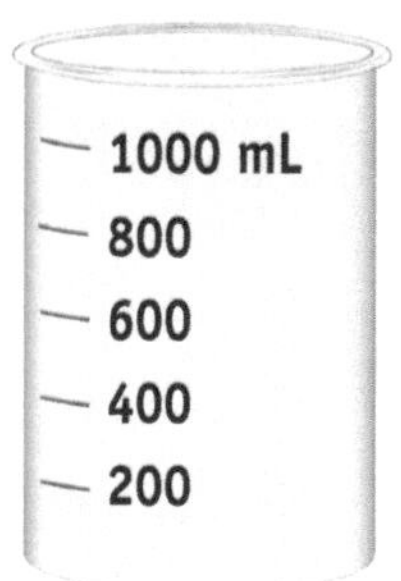

b 5 fl oz

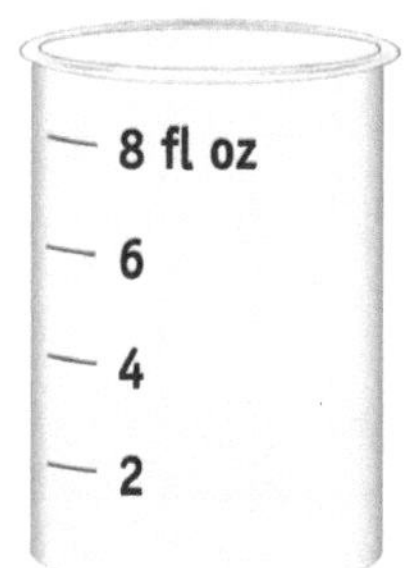

c 6 fl oz

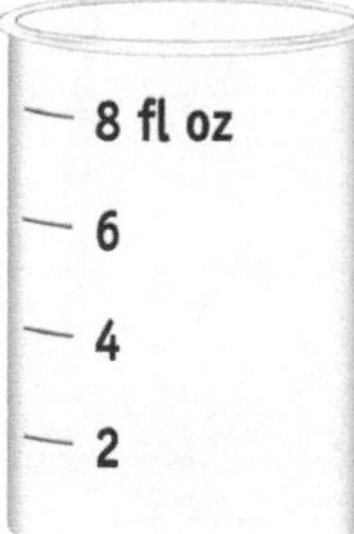

VOLUME AND CAPACITY REVIEW

1 Complete the sentence.

Volume is the amount of ____________ an object takes up.

2 What is the volume of each object?

a Volume = ______ cu. in.

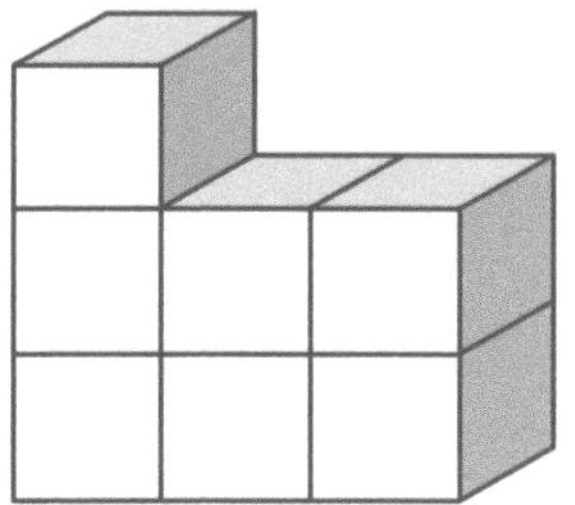

b Volume = ______ cm^3

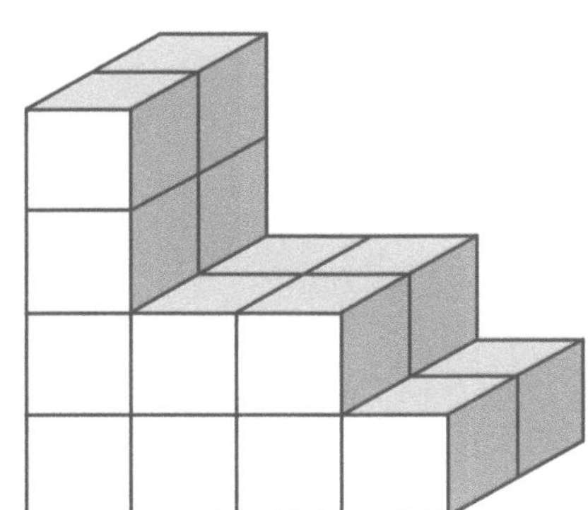

c Volume = ______ cm^3

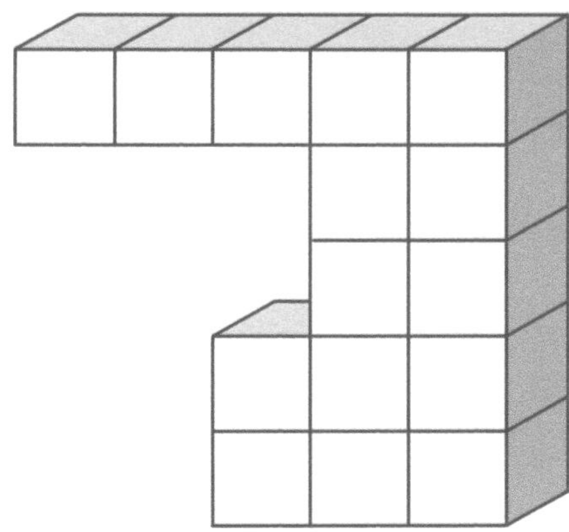

d Volume = ______ cu. in.

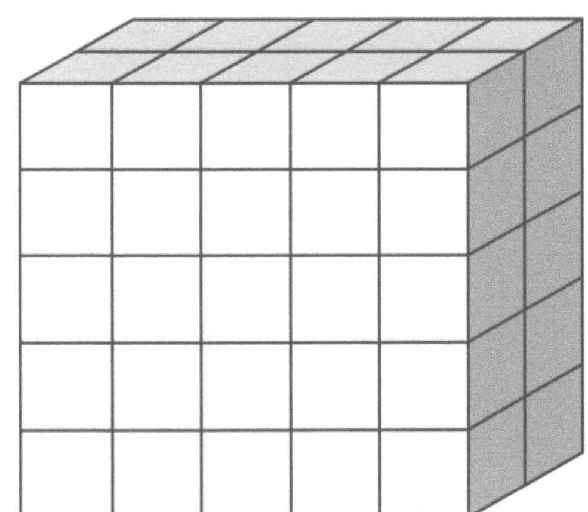

3 What is the difference in volume of the objects in Question 2?

a object **b** and object **c** ______

b object **d** and object **a** ______

REVIEW

4 Circle the containers with the smaller capacity.

a

c

b

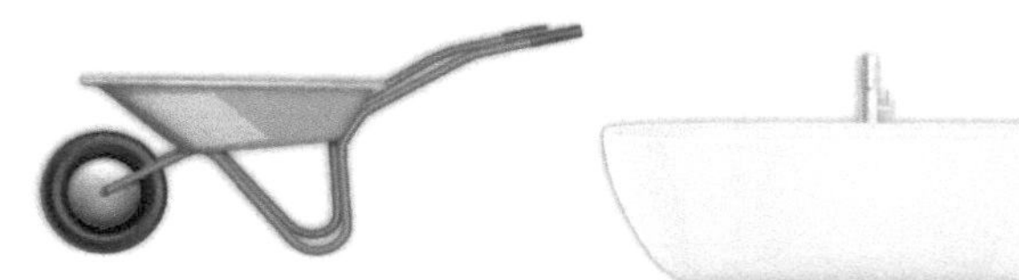

d

5 Order the containers from smallest capacity (1) to largest capacity (5).

a

☐ ☐ ☐ ☐ ☐

b

☐ ☐ ☐ ☐ ☐

c

☐ ☐ ☐ ☐ ☐

6 What is the total capacity of each set of containers?

a ______ L

b ______ gal.

c ______ L

7 List three containers that would hold less than 1 liter.

____

8 List three containers that would hold 1 or more gallons.

____

9 Color each container to show 1 liter.

a

b

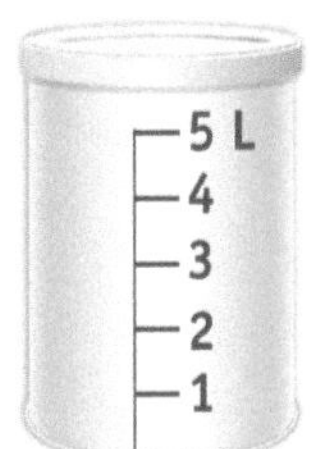

c

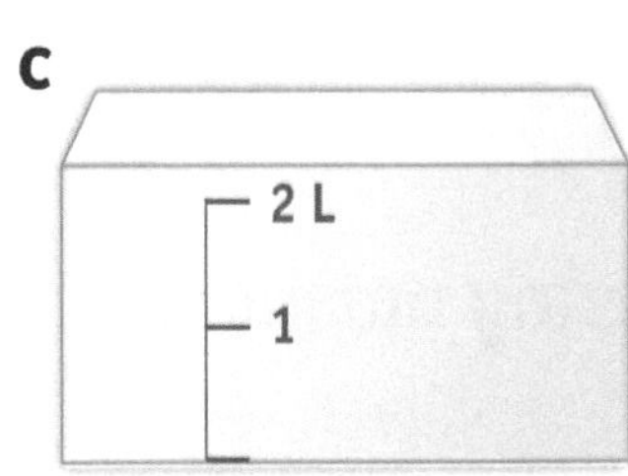

d

10 What amount of liquid is in each container?

a ______

1 gal.

b ______

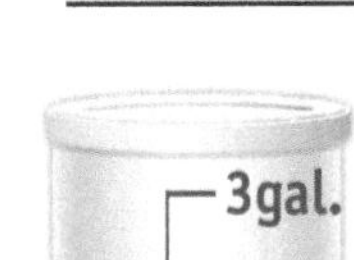

c ______

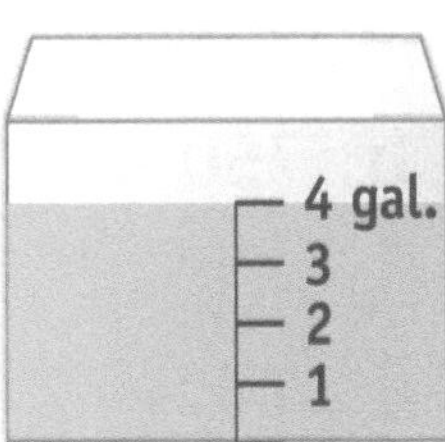

d ______

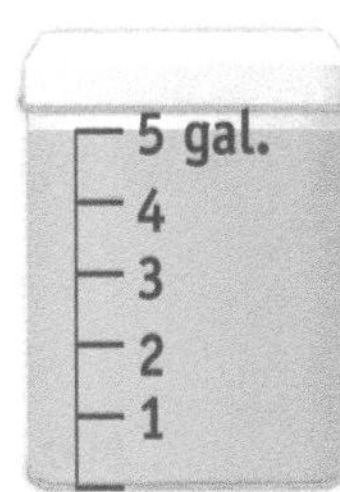

REVIEW

11 Solve. Show your work.

a Danny drinks 1 liter of water on each day of the weekend and 2 liters of water every weekday, except for Wednesday when he drinks 3 liters of water. How much water does Danny drink in one week?	
b Li has a container that holds 3 gallons. How many times does Li need to fill the container to fill a bucket that holds 33 gallons?	
c A bucket holds 10 liters. How many buckets of water will it take to fill Antonia's fish tank, which holds 110 liters?	

12 Write the missing numbers.

a 1,000 mL = _________ L

b 6 fl oz = _________ c

c _________ mL = $\frac{1}{2}$ L

d _________ fl oz = $\frac{1}{4}$ c

13 Color the containers to show the amount.

a 500 mL

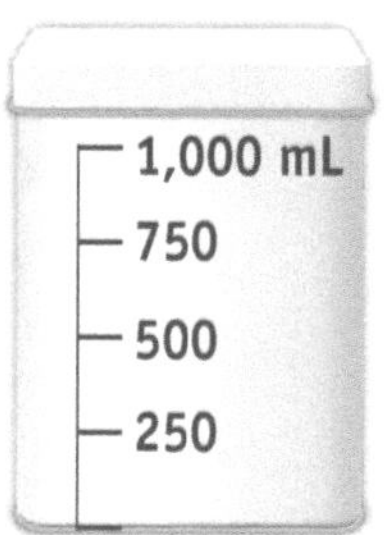

b 750 mL

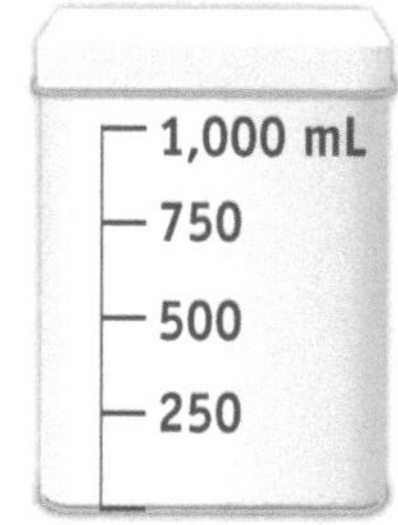

c 6 fl oz

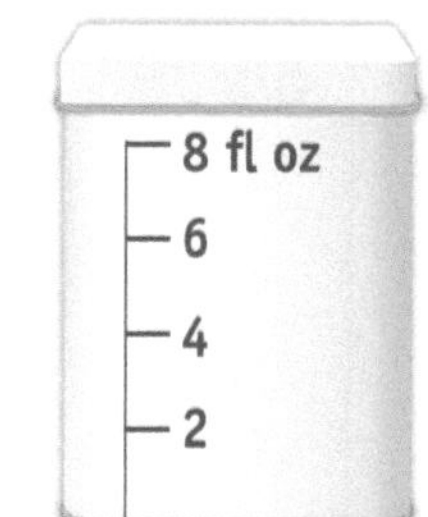

d 8 fl oz

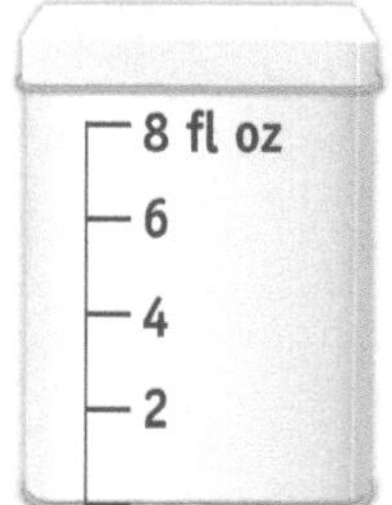

14 Circle the items you would measure in liters or gallons.

a milk in a baby's bottle

b gas in a car

c a cup of tea

d a glass of milk

e drops of food coloring

f water in a swimming pool

15 Write as liters or cups.

a 3,500 mL = __________ L

b 16 fl oz = __________ c

c 1,500 mL = __________ L

d 20 fl oz = __________ c

e 9,250 mL = __________ L

f 28 fl oz = __________ c

16 Write as milliliters or fluid ounces.

a 8 L = __________ mL

b $3\frac{1}{4}$ c = __________ fl oz

c $6\frac{1}{2}$ L = __________ mL

d $2\frac{3}{4}$ c = __________ fl oz

e 9 L = __________ mL

f 3 c = __________ fl oz

17 Number the containers to order them from largest capacity (1) to smallest capacity (5).

a

 ☐

 ☐

 ☐

☐

 ☐

b

 ☐

 ☐

☐

 ☐

 ☐

c

 ☐

 ☐

 ☐

 ☐

 ☐

ANSWERS

1 WHOLE NUMBERS

Place Value THREE-DIGIT AND FOUR-DIGIT NUMBERS

Page 9 – Example(s)

Example 2 (from left to right): hundreds, 0, ones
Example 4 (from left to right): thousands, hundreds, tens, 4

Page 9 – Your Turn

1 a ones
b thousands
c tens
d tens
e ones

2 a 5,921
b 253
c 320
d 4,815

Page 10 – Practice

1 a hundreds
b thousands
c ones
d tens
e hundreds
f tens
g hundreds
h ones
i thousands
j tens
k hundreds
l tens
m ones

2 a 3,458
b 900
c 756
d 1,834
e 235

3 a **8,435**
b **4,756**
c **665**
d **756**
e **837**
f **4,587**
g **926**
h **8,170**
i **6,109**
j **219**
k **2,013**
l **324**
m **596**
n **4,923**

Value THREE-DIGIT AND FOUR-DIGIT NUMBERS

Page 11 – Example(s)

Example 3: 400, 7, 1
Example 4: 8,000, 200, 3

Page 11 – Your Turn

Circle 634, 8,231, 432.

Page 12 – Practice

1 a 4
b 400
c 4
d 40
e 40
f 400
g 4,000
h 400
i 400
j 4,000
k 40
l 4,000
m 40
n 40

2 Adult to check

3 a 530
b 1,037
c 265
d 2,589
e 9,803
f 1,009
g 8,632
h 582
i 471
j 4,936
k 5,419
l 873
m 684
n 3,781
o 9,275

4 a 439, 477, 1,472, 415
b 6,358, 6,426, 6,156
c 1,297, 407, 1,357
d 735, 32, 4,534, 937

Expanded Form THREE-DIGIT AND FOUR-DIGIT NUMBERS

Page 13 – Example(s)

top row: 200, 3
bottom row: thousands, 4

Page 13 – Your Turn

a 400 + 30 + 2
= 4 hundreds + 3 tens + 2 ones
b 3,000 + 60 + 5
= 3 thousands + 6 tens + 5 ones

Page 14 – Practice

1 a 800 + 50 + 7
b 300 + 20 + 9
c 1,000 + 90 + 3
d 1,000 + 800 + 30 + 4
e 500 + 6
f 4,000 + 300 + 70

2 a 300 + 2
b 1,000 + 600 + 40 + 2
c 2,000 + 30 + 7
d 4,000 + 60
e 800 + 50

3 a 1,000 + 400 + 60 + 3
b 700 + 7
c 1,000 + 400 + 90
d 500 + 40
e 6,000 + 800 + 9
f 400 + 20 + 4

Place Value FIVE-DIGIT NUMBERS

Page 15 – Example(s)

Example 2 (top to bottom): 7, 4, 3, 5, 1
Example 3 (top to bottom): ten thousand, thousands, hundred, ten, ones

Page 15 – Your Turn

43,240, **329**, **7,267**, **927**, **1,352**,
672, **93**, **3,289**, **14**, **63,053**

Page 16 – Practice

1 a 42,560
b 95,390
c 59,936
d 99,363
e 38,342
f 67,429
g 84,132
h 53,931
i 19,150
j 10,000
k 35,003
l 62,415
m 71,317
n 59,020

2

	Number	Ten Thousands	Thousands	Hundreds	Tens	Ones
a	63,000	6	3	0	0	0
b	42,618	4	2	6	1	8
c	86,254	8	6	2	5	4
d	38,913	3	8	9	1	3
e	71,352	7	1	3	5	2

3 a ten thousands
b ones
c thousands
d tens
e hundreds
f ten thousands
g thousands
h hundreds
i tens
j ones
k thousands
l hundreds

Value FIVE-DIGIT NUMBERS

Page 17 – Example(s)

Example 2 (counterclockwise): 70,000; 8,000; 400; 90; 6

Page 17 – Your Turn

1 Adult to check
2 54, 64,357, 3,156

Page 18 – Practice

1 a 30,000
b 7
c 50
d 0
e 10,000
f 2,000
g 900
h 10,000
i 40
j 500
k 5,000

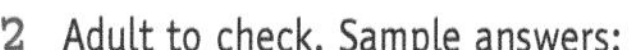

2 Adult to check. Sample answers:
- a 94,258
- b 28,945
- c 24,958
- d 85,249
- e 28,495
- f 89,425
- g 52,948
- h 45,892

3 a 28, 8, 3,428 b 320, 6,320, 0

Expanded Form FIVE-DIGIT NUMBERS

Page 19 – Example(s)

Example 3
(top row) 80,000, 9
(bottom row) 5, 4

Example 4
(top row) 10,000, 60, 5
(bottom row) 6, 2

Page 19 – Your Turn

a 300 b 1,000 c 700 d 30

Page 20 – Practice

1
- a 10,000 + 5,000 + 400 + 70 + 1
- b 3,000 + 500 + 80 + 4
- c 20,000 + 9,000 + 700 + 60 + 2
- d 30,000 + 5,000 + 800 + 40 + 7
- e 50 + 7
- f 100 + 90 + 3
- g 5,000 + 600 + 40 + 9

2
- a 20,000 + 2,000 + 300 + 80 + 7
- b 90,000 + 1,000 + 400 + 70 + 6
- c 80,000 + 9,000 + 200 + 90 + 5
- d 70,000 + 3,000 + 40 + 9

3
- a 70,000, 800, 60
- b 1,000, 60
- c 10,000, 30, 6
- d 300, 8
- e 20,000, 500, 9
- f 200, 7

Greater Than, Less Than, Equal To
THREE-DIGIT, FOUR-DIGIT, AND FIVE-DIGIT NUMBERS

Page 21 – Example(s)

Example 4: is greater than
Example 5: is equal to
Example 6: is less than

Page 21 – Your Turn

a True b True c True d True e True

Page 22 – Practice

1
- a <, less than
- b >, greater than
- c =, equal to
- d >, greater than
- e <, less than

2
- a >
- b <
- c <
- d =
- e <
- f <
- g >
- h >
- i <
- j =
- k =
- l <
- m >
- n >

3
- a ✓
- b ✓
- c ✗
- d ✗
- e ✗
- f ✓
- g ✓
- h ✓
- i ✗
- j ✗
- k ✗

Rounding to the Nearest 100, 1,000, and 10,000

Page 23 – Example(s)

Example 4: 15,500
Example 5: 2,000

Page 23 – Your Turn

a 5,800 b 700

Page 24 – Practice

1
- a 700
- b 1,500
- c 9,900
- d 15,500
- e 59,800
- f 64,300
- g 700
- h 8,900

2
- a 2,000
- b 3,000
- c 7,000
- d 16,000
- e 41,000

3
- a 50,000
- b 50,000
- c 60,000
- d 60,000
- e 10,000

4

	Nearest 100	Nearest 1,000	Nearest 10,000
a 68,437	68,400	68,000	70,000
b 40,305	40,300	40,000	40,000
c 23,036	23,000	23,000	20,000

Factors

Page 25 – Example(s)

Example 2: 21
7
1, 3, 7, 21

Page 25 – Your Turn

a 1, 3, 5, 15 b 1, 3, 9 c 1, 7

Page 26 – Practice

1
- a 1, 2, 7, 14
- b 1, 2, 4, 8, 16
- c 1, 2, 3, 5, 6, 10, 15, 30
- d 1, 2, 4, 8, 16, 32
- e 1, 2, 3, 4, 6, 9, 12, 18, 36
- f 1, 2, 4, 5, 10, 20
- g 1, 2, 11, 22
- h 1, 2, 3, 6

2 Numbers to cross out:
- a 6
- b 3
- c 6
- d 4
- e 7
- f 2
- g 3
- h 2
- i 6
- j 4
- k 10

Greatest Common Factor (GCF)

Page 27 – Example(s)

Example 3: 3
Example 4: 4

Page 27 – Your Turn

a 4 b 3 c 5

Page 28 – Practice

1
- a 14: 1, 2, 7, 14
  21: 1, 3, 7, 21
  7 is the GCF.
- b 21: 1, 3, 7, 21
  24: 1, 2, 3, 4, 6, 8, 12, 24
  3 is the GCF.
- c 18: 1, 2, 3, 6, 9, 18
  36: 1, 2, 3, 4, 6, 9, 12, 18, 36
  18 is the GCF.
- d 10: 1, 2, 5, 10
  24: 1, 2, 3, 4, 6, 8, 12, 24
  2 is the GCF.
- e 16: 1, 2, 4, 8, 16
  20: 1, 2, 4, 5, 10, 20
  4 is the GCF.
- f 22: 1, 2, 11, 22
  33: 1, 3, 11, 33
  11 is the GCF.
- g 10: 1, 2, 5, 10
  30: 1, 2, 3, 5, 6, 10, 15, 30
  10 is the GCF.
- h 9: 1, 3, 9
  27: 1, 3, 9, 27
  9 is the GCF.
- i 12: 1, 2, 3, 4, 6, 12
  18: 1, 2, 3, 6, 9, 18
  6 is the GCF.

Multiples

Page 29 – Example(s)

Example 2: 5; 10; 15; 20; 25
5, 10, 15, 20, and 25

Page 29 – Your Turn

a 3, 6, 9 b 4, 8, 12 c 12, 24, 36

Page 30 – Practice

1 a 2, 4, 6, 8, 10, 12, 14, 16
b 4, 8, 12, 16, 20, 24, 28, 32
c 5, 10, 15, 20, 25, 30, 35, 40
d 7, 14, 21, 28, 35, 42, 49, 56
e 9, 18, 27, 36, 45, 54, 63, 72
f 10, 20, 30, 40, 50, 60, 70, 80
g 11, 22, 33, 44, 55, 66, 77, 88

2 Numbers to cross out:
a 115 b 28 c 20 d 46 e 28 f 23 g 46 h 35 i 37 j 56

Least Common Multiples (LCM)

Page 31 – Example(s)

Example 3: 4

Page 31 – Your Turn

a 12 b 6 c 6

Page 32 – Practice

1 a 3: 3, 6, 9, 12, 15
4: 4, 8, 12, 16
The LCM is 12.

b 5: 5, 10, 15, 20
10: 10, 20, 30, 40
The LCM is 10.

c 2: 2, 4, 6, 8, 10
6: 6, 12, 18, 24, 30
The LCM is 6.

d 3: 3, 6, 9, 12
6: 6, 12, 18, 24
The LCM is 6.

e 1: 1, 2, 3, 4
4: 4, 8, 12, 16
The LCM is 4.

f 4: 4, 8, 12, 16, 20
10: 10, 20, 30, 40
The LCM is 20.

g 3: 3, 6, 9, 12, 15
5: 5, 10, 15, 20
The LCM is 15.

h 2: 2, 4, 6, 8, 10
10: 10, 20, 30, 40
The LCM is 10.

i 3: 3, 6, 9, 12, 15
9: 9, 18, 27, 36
The LCM is 9.

j 4: 4, 8, 12, 16, 20
8: 8, 16, 24, 32
The LCM is 8.

Whole Numbers Review Page 33

1

	Number	Hundred Thousands	Ten Thousands	Thousands	Hundreds	Tens	Ones
a	56	0	0	0	0	5	6
b	250	0	0	0	2	5	0
c	1,346	0	0	1	3	4	6
d	8,007	0	0	8	0	0	7
e	32,430	0	3	2	4	3	0
f	40,003	0	4	0	0	0	3
g	100,200	1	0	0	2	0	0
h	840,937	8	4	0	9	3	7
i	647,300	6	4	7	3	0	0
j	420,030	4	2	0	0	3	0

2 a tens
b ones
c hundreds
d thousands
e hundreds
f hundred thousands
g thousands
h ten thousands
i ones
j ones
k thousands
l tens

3 a 800 b 20 c 20 d 4 e 20,000
f 6,000 g 100,000 h 50,000 i 7 j 500
k 80 l 700,000 m 6 n 90

4 a 328,569 b 674,805 c 635,003 d 270,407

5 a **109,580** b **961** c **7,620** d **87,314** e **89** f **73,554** g **346** h **406,789**

6 Adult to check

7 Adult to check

8 236,400, 23,436, 437, 983,402, 127,483, 1,438

9 a 700 + 20 + 3
b 1,000 + 400 + 30 + 9
c 500 + 30 + 3
d 20,000 + 5,000 + 200 + 90 + 5
e 300,000 + 80,000 + 4,000 + 600 + 20 + 9

10 a 3,526, 5,236, 5,623, 5,632, 6,523
b 14,759, 41,579, 54,791, 75,154, 91,547
c 531,682, 582,316, 613,285, 631,582, 815,632

11 a 9,524, 9,254, 5,429, 4,529, 2,945
b 97,316, 79,613, 69,137, 67,139, 61,379
c 942,355, 495,234, 459,352, 395,542, 253,954

12 a > b < c < d > e > f < g < h = i > j >

13

Round to	a 532,487	b 643,981	c 857,603
nearest 10	532,490	643,980	857,600
nearest 100	532,500	644,000	857,600
nearest 1,000	532,000	644,000	858,000
nearest 10,000	530,000	640,000	860,000
nearest 100,000	500,000	600,000	900,000

14 a 1, 2, 3, 4, 6, 12
b 1, 2, 4, 8, 16
c 1, 2, 3, 6, 9, 18
d 1, 2, 3, 4, 6, 9, 12, 18, 36

15 a 8: 1, 2, 4, 8
12: 1, 2, 3, 4, 6, 12
The GCF is 4.

b 20: 1, 2, 4, 5, 10, 20
24: 1, 2, 3, 4, 6, 8, 12, 24
The GCF is 4.

c 15: 1, 3, 5, 15
18: 1, 2, 3, 6, 9, 18
The GCF is 3.

16 a 2, 4, 6, 8, 10
b 8, 16, 24, 32, 40
c 5, 10, 15, 20, 25
d 9, 18, 27, 36, 45
e 10, 20, 30, 40, 50
f 7, 14, 21, 28, 35

17 a 3: 3, 6, 9, 12, 15
4: 4, 8, 12, 16, 24
The LCM is 12.

b 2: 2, 4, 6, 8, 10
3: 3, 6, 9, 12, 15
The LCM is 6.

2 ADDITION

Adding with and without Regrouping

FOUR-DIGIT NUMBERS

Page 38 – Example(s)

Example 7: 2,635
Example 8: 9,998
Example 9: 8,732

Page 38 – Your Turn

a 2,367 b 6,699 c 12,319 d 1,622 e 8,146

Page 39 – Practice

1 a 6,019 b 5,668

2 a 8,997 b 6,310 c 8,828

3 a 9,532 b 6,163 c 6,428 d 4,723 e 6,110 f 7,109 g 5,159

4 a 6,973 b 9,134 c 17,338 d 14,053 e 10,912 f 12,510 g 12,152

Rounding to Estimate Addition Answers

Page 40 – Example(s)

Example 2: 140; 60; 200
Example 4: 400; 700; 1,100

Page 40 – Your Turn

a 200, 200, 400 b 550, 100, 650

Page 41 – Practice

1 a 60, 50, 110 b 70, 10, 80 c 280, 40, 320 d 30, 580, 610 e 30, 440, 470

2 a 500, 600, 1,100 b 600, 200, 800 c 900, 400, 1,300 d 400, 800, 1,200

Addition Review Page 42

1 a 88 b 79 c 87 d 68 e 108

2 a 856 b 485 c 947 d 874 e 2,793 f 3,788 g 4,765 h 5,247

3 a 113 b 115 c 121 d 93 e 165 f 564 g 1,412 h 1,020 i 1,608 j 1,210 k 1,574 l 8,256 m 12,890 n 14,755 o 14,878 p 10,918

4 a 30, 30, 60 b 50, 60, 110 c 140, 60, 200 d 280, 30, 310

5 a 300, 100, 400 b 500, 300, 800 c 900, 300, 1,200 d 400, 700, 1,100

3 SUBTRACTION

Subtraction with Regrouping

THREE-DIGIT AND FOUR-DIGIT NUMBERS

Page 44 – Example(s)

Example 3: 1,356
Example 4: 3,505

Page 44 – Your Turn

a 5,881 b 2,911 c 4,141

Page 45 – Practice

1 a 2,519 b 6,879

2 a 6,918 b 2,941 c 4,921 d 5,299 e 4,488

3 a 3,831 b 8,109 c 4,949 d 6,619 e 4,427

Subtraction with Regrouping

FIVE-DIGIT NUMBERS

Page 46 – Example(s)

Example 4: 51,271

Page 46 – Your Turn

a 68,496 b 20,862 c 46,106

Page 47 – Practice

1 a 70,996 b 48,817

2 a 11,078 b 48,948 c 18,916 d 78,585 e 34,099

3 a 34,097 b 68,379

4 a 41,382 b 52,493

Regrouping from Larger Place Values

Page 48 – Example(s)

Example 5: 25,405

Page 48 – Your Turn

a 16,580 b 866 c 268

Page 49 – Practice

1 a 67,427 b 4,853 c 6,177 d 19,698 e 125,997 f 24,564 g 44,787 h 5,747 i 268 j 48,528 k 18,996

2 a $36.38 b $6.50 c $44.83 d $47.50 e $44.75 f $205.05 g $12.54 h $102.43

Rounding to Estimate Subtraction Answers

Page 50 – Example(s)

Example 3: 700; 200; 500

Page 50 – Your Turn

1 a 610, 420, 190

2 a 1,600, 200, 1,400

Page 51 – Practice

1 a 740, 260, 480
b 1,360, 240, 1,120
c 43,520, 36,420, 7,100
d 73,430, 34,560, 38,870

2 a 73,600, 21,500, 52,100
b 300, 300, 0
c 6,000, 3,300, 2,700

Subtraction Review Page 52

1 a 32 b 21 c 46 d 37 e 38 f 17 g 552 h 542 i 530 j 541 k 605 l 861

2 a 5,111 b 3,211 c 632 d 1,441 e 6,387 f 4,076 g 13,135 h 18,612 i 81,220 j 21,142 k 26,169 l 30,589

3 a 14 b 115 c 190 d 1,117 e 3,242 f 3,134 g 5,053 h 54,960 i 92,217 j 22,741 k 33,122 l 68,951

4 a 368 b 457 c 32 d 4,847 e 6,417 f 5,579 g 625 h 4,970 i 2,693 j 26,476 k 49,848 l 19,927 m 64,648 n 52,947 o 41,679 p 8,650 q 24,710 r 44,696

5 a 340, 170, 170
b 3,580, 430, 3,150
c 17,440, 1,240, 16,200

6 a 400, 100, 300
b 53,400, 5,400, 48,000

4 MULTIPLICATION

Product, Factors, and Multiples

Page 56 – Example(s)

Example 2: (left column)	(boxes)	(right column)
10	2, 5	2, 5
2, 5		2, 5

Page 56 – Your Turn

1 a 2
b 3

2 a 42
b 23
c 1

Page 57 – Practice

1 a 18
1 2 3 6 9 18
1 × 18 = 18
2 × 9 = 18
3 × 6 = 18

b 7
1 7
1 × 7 = 7

c 24
1 2 3 4 6 8 12 24
1 × 24 = 24
2 × 12 = 24
3 × 8 = 24
4 × 6 = 24

d 16
1 2 4 8 16
1 × 16 = 16
2 × 8 = 16
4 × 4 = 16

2 a 20 b 56 c 108 d 132 e 72

3 a 42, 48, 54, 60, 66
b 28, 35, 42, 49, 56
c 36, 45, 54, 63, 72

4 a 4 b 8 c 60 d 11 e 11 f 8 g 6 h 0

Multiplying 2-Digit by 1-Digit Numbers

Page 58 – Example(s)

(left column)	(middle column)	(right column)
4	2, 4	12 in box
4, 4, 4	12	12
92	92	92

Page 58 – Your Turn

Known facts
30 × 8 = 240
240 + 8 + 8 = 256

Multiply tens then ones
3 tens × 8 + 8 twos
= 240 + 16 = 256

Area model

	30	2
8	240	16

= 240 + 16 = 256

Page 59 – Practice

1 a Known facts
30 × 5 = 150
150 + 5 + 5 + 5 + 5 = 170
Multiply tens then ones
3 tens × 5 + 5 fours
= 150 + 20 = 170
Area model

	30	4
5	150	20

150 + 20 = 170

b Known facts
60 × 8 = 480
480 + 8 + 8 + 8 + 8 + 8 + 8 + 8
= 536
Multiply tens then ones
6 tens × 8 + 8 sevens
= 480 + 56 = 536
Area model

	60	7
8	480	56

480 + 56 = 536

c Known facts
40 × 3 = 120
120 + 3 = 123
Multiply tens then ones
4 tens × 3 + 3 ones
= 120 + 3 = 123
Area model

	40	1
3	120	3

120 + 3 = 123

Standard Algorithms

Page 60 – Example(s)

Example 3: 228
Example 4: 222

Page 60 – Your Turn

1 a

	H	T	O
		$^{1}3$	5
×			2
		7	0

b

	H	T	O
		6	1
×			8
	4	8	8

c

	H	T	O
		7	2
×			3
	2	1	6

d

	H	T	O
		$^{2}2$	3
×			7
	1	6	1

e

	H	T	O
		$^{5}8$	9
×			6
	5	3	4

Page 61 – Practice

1 a 128 c 384 e 736 g 110
b 290 d 729 f 280

2 Score: 5 out of 8
a correct d correct g correct
b correct e correct h incorrect: 488
c incorrect: 360 f incorrect: 140

3 a 1,088 c 2,821 e 7,136
b 1,645 d 3,096

Multiplying 3-Digit and 4-Digit Numbers by 1-Digit Numbers

Page 62 – Example(s)

Example 2: 1,000, 400
5,000, 2,000
7,160

Page 62 – Your Turn

a 631 × 4
Multiply thousands, hundreds, tens, ones
= (600 × 4) + (30 × 4) + (1 × 4)
= 2,400 + 120 + 4
= 2,524
Standard algorithm

	$^{1}6$	3	1
×			4
2,	5	2	4

Area model

	600	30	1
4	2,400	120	4

= 2,400 + 120 + 4
= 2,524

b 742 × 8
Multiply thousands, hundreds, tens, ones
= (700 × 8) + (40 × 8) + (2 × 8)
= 5,600 + 320 + 16
= 5,936
Standard algorithm

	$^{3}7$	$^{1}4$	2
×			8
5,	9	3	6

Area model

	700	40	2
8	5,600	320	16

= 5,600 + 320 + 16
= 5,936

Page 63 – Practice

1 a 1,956 b 7,630 c 3,073 d 47,704

2 a 2,460 b 9,192 c 5,075 d 39,488 e 3,521

3 a 2,928 d 3,352 g 13,230
b 29,640 e 3,542 h 44,970
c 14,675 f 2,481 i 39,746

Multiplying 2-Digit and 3-Digit Numbers by 2-Digit Numbers

Page 67 – Example(s)

Example 3: (bottom left box) 1,400
(top middle box) 1,600
(bottom right box) 16
29,920 + 1,496 = 31,416

Page 68 – Your Turn

a

		$^{1}6$	4
×		1	3
	$^{1}1$	9	2
+	6	4	0
	8	3	2

	60	4	
10	600	40	640
3	180	12	192
			832

b

		$^{6}1$	$^{5}7$	6
×			$^{3}\,^{2}4$	9
	1,	$^{1}5$	8	4
+	7,	0	4	0
	8,	6	2	4

	100	70	6	
40	4,000	2,800	240	7,040
9	900	630	54	1,584
				8,624

c

		$^{3}8$	$^{2}4$	3
×			7	0
		0	0	0
+	5	9,	0	1	0
	5	9,	0	1	0

	800	40	3	
70	56,000	2,800	210	59,010
0	0	0	0	0
				59,010

Page 67 – Practice

1 a 6,360 b 1,863

2 a 2,772 d 3,784 g 33,271
b 6,264 e 47,192 h 60,444
c 16,320 f 12,474

3 a 1,323 c 49,248 e 6,882
b 5,628 d 32,340

Multiplication Review Page 70

1 a 54 c 48 e 72
b 49 d 48 f 30

2 a 6, 12, 18, 24, 30, 36 d 4, 8, 12, 16, 20, 24
b 8, 16, 24, 32, 40, 48 e 7, 14, 21, 28, 35, 42
c 9, 18, 27, 36, 45, 54

3 a 1, 2, 3, 4, 6, 9, 12, 18, 36 c 1, 3, 5, 15
b 1, 2, 3, 4, 6, 8, 12, 16, 24, 48 d 1, 2, 3, 4, 6, 12

4 a 10 d 4 g 9 j 5
b 4 e 56 h 6 k 9
c 9 f 5 i 81 l 4

5 a 511 d 316 g 861 j 4,968
b 147 e 222 h 1,126 k 771
c 738 f 357 i 4,543 l 2,015

6 a 144 b 256 c 301

7 a 702 b 567 c 291

8 a 84 b 294 c 378

9 a 1,448 b 29,070 c 2,865

10 a 2,608 b 23,612 c 4,092

11 a 2,692 b 7,650 c 4,465 d 30,737 e 1,791 f 52,227

12 a 1,288 b 5,166 c 1,050 d 4,416 e 10,738 f 25,757 g 44,992 h 52,080 i 47,304

13 a 2,772 b 3,610 c 32,606 d 5,248 e 1,008 f 34,839 g 1,480 h 46,480 i 15,210

14 a correct b incorrect: 252 c correct d correct e incorrect: 1,540 f correct g incorrect: 7,050

5 DIVISION

Groups and Equal Rows

Page 76 – Example(s)

Example 2:
24
4, 24

Example 4:
24, 4
4, 24

Page 76 – Your Turn

1 a 5
2 a b

Page 77 – Practice

1 a 2, 2 b 9, 9 c 4, 4 d 9, 9 e 2, 2

2 a 3, 3 b 8, 8 c 1, 1 d 2, 2 e 8, 8

Relating × to ÷

Page 78 – Example(s)

Example 2:
15 for red blank
5 for blue blank
Example 3:
10 for both red blanks
2 for blue blank

Page 78 – Your Turn

a 6, 6 b 21, 21 c 100, 100 d 11, 11 e 7, 7

Page 79 – Practice

1 a 45 ÷ 5 = 9 b 2 ÷ 1 = 2 c 64 ÷ 8 = 8 d 42 ÷ 7 = 6

2 a 2 × 6 = 12
6 × 2 = 12
12 ÷ 6 = 2
12 ÷ 2 = 6

b 2 × 9 = 18
9 × 2 = 18
18 ÷ 9 = 2
18 ÷ 2 = 9

c 4 × 5 = 20
5 × 4 = 20
20 ÷ 5 = 4
20 ÷ 4 = 5

d 9 × 8 = 72
8 × 9 = 72
72 ÷ 8 = 9
72 ÷ 9 = 8

e 12 × 10 = 120
10 × 12 = 120
120 ÷ 10 = 12
120 ÷ 12 = 10

3 a 9 × 10 b 5 × 9 c 8 × 5 d 7 × 4 e 6 × 5

Quotient, Divisor, and Dividend

Page 80 – Example(s)

Example 4: 7

Page 80 – Your Turn

1 Adult to check
2 a 48, 6, 8 b 72, 8, 9 c 10 ÷ 5 = 2 d 20 ÷ 10 = 2

Page 81 – Practice

1 a 7 b 2 c 10 d 4 e 7

2 24 ÷ 6, 16 ÷ 4, 28 ÷ 7
3 The first number should be circled in red, and the second number should be circled in blue.
a 3 b 6 c 9 d 4 e 5 f 4 g 9 h 8

4 a 3 b 3 c 7 d 6 e 7 f 11 g 7 h 9 i 5 j 2 k 1 l 11 m 11 n 5 o 10 p 6 q 3 r 5 s 10 t 9 u 12

Standard Algorithm

Page 82 – Example(s)

Example 3: 3; 3
Example 4: 7; 7, 63
Example 5: 7; 7

Page 82 – Your Turn

a 2 b 3 c 6 d 8 e 3 f 4 g 6 h 1

Page 83 – Practice

1 a 4, 4 × 4 = 16 b 9, 2 × 9 = 18 c 4, 5 × 4 = 20 d 4, 6 × 4 = 24 e 7, 4 × 7 = 28

2 a 8 b 44 c 8 d 8 e 10 f 48 g 8 h 6

3 a 8 ÷ 8 = 1, $8\overline{)8}$ with quotient 1 b 20 ÷ 5 = 4, $5\overline{)20}$ with quotient 4 c 63 ÷ 7 = 9, $7\overline{)63}$ with quotient 9 d 120 ÷ 10 = 12, $10\overline{)120}$ with quotient 12

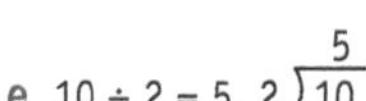

e $10 \div 2 = 5, \overset{5}{2\overline{)10}}$

f $33 \div 11 = 3, \overset{3}{11\overline{)33}}$

g $70 \div 10 = 7, \overset{7}{10\overline{)70}}$

h $72 \div 8 = 9, \overset{9}{8\overline{)72}}$

i $42 \div 7 = 6, \overset{6}{7\overline{)42}}$

Different Ways to Write Division

Page 84 – Example(s)

Example 3: 9, 9
Example 4: 60, 60

Page 84 – Your Turn

a $\frac{43}{2}$ b $\frac{74}{3}$ c $4\overline{)52}$

Page 85 – Practice

1 a $6\overline{)42}$ b $10\overline{)93}$ c $9\overline{)81}$ d $7\overline{)63}$ e $25\overline{)75}$ f $4\overline{)230}$ g $11\overline{)121}$ h $5\overline{)182}$

2 a $\frac{53}{4}$ b $\frac{72}{3}$ c $\frac{37}{4}$ d $\frac{82}{3}$ e $\frac{51}{2}$ f $\frac{95}{3}$ g $\frac{64}{7}$ h $\frac{42}{6}$

3 a $27 \div 3$ b $47 \div 4$ c $64 \div 5$ d $58 \div 4$ e $83 \div 7$ f $62 \div 3$ g $73 \div 4$ h $97 \div 8$

4

	Fraction	$\overline{)\ }$	÷
a	$\frac{61}{4}$	$4\overline{)61}$	$61 \div 4$
b	$\frac{25}{3}$	$3\overline{)25}$	$25 \div 3$
c	$\frac{72}{6}$	$6\overline{)72}$	$72 \div 6$
d	$\frac{49}{7}$	$7\overline{)49}$	$49 \div 7$
e	$\frac{81}{9}$	$9\overline{)81}$	$81 \div 9$

f	$\frac{74}{5}$	$5\overline{)74}$	$74 \div 5$
g	$\frac{69}{9}$	$9\overline{)69}$	$69 \div 9$
h	$\frac{22}{3}$	$3\overline{)22}$	$22 \div 3$
i	$\frac{16}{4}$	$4\overline{)16}$	$16 \div 4$

Division with Remainders

Page 86 – Example(s)

Example 3: 3, 4
3, 18
18, 22

Page 86 – Your Turn

a 3 remainder 3 b 8 remainder 4 c 6 remainder 1

Page 87 – Practice

1 a 7 r 7 b 6 r 3 c 8 r 3 d 7 r 6 e 8 r 1 f 9 r 2 g 7 r 2 h 9 r 4 i 5 r 7

2 a 4 r 1 b 7 r 2 c 5 r 3 d 9 r 5

3 a $25 \div 4 = 6$ r 1
b $70 \div 6 = 11$ r 4
c $84 \div 9 = 9$ r 3
d $148 \div 12 = 12$ r 4
e $106 \div 10 = 10$ r 6
f $62 \div 5 = 12$ r 2
g $29 \div 6 = 4$ r 5
h $78 \div 8 = 9$ r 6

Division of 2-Digit Numbers

Page 88 – Example(s)

Example 2:
(middle box) 10; 20
(right box) 6
Example 3: 12
Example 4: 13
Example 5: 16

Page 88 – Your Turn

a 12 b 21 c 11 d 22 e 11

Page 89 – Practice

1 a 11 b 13 c 11 d 11 e 11 f 12 g 13

2 a 17 b 14 c 17 d 12 e 17 f 13 g 29 h 15 i 28 j 14 k 13 l 18 m 16 n 27 o 18

3 a 19 b 26 c 37 d 15 e 32 f 13 g 11

Division of 3-Digit Numbers

Page 90 – Example(s)

Example 6: 432
Example 7: 123
Example 8: 52

Page 90 – Your Turn

a 212 b 242 c 111 d 211 e 341 f 120 g 120

Page 91 – Practice

1 a 135 b 124 c 159 d 321 e 142 f 98 g 84 h 27 i 56 j 98 k 65

2 a 117 r 1 b 188 c 150 r 3

3 a 90, 100, 120, 40, 300
b 90, 20, 80, 70, 60
c 70, 110, 30, 60, 50

Recording Remainders as Fractions and Decimals

Page 92 – Example(s)

Example 3: $\frac{3}{4}$, $\frac{1}{2}$, 54.5

Page 92 – Your Turn

a 74 r 1 = $74\frac{1}{2}$ = 74.5
b 45 r 1 = $45\frac{1}{3}$ = 45.33
c 129 r 2 = $129\frac{2}{5}$ = 129.4

Page 93 – Practice

1 a 49 r 1 = $49\frac{1}{3}$
b 111 r 3 = $111\frac{3}{4}$
c 173 r 1 = $173\frac{1}{2}$
d 63 r 2 = $63\frac{1}{2}$
e 171 r 2 = $171\frac{2}{3}$

2 a 54 r 3 = 54.75
b 62 r 2 = 62.4
c 43 r 5 = 43.625

3

	Dividend	Divisor	Quotient	Remainder	Quotient and Remainder as a Fraction	Quotient and Remainder as a Decimal
a	15	2	7	1	$7\frac{1}{2}$	7.5
b	32	5	6	2	$6\frac{2}{5}$	6.4
c	57	8	7	1	$7\frac{1}{8}$	7.125
d	38	3	12	2	$12\frac{2}{3}$	12.67

Division Review Page 94

1 a 5, 5 b 4, 16, 4 c 3, 24, 3

2 a 7, 7 b 5, 5 c 6, 6

3 a 48 ÷ 6 = 8; 48 ÷ 8 = 6
b 72 ÷ 8 = 9; 72 ÷ 9 = 8
c 10 ÷ 2 = 5; 10 ÷ 5 = 2
d 28 ÷ 7 = 4; 28 ÷ 4 = 7
e 12 × 10 = 120; 10 × 12 = 120
f 3 × 12 = 36; 12 × 3 = 36
g 8 × 8 = 64
h 4 × 12 = 48; 12 × 4 = 48
i 9 × 7 = 63; 7 × 9 = 63
j 12 × 12 = 144
k 7 ÷ 1 = 7; 7 ÷ 7 = 1
l 7 × 6 = 42; 6 × 7 = 42

4 a 6 × 4 = 24
4 × 6 = 24
24 ÷ 4 = 6
24 ÷ 6 = 4
b 7 × 3 = 21
3 × 7 = 21
21 ÷ 3 = 7
21 ÷ 7 = 3
c 7 × 8 = 56
8 × 7 = 56
56 ÷ 8 = 7
56 ÷ 7 = 8

5 a 6 × 7 b 11 × 9 c 2 × 8 d 8 × 6 e 5 × 8 f 7 × 7 g 4 × 8 h 6 × 6 i 11 × 11

6 a 4 b 8 c 10 d 8 e 12 f 12 g 4 h 10 i 7

7 36 ÷ 3, 12 ÷ 1, 24 ÷ 2

8 a $6\overline{)42}$ b $9\overline{)27}$ c $9\overline{)81}$ d $2\overline{)127}$ e $4\overline{)464}$ f $3\overline{)721}$

9 a $\frac{25}{5}$ b $\frac{36}{4}$ c $\frac{24}{6}$ d $\frac{72}{8}$ e $\frac{9}{9}$ f $\frac{63}{7}$ g $\frac{40}{4}$ h $\frac{32}{8}$ i $\frac{10}{2}$

10 a 24 ÷ 3 b 42 ÷ 6 c 49 ÷ 7 d 121 ÷ 11 e 80 ÷ 8 f 90 ÷ 9

11 a 4 b 6 c 6 d 7 e 12 f 5 g 9 h 10

12 a 3 r 6 b 10 r 2 c 3 r 0 d 4 r 3 e 1 r 2 f 5 r 1 g 5 r 3 h 7 r 2 i 4 r 0 j 9 r 1

13 a 7 r 1 b 8 r 2 c 9 r 6 d 4 r 5

14 a 18 ÷ 4 = 4 r 2
b 134 ÷ 12 = 11 r 2
c 109 ÷ 10 = 10 r 9
d 79 ÷ 8 = 9 r 7
e 28 ÷ 6 = 4 r 4

15 a 31 b 12 c 24 d 21 e 43 f 12 g 13 h 17 i 15 j 29 k 16 l 14

16 a 17 b 20 c 14 d 18

17 a 5 r 2 b 15 r 4 c 9 r 3 d 9 r 5 e 14 r 0 f 8 r 1

18 a 421 b 213 c 122 d 111 e 234 f 332

19 a 321 r 1 b 116 r 6 c 119 r 3 d 181 r 1 e 343 r 1 f 129 r 4

20 a 127 r 2 b 118 r 1 c 106 r 1 d 127 r 4

21 a 4, 6, 8, 14, 22
b 6, 1, 7, 2, 11
c 1, 3, 6, 8, 5
d 1, 4, 8, 10, 9

22 a $155\frac{3}{4}$ b $106\frac{2}{5}$ c 126 d $156\frac{1}{6}$ e $95\frac{8}{9}$ f $193\frac{3}{4}$ g $83\frac{1}{5}$ h $109\frac{1}{3}$ i 347 j $121\frac{5}{7}$ k $64\frac{1}{4}$ l $48\frac{1}{2}$

23 a 197.5 b 156.8 c 168.75 d 281.5 e 224.75 f 124.33 g 52.25 h 64.8 i 196.2 j 158.5 k 151.33 l 60.5

24 a correct
b correct
c incorrect, 90 r 5
d incorrect, 110 r 4
e incorrect, 71
f correct
g incorrect, 92 r 6
h correct

6 FRACTIONS

Comparing Fractions

Page 102 – Example(s)

Example 3: six, 6
Example 4: two, 2

Page 102 – Your Turn

1 Adult to check
2 a 1 b 2 c 2

Page 103 – Practice

1 a $\frac{1}{4}$ (1), $\frac{2}{3}$ (5), $\frac{3}{5}$ (3), $\frac{5}{8}$ (4), $\frac{3}{4}$ (6), $\frac{1}{3}$ (2)
b $\frac{1}{3}$ (2), $\frac{1}{4}$ (1), $\frac{2}{3}$ (3), $\frac{3}{3}$ (6), $\frac{4}{5}$ (5), $\frac{6}{8}$ (4)

2 Adult to check
3 Adult to check
4 a > b = c > d < e = f < g = h < i > j < k <

Proper and Improper Fractions

Page 104 – Example(s)

Example 3: any number greater than 2

Example 4: any number greater than 2

Page 104 – Your Turn

Improper: $\frac{8}{2}$, $\frac{7}{3}$, $\frac{10}{4}$, $\frac{9}{6}$ Proper: $\frac{2}{8}$, $\frac{4}{9}$, $\frac{5}{10}$, $\frac{1}{4}$

Page 105 – Practice

1 a $\frac{1}{2}$ b $\frac{2}{3}$ c $\frac{2}{8}$ d $\frac{12}{24}$ e $\frac{53}{60}$

2 a $\frac{8}{5}$ b $\frac{3}{1}$ c $\frac{5}{3}$ d $\frac{81}{41}$ e $\frac{53}{24}$

3 Adult to check

4 Adult to check

Mixed Numbers

Page 106 – Example(s)

Example 3: $3\frac{2}{3} = 3 + \frac{2}{3}$

Example 4: $2\frac{1}{2} = 2 + \frac{2}{2}$

Page 106 – Your Turn

1 a b

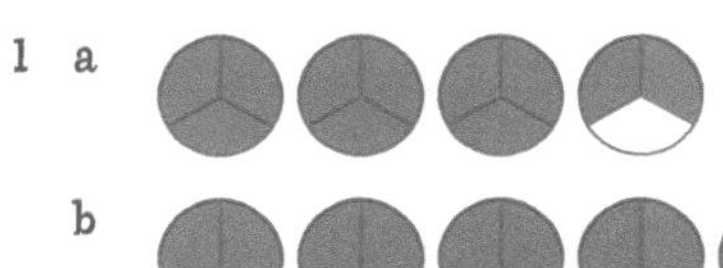

c

Page 107 – Practice

1 a b c

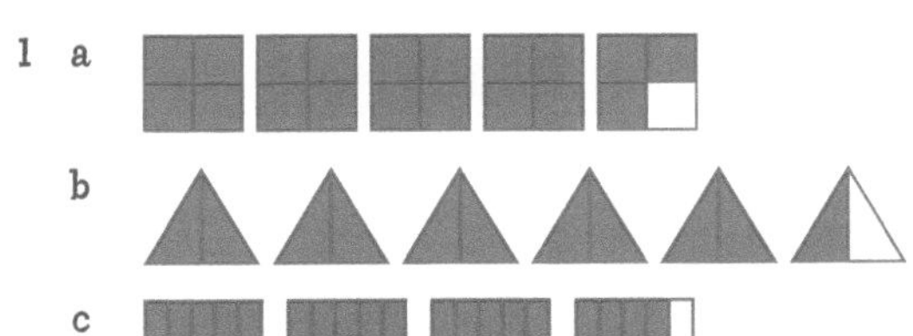

2 a $4\frac{4}{5}$ b $5\frac{2}{8}$ c $1\frac{1}{3}$

Improper Fractions and Mixed Numbers

Page 108 – Example(s)

Example 2: 11, 11

Example 4: 9, 2; 9, 2

Page 108 – Your Turn

a 18, $4\frac{2}{4}$ b 13, $1\frac{5}{8}$ c 11, $5\frac{1}{2}$

Page 109 – Practice

1 a $\frac{7}{2}$ b $\frac{16}{6}$ c $\frac{11}{3}$ d $\frac{7}{4}$ e $\frac{17}{3}$ f $\frac{13}{2}$ g $\frac{9}{2}$ h $\frac{12}{5}$

2 a $3\frac{1}{3}$ b $1\frac{2}{5}$ c $1\frac{2}{3}$ d $4\frac{1}{2}$ e $1\frac{2}{4}$ f $1\frac{2}{10}$ g $5\frac{1}{4}$ h $10\frac{2}{3}$

3 a $3\frac{4}{7}$ b $5\frac{5}{9}$ c $3\frac{5}{10}$ d $8\frac{3}{8}$ e $7\frac{3}{6}$

4 a $\frac{18}{5}$ b $\frac{39}{8}$ c $\frac{20}{3}$ d $\frac{12}{9}$ e $\frac{39}{7}$ f $\frac{36}{5}$ g $\frac{21}{8}$

Add and Subtract Fractions with the Same Denominator

Page 110 – Example(s)

Example 2: 4

Example 3: 5

Example 5: 5

Example 6: 2

Page 110 – Your Turn

a 3 b 4 c 4 d 7 e 4

Page 111 – Practice

1 a $\frac{2}{3}$ b $\frac{5}{8}$ c $\frac{5}{8}$ d $\frac{5}{10}$ e $\frac{2}{2}$ f $\frac{8}{10}$ g $\frac{4}{5}$ h $\frac{4}{6}$ i $\frac{9}{10}$ j $\frac{7}{8}$ k $\frac{8}{10}$

2 a $\frac{4}{10}$ b $\frac{3}{8}$ c $\frac{4}{8}$ d $\frac{5}{10}$ e $\frac{1}{3}$ f $\frac{1}{4}$ g $\frac{2}{8}$ h $\frac{2}{5}$ i $\frac{6}{10}$ j $\frac{4}{8}$ k $\frac{4}{12}$

3 a $\frac{7}{10}$ b $\frac{7}{8}$ c $\frac{2}{4}$ d $\frac{1}{10}$ e $\frac{3}{4}$

Fractions Review Page 112

1 a $\frac{3}{4}$ b $\frac{4}{5}$ c $\frac{5}{8}$ d $\frac{3}{6}$

2 a $\frac{5}{8}$ b $\frac{1}{5}$ c $\frac{5}{8}$ d $\frac{5}{10}$

3 a 6 b 5 c 4 d 2 e 1 f 6 g 1 h 1 i 4 j 1 k 8 l 2 m 8 n 4 o 5

4 a $\frac{3}{2}$ b $\frac{4}{2}$ c $\frac{4}{3}$ d $\frac{5}{1}$ e $\frac{3}{2}$ f $\frac{5}{4}$ g $\frac{45}{30}$ h $\frac{51}{30}$

5 a b c d

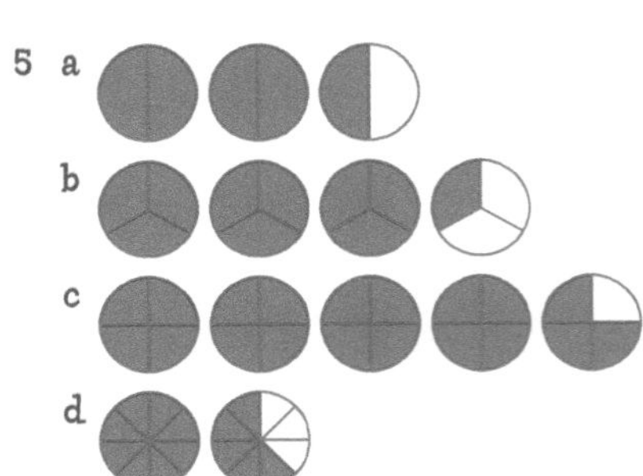

6 a $2\frac{2}{3}$ b $3\frac{3}{4}$ c $2\frac{4}{8}$ d $3\frac{3}{5}$

7 a $\frac{10}{3}$ b $\frac{15}{6}$ c $\frac{13}{8}$ d $\frac{13}{3}$ e $\frac{21}{2}$ f $\frac{59}{8}$ g $\frac{18}{7}$ h $\frac{9}{4}$

8 a $2\frac{2}{4}$ b $2\frac{1}{7}$ c $4\frac{1}{5}$ d $3\frac{2}{10}$ e $7\frac{1}{9}$ f $10\frac{2}{3}$ g $9\frac{4}{5}$ h $8\frac{1}{2}$

7 DECIMALS

Writing Decimals

Page 114 – Example(s)

Example 3: $\frac{62}{100} = 0.62$

Example 4: $\frac{259}{100} = 2.59$

Page 114 – Your Turn

	Fraction	Decimal	Out of 100
a	$\frac{32}{100}$	0.32	32 out of 100
b	$\frac{57}{100}$	0.57	57 out of 100
c	$\frac{93}{100}$	0.93	93 out of 100
d	$\frac{22}{100}$	0.22	22 out of 100
e	$\frac{138}{100}$	1.38	138 out of 100
f	$\frac{365}{100}$	3.65	365 out of 100

Page 115 – Practice

1 a (124).(35) b (20).(34) c (82).(10) d (64).(39) e (913).(26) f (1).(34) g (52).(45) h (142).(53) i (106).(50)

2

	Tens	Ones	.	Tenths	Hundredths
a	1	3	.	7	8
b	4	6	.	2	4
c	5	1	.	0	3
d	3	0	.	0	8

3 a 8 ones + 2 tenths + 3 hundredths
b 4 ones + 5 hundredths
c 7 tenths + 6 hundredths

4 a 1.27, 2.17, 2.71, 7.12, 7.21
b 0.30, 0.33, 3.03, 3.30, 3.31
c 1.8, 1.85, 5.18, 8.15, 8.51
d 3.67, 3.76, 6.37, 6.73, 7.63

Relating Tenths to Hundredths

Page 116 – Example(s)

Example 5: 7

$\frac{7}{10} = 0.70$

Example 6: 1 tenth, 5 hundreths; 15, $\frac{15}{100} = 0.15$

Page 116 – Your Turn

1 a 9, 0.90 b 64, 0.64 c 33, 0.33

Page 117 – Practice

1 a

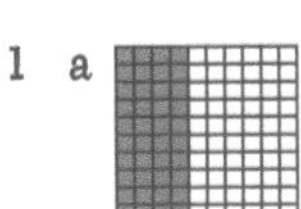

b

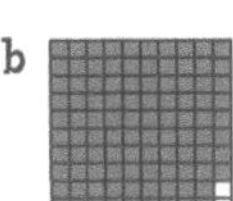

c

2 a 0.13 b 0.80 c 0.07

3

	Words	Diagram	Fraction	Decimal
a	sixty hundredths		$\frac{60}{100}$	0.60
b	forty-two hundredths		$\frac{42}{100}$	0.42
c	ninety-three hundredths		$\frac{93}{100}$	0.93
d	one hundredth		$\frac{1}{100}$	0.01
e	eighteen hundredths		$\frac{18}{100}$	0.18

Decimals and Fractions in Words

Page 118 – Example(s)

Example 3: eighty-two; sixty-nine; hundredths; 8,269; eight; two; sixty-nine
Example 4: zero; nine; nine; 99; ninety-nine

Page 118 – Your Turn

	Fraction	Fraction in Words	Decimal
a	$\frac{84}{100}$	eighty-four hundredths	0.84
b	$\frac{36}{100}$	thirty-six hundredths	0.36
c	$\frac{139}{100}$	one hundred and thirty-nine hundredths	1.39

Page 119 – Practice

1 a two and ninety-four hundredths
b zero and eighty-two hundredths
c eight and ninety-three hundredths
d one and thirty-seven hundredths
e two and forty hundredths
f ten and seventy-three hundredths
g twenty and two hundredths

h zero and sixteen hundredths

i twenty-nine and six hundredths

j forty-three and forty-four hundredths

2 a $\frac{6}{100}$ b $\frac{23}{100}$ c $\frac{42}{100}$ d $\frac{89}{100}$

e $\frac{102}{100}$ f $\frac{712}{100}$ g $\frac{963}{100}$ h $\frac{890}{100}$

i $\frac{701}{100}$ j $\frac{547}{100}$ k $\frac{800}{100}$ l $\frac{320}{100}$

Thousandths

Page 120 – Example(s)

Example 3: 8, 2, 9, 6

Example 4: 4, 7, 6, 0, 9

Page 120 – Your Turn

1 a 7, 3, 8, 2
b 5, 4, 1, 0
c 9, 7, 3, 4
d 8, 5, 3, 2
e 6, 5, 9, 3
f 7, 1, 1, 3

Page 121 – Practice

1 a 6 b 2 c 4

2 a 9 b 3 c 7

3 a 8.691 b 4.385 c 6.702

4 a 1.672
b 5.381
c 9.035
d 8.354
e 7.438
f 1.085
g 1.006
h 6.952
i 2.010
j 2.340
k 5.000
l 6.100
m 7.467

Place Value

Page 122 – Example(s)

Example 2: 3, 2, 5, 1, 9, 4

Example 3: 1, 4, 3, 1, 0, 9

Page 122 – Your Turn

1 a 62.493 b 25.620 c 7.358

2 a 1.246 b 29.368 c 84.721

3 a 32.739 b 1.435 c 0.583

4 a 73.282 b 1.122 c 40.475

5 a 10.650 b 74.009 c 21.436

Page 123 – Practice

1 a thousandths
b tens
c hundredths
d tenths
e tenths
f thousandths
g hundredths
h tenths
i tens
j hundredths
k ten thousandths

2 a **21.350**
b **71.4583**
c **0.359**
d **54.9252**
e **99.9999**
f **64.381**
g **82.563**
h **0.5034**
i **17.32**
j **53.1**
k **80.0019**

3

	Decimal	Tens	Ones	.	Tenths	Hundredths	Thousandths	Ten Thousandths
a	43.246	4	3	.	2	4	6	
b	74.9783	7	4	.	9	7	8	3
c	87.903	8	7	.	9	0	3	
d	95.0902	9	5	.	0	9	0	2
e	16.10	1	6	.	1	0		
f	24.649	2	4	.	6	4	9	
g	30.2587	3	0	.	2	5	8	7
h	61.082	6	1	.	0	8	2	
i	53.942	5	3	.	9	4	2	
j	60.4365	6	0	.	4	3	6	5

Decomposing Decimals

Page 124 – Example(s)

Example 2: 2, 4, 9, 3; 493

Example 3: 457; 5, 4, 5, 7
5, 457

Page 124 – Your Turn

a 2, 7
b 3, 2, 7
c 43, 4, 3
d 103, 4, 1, 0, 3

Page 125 – Practice

1

	Decimal	Mixed Number	Wholes	Tenths	Hundredths	Thousandths
a	4.175	$4\frac{175}{1,000}$	4	$\frac{1}{10}$	$\frac{7}{100}$	$\frac{5}{1,000}$
b	6.157	$6\frac{157}{1,000}$	6	$\frac{1}{10}$	$\frac{5}{100}$	$\frac{7}{1,000}$
c	1.493	$1\frac{493}{1,000}$	1	$\frac{4}{10}$	$\frac{9}{100}$	$\frac{3}{1,000}$
d	8.459	$8\frac{459}{1,000}$	8	$\frac{4}{10}$	$\frac{5}{100}$	$\frac{9}{1,000}$
e	3.237	$3\frac{237}{1,000}$	3	$\frac{2}{10}$	$\frac{3}{100}$	$\frac{7}{1,000}$
f	7.368	$7\frac{368}{1,000}$	7	$\frac{3}{10}$	$\frac{6}{100}$	$\frac{8}{1,000}$
g	9.945	$9\frac{945}{1,000}$	9	$\frac{9}{10}$	$\frac{4}{100}$	$\frac{5}{1,000}$

2

	Decimal	Mixed Number	Wholes	Thousandths
a	5.324	$5\frac{324}{1,000}$	5	$\frac{324}{1,000}$
b	6.173	$6\frac{173}{1,000}$	6	$\frac{173}{1,000}$
c	4.159	$4\frac{159}{1,000}$	4	$\frac{159}{1,000}$
d	3.438	$3\frac{438}{1,000}$	3	$\frac{438}{1,000}$
e	6.805	$6\frac{805}{1,000}$	6	$\frac{805}{1,000}$
f	7.590	$7\frac{590}{1,000}$	7	$\frac{590}{1,000}$
g	9.720	$9\frac{720}{1,000}$	9	$\frac{720}{1,000}$

Decimals Review Page 126

1 a (24).(20)
b (63).(58)
c (0).(30)
d (58).(37)
e (70).(59)

2

	Tens	Ones	.	Tenths	Hundredths	Thousandths
a	3	5	.	6	5	1
b	0	8	.	5	6	2
c	6	9	.	8	3	9
d	7	6	.	5	8	6
e	3	9	.	1	5	6
f	1	0	.	4	9	7

3 a 4.32, 3.42, 3.24, 2.43, 2.34
b 7.317, 4.371, 3.174, 1.734, 1.473
c 8.965, 8.695, 6.895, 5.968, 5.698
d 9.34, 9.304, 9.034, 4.093, 3.904
e 9.529, 9.501, 5.243, 3.781, 3.331

4 a 8 ones + 2 tenths + 3 hundredths + 4 thousandths
b 5 ones + 4 tenths
c 2 tens + 4 ones + 7 hundredths
d 5 tens + 1 one + 7 tenths + 8 hundredths
e 4 ones + 7 tenths + 3 hundredths + 8 thousandths
f 2 tens + 4 ones + 8 tenths + 2 hundredths + 5 thousandths

5 a 0.80
b 0.73
c 0.04
d 0.13
e 2.38
f 1.34

6 a 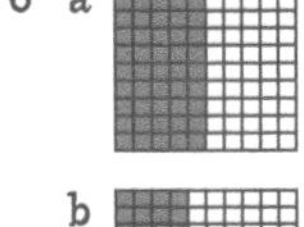

b

c 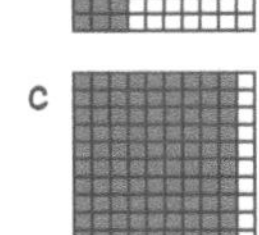

d 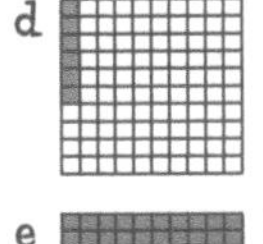

e

f 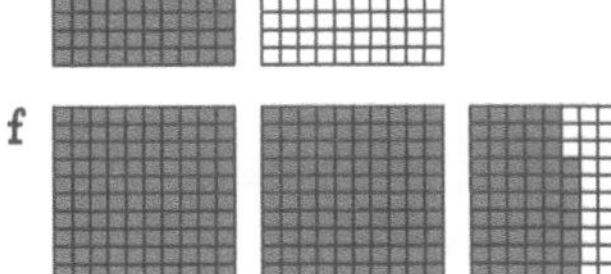

7

	Fraction	Fraction in words	Decimal
a	$\frac{29}{100}$	twenty-nine hundredths	0.29
b	$\frac{38}{100}$	thirty-eight hundredths	0.38
c	$\frac{197}{100}$	one hundred ninety-seven hundredths	1.97
d	$\frac{254}{100}$	two hundred fifty-four hundredths	2.54
e	$\frac{6,348}{1,000}$	six thousand, three hundred forty-eight thousandths	6.348
f	$\frac{241}{1,000}$	two hundred forty-one thousandths	0.241
g	$\frac{6,846}{1,000}$	six thousand, eight hundred forty-six thousandths	6.846
h	$\frac{483}{100}$	four hundred eighty-three hundredths	4.83

8 a six and five hundred ninety-three thousandths
b zero and seven hundred forty-two thousandths
c three and five hundred sixty-one thousandths
d zero and eight hundred three thousandths
e two and forty-one hundredths

9 a 5
b 9
c 3
d 0
e 6

10 a 4
b 7
c 6
d 3
e 8

11 a 4
b 2
c 9
d 8

12 a 3.768
b 69.178
c 52.834
d 80.927
e 64.085

13 a 5.935
b 6.710
c 8.423
d 2.872
e 4.731
f 6.481
g 3.7
h 5.49
i 4.907
j 8.034

14 a 0.2
b 3.75
c 1.47
d 0.9
e 7.33
f 0.6
g 8.43
h 1.25

15

	Decimal	Tens	Ones	.	Tenths	Hundredths	Thousandths
a	15.723	1	5	.	7	2	3
b	74.978	7	4	.	9	7	8
c	73.098	7	3	.	0	9	8
d	3.432	0	3	.	4	3	2
e	5.24	0	5	.	2	4	0
f	6.13	0	6	.	1	3	0
g	8.354	0	8	.	3	5	4
h	91.407	9	1	.	4	0	7
i	70.320	7	0	.	3	2	0
j	90.004	9	0	.	0	0	4

16 a $2 + \frac{6}{10} + \frac{3}{100}$
b $7 + \frac{3}{10} + \frac{0}{100}$
c $1 + \frac{1}{10} + \frac{7}{100}$
d $5 + \frac{0}{10} + \frac{8}{100}$

17 a $6 + \frac{28}{100}$
b $8 + \frac{48}{100}$
c $4 + \frac{3}{100}$
d $3 + \frac{50}{100}$

18 a $2 + \frac{6}{10} + \frac{2}{100} + \frac{4}{1,000}$
b $8 + \frac{1}{10} + \frac{8}{100} + \frac{3}{1,000}$
c $9 + \frac{7}{10} + \frac{5}{100} + \frac{9}{1,000}$
d $4 + \frac{9}{10} + \frac{2}{100} + \frac{3}{1,000}$
e $15 + \frac{4}{10} + \frac{0}{100} + \frac{9}{1,000}$
f $10 + \frac{7}{10} + \frac{9}{100} + \frac{0}{1,000}$

19 a $3 + \frac{729}{1,000}$
b $8 + \frac{430}{1,000}$
c $5 + \frac{745}{1,000}$
d $14 + \frac{657}{1,000}$
e $20 + \frac{130}{1,000}$
f $39 + \frac{429}{1,000}$

8 PATTERNS AND ALGEBRA

Number Patterns

Page 132 – Example(s)

Example 5: Add 3
Example 6: Subtract 6

Page 132 – Your Turn

a 16, 32, 64, 128
b 132, 120, 108, 96
c 48, 24, 12, 6
d 73, 79, 85, 91
e 18, 54, 162, 486

Page 133 – Practice

1 a 2,000, 1,000, 500, 250, 125
b 2,002, 2,004, 2,006, 2,008, 2,010
c 188, 191, 194, 197, 200
d 1,017, 1,025, 1,033, 1,041, 1,049

2 a − 3
b × 2
c × 5
d + 11
e × 6
f ÷ 2

3 a 14, 26, 50, 98, 194
b 13, 25, 49, 97, 193
c 68, 36, 20, 12, 8
d 38, 62, 110, 206, 398

4 a 54, 45, 36. Rule: − 9
b 500, 2,500, 12,500. Rule: × 5
c 61, 57, 53. Rule: − 4

5 a ● − ■ = ▲
b D × E = F
c ▲ ÷ ■ = ★
d G ÷ H = L
e X + A = ⬢

Pattern Grids

Page 135 – Example(s)

Example 3: (top row) 30, 24
(bottom row) 11, 9
Example 4: (top row) 99
(bottom row) 92, 96

Page 135 – Your Turn

a 8, 16, 24, 32, 40
b 0, 5, 10, 15, 20
c 3, 6, 9, 12, 15

Page 136 – Practice

1 a 12, 14, 16, 18, 20, 24, 26

2 a D = B ÷ 4
b K = C × 11
c ▲ = ■ ÷ 3

3 a 46, 106, 226, 466
b 20, 28, 44, 76
c 68, 260, 1,028, 4,100

4 a

÷ 3	9	6	1	3	4	21
+ 7	34	25	10	16	19	70

b

÷ 5	5	1	13	2	12	4
+ 8	33	13	73	18	68	28

c

+ 12	19	20	22	23	25	21
− 7	0	1	3	4	6	2

Equivalent Expressions

Page 137 – Example(s)

Example 5: 8
Example 6: 18

Page 137 – Your Turn

a 20
b 3
c 20
d 4
e 100
f 25
g 50
h 8
i 36

Page 138 – Practice

1 a 4
b 16
c 3
d 4
e 34
f 7
g 9
h 10
i 4
j 20
k 5

2 Adult to check

3 a 3
b 22
c 45
d 3
e 2
f 5
g 26

Equations and Patterns with Fractions and Decimals

Page 139 – Example(s)

Example 5: 15
Example 6: Add 0.3

Page 139 – Your Turn

a 1.1
b 12
c 16
d 3.6

Page 140 – Practice

1 a 3.2
b 1.2
c 2.4
d 1.1
e 4
f 1.5
g 2
h 2.2
i 3
j 4.8
k 8
l 0.9
m 2
n 4.1

2 a 4
b 16
c 6
d 6
e 12
f 12
g 4
h 1
i 18
j 8
k 9

3 a 3
b 12
c 20
d 6
e 10

4 a 1.8, 1.5, 1.2
b 3.5, 3.7, 3.9
c 1.0, 1.2, 1.4
d 2.5, 2.7, 2.9
e 4.9, 4.5, 4.1
f 9.4, 9.0, 8.6
g 7.9, 7.6, 7.3

Patterns and Algebra Review Page 141

1 a 18, 54, 162, 486
b 104, 106, 108, 110
c 1,250, 250, 50, 10
d 85, 79, 73, 67

2 a + 7
b − 3
c × 2
d − 4

3 a 10, 18, 34, 66, 130
b 45, 18, 9, 6, 5
c 16, 36, 76, 156, 316

4 a A × B = C
b ▲ − ● = ■
c D × F = E

5 a 45, 35, 25, 15, 5, 0
b 12, 32, 44, 60, 80, 88

c

÷ 5	12	10	5	2	3
+ 9	69	59	34	19	24

d

× 7	35	49	63	77	42
− 4	1	3	5	7	2

6 a 3
b 13
c 12
d 7
e 40
f 8

7 a 8
b 11
c 17
d 9
e 70
f 12

8 a 12
b 16
c 20
d 48
e 96
f 3

9 a 6 b 1.2 c 9 d 8 e 2 f 4.8

10 a 2.8, 3.1, 3.4 b 9.4, 9.0, 8.6 c 10.5, 13, 15.5 d 4.2, 5.2, 6.2 e 8.5, 10, 11.5 f 5.4, 4.3, 3.2

9 LENGTH

Meters and Feet

Page 144 – Example(s)

blue: *b, d, e*
red: *a, c, f*

Page 144 – Your Turn

Adult to check

Page 145 – Practice

1 Circle: car, plane, cruise ship, kayak
2 Circle: house, boat, tree, pool
3 Adult to check

Centimeters and Inches

Page 146 – Example(s)

Mark *a, c, e, f*

Page 146 – Your Turn

a 6 b 9

Page 147 – Practice

1 Adult to check
2 a 1 in. b 3 in. c 2 in. d 5 in.

3 a 9 cm b 12 cm c 8 cm

4 a green
b orange
c orange, blue, pink, green

Millimeters and Quarter-Inches

Page 148 – Example(s)

a 45 b 83 c 121

Page 148 – Your Turn

1 a $2\frac{3}{4}$ in. b $4\frac{1}{4}$ in. c $5\frac{1}{4}$ in.

2

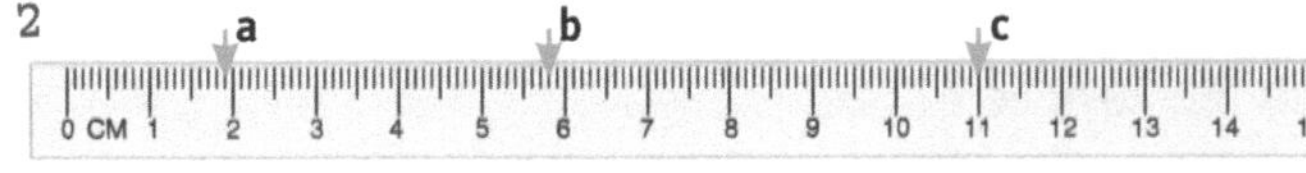

Page 149 – Practice

1 Adult to check
2 a 44 mm b 126 mm c 13 mm d 95 mm

3 13 mm, 44 mm, 95 mm, 126 mm

4 a $3\frac{1}{2}$ in. b $5\frac{1}{4}$ in. c $4\frac{3}{4}$ in. d $1\frac{3}{4}$ in.

5 $1\frac{3}{4}$ in., $3\frac{1}{2}$ in., $4\frac{3}{4}$ in., $5\frac{1}{4}$ in.

Converting Measurements

Page 150 – Example(s)

b 4 c 6 d 72 e 1,200 f 1,600 g 240 h 8

Page 150 – Your Turn

a cm to m	
400	4
350	3.5
680	6.8
1,200	12

b ft. to in.	
8	96
$3\frac{1}{2}$	42
12	144
$1\frac{1}{2}$	18

Page 151 – Practice

1 a 72 b 1 c 120 d 5 e 18 f 3 g $2\frac{1}{2}$

2 a 300 cm b 50 mm c 12 cm d 4 cm e 10 cm f 8 m g 17 cm

3 a No b Yes c Yes d Yes e No f Yes g No h No i Yes

4

a mm to cm	
60	6
130	13
280	28
1,490	149

b ft. to in.	
8	96
$2\frac{1}{2}$	30
11	132
$5\frac{1}{2}$	66

c in. to ft.	
72	6
66	$5\frac{1}{2}$
24	2
78	$6\frac{1}{2}$

d m to cm	
24	2,400
56	5,600
740	74,000
153	15,300

Kilometers and Miles

Page 152 – Example(s)

Mark: *a, c, d, f*

Page 152 – Your Turn

1 a 7,000 m b 10,560 ft. c 14,000 m d 21,120 ft. e 315,000 m

2 a 9 km b 1 mi. c 34 km d 2 mi. e 537 km

Page 153 – Practice

1 Adult to check
2 a 5,000 b 10,560 c 1,000 d 15,840 e 5,280 f 8,000 g 22,000

3 a 6.25 km b 2,000 m c 3.5 km d 4,500 m e 53 km

Perimeter

Page 154 – Example(s)

18

Page 154 – Your Turn

a P = 5 in. + 1 in. + 5 in. + 1 in. = 12 in.
b P = 4 m + 2 m + 5 m + 5 m = 16 m

Page 155 – Practice

1 a P = 10 in. b P = 20 cm c P = 8 ft. d P = 15 m e P = 12 ft. f P = 32 cm

2 Adult to check

3 a 26 m b 20 m c 18 m

4 a Yes b No c Yes d Yes

5 1 Trees and herbs
2 Palms
3 Succulents
4 Citrus
5 Roses
6 Pots and planters
7 Outdoor furniture
8 Indoor plants

6 a 4 ft. b 30 mm c 8 in. d 18 in. e 8 m f 18 ft. g 17 mm

7 a P = 26 ft. b P = 28 cm c P = 20 in. d P = 40 cm

Length Review Page 158

1 a 10 cm b 14 cm c 2 cm d 8 cm

2 2 cm, 8 cm, 10 cm, 14 cm

3 Adult to check

4 a cm b cm c mm d cm e mm f cm

5 a 14 b 42 c 95 d 133

6 Adult to check

7 a 4 in. b 6 m c 300 ft. d 1 mm e 6 in.

8 a 7 b 40 c 2,000 d 1 e 600 f 13.6 g 24 in. h 4 ft. i 5 ft. j 36 in. k 30 in. l $3\frac{1}{2}$ ft.

9 a 6,000 b 8,000 c 17,000 d 5,280 e 15,840 f 10,560

10 a 7 b 11 c 2 d 2 e 1

11 a P = 12 ft. b P = 16 cm c P = 14 cm d P = 17 in. e P = 20 ft. f P = 22 cm

12 Adult to check

13 a 11 b 28 c 16 d 10 e 13 f 12 g 70 h 22 i 10 j 102

14 a P = 28 m b P = 18 in.

10 ANGLES

Angles

Page 162 – Example(s)

Adult to check

Page 162 – Your Turn

Adult to check

Page 163 – Practice

1 Adult to check

2 a 4, 3, 5, 2, 1 b 2, 1, 4, 5, 3 c 1, 5, 2, 4, 3

3 Adult to check

Right Angles

Page 164 – Example(s)

a right b not right c right d not right e right f right

Page 164 – Your Turn

Adult to check

Page 165 – Practice

1 Adult to check

2 Adult to check

3 a = b < c > d = e = f = g <

4 a

c 

e 

b 

d 

Acute and Obtuse Angles

Page 166 – Example(s)

c 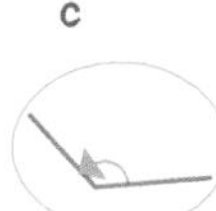

e 

g 

i 

d 

f 

h 

Page 166 – Your Turn

Adult to check

Page 167 – Practice

1 a ∠DEF or ∠FED, Acute
b ∠PQR or ∠RQP, Obtuse
c ∠CAT or ∠TAC, Obtuse
d ∠PMN or ∠NMP, Acute
e ∠IHG or ∠GHI, Obtuse

2 a 4, 3, 2, 1, 5 b 5, 1, 2, 3, 4 c 4, 3, 5, 1, 2

3 a 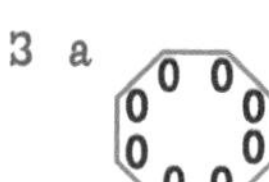

c 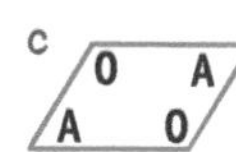

b 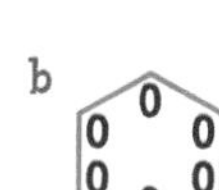

d O A
A O

Straight, Reflex, and Revolution Angles

Page 168 – Example(s)

b straight　c reflex　d revolution

Page 168 – Your Turn

Adult to check

Page 169 – Practice

1 Reflex angles: c, d, g
Straight angles: a, f
Revolutions: b, e
2 Adult to check
3 a A　b E　c B　d D　e C
4 Adult to check
5 Adult to check

Using a Protractor

Page 170 – Example(s)

Adult to check

Page 170 – Your Turn

a Inside　b Inside

Page 171 – Practice

1 a 105°　b 170°　c 15°　d 65°　e 145°

2 a 25°　b 45°　c 160°　d 117°　e 30°　f 142°　g 155°

3 Adult to check

Angle Sum of a Triangle

Page 173 – Example(s)

b right　c isosceles　d equilateral

Page 173 – Your Turn

a 70°　b 50°　c 50°

Page 174 – Practice

1 a 40°, isosceles　b 50°, right　c 60°, equilateral　d 115°, scalene　e 60°, right

2 a 200 ✘　b 190 ✘　c 180　d 180　e 180

Angle Sum of Quadrilaterals

Page 175 – Example(s)

Adult to check—each figure should have a line connecting two opposite vertices.

Page 175 – Your Turn

1 a 135°　b 85°　c 90°　d 80°　e 75°

Page 176 – Practice

1 a 55°　b 61°　c 34°　d 90°　e 242°　f 42°　g 100°　h 120°　i 78°　j 30°　k 112°

Angles Review Page 177

1 a turn, arms
b right, ninety
2 Adult to check
3 Adult to check
4 a 

b 

c 

d 

e 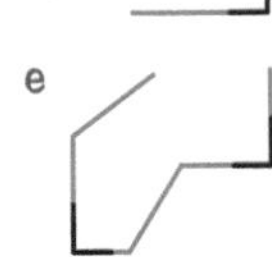

f 

5 Adult to check
6 a ∠ABC or ∠CBA, Acute
b ∠CDE or ∠EDC, Obtuse
c ∠PQR or ∠RQP, Obtuse
d ∠FGH or ∠HGF, Acute
e ∠STU or ∠UTS, Obtuse
f ∠VWX or ∠XWV, Straight
7 Acute: a, f; Obtuse: c, h; Reflex: e; Straight: d; Revolution: b, g
8 a A　b C　c D　d B　e E
9 Adult to check
10 Adult to check
11 Adult to check
12 a 50°　b 165°　c 140°　d 90°
13 a 135°　b 170°　c 90°　d 115°　e 45°
14 Adult to check
15 a 60°, equilateral　b 50°, scalene　c 90°, right　d 60°, scalene　e 30°, isosceles　f 20°, right
16 a 131°　b 141°　c 90°　d 67°　e 105°　f 233°

11 SHAPES

Shapes

Page 182 – Example(s)

d 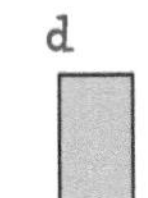
e 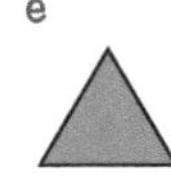
f 

Page 182 – Your Turn

a square (regular quadrilateral)
b irregular pentagon
c irregular triangle
d rectangle (irregular quadrilateral)
e regular triangle
f irregular hexagon

Page 183 – Practice

1 a regular pentagon
b rectangle (irregular quadrilateral)
c irregular hexagon
d irregular octagon
e regular hexagon

2

	Name	Letters that help identify polygon	Angles	Sides
a	triangle	tri	3	3
b	pentagon	pent	5	5
c	hexagon	hex	6	6
d	heptagon	hept	7	7
e	octagon	oct	8	8
f	nonagon	non	9	9
g	decagon	deca	10	10

Types of Lines

Page 184 – Example(s)

b horizontal

c vertical

d perpendicular

Page 184 – Your Turn

1 Vertical lines: a, d, g; Horizontal lines: b, c, i; Parallel lines: b, f, g; Perpendicular lines: e, h

Page 185 – Practice

1 Adult to check 2 Adult to check 3 Adult to check

Triangles

Page 186 – Example(s)

a 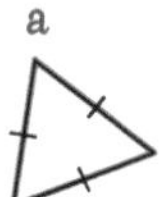

b 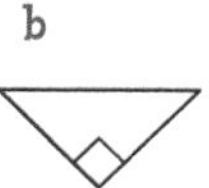

c 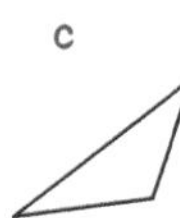

d 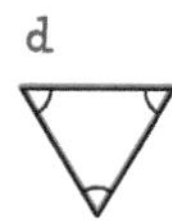

e 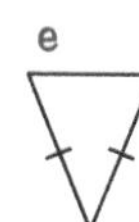

Page 186 – Your Turn

Equilateral triangles: c, d, g

Isosceles triangles: f

Scalene triangles: a

Right triangles: b, e

Page 187 – Practice

1 a equilateral

b scalene

c right

d scalene

e right

f equilateral

g isosceles

2 Adult to check

3 Adult to check

Quadrilaterals

Page 188 – Example(s)

b irregular

c regular

d irregular

Page 188 – Your Turn

a trapezoid

b kite

c square

d parallelogram

Page 189 – Practice

1

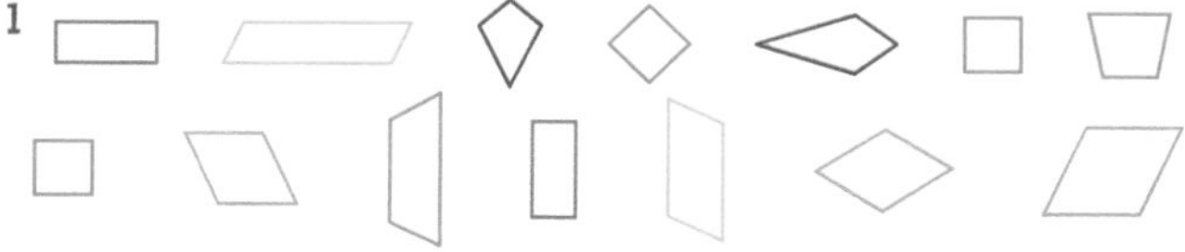

2 Adult to check

3 Adult to check

Polygons

Page 190 – Example(s)

b irregular octagon

c irregular heptagon

d regular pentagon

Page 190 – Your Turn

a 7 (irregular heptagon)

b 10 (irregular decagon)

c 9 (regular nonagon)

d 12 (regular dodecagon)

Page 191 – Practice

1 Adult to check

2 a regular pentagon

b irregular hexagon

c regular hexagon

d regular triangle

e irregular hexagon

f regular pentagon

g irregular pentagon

3 a regular heptagon

b irregular octagon

c irregular heptagon

d regular octagon

e regular heptagon

f irregular octagon

4 a regular decagon

b regular dodecagon

c irregular decagon

d irregular nonagon

e regular nonagon

f regular decagon

g irregular dodecagon

Symmetry

Page 192 – Example(s)

b 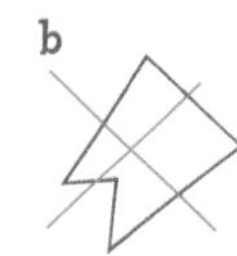

c 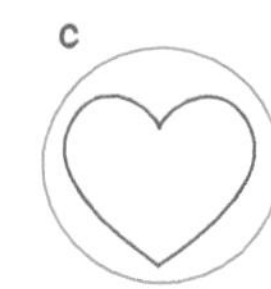

d 

e 

Page 192 – Your Turn

a 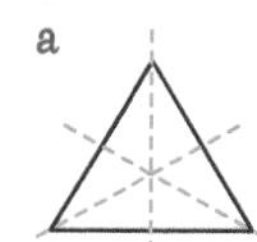

b 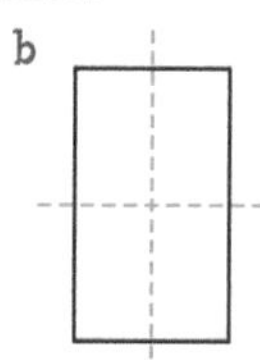

c 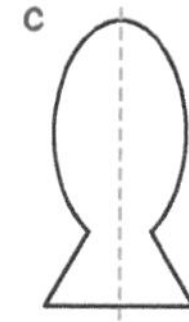

Page 193 – Practice

1 Adult to check

2 Adult to check

3 ✔ ✔ ✔ ✘ ✔ ✔ ✘ ✔

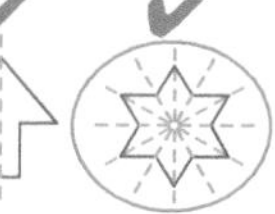

4 a

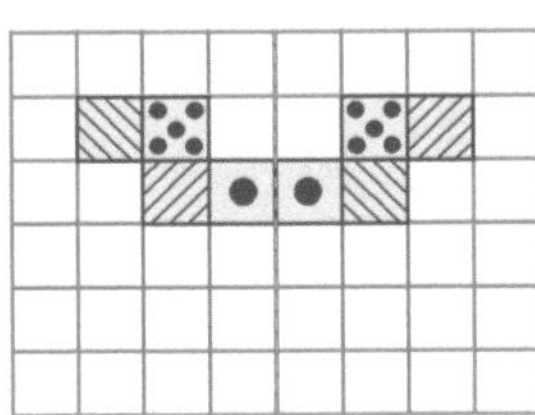

b

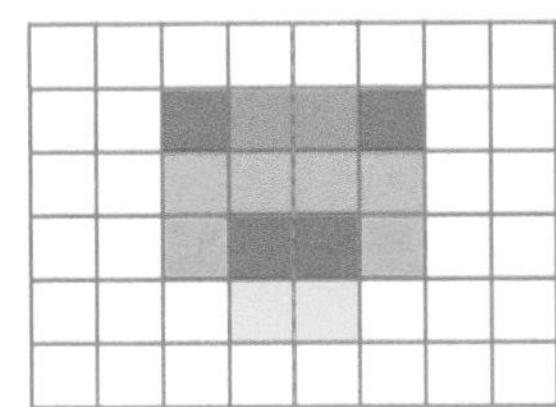

Shapes Review Page 194

1 a irregular octagon
b regular hexagon
c regular dodecagon
d irregular dodecagon
e regular decagon
f regular triangle
g rectangle (irregular quadrilateral)
h regular heptagon
i regular nonagon
j irregular octagon
k regular pentagon
l square (regular quadrilateral)
m irregular pentagon
n irregular heptagon
o regular octagon

2 a horizontal
b parallel
c horizontal
d perpendicular
e vertical
f parallel
g vertical
h perpendicular
i parallel
j vertical

3 Adult to check

4 a right
b isosceles
c equilateral
d scalene

5 Equilateral triangle: All sides the same length, All angles the same size
Isosceles triangle: Two sides the same length, Two angles the same size
Scalene triangle: All sides different lengths, All angles different sizes
Right triangle: One right angle

6 a parallelogram
b rhombus
c square
d kite
e trapezoid
f rectangle

7 a parallelogram, rhombus, square, trapezoid, rectangle
b square, rectangle

8 a 8
b 9
c 7
d 12
e 10
f 4
g 5
h 6
i 7
j 3

9 half, reflection (or mirror image)

10 Adult to check

11 a

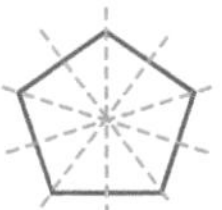

b

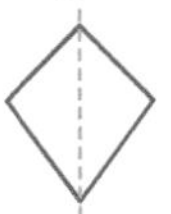

c

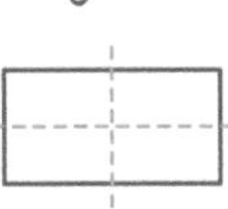

d

e

12 a

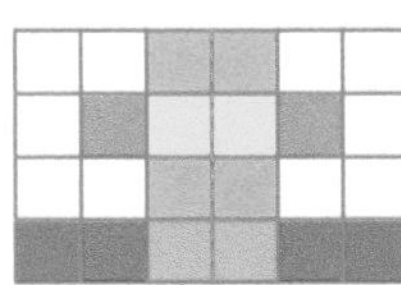

b

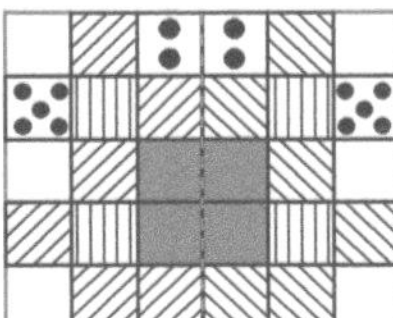

c

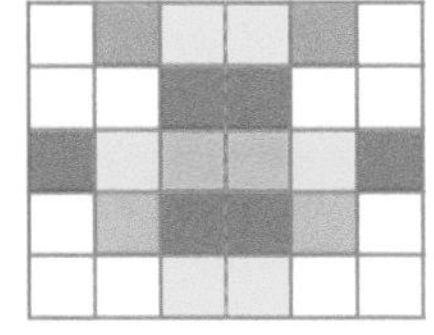

12 AREA

Square Centimeters and Inches

Page 198 – Example(s)

b 10
c 9

Page 198 – Your Turn

a 8 cm^2
b 18 cm^2

Page 199 – Practice

1 a 10 cm^2
b $8\frac{1}{2}$ cm^2
c 12 cm^2
d $9\frac{1}{2}$ cm^2
e 12 cm^2
f 14 cm^2
g 11 cm^2

2 a 7
b 4 and 6
c $3\frac{1}{2}$ cm^2
d 7
e 5
f $4\frac{1}{2}$

3 Adult to check

Square Meters and Feet

Page 200 – Example(s)

b 12
c 15

Page 200 – Your Turn

a 12 sq. ft.
b 4 sq. ft.

Page 201 – Practice

1 Circle: door, screen, bed, fence
2 Adult to check
3 a 12 m^2
b 24 m^2
c 12 m^2
d 9 m^2
e 2 m^2

4 No

Square Kilometers and Miles

Page 202 – Example(s)

Mark *a, b, d*

Page 202 – Your Turn

Adult to check

Page 203 – Practice

1 a 12
b $9\frac{1}{2}$
c 8
d 10
e 7
f 8
g 6

2 a Australian Capital Territory
b Western Australia
c Western Australia

Area – Using Multiplication

Page 204 – Example(s)

length, 5 in., 15

Page 204 – Your Turn

a Area = length × width
= 2 ft. × 4 ft.
= 8 $ft.^2$

Page 205 – Practice

1 a Area = length × width
= 5 ft. × 4 ft.
= 20 $ft.^2$

b Area = length × width
= 6 m × 1 m
= 6 m^2

c Area = length × width
= 4 in. × 3 in.
= 12 $in.^2$

2 a Area = l × w
= 7 in. × 7 in.
= 49 in.²

b Area = l × w
= 3 cm × 6 cm
= 18 cm²

c Area = l × w
= 5 ft. × 2 ft.
= 10 ft.²

d Area = l × w
= 6 m × 6 m
= 36 m²

e Area = l × w
= 1 in. × 1 in.
= 1 in.²

Perimeter

Page 206 – Example(s)

18

Page 206 – Your Turn

a P = 4 ft. + 1 ft. + 1 ft. + 1 ft. + 1 ft. + 1 ft. + 1 ft. + 1 ft. + 1 ft. + 4 ft.
= 16 ft.

Page 207 – Practice

1 a P = 2 in. + 4 in. + 2 in. + 4 in.
= 12 in.

b P = 1 cm + 2 cm + 1 cm + 4 cm
= 8 cm

c P = 2 ft. + 2 ft. + 2 ft. + 2 ft. + 2 ft.
= 10 ft.

d P = 1.5 cm + 3 cm + 1.5 cm + 3 cm
= 9 cm

e P = 1.5 m + 1.5 m + 1.5 m + 1.5 m
= 6 m

f P = 2.5 m + 2.5 m + 2.5 m + 2.5 m + 2.5 m + 2.5 m
= 15 m

g P = 5 in. + 2 in. + 1 in. + 1 in. + 1 in. + 1 in. + 3 in. + 2 in. + 6 in. + 6 in.
= 28 in.

h P = 4 ft. + 7 ft. + 4 ft. + 1 ft. + 3 ft. + 1 ft. + 3 ft. + 3 ft. + 3 ft. + 1 ft. + 3 ft. + 1 ft.
= 34 ft.

Area Review Page 208

1 a 8 b 7 c 8 d $7\frac{1}{2}$

2 Adult to check

3 Mark: a, c, d, g, h

4 a 20 b 10 c 12 d 11 e 20 f 18 g 11 h 11

5 a D, G, H b A, E, F c A, E d F e 10 m²

6 a 24 ft.² b 9 ft.² c 5 ft.² d 9 ft.² e 3 ft.² f 9 ft.² g 6 ft.² h 6 ft.²

7 71 ft.²

8 Adult to check

9 a 24,429 km² b 5,455 km² c 11,075 km² d 19,054 km²

10 a Area = length × width
= 1 m × 1 m
= 1 m²

b Area = length × width
= 1 in. × 7 in.
= 7 in.²

c Area = length × width
= 3 ft. × 3 ft.
= 9 ft.²

d Area = length × width
= 3 cm × 5 cm
= 15 cm²

e Area = length × width
= 8 ft. × 2 ft.
= 16 ft.²

f Area = length × width
= 5 cm × 5 cm
= 25 cm²

g Area = length × width
= 4 in. × 3 in.
= 12 in.²

h Area = length × width
= 6 cm × 6 cm
= 36 cm²

11 a P = 3 m + 5 m + 3 m + 5 m
= 16 m

b P = 4 in. + 4 in. + 4 in. + 4 in.
= 16 in.

c P = 4 m + 4 m + 1 m + 3 m + 1 m + 3 m + 1 m + 3 m + 1 m + 7 m
= 28 m

d P = 2 ft. + 2 ft. + 2 ft. + 2 ft.
= 8 ft.

e P = 6 cm + 3 cm + 6 cm + 3 cm
= 18 cm

f P = 8 ft. + 6 ft. + 3 ft. + 3 ft. + 5 ft. + 1 ft. + 5 ft. + 1 ft. + 5 ft. + 1 ft.
= 38 ft.

g P = 10 cm + 2 cm + 3 cm + 5 cm + 3 cm + 2 cm + 1 cm + 2 cm + 3 cm + 7 cm
= 38 cm

13 VOLUME AND CAPACITY

Volume

Page 213 – Example(s)

a 3, 3 b 8, 8

Page 213 – Your Turn

a 5 b 11

Page 214 – Practice

1 a 7 cu. in. b 7 cm³ c 32 cu. in. d 32 cm³

2 a 3 b 22

3 object 4

Capacity

Page 215 – Example(s)

c 

Page 215 – Your Turn

Adult to check

Page 216 – Practice

1 a 1, 2, 4, 3, 5 b 5, 3, 1, 2, 4 c 4, 5, 3, 2, 1

2 a 15 gal. b 13 gal. c 14 L d 7 L e 14 gal.

Liters and Gallons

Page 217 – Example(s)

b 1 c 1 d 5

Page 217 – Your Turn

a 12 b 9 c 6 d 8,000 e 6 f 500,000 g 8

Page 218 – Practice

1 a 4 b 4 c 15,000 d 8 e 16

2 Adult to check

3 Adult to check

4 a 10 b 27

5 a b c

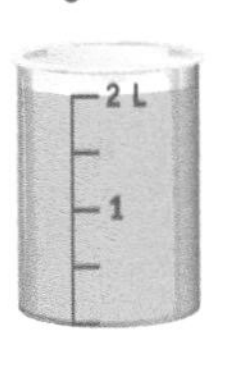

6 a 10 b 1 c 4 d 3 e 3 f 1 g 6

7 a b c

8 a c b a c b d a

9 a 2 gal. b 5 gal. c 4 gal. d 1 gal.

10 a 20 containers b 30 buckets of water c 48 oranges d 10 gal. of juice

Milliliters and Fluid Ounces

Page 221 – Your Turn

a

c

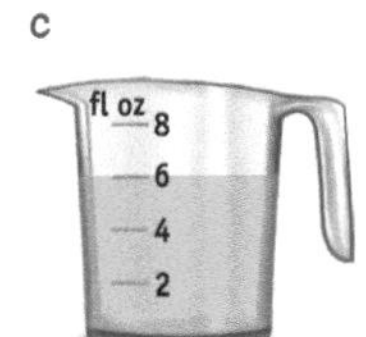
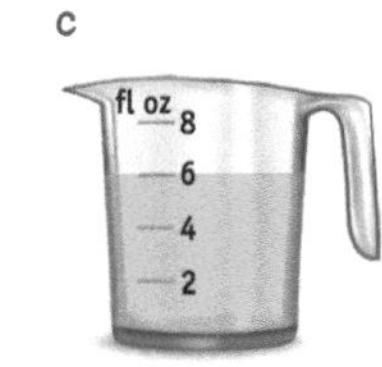

e

b

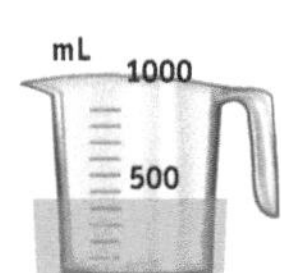

d

Page 222 – Practice

1 b, c, f, g

2 a 1 L b 2 c c $9\frac{3}{4}$ L d $1\frac{1}{2}$ c e $8\frac{1}{2}$ L f 3 c g 10 L h $2\frac{1}{2}$ c

3 a 4,000 mL b 26 fl. oz. c 3,500 mL d 10 fl. oz. e 1,750 mL f 24 fl. oz. g 6,750 mL h 44 fl. oz.

4 a c e

Volume and Capacity Review Page 223

1 space

2 a 7 b 18 c 15 d 50

3 a 3 cm^3 b 43 cu. in.

4 a left b left c right d left

5 a 1, 3, 5, 4, 2 b 2, 1, 3, 5, 4 c 5, 3, 2, 1, 4

6 a 8 b 6 c 21

7 Adult to check

8 Adult to check

9 a b c d

10 a 1 gal. b 2 gal. c 4 gal. d 5 gal.

11 a 13 L b 11 times c 11 buckets of water

12 a 1 b $\frac{3}{4}$ c 500 d 2

13 a b c d

14 b, f

15 a $3\frac{1}{2}$ L b 2 c c $1\frac{1}{2}$ L d $2\frac{1}{2}$ c e $9\frac{1}{4}$ L f $3\frac{1}{2}$ c

16 a 8,000 mL b 26 fl. oz. c 6,500 mL d 22 fl. oz. e 9,000 mL f 24 fl. oz.

17 a 5, 4, 2, 3, 1 b 1, 4, 3, 5, 2 c 4, 2, 3, 5, 1